The Unaccountables

The Unaccountables

The powerful politicians and corporations who profit from impunity

Edited by Michael Marchant, Mamello Mosiana,
Ra'eesa Pather and Hennie van Vuuren

Contributors: Daniel Beizsley, Caryn Dolley, Paul Holden, Michael Marchant, Zen Mathe, Abby May, Mamello Mosiana, Lehlohonolo Ndlovu, Lucas Nowicki, Luvano Ntuli, Ra'eesa Pather, Neroli Price, Meghan Samaai, Erin Torkelson and Hennie van Vuuren

First published by Jacana Media in 2022

10 Orange Street
Sunnyside
Auckland Park 2092
South Africa
+2711 628 3200
www.jacana.co.za

© Open Secrets, 2022

All rights reserved.

ISBN 978-1-4314-3295-0

Infographics by Gaelen Pinnock
Cover design by publicide
Editing by Lara Jacob
Proofreading by Megan Mance
Indexing by Adrienne Pretorious
Set in Ehrhardt 11/15pt
Printed and bound by ABC Press, Cape Town
Job no. 003953

See a complete list of Jacana titles at www.jacana.co.za

Contents

Acronyms 9
Contributors 11
Challenging impunity: The Unaccountables 13

Section 1: Apartheid Profiteers

Introduction 21
1. Who bankrolled the National Party? 23
2. Naspers: The taproot of the National Party 29
3. Swiss bankers 35
4. KBC and KBL/Quintet banks: The arms money machine 39
5. Dame Margaret Hodge MP: A very British apartheid profiteer 47

Section 2: War Profiteers

Introduction 57
1. Jacob Zuma and Thales: Comrades in arms 61
2. BAE Systems: The great British rip-off 69
3. John Bredenkamp: BAE's bagman 77
4. Fana 'Styles' Hlongwane: BAE agent 83
5. Siphiwe Nyanda and the BAE corruption bombshell 91
6. RDM and the NCACC: Profiting from misery in Yemen 101

Section 3: State Capture Profiteers

Introduction 113
1. The Chinese Railway Rolling Stock Corporation:
   China Inc boards the state capture train 115
2. Prasa: Looted and left for scrap 123
3. Auswell Mashaba and Vossloh: The middleman and
   German rail company that derailed Prasa 131
4. Roy Moodley: The owner of Prasa? 141
5. Sfiso Buthelezi: The board chair who derailed Prasa 149
6. Refiloe Mokoena: The attorney on the wrong side of
   the law 157

Section 4: Welfare Profiteers

Introduction 167
1. Liberty: Profit over pensioners 169
2. Captured regulator?: The FSCA and Dube Tshidi 175
3. Net1 and CPS: Welfare profiteers 183

Section 5: Bad Bankers

Introduction 195
1. Nedbank and the Bank of Baroda: Banking on state capture 197
2. HSBC: The world's oldest cartel 205
3. Estina's banks: FNB and Standard Bank 213
4. Credit Suisse and VTB Capital: Enablers of mega looting
   in Mozambique 223

Section 6: Failing Auditors

Introduction 235
1. Deloot 237
2. EY and those fishy $2.2 billion scams 245
3. KPMG: At the heart of state capture 253
4. PwC and Nkonki asleep in the cockpit of SAA 263
5. IRBA: Soft touch audit regulator in turmoil? 271

Section 7: Conspiring Consultants

Introduction 281
1. McKinsey: Profit over principle 283
2. Bain & Company: The 'KGB of consulting' 291
3. BCG Consulting: Consultant to Kleptocrats 299

Section 8: Bad Lawyers

Introduction 309
1. The national postponement authority 313
2. Andrew Chauke: Joburg's king of public prosecutions 325
3. Sello Maema: the NPA's deputy prosecutions boss in the
   North West 333

We have not forgotten 343
Acknowledgements 349
Notes 351
Index 417

Acronyms

AFU	Asset Forfeiture Unit of the NPA
AML	Anti-Money Laundering
BBBEE	Broad-Based Black Economic Empowerment
BEC	Bid Evaluation Committee
CFSC	Cross Functional Sourcing Committee
DPCI	Directorate for Priority Crimes Investigation (the Hawks)
DPP	Director of Public Prosecutions
FIC	Financial Intelligence Centre
FICA	Financial Intelligence Centre Act
FSB	Financial Services Board
FSCA	Financial Sector Conduct Authority
FNB	First National Bank
ID	Investigating Directorate of the NPA
IMF	International Monetary Fund
IRBA	Independent Regulatory Board for Auditors
MK	Umkhonto weSizwe
NCACC	National Conventional Arms Control Committee
NDPP	National Director of Public Prosecutions
NPA	National Prosecuting Authority
OCCRP	Organised Crime and Corruption Reporting Project
OUTA	Organisation Undoing Tax Abuse
PFMA	Public Finance Management Act
Prasa	Passenger Rail Agency of South Africa

SAA	South African Airways
SCA	Supreme Court of Appeal
SDPP	Strategic Defence Procurement Package
SETA	Sector Education and Training Authority
SIU	Special Investigating Unit
SOEs	state-owned enterprises
SCM	Supply Chain Management
SWI	Shadow World Investigations
UBC	Unpaid Benefits Campaign

Contributors

THIS BOOK REPRESENTS THE collective effort of the small, tenacious and dedicated team at Open Secrets. Many colleagues at Open Secrets, past and present, contributed to the investigations and writing contained in this book. We would like to thank and acknowledge the following Open Secrets contributors:

- Caryn Dolley
- Michael Marchant
- Zen Mathe
- Abby May
- Mamello Mosiana
- Lehlohonolo Ndlovu
- Lucas Nowicki
- Luvano Ntuli
- Ra'eesa Pather
- Neroli Price
- Meghan Samaai
- Hennie van Vuuren

Many of the profiles in this book are also the result of collaboration with activists, investigators, academics and partners in civil society. We wish to acknowledge the investigative and writing contributions of the following individuals and their organisations:

- Paul Holden: Paul is the Director of Investigations at Shadow World Investigations (SWI) in the United Kingdom. He is the author of

several books on the arms deal and was a key witness at the Zondo Commission of Inquiry into State Capture. Paul contributed to the writing of several chapters in the War Profiteers and State Capture Profiteers sections, and we have referenced his work extensively throughout.
- Dr Erin Torkelson: Erin is a lecturer in human geography at Durham University. She is an expert on social grants and cash transfers in South Africa, and has written extensively on the role of Net1 and CPS in profiting from the unlawful contract with SASSA to distribute social grants in South Africa. Erin is the lead author of the chapter in this book on Net1 and CPS.
- Daniel Beizsley: Daniel is an associate at the UK-based organisation Spotlight on Corruption. Daniel is a criminologist whose PhD is in the role of international financial institutions' role in corruption in Europe and the developing world. Daniel is a co-author of the chapter on EY in this book.

Challenging impunity: The Unaccountables

SOUTH AFRICA IS A wealthy country. The 2022 *Africa Wealth Report*, published by private wealth advisors Henley & Partners and New World Wealth, estimated total private wealth in South Africa to be over $651 billion, more than R10 trillion.[1] When it comes to the number of US dollar millionaires, South African ranks 28th in the world. It is a dwindling crop in a world in which rich folks are attracted to domiciles in very rich countries, but South Africa is home to more than twice as many high-net-worth individuals than any other African country.[2]

This wealth is heavily concentrated. Research by the Southern Centre for Inequality Studies and World Inequality Database in 2020, showed that in a population of 60 million people, just 3,500 people held 15 per cent of all wealth.[3] This is the equivalent to the total wealth held by 90 per cent of people in the country.[4] The consequence of this is that despite the wealth and resources available in the country, poverty is pervasive. Millions of South Africans go hungry every day, and more than half of the population live in 'chronic poverty'.[5]

There is not one single explanation for this state of affairs, but a key cause of the entrenched and worsening inequality in South Africa is endemic corruption and economic crime. It undermines human rights and deepens inequality. Such acts of violence by powerful individuals and corporations drive millions into poverty in a country like South Africa. In turn, our inability to challenge these crimes is in large part explained by a long-running failure to hold the powerful and wealthy to account for the crimes that they profit from. Economic crimes and corruption are committed by a small band of the powerful, but they pose fundamental threats to democracy and social justice. They result in the looting of public funds, the destruction of democratic institutions, the erosion of basic public services, and ultimately the infringement of the human rights of millions of people. Powerful economic elites are the key enablers of these crimes. Indeed, throughout South Africa's history, criminal regimes and corrupt networks have relied on a network of politicians, corporate CEOs, arms dealers and smooth-talking fixers. These actors have used the proceeds to build a system to ensure their impunity.

Open Secrets has a mission to disrupt these networks and pursue accountability. We do so because we want a society in which the powerful do not monopolise resources and influence. One of the ways in which we seek to disrupt networks of power is by investigating and exposing the powerful and well-resourced profiteers who are implicated in various economic crimes. Much of this work is contained in this book. *The Unaccountables* contains thirty-five profiles of unaccountable corporations and private individuals, as well as politicians and state institutions. All of them have played a role in crimes that have had grave social consequences. None of them have been properly held to account.

Each individual, company and institution in the book has a single short chapter that tells its story, and these chapters are grouped into eight sections. Section 1 discusses the apartheid profiteers – those individuals, spies, politicians and companies that funded, supported and profited from the crime of apartheid. Section 2 contains the war profiteers – those politicians, fixers and arms companies who corrupted democratic politics by their involvement in the 1999 arms deal, as well as the South African arms companies that continue to profit from exporting arms for use in the war zone of Yemen today. Section 3 turns to contemporary state capture, and profiles the global companies and local politicians and middlemen who have wrought devastation on the state, and in particular both passenger and commercial rail in South Africa. Section 4 discusses what we call welfare profiteers, the financial companies that have made a killing from their role in managing social grants and private pension funds in South Africa, often at great cost to pension fund members and social grant beneficiaries. Section 5 turns to the banks – those South African and global banks that were crucial to enabling state capture in South Africa, as well as similar grand corruption in Mozambique. Section 6 discusses the role of the auditors; each of the 'Big Four' audit firms is profiled in relation to their role as guns for hire for corporations and state actors, and their willingness to look the other way despite their professional duties. Section 7 discusses the consultants; it profiles the 'Big Three' consulting firms and the role of some in South African state capture, as well as the pattern of the industry's involvement with kleptocrats around the world. Section 8 is the final section and profiles the 'bad lawyers', those prosecutors within the National Prosecuting Authority (NPA) who have delayed justice and acted as obstacles to accountability.

Thirty-five individual stories, grouped into eight sections, and with a central common theme – the impunity of the powerful and the need to end it. Yet, there are other themes that emerge from these stories and who we chose to profile in this book. Inevitably, the book cannot contain all of the rogues who are implicated in corruption in South Africa and remain unaccountable. This is a slice of a significant cohort of politicians and individuals whose conduct, we believe, helps us understand the phenomenon of power and impunity; it is not meant to be encyclopaedic. However, for the readers who themselves are implicated in economic crimes – your omission should not be read as undermining of your offence, nor a clean bill of health given your crimes. Our advice: do not be impatient if your infamy is not sufficiently recognised, rather be assured you are on the list of future investigations.

The choices we have made on who to include helps to show the following important things:

The long shadow of economic crime in South Africa

With the exhausting pace of the news cycle and the sheer number of scandals in South Africa, it is easy for calls for accountability to fade over time. This is a grave error. We have deliberately chosen to dedicate profiles to apartheid profiteers as well as those implicated in corruption in the arms deal in the 1990s, alongside numerous profiles that focus on contemporary state capture. We do so for two main reasons. The first is that the need for justice and accountability does not fade with time. It is as urgent today as ever to use the evidence available to hold companies and individuals accountable for their complicity in the crime of apartheid. This is important to protect the victims' right to truth and justice, but also to send a message that one's ability to evade accountability, even for long periods, is never a guarantee of impunity.

The second reason is that those who profit from crimes in one era retain powerful positions in the future, not only perpetuating networks of criminality in the present, but actively undermining institutions that might hold them to account. A failure to act against those engaged in crimes in the past can have devastating long-term impacts on the rule of law, and guarantees the recurrence of similar crimes in the future. The only way to stop this is to disrupt criminal networks through accountability. One only needs to look at the destruction wrought by former president Jacob Zuma, in large part to avoid accountability for alleged crimes committed twenty-five years ago, to see this. Zuma is alleged to have accepted bribes from a French arms company that had propped up apartheid with illicit weapons along with a range of other European arms companies profiled in this book. The long shadow is clear to see.

Politicians and corporations united in impunity

A deeply unhelpful but unfortunately popular debate in South Africa concerns whether it is politicians or private actors who are predominantly to blame for economic crime and corruption, and thus who should be the primary focus of efforts to pursue accountability. This is often used by reactionary and opportunistic players to distract from their role in criminality.

Our choice of who to profile in this book makes it clear that to fully understand and dismantle these criminal networks it is imperative to pay full attention to the role all the actors – public and private – in economic crime. The sections that focus on contemporary state capture provide perhaps the clearest for this. The looting of Transnet and the Passenger Rail Agency of South Africa (Prasa) relied on ministers, board members at state-owned enterprises (SOEs), global rail companies, global and local banks, mega consulting firms, businesspeople, auditors and politicians to pull it off. They all got a lucrative cut and walked away from the carnage while members of the public bore the great cost. These crimes also required Members of Parliament and officials in law enforcement and the National Prosecuting Authority (NPA) to fail to act. Accountability of any one of these individuals, companies or institutions is not more important than any other. Our efforts to pursue accountability and reforms must tackle all of those who are complicit in economic crime.

We can do something about it

The title of the book – *The Unaccountables* – and the content of this introduction points to a focus on impunity and a failure of accountability. It is thus no surprise that much of the analysis in the profiles focuses on the extensive public evidence of corruption or other economic crimes, and yet a failure to take any action. However, this is not at all suggesting that the situation is hopeless. To the contrary, the hope remains that this book and the stories in it can contribute to accountability and action against those implicated. This is why, in each chapter, we identify the possible routes to pursuing accountability, along with the important reforms and actions by relevant regulatory bodies or law enforcement that would make accountability possible. In doing so, we hope that the book makes a strong argument for disrupting the status quo and shows that action to do so is possible.

It is important to acknowledge that the possibilities to pursue accountability exist because of the extraordinary work of activists, civil society, investigative journalists, academics and whistleblowers. Their fearless work over many generations has always challenged the powerful, and provides the evidence we need to continue that struggle. While the profiles in this book are based on Open Secrets' investigations, all of them rely heavily on others. That is why we have referenced this book thoroughly, and encourage readers to follow the notes to dig into more detail on these stories.

1
APARTHEID PROFITEERS

Introduction

THE LAST APARTHEID PRESIDENT, FW de Klerk, gave his final, sort of, apology for apartheid from the grave in 2021. In an eery recorded message the erstwhile enforcer of apartheid denied that he supported apartheid for most of his political career, but conceded that apartheid was 'wrong'.[1] De Klerk, from a family of National Party aristocrats, happily lined his pockets and that of his family with monthly wages from the apartheid state. For many years this was his reward for an unfailing loyalty to the apartheid system. His latter day *mea culpas*, whether by genuine intention or cynical calculation, ensured him a Nobel Peace Prize and a steady income stream from speaking tours on campuses in the USA and elsewhere for more than two decades after the end of white minority rule.

In his farewell video to South Africa, De Klerk is flanked by a painting by artist Maggie Laubser featuring a black women in a yellow head scarf.[2] The other woman in the frame is his wife Elita de Klerk, who had previously been married to Tony Georgiades, a Greek shipping magnate who became rich off apartheid oil sanctions busting and later acted as one of the middlemen in the corrupt arms deal of the Mandela/Mbeki administrations.[3]

De Klerk died a wealthy man with a deeply contested legacy. While he craved political attention, there was no outpouring of public emotion, unlike when fellow Nobel Laureate Nelson Mandela passed away in 2013. In the days after Mandela's death journalists pounded the pavement outside his house and interviewed members of the public and neighbours who came to drop off flowers or cards on the pavement of his home. Many of his admirers had encountered Mandela on the street or in public life, and had stories to share of the importance of these moments. Mandela was after all a politician who sought to connect with people, including his opponents whom he so successfully disarmed. In contrast, *News24* managed to speak to only one of De Klerk's neigbours in the wealthy Cape Town suburb of Fresnaye. Neighbour Steven Chasen recalled their only interaction, 'I think he waved to me once on his way to church.'[4] Chasen seemed most enamoured by the extra security detail afforded to the ex-president and by extension his neighbours: 'I've never felt so safe.'[5]

Impunity for apartheid crimes, whether economic or political, set the tone for the many troubles faced in South Africa's democratic politics over the past three decades. The real beneficiaries of apartheid's horrors and violence have not been held to account. The apartheid corporate profiteers never had their riches taxed as should have been the case at the onset of democracy. Many have used this foundational wealth to build large multinational empires.

This chapter examines a handful of these profiteers, some of whom featured in the book *Apartheid Guns and Money: A Tale of Profit*. They include the corporations who tithed to the National Party and kept them sweet in return for sweetheart deals, and the media giant Naspers which finally gave a whimpering apology for its central role in the apartheid machinery in 2015. We focus on international banks in Luxembourg, Switzerland and Belgium that grew fat off apartheid profits and kept the war machine functioning. We also look at one unlikely beneficiary of apartheid profits – a British Labour Party MP who made a name for herself fighting illicit financial flows. What they all have in common is that none of them have been held to account for the profits generated from a crime against humanity.

ONE
Who bankrolled the National Party?

THE APARTHEID REGIME'S staying power was enabled by a control of guns, police officers' truncheons and the people who wielded them. However, the system of white supremacy always required cash. During the British colonial period local business would pay fealty to the crown by stocking the tower of London with diamonds and gold. In return they made hay in the colonies through state-sanctioned dispossession and oppression.

By the 1980s the way in which election campaigns were conducted in South Africa required money and lots of it. While it pales in comparison with cash gorging in modern US or South African elections, what it has in common is a reliance on the funds of rich powerful corporations and people. The National Party, who had been in power for close to forty years, needed to spend more money on elections to ensure that its claim to power was legitimised by the majority of the white electorate. Who would bankroll the campaigns? This was a secret for many years and for good reason. Political party funding is a neat way for business and political elites to sign a secret accord. In return for cash, the politicians provide access to power and potentially a nod in the right direction to ensure the donors are first in line when new state contracts are awarded. While this corrupt relationship has come to dominate party politics, in South Africa under apartheid paying cash to the Nats meant you had chosen to back a racist regime. These are all facts that the business elite wished to have neatly swept under the carpet in the wake of South Africa's liberation and first democratic elections in 1994.

A book of names

A book of names, or pages thereof, does exist and Open Secrets tracked it down in Bloemfontein. The Archive for Contemporary Affairs, a four-storey, brown face-brick building at the University of the Free State in Bloemfontein is an unassuming place. Yet its 3.5 kilometre-long shelves of files contain some of the shadiest secrets from South Africa's past. Many of the National Party's (NP) most prominent politicians sent their collections, including official NP documents, to this archive. There is no longer a National Party, and it is unclear whether anyone really wants to 'own' this memory of oppression that delivered so much paperwork. It is nonetheless worthy of far more attention by researchers from across the country.

Despite reading through hundreds of folders from PW Botha's and FW de Klerk's archives, the Open Secrets team working on research for the book *Apartheid Guns and Money*[6] never expected to be delivered a series of folders marked 'National Party donations'. Out of the folders came the signed cheques, fawning letters of thanks and promises of anonymity that secretive party funding demands. Around 70 individual donors were identified in these pages.

Sharing the apartheid gravy train

The names in the folders? – some of South Africa's most prominent businessmen, past and present. While the story of party finance is often revealed only through whispers, in this unassuming archive we had found indisputable documentary evidence. The letters featured here provide a glimpse into the complicity between big business and the oppressive apartheid regime that was until now kept secret.

Some donors were unsurprising, given their long-term complicity with the regime. In a letter written in 1988, De Klerk informed Botha of a R50,000 donation from Barlow Rand (now trading as the large conglomerate, Barloworld).[7] De Klerk notes that, 'They prefer to keep their contribution confidential...' before stating that one of the company's directors, Derek Cooper – who continued to play a prominent role in South African business until his retirement as Standard Bank chairman in 2010 – would handle the donations.[8] Barlow Rand was one of the chief suppliers of technology for military use to the government. Between the 1960s and 1980s the corporation's leadership sat on Botha's Defence Advisory Board all the while presenting itself as an enlightened opponent of apartheid. The two-faced nature of many of these corporations and their executives is a theme that runs throughout this book.

Sanlam, a cornerstone of support to the National Party for decades, gave generously and received favours in return. At least six payments were made by the Sanlam group, totalling R220,000 (R4.2 million today). In 1983, the Sanlam chairman, Fred du Plessis, who also served on PW Botha's Defence Advisory Council, wrote to Botha to assure him of his company's 'moral support in carrying out the demanding tasks which rest on his shoulders'.[9]

For good measure, Du Plessis threw in a company-branded pocket diary. Botha responded to his friend and indicated that it had been brought to his attention that state-owned corporations were operating in a manner that discriminated against Sanlam. He intended to remedy this: 'I have now given orders that Sanlam and its affiliates are properly considered in the awarding of any business by State-Owned Enterprises.'[10]

Another name in these documents who has continued making super profits in a democratic South Africa is Shoprite businessman, Christo Wiese. A plutocrat, although he recently shaved off a chunk of his fortune by backing Steinhoff and its CEO, international fraudster Markus Jooste, Wiese remains ensconced in his luxury Clifton pad in Cape Town with a view towards Robben Island. Wiese was also eager to support the NP and 'anxious' to have this support made known to the president.[11] In 1989, Minister Kent Durr sent a letter to the newly appointed president, FW de Klerk, informing him of Wiese's financial support. Durr fondly describes Wiese, then the director of the clothing retail giant Pepkor, as 'an old friend and supporter of the National Party'.[12]

Of course, as the Guptas' former state capture shebeen at Saxonwold has shown us, these relationships also require a more personal touch.

This is captured perfectly in a letter sent by prominent PG Glass executive chairman, Bertie Lubner. In the letter, written to PW Botha dated 23 June 1982, Lubner writes to thank the prime minister for 'a very wonderful evening which we spent with you, charming members of your family and other guests'.[13] He proceeds to write of how much he admires Botha's leadership of the country: 'It is men with such high ideals and determination like yourself that create history.'[14] Post-apartheid amnesia ensured that at the time of his death in 2016, Lubner was praised only as a beloved philanthropist and iconic business leader, with far too little said about his support for the establishment during apartheid.

This letter and others of a similar nature from Bennie Slome[15] of Tedelex and Macsteel's Eric Samson[16] were some of the more surprising finds in the archive. This is because these men were widely known as part of the self-proclaimed liberal English-speaking business elite of the time. Though perhaps this surprise is misplaced – big business motivated by profit notoriously funds whoever is in power.

We also found letters of support from Altech (now electronics giant Altron) head, W.P. (Bill) Venter. A long-time ally of the apartheid military, Venter made profits supplying the military with missile systems and other key technology at the height of apartheid's war in Angola and cross-border raids. To return the favour, Venter made hefty donations to the NP. In 1982 he pledged R150,000 (R3.2 million in today's terms)[17] with promises of more to come, which he honoured in 1985 and 1989 with generous donations of R200,000 (R3 million in today's terms).[18] In the letter Venter points out the success that his company has achieved, adding that, '…we believe that we would be able to achieve very little without the firm support of the current [NP] government…'.[19]

In 2017, Venter finally stepped down as Altron chair and was praised for his contribution to the South African economy. His collaboration with the apartheid state was conveniently ignored.

Venter was not the only donor with links to the arms trade. Weapons dealer Dan Maartens of the Intertechnic group and Giovanni Mario Ricci, an Italian fraudster and sanctions buster who worked closely with Craig Williamson, also made donations. Ricci, who relied heavily on the government's covert business, provided the NP with R250,000 in 1987 (R2.7 million today).[20]

The gravy train rolls on

The Truth and Reconciliation Commission (TRC) concluded that many businesses 'benefited financially and materially from apartheid'.[21] While many businesses presented themselves as victims of apartheid and part of an enlightened opposition to apartheid, these letters tell a different story. They reveal a complicity with the NP government and show that a significant portion of the business elite kept the taps open to the party at the height of domestic repression and foreign wars. It also allows us to go beyond the broad brushstrokes of the TRC and have a more nuanced conversation about the degrees of complicity within the private sector.

In the post-state capture period, when South Africa is still struggling with the undue influence of the private sector in politics, it is vital to understand the nature of these networks. South Africa desperately needs a private sector that can create jobs – but it also requires far more effective enforcement of the laws governing private sector misconduct. The Zondo Commission of Inquiry into State Capture has singled out the issue of party funding as an 'existential threat to democracy' if not effectively regulated.[22]

In 2021, following years of hand-wringing by Parliament, a new Political Party Funding Act came into force, which for the first time regulates the private funding of political parties. The success of this process and the enforcement of these rules is vital to ensure that the powerful and corrupt are limited in their use of secret funding to undermine democratic politics and buy political favours. It took a democratic South Africa twenty-seven years to finally attempt to harness a corrupt force in politics, which has seen big corporations, tobacco smugglers and state capture looters buy an entrance ticket to the golden circle of political power through the back door. It was a neat continuation of bad policies favoured by the National Party elite.

Has the door finally been closed on these Unaccountables? In 2022 some senior ANC leaders have proposed the curtailing of the powers of the Funding Act, which they see as an unnecessary hassle. They wish for a return to business as usual, which, if National Party leader FW de Klerk and his party treasurers were alive would no doubt be greeted with a cheery 'hear-hear'.

TWO

Naspers: The tap root of the National Party

Naspers is a savvy international media giant with roots in South Africa. The Cape Town-based company is ranked 446th in the Forbes list of global corporations, pipping all the banks, finance houses and behemoths like Sasol and MTN to be crowned the largest company in South Africa.[23] Its assets, valued at over R1.1 trillion,[24] include Media24 and Takealot in South Africa and Prosus (owned through a cross-holding), which is said to be the largest consumer internet company in Europe. Not bad for a South African company established in 1914 to further the cause of Afrikaner nationalism and once described by its top management as one of the 'tap roots of the National Party power'.[25]

A crucial catalyst for Naspers' fortunes was its close relationship with the National Party of PW Botha. This pivoted the successful newspaper and textbook publishing company to establish only the second subscription television station outside of the United States, thereby opening the door to a set of deals during the 1990s in China and elsewhere that would turn the Naspers princes into plutocrats.

Information warriors

In 1981, South Africa was ramping up conflict in Southern Africa. The ruling National Party (NP) also faced increasing internal resistance, both from the liberation movements and South African civilians.

Even as the turmoil grew, President Botha knew that there was an information war to be won and his first prize was the white National Party voters. Botha took time out of the war in Angola to write to Piet Cillié, the chairperson of media giant Nasionale Pers (Naspers) to complain about the 'leftist propaganda' of the popular women's magazine *Fair Lady*. In a letter marked 'personal and confidential', Botha chastised Cillié about an article on Bishop Desmond Tutu and his wife Leah, published by editor Jane Raphaely.[26] At the height of apartheid, all dissenting voices, especially those of the likes of Tutu, had to be muzzled.

Botha expressed the government's disappointment in the piece and demanded that Naspers 'put an end to Jane Raphaely's leftist politics'.[27] He added, 'I think that there is sufficient Nationalist sentiment amongst the Naspers management to put pay to these type of activities.'[28] The acquiescent Cillié wrote back to signal his agreement noting that, 'I trust in future there will be fewer reasons for disagreement'.[29]

This is one of many letters where PW Botha berated media owners and editors alike about their content. Responses were usually timid apologies. This desperation to control information is familiar. The echoes of the past resonate powerfully today as we again face threats to media freedom. The NP, like some of the political elites today, relentlessly pursued control over public opinion. Propaganda and censorship were the order of the day.

With the SABC as state broadcaster firmly in the NP's pocket, influence over all aspects of the privately owned press became the primary target. Naspers and its stable of Afrikaans-language newspapers was a key to the NP's voter base. As leader of the Cape NP, Botha had sat on Naspers's board from 1966 until 1977, shortly before becoming prime minister. In addition, documents obtained by Open Secrets show that the NP also held 74,000 shares in Naspers (in 1984), and so the fortunes of the ruling party and one of the dominant media houses were intertwined.[30] Both prospered off the others' fortune. These relationships are toxic not only because they allow those in power to control the media, but also because they allow private media companies to wield influence within government.

During the most recent period of state capture in a democratic South Africa, the Gupta family-owned *ANN7* and *New Age* were both backers of President Zuma's clique and beneficiaries of their largesse through access to state resources. This is a powerful reminder of the deeply toxic nature of such relations.

Payola TV?

Naspers was one of the most significant donors found in party files at the University of the Free State Archives. In a letter written to FW de Klerk on 17 August 1989, Naspers Managing Director Ton Vosloo reaffirmed the company's support of the NP.[31] Vosloo reminded De Klerk of a donation of R150,000 (approximately R1.6 million today) made to the NP before the 1987 elections. He also pledged a further R220,000 (approximately R2 million today) in support of the NP ahead of South Africa's last race-based general elections in September 1989. Vosloo ended his letter promising funding to the NP in Transvaal by adding that 'our newspaper *Beeld* in the Transvaal is your ally and we trust that this formidable combination will wipe out the competition'.[32]

In return for its financial loyalty, Naspers could count on revenue from government advertising and lucrative school textbook contracts. Yet, there was a much bigger prize at stake. By the mid-1980s, Naspers had their sights fixed on a big portion of the licence to start South Africa's first paid television service – M-Net (the forerunner of the African continental DSTV network). In a 1985 letter to Pik Botha, the minister in charge of the TV licensing process, and copied to PW Botha, Ton Vosloo forcefully lobbied for the contract, and unambiguously linked it to the ongoing propaganda work that Naspers could provide in supporting newspapers that would serve as pro-government mouth pieces.[33]

This lobbying had its desired effect and the government awarded Naspers a 26% stake in the country's first commercial TV service, M-Net.[34] Vosloo was quick to thank PW Botha. In a July 1985 letter that also discussed strengthening support for the pro-government *Citizen*, Vosloo wrote: 'Thank you for your leadership on the TV matter and your quick decision. I appreciate it. The decision now places the matter in a more certain trajectory.'35

This deal proved to be incredibly lucrative for Naspers who grew its business into the DSTV behemoth today. These fortunes multiplied when Naspers bought close to a 50 per cent share in the Chinese internet company Tencent in 2001.36 While it is now Africa's largest media and internet company with a global outlook, Naspers's profits are undoubtedly rooted in the apartheid economy.

In 2017 Ton Volsoo published a memoir *Across Boundaries* in which he attempts to set the record straight, following Open Secrets revelations of the details of NP funding in the book *Apartheid Guns and Money*. He candidly admits that, 'Nasionale Pers [now Naspers] was a supporter of the National Party from its inception in 1915. Over the years the group's publications supported and built the NP with a political ideal in mind. There was also financial donations.'37 There is no contrition or regret in Vosloo's tone and not even the admission that he and other Naspers 'leaders' were not journalists in the true sense but rather simple scribes for a racist regime.

Plutocrats do not apologise for apartheid

Two men who shaped Naspers in the 1980s and beyond are businesspeople Ton Vosloo and Koos Bekker. It was Vosloo, as the story goes, who brought Bekker into the company as a young US graduate in the 1980s to help establish its television empire. When Vosloo resigned as CEO in 1997, Bekker succeeded him, with Vosloo backing Bekker from his new position as executive chair of the Naspers board. Bekker is today one of the top five richest people in South Africa and, according to the *Forbes* rich list, has accumulated a fortune of R40 billion.38

What is forgotten is that the biographies of both men are deeply intertwined with the apartheid state machinery. Koos Bekker's father Cor Bekker was a top government spy in the 1970s and 1980s – a civil servant who worked in the Bureau of State Security (BOSS) and would become number two of the National Intelligence Service, acting as the efficient deputy to Neil Barnard during the crucial period of early clandestine negotiations between the NP regime and the liberation movement.39 These connections could not have gone unnoticed at Naspers HQ. If you live in a garrison state then fortune is likely to favour the offspring of one of the country's top securocrats.

Similarly Ton Vosloo was a Naspers newspaperman from the mid-1950s and only retired as non-executive director in 2015. His rapid rise through Naspers coincided with the role of its daily newspapers as the 'official mouthpiece' of the National Party, as Vosloo wrote in his memoir. In companies like Naspers during the height of apartheid, anyone with a liberal outlook or commitment to anti-racism had little prospect for career success in the mould of Vosloo.

As Professor Anton Harber, editor of the regime-critical *Weekly Mail* in the 1980s, remarked when reviewing Vosloo's book, 'The gravest sin of the Afrikaans media was not what it said but what it systematically hid from its public: the forced removals, the prison torture, the slave working conditions, the censorship, the petty segregation, the daily humiliations – all the conditions that defined apartheid and made it so horrifying to the rest of the world.'[40] Such is the legacy of Vosloo and the remaining acolytes at Naspers who defend his legacy.

Did the advent of democracy make Vosloo any more reflective? One little noticed detail provides important insight. In 2002 Vosloo published a memoir of his father-in-law Judge Jan Strydom (Vosloo and Anet Strydom were married in 2001). While such a self-published monograph shouldn't warrant much attention – Strydom was a vile judge with Nazi sympathies and responsible for racist judgments. The book, which Vosloo published, is focused on the period in which Strydom was interned as a Nazi sympathiser and member of the fascist Ossewabrandwag movement in South Africa during the Second World War.[41] Strydom was also notorious for numerous racist judgments during the apartheid period and was loathed by many of his judicial peers. This included an infamous 1988 judgement in which a young white man was given only a five-year suspended sentence for tying a black farm worker, Mr Eric Sambo, to a tree and beating him to death over a period of two days.[42] In the words of Vosloo, his father-in-law was 'swept up in the tumult of his time, just as happened to later struggle people'.[43] It is a startling claim to be made in 2000, equating the conduct of men who anticipated liberation from Nazi Germany with people who struggled against white supremacy.

It might therefore come as little surprise that under Vosloo's leadership as Naspers chair, Naspers management refused to appear before the TRC media hearings. This led the TRC chairperson, Archbishop Desmond Tutu, to ask, 'Is silence from that quarter to be construed as consent, conceding that it was a sycophantic handmaiden of the apartheid government?'[44] The atonement was left to 150 conscientious Naspers journalists who broke rank with management and submitted to the TRC that their newspapers had acted as an NP mouthpiece.[45]

In 2015, at the time of Naspers's centenary and shortly after Vosloo retired, Naspers relented and apologised for its role in supporting apartheid.[46] This corporate concession is rightly considered by many to be too little, too late.

The interests of media owners and that of politicians continue to overlap today. Naspers deserves singling out because it profited off apartheid. However, today Iqbal Survé's Independent group of newspapers and until recently the Gupta-owned media stable continue the practice of using the newsrooms to their own advantage.

South Africa deserves a far more democratic media landscape, which is not beholden to corporate interests or the whims of politicians who continue to hang the sword of further 'regulation' over editors. These are not just veiled threats to media freedom, but ultimately undermine our constitutional right to know. An informed public is far more likely to be able to tell the difference between disinformation and the #GuptaLeaks. This is what many politicians and media bosses fear the most.

At the time of his retirement from Naspers in 2015, Ton Vosloo reportedly said, 'Journalism is the last line of opposition against the powerful, corruption and misdeeds. May our knees never weaken.'

Maybe he should have added 'again'.

THREE
Swiss bankers

IT IS NO SECRET THAT SWISS banks have a particularly bleak history of putting profit over people. Their role in selling apartheid gold, and providing extensive loans to the regime in times of crisis, is well documented. Yet Swiss archival documents obtained by Open Secrets and first published in *Apartheid Guns and Money* speak to a far deeper complicity between the Swiss banks, their executives and the apartheid state and private sector. Was their relationship so cosy, in fact, that in the case of a nuclear war the Swiss had their eye on the highveld for a fresh start?

At the turn of the 21st century, Swiss banks faced multiple lawsuits for their role in accepting and laundering the assets of victims of the Nazi orchestrated Holocaust. At the time the Swiss Banking Association declared in adverts that 'Secrecy is as vital as the air we breathe'.[47] It also lobbied hard to ensure the Swiss government put a blanket ban on access to any documents which spoke to Swiss corporations' links with apartheid South Africa. Despite its policy of neutrality, Switzerland clearly chooses to side with profit. This behaviour requires secrecy to thrive. So it should come as no surprise that, in addition to Nazi gold, Swiss bank vaults also housed apartheid profits.

Swiss secrets

After decades of blocking access, the Swiss government finally released documents detailing its corporations' economic ties with apartheid South Africa in June 2014. Cynically, it was the dismissal in late 2013 by the New York Appeals Court of a class action lawsuit against corporations involved in aiding and abetting gross human rights violations during apartheid that was no doubt central to the eventual release.[48] The case, brought by an organisation of apartheid victims, Khulumani Support Group, originally included the Swiss banks, the Unition Bank of Switzerland (UBS) and Credit Suisse.[49] Assured that the risk of being held to account had diminished considerably, Swiss authorities finally agreed to open up the archive.

Open Secrets researchers visited the Swiss Federal Archives in Bern shortly after the apartheid documents were made publicly accessible. One of the most intriguing finds was a 1960 government letter addressed to the Swiss mission in Pretoria, which identified South Africa as a possible refuge in the event of a third world war. A file called *'Sitzenverlegung'* (head office relocation) identified South Africa, Canada and New Zealand as possible safe havens for Swiss companies and politicians in the event of a nuclear war. Reasons in favour of South Africa, the Swiss secretary of foreign affairs wrote, are 'that it is relatively liberal, welcoming of investment by foreign corporations, and geographically located far away from the likely main theatre of war'.[50] Evidently 'relatively liberal' is a matter of interpretation.

On 21 March 1960, the South African police shot and killed 69 protesters in Sharpeville. In its wake, the apartheid government declared a state of emergency, banned the African National Congress and Pan Africanist Congress and imprisoned 18,000 people, many of whom were kept in solitary confinement. Against this violent crackdown and militarisation of the state, a Swiss official based in Cape Town was at pains to reassure the Swiss Department of Foreign Affairs that South Africa was still a good option for refuge. In a letter dated 5 May 1960 – less than two months after the massacre – the official wrote, 'There is no doubt that the South African government is committed to ensuring peace and order and security under all circumstances. We can also expect positive efforts to be made to maintain good relations between the races. Under these circumstances, it appears justified to continue the discussions with South African officials.'[51]

From Heidi to the highveld

By the early 1980s, with the fear of nuclear war undiminished, key apartheid ally UBS still had its eye on a safe haven in the highveld. A confidential memo dated 30 November 1982 contains details of a meeting between the Swiss Ministry of Foreign Affairs, the head of UBS – Dr FG Gygax – and representatives from UBS's fund management company – Intrag AG.[52] The memo reveals that, in the meeting, an 'emergency agreement' for the UBS-controlled South African Trust Fund (SAFIT) was finalised. The fund was set up in 1948 and was central to the sale of South African gold facilitated by Switzerland. The agreement, which would come into effect through a telex-communicated codeword, would see the Swiss Union Trust for South Africa take over management of UBS. All these plans were in place to safeguard Swiss corporate wealth in the event of an escalation of the Cold War. An agreement, wrote the manager of the UBS office in Johannesburg to the Swiss embassy in Pretoria, that we hope 'will never be put into force.'[53]

Swiss bankers had the regime's back

Apartheid survived as long as it did because it was never truly isolated. An international network of economic and diplomatic allies played a substantial role in keeping it afloat. Of the international banks, the Swiss commercial banks were among the most significant and long-standing supporters of the apartheid regime. Not only did they do business with apartheid South Africa, they also protected the regime by lobbying the Swiss government. In turn, they profited handsomely through the Zurich Gold Pool which became a central node for the sale of apartheid gold. This relationship was worth protecting. South Africa borrowed money at a premium and its debt was backed up by gold. Gold whose extraction over time has relied on the exploitation of poorly paid black mineworkers working in hazardous conditions to grow the fortunes of a few.

When we quizzed former Minister of Finance Barend du Plessis on the plan for Swiss banks to relocate to the highveld, he was surprised but 'delighted' – saying that it was a reminder of the great 'century-long' relationship between Swiss banks and South Africa.⁵⁴ In an aside, reflecting on the ability of the apartheid government to call in favours from their powerful Swiss allies, Du Plessis recalled a moment during the debt crisis of the mid-1980s; 'One of our South African Airways Boeings landed in Switzerland with gold. A very small bank that was a creditor wanted to confiscate the airplane with the bullion on board. During the course of that day Dr Senn of UBS, who was a great friend of SA, bought the bank. He never told me the name of the bank as it was confidential at the time – and he fired the very brave CEO.'⁵⁵

In 1994, democratic South Africa inherited the mountainous debt owed to the financial institutions that bankrolled apartheid. The Swiss banks were among the debt collectors that came knocking. For decades, these banks knowingly propped up the regime that they saw as creating enough order for them to use the country as back-up for their corporations in times of war. When that regime was dismantled, they demanded repayment from all South Africans. These banks have never been forced to account for their role in funding oppression.

Without a hint of irony, the right-leaning Swiss People's Party (SVP), run in part by private bankers, announced in August 2017 that it will seek support in the Swiss parliament to stop the sharing of tax information with countries like South Africa because of 'corruption' in those countries.⁵⁶ This data-sharing commitment was designed to help countries like South Africa tackle money laundering and tax evasion by the super wealthy and corrupt, including Swiss companies operating from South Africa.

FOUR
KBC and KBL/Quintet banks: The arms money machine

In 1977 the United Nations Security Council imposed a mandatory arms embargo on apartheid South Africa. This was a potential blow to the war economy, and the apartheid regime needed a plan. Over the next seventeen years, their solution allowed them to move over R650 billion (in today's terms) around the world in near complete secrecy. With this they procured the weapons and technology that fuelled wars in Southern Africa, and domestic repression. This is the story of the banks behind the apartheid arms money machine.

Belgium's dirty secrets

To do this, in addition to arms companies and foreign governments willing to bust the embargo, the apartheid military state needed an invisibility cloak for the movement of the cash. Who better to provide one than Kredietbank, a powerful Belgian bank headed up by key apartheid ally André Vlerick, who was deeply embedded in the Belgian moneyed elite.[57] Vlerick was associated with the Flemish Christian People's Party and, in 1972, was appointed as the Belgian minister of finance. In 1974 he joined Kredietbank, one of Europe's largest banks that benefited from its close relationship with the politically well connected in the

Flemish North of Belgium. Vlerick served as Kredietbank's deputy chairman until 1980 when he became chairman, a position he held until his retirement in 1989.[58] Kredietbank and its subsidiary in Luxembourg (Kredietbank Luxembourg) were central to apartheid's secret global financial architecture.[59]

Vlerick could be characterised as quasi ambassador at large for the apartheid regime. He would frequently travel to South Africa to meet with various political and business leaders. In addition he also helped establish pro-apartheid lobby groups in Belgium and across Europe. One such group in Belgium was Protea, a pro-Pretoria propaganda mouthpiece. With Vlerick at its helm for thirteen years, it drew its membership from Belgian conservative senators as well as two of Belgium's two main banks, Kredietbank and Banque Paribas.[60] Vlerick's lobbying efforts extended to a pan-European formation called EUROSA. In addition to Protea in Belgium, there were 'sister organisations' in Austria, Britain, Denmark, France, Italy, the Netherlands, Switzerland and West Germany. Evidence collected from Vlerick's archive has established that Eurosa received direct funding from the apartheid government.[61]

All roads lead to Luxembourg

As if ideological alignment wasn't enough, Kredietbank had a subsidiary in Luxembourg, KBL, whose presence in the wealthy tax haven was key to this money-laundering operation. Kredietbank and KBL were not the only banks that formed part of this arms money machine, but evidence shows that they were one of the most significant players in this scheme.[62]

This channel for moving large sums of money in secret was so successful, in fact, that the South African state-owned arms company Armscor was worried that it was being over-utilised, leaving them vulnerable in the case of detection. In a newly declassified report from 1980 found in the military archives, Armscor officials stress the need to diversify Armscor's payment channels given reliance on the 'overutilised Kredietbank Luxembourg channel'.[63] 'As a result of the circumstances [sanctions]', the report continues, 'the Paris [Armscor] office made significant use of the services of Kredietbank Luxembourg to make payments. The high concentration of payments through this channel is regarded as risky in the event that the implicated individuals at the bank should be identified.' The same report reveals that Kredietbank was also Armscor's most significant source of foreign loans in this period, making up a full 25 per cent of the arms company's foreign loan portfolio.[64]

The Paris office referenced here is Armscor's clandestine office situated on the top floor of the South African embassy in Paris; staffed with Armscor officials, whose sole job was to manage illegal arms purchases throughout Europe.

The arms money machine at work

These secret channels formed part of what we call the arms money machine, a sophisticated international system designed specifically to bust sanctions. For over two decades, this criminal enterprise laundered money through a global corporate and banking architecture involving hundreds of front companies in the secrecy jurisdictions of Panama and Liberia. Former Armscor officials have argued that it acted as conduit for 70 per cent of the cash used by South Africa to illegally buy weapons.[65]

As we can see in the Armscor documents, at the centre of this criminal enterprise was Kredietbank's subsidiary in Luxembourg (KBL). The bank did not just provide hundreds of numbered accounts, but was an active accomplice in the conspiracy by setting up the front companies and providing nominee directors, some of whom were employees of the bank. Unsurprisingly, former officials who operated in the Paris office have alleged that the senior managers at KBL were intimately aware of this conduct.

As has been detailed in the book *Apartheid Guns and Money*, KBL managed payments through approximately 850 bank accounts. According to Martin Steynberg, an ex-Armscor official based in Paris, most of this money originated from Armscor's accounts at Volkskas bank (now part of ABSA) in Pretoria.[66] With the sign off of the South African Reserve Bank, it then moved through a series of accounts held by various international banks to Luxembourg. Some of these accounts were in the name of front companies while others were numbered

THE ARMS MONEY MACHINE:

A tale of banks and front companies

③ Paris Embassy: Armscor's secret hub responsible for all weapons trade with France and Europe. They managed 487 Armscor bank accounts, mostly with Kredietbank.

Kredietbank Belgium: The bank's senior managers included pro-apartheid lobbyists. They owned KBL – the primary conduit for Armscor's money-laundering network.

Kredietbank Luxembourg (KBL): Armscor's main bank in Europe provided hundreds of untraceable accounts. KBL officials assisted in the formation of Armscor's front companies.

At least 39 Armscor front companies were set up in Panama between 1978 and 1991.

Front companies registered here were used to hide payments made to bank accounts controlled by Armscor in Europe.

② Panama

USA

Chile

'One of the most important global money-laundering schemes ever'
~ Professor Mark Pieth

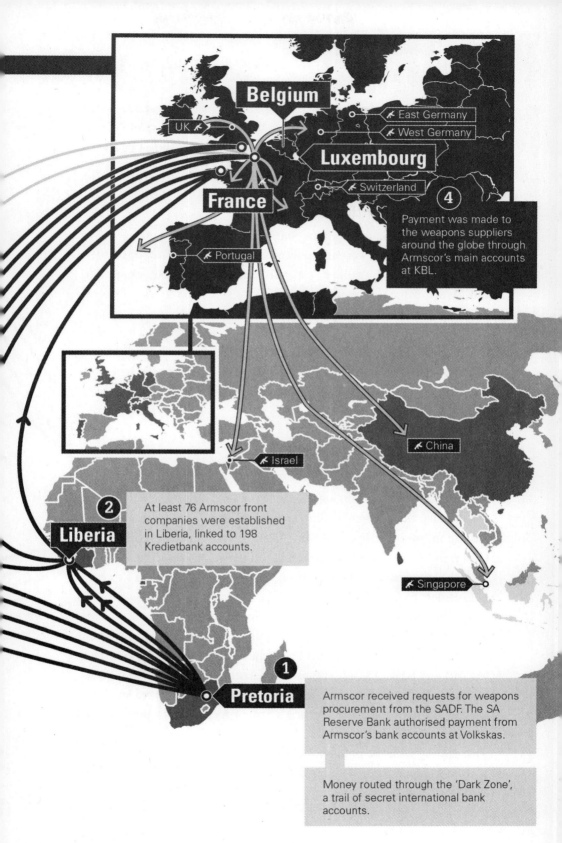

accounts held by KBL. The money would eventually be consolidated in KBL and Kredietbank accounts (so-called Armscor 'main accounts') before being paid to the arms suppliers. The purpose of this roundabout trail was to break and obscure the cash flow so that it couldn't be traced back to South Africa.[67]

Criminal trade with Beijing

Open Secrets found traces in the South African Defence Force archives of how KBL accounts were allegedly used for clandestine weapons trades. In 1983 and 1984, the military was purchasing small arms, ammunition and bombs from Communist China. To do so, they required falsified End User Certificates (EUC) from Zaire (now the Democratic Republic of the Congo) to hide the fact that the weapons were destined for South Africa.[68] In February 1984, two EUCs were purchased through a front company called Adam Export. As the invoices show, payment had to be made to numbered accounts held by KBL.[69]

The Armscor connections

It seems likely that André Vlerick's close connection to the National Party and senior officials like PW Botha in the 1970s and 1980s played a key role in bringing Kredietbank and its subsidiary close to the military establishment. However, KBL also needed a man on the ground in South Africa. Searching through PW Botha's archive at the University of the Free State, the SADF archive in Pretoria and André Vlerick's personal archive in Leuven, Open Secrets identified this man as Leendert Dekker.[70]

A chartered accountant by profession, Dekker was a long-time senior director at Armscor before becoming a Pretoria-based consultant to a range of international banks, including Armscor's international banking ally KBL. He was appointed to Armscor in 1968 by PW Botha and served as its CEO from 1977 until 1979. In addition, from late 1977 Dekker helped to reshape Pretoria's arms procurement operations as part of a small team based in the Department of Commerce and tasked with dealing with the problems posed by sanctions.[71]

In correspondence between PW Botha and Dekker, it is clear that the two had a close relationship. At the time of Dekker's resignation from Armscor, Botha wrote to thank him for his service. In the letter written in 1979, Botha writes, 'You have made a great contribution to your country and more specifically Armscor, there is great appreciation for this. Your goodwill towards me will always remain a pleasant memory.'[72] Dekker responded to thank Botha. In a handwritten note scrawled by Botha at the top of this letter from Dekker, Botha wrote, 'NB: Remember him. We will need him later on.'[73]

After leaving Armscor, Dekker set up a consultancy specialising in representing foreign commercial and financial institutions in South Africa. Shortly afterwards, Dekker became a Johannesburg- and Pretoria-based representative for none other than KBL, a position, according to the records, he held from 1982 until 2001.[74] Dekker declined a request for an interview for *Apartheid Guns and Money*, arguing that he was still bound by Armscor's secrecy provisions. He did deny that Kredietbank played any role in weapons procurement for apartheid, or in assisting in the provision of loans to Armscor, despite documentary evidence to the contrary.[75]

In pursuit of accountability

Today Kredietbank is known as KBC Bank and is the 28th largest bank in Europe in 2022 by measured assets (close to R6 trillion) with 41,000 employees across the globe.[76] It survived the 2008 financial crisis through a Belgian government bailout and by selling off KBL to Qatari investors for over €1 billion (R15 billion).

These powerful European banks have never been held to account for their role as accomplices in the crime of apartheid. The scope and scale of their involvement stands shoulder to shoulder with the role of banks such as HSBC and many local banks given their role in enabling the state capture project under Jacob Zuma's ANC. The extensive collaboration of international financial institutions in our violent past and present means we need to work harder in order to hold them to account.

Open Secrets has taken steps towards holding the apartheid banks to account. In 2018 Open Secrets, together with Centre for Applied Legal Studies (CALS), laid a complaint with the Organisation for Economic Co-operation and Development (OECD) national contact points

(NCPs) in the Belgian and Luxembourg governments.[77] This concerned the conduct of KBC (Belgium) and KBL (Luxembourg – which has since rebranded as Quintet bank following a takeover by the Qatari royal family) and their impact on human rights in Southern Africa. Juan Pablo Bohoslavsky, a UN Independent Expert on the Effects of Foreign Debt, made a powerful submission to the Belgium and Luxembourg OECD NCPs, which supported our complaint and called for the NCPs to investigate the matter.[78] This complaint was rejected on spurious grounds and Open Secrets has shown that the process in Belgium in particular was unsuccessful in large part because the banks had asserted themselves in the adjudication process.[79]

In 2019, following the flawed decision by the NCPs, Open Secrets submitted a detailed docket to the National Director of Public Prosecutions (NDPP) and the head of the Hawks General Godfrey Lebeya.[80] The docket was accompanied by a letter of support and various petitions by eight former TRC commissioners, three TRC members, and twenty-two civil society originations. A letter from Professor John Dugard, emeritus professor of law, called for a full investigation of the banks with a view towards their prosecution. At the time of writing this book, twenty-four months have passed without the NPA or Hawks providing a clear plan to investigate one of the most significant financial crimes in South Africa's history.

Open Secrets is committed to continuing a decade-long battle for accountability in this matter. Such efforts are important because those who profited from serious international crimes like apartheid must be held to account and because we must send a message to banks across the globe that their role as collaborators in corruption and state capture will no longer be ignored.

FIVE
Dame Margaret Hodge MP: A very British apartheid profiteer

It is amazing how many friends and admirers Nelson Mandela had, particularly after his release. The people and institutions that supported apartheid, while claiming to do the opposite, are foremost among those who deserve, at the very least, a public accounting of their behaviour.

In June 1994, only two months after South Africa's first post-apartheid election, Margaret Hodge gave an interview to the *New Statesman*.[81] Hodge had just been elected as the Member of the British Parliament for the safe Labour seat of Barking. Asked what had had the greatest impact on her political beliefs, Hodge replied that 'the ending of apartheid and the holding of democratic elections in South Africa have restored a sense of optimism and hope that I was in danger of losing'.[82] Asked 'which political figure – living or dead – do you most admire?' – well, you can guess who she answered.

A little known fact, until Open Secrets started digging, is that her family's very successful company ran a highly profitable joint-venture partnership in South Africa for the majority of the 1970s and 1980s: precisely the period in which the anti-apartheid movement had called for extensive economic sanctions and disinvestment. For the life of this joint venture, she saw fit to hold shares in the special purpose vehicle that held her family's slice of the pie.

Hodge's assistant Alex Conneely Hughes, in response to questions from Open Secrets, conceded that she was aware of her family's business in apartheid South Africa.[83] We were told that Hodge and her sisters protested this in a letter to their father in 1973. We were, however, not provided with a copy of the letter following a request to do so. According to Hodge their father took no heed of this call. She further claimed that all profits she derived from the South African business between 1973–1994 were given to a charity.

However, Hodge claims through her spokesperson not to have any recollection of the charities to which she donated her apartheid profits for a period of over twenty years. The spokesperson also couldn't say how Hodge was able to determine what part of her dividends were made up of profits from South Africa and profits from other jurisdictions.

And while Hodge may have paid dividends to charities she can't recall, she chose not to sell shares held in her own name. These shares would have increased in value as her family's company thrived, including in apartheid South Africa.

Another Oppenheimer makes a fortune in South Africa

Apartheid's depredations were obvious, many and utterly vile. This ensured that the international community was in no doubt as to what apartheid was, who was responsible for it and how soon it needed to be ended. The call for sanctions and disinvestment was loud and clear, and the anti-apartheid movement was diligent in ensuring that lists of international companies with South African subsidiaries were widely distributed.

Yet, apartheid continued – flourished, even – during the 1970s and into 1980s. It did so largely because it was profitable, both for local and international business. The opportunity for making a buck in South Africa on the back of black labour was enticing enough to ensure that, the opprobrium shown towards the country on the international stage notwithstanding, the apartheid government never ran short of businesses and governments willing to look the other way.

One of the companies that would make hay under apartheid's glaring sun was Coutinho, Caro & Co (London) (CCC).[84] CCC had been formed in 1951 by Hans Oppenheimer (no relation to the South African mining family of the same name), a German immigrant who had settled in London following a stint in Egypt, and was a subsidiary of a German steel trader of the same name.

Hans Oppenheimer – Margaret Hodge's father – was joined in managing the company by his son, Ralph (Hodge's brother), in the late 1960s. Ralph helped to oversee the rapid expansion of the company, which was renamed Stemcor, a contraction of Steel Marketing Corporation, when the family took 100 per cent control in 1987.[85] By 2000 Stemcor had a turnover of £1 billion and a decade later was ranked as the world's largest independent steel trader.[86]

From at least 1973 onwards, the Oppenheimer family held their share of CCC through a special-purpose vehicle called Irene Securities. Margaret Watson, as Hodge was then known, held over 6 per cent of the shares in Irene Securities for the remainder of the 1970s and 1980s.[87]

In 1973, CCC formed a joint venture in South Africa with the multi-sector conglomerate Protea Holdings. The joint venture was called, creatively, Protea International. Company records for Protea International show that, in July 1973, the company issued 10,000 shares. CCC held 4,999 'B' shares and Protea Holdings held 4,999 'A' shares – cementing the 50/50 split in ownership between the two companies in Protea International. In addition, CCC was represented on the board of Protea International by Herbert Edmonds, a top CCC company man for close to three decades.[88]

CCC's shareholding in Protea International would not go unnoticed by the activist community. The information was not hard to find – Protea International was listed as a subsidiary in every CCC annual report from the year it was formed, as was its location in South Africa. By 1988, the UK-based Anti-Apartheid Movement included CCC and Protea International in a call for the 'complete withdrawal of all foreign firms from South Africa and Namibia', motivated by 'the particular role which foreign investment plays in supporting the apartheid system'.[89]

Apartheid profits: 'Highly satisfactory'

It is difficult, based on the available documents, to quantify exactly how well Protea International did. The remaining records of Protea International are scattered across in archives in South Africa, and none of the surviving records indicate how much money flowed through the company. The records of CCC, available from Companies House in the UK and considerably more fulsome, provide a limited window. Between 1982 and 1987, CCC's company statements record turnover by segment and geographical area, including for the whole of Africa. They show that, between 1982 and 1987, CCC recorded a hefty turnover in Africa worth £73,399,554 – equal to over £240 million in 2022, or about R4.9 billion.[90]

During this period, CCC also had a subsidiary and office in Kenya, meaning that we cannot calculate the exact proportion of African turnover earned by Protea International. We do know, however, that it would have been very substantial. Indeed, in 1987, in Stemcor's first annual statement, Ralph Oppenheimer wrote a chairman's statement that provided an overview of the company's prospects. 'Protea International (Pty) Limited had another highly satisfactory year in 1987,' Oppenheimer wrote. 'Protea has been one of our most successful investments since we first established the company in 1973 as an equal partnership with Protea Holdings.'[91]

Protea: Forged from steel

Protea International's success was predicated, at least in part, on its ability to integrate itself into the apartheid economic machine at the highest and most influential levels. In January 1980, South Africa's *Sunday Times* newspaper ran a rare and detailed profile of Protea International, giving a unique insight into where and how the company made its money. The profile was written following a South African government-backed trade delegation to South America, which was led by John Kopiski, Protea International's managing director.[92]

Initially, Protea International worked primarily as an importer, bringing steel into the South African market. But, from 1976 onwards, this situation was reversed, and the company became a net exporter of South African steel.

Like CCC and Stemcor, Protea International produced none of its own steel, rather acting as an international agent for existing steel producers. Protea sourced its steel in South Africa from a number of sources, of which Iscor appears to be most prominent. Iscor was the South African state-owned steel giant and one of the major economic pillars of South Africa's resource-heavy economy.

Protea International's rapid growth was attributed to its particular acuity in expanding into Central and South America, where, by 1980, it was selling R100-million worth of South African steel and other products, serviced by a network of facilities across the continent. For example, Protea International opened marketing offices in Buenos Aires and Sao Paulo – both then under the rule of military dictatorships.

The company also maintained permanent representatives in both Peru and apartheid's ally Chile, run by Augusto Pinochet, a violent dictator.[93] Protea International – and CCC – was thus turning healthy profits selling apartheid steel to Pinochet's Chile.

The apartheid military ties

For a company formed in 1973, Protea International had, by the late 1970s and early 1980s, reached impressive heights. And while the company may well have been uniquely staffed with excellent salespeople, it must surely also have benefited from the close connections between the apartheid regime and its other parent company, with whom CCC had got into bed in 1973: Protea Holdings.

From its very earliest days, Protea Holdings, a sizeable industrial conglomerate, could count on the support of Richard Lurie, who would become a major investor and director. Lurie, who died in 2007, was the archetypal self-made man.[94] Starting as a lowly 'tea boy' at the Johannesburg Stock Exchange (JSE), he eventually worked his way up the ladder and was appointed president of the JSE on four occasions between the 1960s and 1980s.

Archival documents show that Lurie's prominence extended into the heart of the apartheid political and military machine. In April 1980, Lurie was invited to join the so-called Defence Advisory Board for two years by PW Botha, at the time the prime minister of South Africa. It was under Botha's watch, first as minister of defence and then prime minister, that apartheid's military machine expanded to eventually swallow a substantial portion of South Africa's economic output – and in which the military would wreak havoc in Angola and Mozambique and be mobilised to violently suppress the protests in the townships.

In the letter, Botha justified the appointment of the council by citing the 'escalating military situation in southern Africa and the possible consequences for the RSA in combating this threat, especially with regard to the effect this may have on the economy and manpower situation'.[95]

Incidentally, the man listed below Lurie in the invitation letter was none other than Basil Hersov. Hersov, a darling of the apartheid business world and a military man himself, was one of the agents paid millions in commissions by BAE Systems in the infamous 1999 Arms Deal[96] – itself a live and active cautionary tale of how apartheid corruption continues to infect the present.

Unsurprisingly for a company that turned a profit under apartheid, Protea Holdings was linked to serious gross human rights violations in the 1970s. In 1971, for example, the South African Institute of Race Relations conducted a survey which found that Protea Holdings was found to be paying poverty wages to its black staff.[97]

But a far more horrifying – and public – story would come to prominence in 1975. The roots of the story stretched back to 1963, when the South African government agreed to allow private companies to set up psychiatric camps on its behalf. By 1975, 11,000 mentally ill persons were housed in these private camps, of which 9,000 were black patients. Public leaks, parliamentary questions in the UK and a detailed investigation in the UK's *Observer* revealed the horror of the prevailing conditions. Black patients were made to sleep thirty to a room on flimsy mats. They were treated by part-time physicians with ghoulish attitudes to African psychiatric patients. The death rates were alarming: in 1973, at one facility called Randwest, 207 of the 3,200 black inmates died.[98]

The source of the influx of black patients was equally disturbing. By and large the populations of the camps were made up of the detritus of apartheid's devastation, 'those who are found wandering, drunk, or collapsed in the streets'. A brief review by a white psychiatrist and a rubber stamp from a magistrate was all that was required to declare the thousands of black Africans insane, rather than simply indigent. After being admitted, they were put to work, making leg irons and coathangers, or sent out as a private labouring army.[99]

Contemporaneous investigators dug deep to find the primary corporate power behind the camps, a company called Intrinsic Investments, of which Lurie was a director. According to an investigation in the US, led by the Congressional Black Caucus, Intrinsic 'was linked to Protea Holdings, specialising in chemicals, drugs, hospitals and medical supplies'.[100]

The story reared its head again in 1979, following a series of site visits by the American Psychiatric Association, the results of which were again reported on in the UK's *Observer*. Their investigation concluded that 'these findings substantiate allegations of social and political abuse of psychiatry in South Africa'.[101]

Giving an interview to the journal *Science News*, the association's President Alan Stone, who led the visits, commented further that 'the most shocking finding of our investigation was the high number of needless deaths among black patients. There was evidence of patients being allowed to die who had treatable illnesses'.[102]

So, at the very time that CCC was working with the apartheid government and Protea Holdings to grow their business, their partner, Intrinsic Investments, was being publicly linked to serious human rights violations in both the South African and British press.

Business the British way?

'Why Margaret Hodge?', you may be asking. Aren't there other examples of equally, if not more, egregious profiteering and double-speak? Hodge symbolises the historical relation between South Africa and Britain which was built on extraction and the creation of wealth in the United Kingdom. From the extraction of minerals built on the brutal migrant labour system to the British government and elite attitudes towards apartheid, oppression has long characterised the UK-South African relationship. Some mealy-mouthed objections aside, Britain was the largest foreign direct investor in the apartheid period and, when it really mattered, Pretoria could rely on Thatcher and the Tories to back the regime.

There is much to lay at the door of the British in the post-apartheid period too. It was BAE Systems, receiving the full diplomatic support of the British government, which was the biggest beneficiary of the Arms Deal. It was also the biggest payer of bribes. Documentary evidence shows that the company was ruthless in finding officials and politically connected comrades to bribe as apartheid ended.

It was Bell Pottinger, a British company set up by Thatcher's spin doctor, which tried to stoke racial discord in defence of the Guptas' outright looting of the South African purse during state capture. In a remarkable turn of events, it was Fana Hlongwane, the most well-known agent paid by BAE Systems in the Arms Deal, who introduced the Guptas to Bell Pottinger on the recommendation of a former BAE executive.

This culture of unaccountability in relations between South Africa and Britain must come to an end. It is time that the British electorate (and the Labour Party) holds people like Hodge accountable for knowingly profiteering at such great human cost. Hodge has clothed herself in the claim that she has dedicated her life to fighting racism – that her very 'being' was anti-racist. The facts suggest otherwise.[103]

2
WAR PROFITEERS

Introduction

THE GLOBAL ARMS TRADE has corruption coursing through its veins. It is a cynical business whose primary target is almost always innocent civilians. The burdens they carry are not only in the physical manifestation of wars that are mostly unjust, but in the violence created by war profiteers who peddle their wares at great cost to societies and democratic institutions across the globe. This chapter focuses on two prominent examples of this – the 1999 arms deal in South Africa and the ongoing sale of South African weapons to countries in the Middle East that are being used against civilians in Yemen.

As the People's Tribunal on Economic Crime found, the 1999 arms deal, instigated by Thabo Mbeki and others, was the bridge between the economic crimes of apartheid and the state capture of recent years.[1] The final agreement sealing the 1999 Strategic Defence Procurement Package – the infamous 'arms deal' – was signed on 3 December 1999. It was a deal that locked South Africa into two decades of insurmountable debt in the form of loan repayments and interest fees. At the time, the arms deal, already surrounded by controversy and allegations of fraud, corruption and impropriety, was the largest foreign procurement undertaken by South Africa's democratic government. At the time, R30 billion was spent on the deal. However, this value was at the 1999 exchange rate and did not include two decades' worth of costs related to the financing of the deal such as fluctuating interest rates, transfer costs and other repayment fees. The arms deal made arms companies and banks very rich. Arms deal expert Paul Holden calculated that a staggering R142 billion had been spent on all arms deal-related costs by October 2020 when final payments were made.[2]

If we take the upper figure, it is equivalent to every South African alive today forking out close to R24,000 for a corrupt project that has damaged our democracy and its people. A measure of the social cost of the arms deal is that it would cover the cost of one year of the Basic Income Grant for all citizens.[3] This is a sum that the Minister of Finance and many corporate bigwigs claim is currently unaffordable. This multi-billion-rand deal was made at a time when South Africa should have been ramping up efforts to combat its growing HIV/AIDS epidemic. It was just years before that then health minister, Nkosazana Dlamini-Zuma, claimed that an ARV programme that would combat mother-to-child transmissions was too expensive to contemplate.[4] At the time, for every R1 spent on the HIV/AIDS programme (including providing anti-retrovirals), R7.63 was spent on the arms deal.[5]

Apart from the extortionate cost, it is unclear if the weapons were needed at all. The White Paper on National Defence presented by Parliament and approved by Cabinet in 1996 – one year before the 1997 official start of the arms deal acquisition process – clearly acknowledged that there was no military threat to South Africa. In fact, the White Paper emphasised that South Africa's focus had shifted from a military offensive approach to an approach that allowed for the needs of the population to be prioritised as 'poverty [w]as SA's biggest risk to national security'.[6] Yet, as is too often the case, profit was placed above the most basic needs of South Africans. The notoriously dirty global arms trade, where arms companies dole out billions in bribes as a cost of doing business, ensured ample opportunities for self-enrichment by politicians, corporations and middlemen. This trumped the need for social welfare and housing projects.

This section delves into some of the key corporations and individuals implicated in corruption in the arms deal who should be held to account. There are indeed many, many more – but these would represent a powerful start.

We also probe the world's worst humanitarian crisis – the war in Yemen, which South African-German arms company Rheinmetall

Denel Munition and others have used to rake in profits while their wares can be linked to the murder of civilians in a faraway land that receives relatively little media attention.

Collectively these war profiteers are all engaged in violence and human rights abuse for which they should be held to account.

ONE
Jacob Zuma and Thales: Comrades in arms

AFTER A DECADE OF JACOB Zuma's scandal-ridden presidency, and the catastrophic impact of state capture under his watch, it is easy to forget that his efforts have been almost entirely dedicated to ensuring he remains unaccountable for alleged crimes committed *before* he was president. Zuma's long and most tumultuous run-in with the law actually relates to his role in the 1999 arms deal, not his relationship with the grifters in the Gupta family. He currently stands accused of eighteen charges of fraud, corruption, racketeering and money laundering, related to 783 payments made to him by convicted fraudster Schabir Shaik. His co-accused is the South African subsidiary of the mega French arms company Thales (previously known as Thomson-CSF), alleged to have bribed Zuma to protect itself from prosecution in relation to the deal.

The failure to hold Zuma and these corporations to account for their alleged crimes has had far-reaching consequences for South Africa's young democracy. Zuma and his allies inside and outside the state have contributed to delaying legal processes, deferring justice and undermining key institutions. Together, this has created a culture of impunity which has enabled opportunities for current-day state capture.

Schabir Shaik: Part-time businessman, full-time fraudster

Allegations of corruption related to the role of Zuma and Thales in the arms deal have been ventilated in South African courts. In 2005, Judge Hilary Squires convicted Schabir Shaik on charges of fraud and corruption, and described the relationship between Shaik, Zuma and Thales as a 'mutually beneficial symbiosis'.[7] As Zuma's close friend and financial adviser, as well as Thales's South African BEE partner in the bid to win the contract to supply the weapon systems for South Africa's newly acquired warships, Shaik was perfectly positioned to act as middleman between the two, protecting their respective interests, and his own.

Shaik was charged on two counts of corruption for his role in the arms deal, both of which related to undue payments by him to Zuma, both before and after he became the deputy president of South Africa. He also faced a third count of fraud for misrepresentation of financial records related to an arm of his Nkobi group of companies.

Shaik's first charge of corruption related to what the state called a 'generalised pattern of corrupt behaviour between [Shaik] and Zuma'.[8] The court found that, from 1995 to 2002, an already cash-strapped Shaik, either directly or through his companies, made numerous scheduled payments to Zuma totalling R1,282,027.63, while having full knowledge of Zuma's financial state and inability to pay him back.

Given all of this, the court found that the 'irresistible' inference was that Shaik made the payments in anticipation of some business-related benefit that Zuma could deliver through his name, the backing of his political office and vast 'political connectivity'. In its findings, the court ruled that Shaik must have foreseen that, by making these payments to Zuma, the latter would continue to provide support upon which Shaik and his companies were entirely dependent.

Shaik's second charge related to the arranged payment of R500,000 per year to Zuma from French arms company Thales. The purpose of this alleged bribe, facilitated by Shaik, was clear. In the face of looming pressure and impending investigations, Thales was to pay Zuma in order to ensure that Zuma would use his political influence to provide protection from investigative processes and to ensure that Thales would be looked at favourably for future South African projects. The alleged payment was to buy impunity and enable continued profits.

Again, such practices are standard in the world of grand corruption, where large corporations often buy politicians through campaign contributions or 'brown envelopes' with an understanding that favours will be returned when needed.

Thales: The French connection

It is for this reason that Thales stands in the dock as Zuma's co-accused. But as Open Secrets has shown through its investigations, Thales has a long history of flouting international laws to profit from its links to South Africa; its predecessor Thomson-CSF had a long and profitable relationship with the apartheid military and political elite, despite the compulsory UN arms embargo.[9]

It is alleged that Jacob Zuma first entered into a formal agreement with the director of Thales's South African subsidiary, Alain Thétard, and Schabir Shaik at a meeting in Durban in March of 2000. This was the meeting in which it was agreed that R500,000 per year would be paid to Zuma by Thales. The payments would be made through a network of Shaik's business accounts. This agreement was reached as calls from within government and from civil society groups for an investigation into irregular procurement processes related to the arms deal were growing in urgency.

During Shaik's trial, all parties denied that this meeting took place and that any such agreement was made. However, Sue Delique, Thétard's former secretary, was able to provide evidence in the form of the now infamous encrypted fax sent by Thétard to Thales's sales director for Africa. The fax not only confirmed that the meeting had indeed taken place, but also that an agreement had been reached with Zuma.

In the Shaik trial, Judge Squires concluded that all parties present at this March 2000 meeting knew exactly what it was that they were agreeing to and that this payment was clearly made to ensure the protection of Thales from investigation and prosecution. The parties even concocted a code phrase fit for a cheap spy thriller to seal the deal – Zuma was to confirm his acceptance of the bribe by saying 'I see the Eiffel Tower lights shining today'.[10]

Another day in Stalingrad: The state vs Zuma

The successful prosecution of Shaik should have opened the doors for the National Prosecuting Authority (NPA) to pursue a case against Zuma himself. In fact, the final judgment mentioned Zuma's name 471 times.[11] However, the NPA chose not to pursue a case against Zuma immediately on the basis that the prospects of success were not strong enough.[12]

For the last two decades, both Zuma and various elements in the state have been responsible for delaying processes and dragging this case out for the last two decades, all while sowing seeds of doubt and mistrust of legal systems and investigative bodies in the minds of many South Africans.

In 2006, after his involvement in Shaik's web of fraud and corruption was laid out in the courts, Zuma was himself charged with numerous counts of corruption, fraud and racketeering. However, after months of postponements, these charges were struck off the roll by Judge Herbert Msimang as prosecutors made repeated requests for further delays in the case, citing their unreadiness.[13]

In 2007, the Scorpions – the predecessor to the Hawks and a successful independent agency that investigated and prosecuted organised crime and corruption – indicted Zuma on various counts of racketeering, money laundering, fraud and corruption. However, the charges were again thrown out by the courts as Judge Chris Nicholson ruled that the National Director of Public Prosecutions (NDPP) did not give Zuma a chance to make representations before charges were filed against him. In 2009, the Supreme Court of Appeal (SCA) rejected this argument, finding that there was no need for Zuma to be allowed to make representations before he was charged, thus allowing the NDPP to revisit charges against Zuma.

However, shortly after this ruling, the spy tapes scandal emerged. The 'spy tapes' referred to the secretly recorded conversations between the former NDPP Bulelani Ngcuka and Scorpions head Leonard McCarthy, that Zuma's legal defence would use as evidence of collusion. The mysterious and well-timed emergence of these spy tapes resulted in the conspiracy theory that the decision to bring charges against Zuma was politically motivated. Zuma and his lawyers argued that there had been an abuse of process on the part of Ngcuka and McCarthy, and that the timing of the charges had been manipulated for ends other than the legitimate purpose of a prosecution.[14] Again, these charges were taken off the table by the acting NDPP, Mokotedi Mpshe, who rejected arguments made by his own prosecutors that the 'spy tapes' were immaterial to the actual charges.

One would assume that evidence of a conspiracy to quell Zuma's aspirations of the presidency would be something he would want in the public domain. However, Jacob Zuma, his legal team and Mpshe fought to ensure that the spy tapes be kept under wraps. This prompted a near decade-long battle to have the tapes released and the charges reinstated. The reason for this fight was at least partly because their disclosure shows that the tapes had nothing to do with the substance of the corruption charges facing Zuma.

Judge Seriti's corruption cover-up commission

While the spy tapes battle raged on, President Zuma, in October 2011, announced a commission of inquiry headed by Judge Willie Seriti to investigate allegations of corruption in the arms deal. The Commission, marred by numerous high-level resignations and allegations of hidden political agendas, was labelled by many civil society organisations a whitewash. Four years and R137 million later, the Commission, which failed to consider key evidence or call important witnesses – including Zuma or Schaik – produced a report that exonerated all parties.[15] This report has been used by Zuma and his allies to further bolster their defence. That is, until 2019, when the North Gauteng High Court set aside the findings of the Commission, ruling in favour of the application by civil society groups Corruption Watch and the Right2Know Campaign. The court found that the Commission had fundamentally failed to do its job by finding 'a clear failure [by the Seriti Commission and its judges] to test evidence of key witnesses [and] a refusal to take account of documentary evidence which contained the most serious allegations'.[16]

In an effort to pursue accountability for the cover-up at the Arms Deal Commission, Open Secrets and Shadow World Investigations submitted a complaint concerning the conduct of both judges, Judge Seriti and Judge Musi, to the Judicial Services Commission, which referred the matter to the Judicial Conduct Committee in 2021 for review.[17] At the time of writing, the two judges were attempting to avoid any sanction of their conduct through representations in court, mounting a Stalingrad strategy of their own.

The NPA gets back in the ring

A major blow was dealt to Zuma's obfuscations when, in 2017, the high court in Pretoria and SCA ruled that the decision to withdraw the charges against Zuma and Thales had been irrational, and that the NPA must reconsider the decision. The court held that Mpshe's decision was irrational because the contents of the tapes did not negatively impact the validity of the investigation, the weight of the evidence or the merits of the prosecution. In a radical about turn, and further evidence of Zuma's cynical legal strategy, Zuma's legal team conceded to the SCA that they agreed that the decision, which they had so vigorously defended for a decade at huge cost to the taxpayer, had been irrational. The NPA formally reinstated the charges in March 2018.

Ironically, given their complicity in the delays and the fact that the alleged corruption was precisely to ensure avoidance of prosecution, both Zuma and Thales have continued to argue that they are unable to receive a fair trial, partly because of this delay. Both parties have submitted requests for a permanent stay of prosecution on this basis. Crucially, in October of 2019, the KwaZulu-Natal high court rejected Zuma and Thales's respective applications for a permanent stay of prosecution. The judgment stated that the seriousness of the offences faced by Zuma outweighs any prejudice that he claims he will suffer if the trial proceeds.[18] The parties appealed to the SCA, but the appeal was thrown out without hearing arguments on the basis that it had no prospects of success.[19]

In 2020, Zuma's legal team made a 'a damaging admission', explaining that Zuma would only have taken the stand at Shaik's trial in 2005 if he had been guaranteed immunity from prosecution, adding that testifying 'would have been ill-conceived and highly risky [...] without waiving [his] guaranteed constitutional rights, including rights to silence and against self-incrimination'.[20] This statement infers that Zuma, contrary to what he has argued for at least fifteen years, is aware of his role in the crimes of which Shaik has been prosecuted. This repositioning on the part of Zuma and his lawyers may well come back to haunt them if and when his trial continues.

Justice down but not out

In 2021 Zuma's legal team lead by Dali Mpofu SC took South Africans deeper into the Stalingrad legal territory. It is an approach that worked well for Zuma's late Counsel Kemp J. Kemp and Mpofu has become a latter-day tactician at such legal battles, which seemingly achieve little other than the delay of justice.

The current iteration of the Stalingrad strategy is focused on the contention that the lead state prosecutor Adv. Billy Downer lacks '"independence and impartiality" and that the impending trial has already been tainted by political and unlawful meddling, specifically involving the National Prosecuting Authority. Downer would thus be unable to conduct a "lawful prosecution" that would uphold Zuma's constitutional rights to a fair trial.'[21] There are many reasons why Zuma and by extension Thales no doubt fear Downer, and high up on that list is that he successfully led the legal team that ensured Shaik's conviction in 2005.

Despite these delay tactics, the Zuma-Thales trial is likely to go ahead in 2023. If it does it will be the result of years of relentless hard work and toil by those in civil society and state institutions who have gathered the evidence and struggled against those who would rather entrench secrecy and impunity.

TWO

BAE Systems: The great British rip-off

UK MEGA ARMS CORPORATION BAE Systems used its network of covert partners, offshore companies and secretive, but highly lucrative, money transfers firstly to ensure it won the most lucrative part of the 1999 arms deal, and then later to avoid accountability for the alleged bribe payments upon which its selection relied. With its modus operandi laid bare, and the evidence overwhelming, there is no reason for BAE to remain unaccountable.

BAE's dodgy business background

BAE Systems, previously known as British Aerospace, is a British behemoth in the notoriously corrupt global arms trade. The UK-based company has and continues to supply arms to war-torn regions across the globe, seemingly with little regard for the lived realities of the civilians who suffer as BAE's jets drop bombs on them. The most recent example of BAE's willingness to put profit before their human rights obligations is their continued supply of weapons to Saudi Arabia despite the Saudis' ongoing human rights abuses in Yemen. This was affirmed by a June 2019 UK court ruling which declared UK arms sales to Saudi Arabia unlawful. Not even this has stopped BAE from continuing its supply.²² The company has continued to make its regular flights from England to Saudi Arabia with the cargo and the expertise needed to continue the indiscriminate bombing of Yemeni civilians.²³

BAE has a long and lucrative history with Saudi Arabia, assisted along the way by the British political establishment. In 1985, BAE entered into a deal to supply Saudi Arabia with fighter jets and other aircraft. The deal, known as the Al-Yamamah deal, was sanctioned by Margaret Thatcher and would come to be known as the most corrupt transaction in commercial history.²⁴ At the time, the deal was worth about £43 billion.²⁵ It later emerged, during an investigation by the UK Serious Fraud Office (SFO), that BAE had paid more than £6 billion in bribes to UK and Saudi politicians and middlemen in order to secure the deal.

However, as the SFO investigation started gaining traction, the UK government, pressured by threats of 'repercussions' from the Saudis, made the call to halt the SFO's investigation, claiming that prosecution would be unlikely.²⁶ It later emerged that this decision was made after direct intervention by then Prime Minister Tony Blair, who insisted that the investigation into BAE's conduct in relation to the Saudi Kingdom be stopped.

Despite two decades of denying any wrongdoing in their global operations, including in Saudi Arabia, BAE did acknowledge a 'serious accounting offence' regarding their activities in Tanzania. It settled that case with the SFO for a mere £30 million, a fraction of what it made from the deal. In a separate settlement with the United States government, BAE paid $400 million for violations of laws that bar the use of bribe payments to secure deals in Saudi Arabia, the Czech Republic, Hungary and other countries.²⁷

This was a mere slap on the wrist. Arguably, this failure to pursue real accountability cemented a culture of impunity and allowed BAE to continue to operate its network around the globe and eventually expand its business to South Africa.

BAE Systems: Big game hunting in South Africa

On 3 December 1999, when the final agreements related to South Africa's multi-billion-rand Strategic Defence Package were signed,

BAE Systems had secured itself the largest and most lucrative of all the contracts. It was awarded the contract to supply the South African Air Force with 24 Hawk trainer aircrafts, as well as a second contract – along with Swedish defence company SAAB – to supply 26 Gripen fighter jets. Together, these contracts were worth R15.77 billion (valued at about R45 billion today), which was more than half the total cost of the arms deal at the time.

However, as set out below, the process to ensure BAE's selection as South Africa's preferred supplier of these aircrafts was long and riddled with procedural inconsistencies and irregularities.

BAE, with the help of the UK government, had in fact been lobbying key South African figures from as early as 1993. It is reported that the former UK Prime Minister John Major met with President Nelson Mandela in September of 1994, armed with a letter lobbying on behalf of the UK arms industry which, in the wake of apartheid, had identified South Africa as a potential new arms purchaser.[28] This was three years before then Deputy President and head of the Cabinet sub-committee on acquisitions, Thabo Mbeki, formally announced tender invitations for what would be the most expensive post-apartheid government acquisition.[29]

With the support of the British government, through the Defence Export Service Organisation (DESO), BAE, along with other British suppliers, was able to get its products and proposals in front of the Department of Defence before there was even a deal to speak of. By the time the arms deal was announced, a network of questionable relationships had been formed.

Selling South Africa weapons it did not need, nor could afford

By 1994 the South African Air Force (SAAF) was reconsidering its system, which required three different types of aircrafts at three different skill levels. It first decided that only the mid-tier aircrafts needed to be replaced as the aircrafts at the other tiers were still fully operational with a considerable lifespan remaining; it then decided to transition to a two-tier system. Under the two-tier system, pilots would first train on Pilatus trainers and then move onto a fighter jet that could work as both a jet fighter and as a trainer.[30] Under the two-tier system, BAE would not have had a chance – they were offering trainer and fighter jets separately, rather than a multi-role trainer/fighter.

The SAAF invited the submission of tenders from international suppliers. By March 1997, twenty-three bids had been received and narrowed down to four preferred suppliers. Notably, BAE, who had submitted tenders for both its Hawk and Gripen crafts, did not make the shortlist. The Hawk was rejected because it did not meet the operational requirements, and the Gripen was rejected because it was too expensive.

BAE did not take this failure lying down. Insistent on expanding its market, it embarked on an intensive lobbying process. Soon thereafter, then Minister of Defence Joe Modise intervened to change SAAF's system back to a three-tier system, thus creating a space in which BAE's Hawk and Gripen could be reconsidered and ultimately selected.

The final selection of BAE and SAAB's Gripen eventually came down to a technicality.[31] The bids were evaluated on three criteria: technical, financing and offsets. However, mysteriously, neither of the other suppliers under consideration submitted the necessary financing information.

Why would two bidders at the final stage of a multi-billion-rand acquisition process fail to submit documents needed to possibly secure a lucrative deal? Despite claims by South African officials that repeated requests were made to these arms companies to submit their information, representatives of the losing bidders have alleged that no requests were made for additional information.[32]

As was the case with the Gripen, BAE's Hawk bid was evaluated on three criteria. However, the Hawk faced even bigger obstacles to selection, as it was both technically less impressive than the other options and more expensive. BAE's Hawk ultimately only won the contract after the direct intervention of then Minister of Defence Joe Modise. In an April 1998 meeting of the Arms Acquisition Council, Modise called for a 'visionary approach' to be adopted and that cost as a criterion in the evaluation of the bids be removed.[33] Or, in other words, one of South Africa's most expensive post-apartheid contracts would be decided with cost excluded. This was good news for BAE whose offer was twice as expensive as its nearest competitor.

Moreover, the offsets offered by BAE were given a huge score that dwarfed its competitors. Offsets were one of the major incentives offered to ensure the public's approval of the vast amount of money that the arms deal would cost South Africa. The offsets were developmental kickbacks meant to promote economic growth and industrial development within South Africa, though few ever materialised.

The World Trade Organization (WTO) generally prohibits using 'offsets' as a selection criterion within procurement processes, as they have been argued to constitute 'legal bribery'.[34] Remarkably, though, the arms industry, an industry which is said to contribute 40 per cent of all corrupt transactions globally[35] is exempt from this rule, and has come to rely on offset programmes to secure contracts.

In this case, BAE submitted an offset proposal that was roughly ten times larger than that of any of their competitors. However, it would later be confirmed that the offset benefits offered by BAE under the Hawk agreement were grossly miscalculated.[36] Their promise of R10 billion actually only equated to R1.5 billion in offsets. The Hawk was thus selected on the basis of egregiously wrong information. While this information would usually be enough to cancel or re-evaluate the contracts, no effort was made by the acquisition committee to do either.

BAE bags big trophies

As we detail in the next chapters, BAE relied on a number of overt and covert agents in their vast network to advance their business interests across the world.

This network was blown wide open in November 2008 when the Scorpions raided the properties of BAE Systems South Africa and their key agents, Fana Hlongwane and the late John Bredenkamp. In order to secure the search warrants necessary for the raids to take place, the Scorpions relied heavily on an affidavit from the United Kingdom's Serious Fraud Office (SFO).[37]

The SFO affidavit outlined how BAE had allegedly run a system of agents in South Africa in an effort to secure contracts in the arms deal. This system operated with the explicit intention to facilitate payment of massive 'commissions' – totalling £115 million – by BAE to various agents.[38]

This network not only ensured that BAE could continue to maximise its profits, but also that it could avoid any scrutiny from investigative authorities, and that payments could be made to those in positions of power without being traced.

According to the SFO affidavit, in the 1990s BAE was looking for a system to conceal payments to its system of agents following concern that payments they had been making to Chilean dictator Agusto Pinochet might be discovered. By 1998, Red Diamond Trading Limited was established in the notorious tax haven of the British Virgin Islands for this purpose. The company was set up specifically to make payments to covert agents, as records show that BAE's overt agents continued to be paid through normal BAE channels. The SFO rejected the defence presented by BAE executive Mike Turner that these payments were made solely to avoid scrutiny from media and anti-arms campaigners. Instead, the SFO concluded that Red Diamond was primarily used with the explicit intent to ensure that corrupt payments could be made without raising any alarms within law enforcement agencies.[39]

BAE's beneficiaries included the following powerful South African politicians:

Joe Modise

Joe Modise was the defence minister at the time of the arms deal. As noted above, before his death in 2001, Modise was accused of altering procurement processes during the arms deal, specifically to ensure BAE's selection. His interventions in this regard are discussed above, and included demanding that the acquisition process ignore the issues of cost. He was also accused of failing to declare clear conflicts of interest; companies in which he held shares stood to profit approximately R20 million from contracts related to the fulfilment of BAE's offset obligations. Whilst there was considerable suspicion related to his role in the BAE network, investigation into the former defence minister ceased after his death.

Stella Sigcau

The late Stella Sigcau was the Minister of Public Enterprise at the time of the deal. Sigcau was one of five members of the Cabinet sub-committee in charge of the acquisition process, along with Thabo Mbeki, Joe Modise, Trevor Manuel and Alec Erwin.

In 2013, evidence emerged that Sigcau was another player that BAE provided benefits to in order to advance its arms deal bid.[40] Fax messages dated September 1998,[41] uncovered during the SFO investigation, indicate that BAE's representative in South Africa, Alan McDonald, had helped to arrange for Sigcau's daughter to be given a job in the United Kingdom, as well as further assistance for Sigcau's grandchildren.

Was this assistance related to the deal? In the fax, McDonald asks for assistance in ensuring that Sigcau is given the support that she requested for a personal family matter. Conveniently, McDonald prefaces his request by stating that

> the fact we have got Hawk on to the final list is very much due to our friends in the country rather than the quality of our ITP [Invitation To Prequalify] response. One friend who has, and remains, absolutely critical to our ultimate success for both Hawk and Gripen is Minister Stella Sigcau.[42]

Not only does McDonald acknowledge BAE's reliance on local agents and their favours to ensure selection, but he also seemingly acknowledges the poor quality of their bid.

Additional correspondence between Portia Ndzamela, Sigcau's daughter, and a BAE representative confirms that efforts were made to secure a job as well as a residence for Ndzamela and her children in London.[43] In that correspondence, Ndzamela not only thanks the BAE representative for the support services during her trip to London, which she describes as 'outstanding and of the highest order', but also says that she looks forward to making the move to London and 'developing a friendly and professional relationship that will be mutually beneficial'.[44]

It is clear from these fax messages that BAE understood that, by providing Sigcau with the requested support for her daughter, their bid would be favourably considered or even prioritised.

BAE: A response and no responsibility

When Open Secets first published some of the details of the involvement of BAE agents in the deal, BAE offered a statement in response to Open Secrets's calls for arms deal-era accountability which read:

> *Our settlements with the [UK Serious Fraud Office] SFO and [US Department of Justice] DOJ a decade ago followed long investigations by those authorities relating to a number of countries, including South Africa. Neither settlement involved charges of bribery or corruption relating to South Africa or any other country.*

BAE's response conveniently ignores a third settlement – a 2011 settlement with the US Department of State. In that settlement, BAE admitted to using their Red Diamond system to pay agents in South Africa. Yet in the earlier DOJ settlement, they had admitted that the payments through Red Diamond were made with the knowledge that they 'would be used to ensure BAE was favoured in foreign government decisions regarding the sale of defence articles'.[45] Read together, the two settlements provide the irresistible inference that the payments made through Red Diamond to agents in South Africa were made to influence the South African government.

Like many of those implicated in arms deal-era corruption, BAE has managed to escape accountability for its role in the erosion of South Africa's democratic institutions and citizens' trust. They took advantage of a country in transition in order to further their own profits. BAE should be one of the first mega corporations to account for its role in this story. Its deep pockets also mean it is well placed to pay back the money.

THREE
John Bredenkamp: BAE's bagman

BAE MANAGED TO LAND one of the most lucrative arms deal contracts despite protests from heads of both the South African Air Force and the South African National Defence Force, who expressed their concerns about the exorbitant cost of BAE's Gripen and Hawk, and its failure to meet the full requirement specifications.[46] So, how did BAE manage to secure these deals when the very institutions for which these aircrafts were being purchased were in protest? The controversial choice only starts to make sense when examining the influential middlemen they had on their side.

Enter, John Bredenkamp.

The flamethrower salesman

John Bredenkamp is deserving of the infamy that polite company fastidiously reserves for the corrupt Gupta family. He is a notorious figure in the world of international clandestine deals. A known smuggler, tobacco and arms trafficker, sanctions-buster and occasional businessman, Bredenkamp has made a fortune across various industries despite being at the centre of numerous criminal allegations throughout his career.

Bredenkamp is alleged to have assisted numerous pariah states to bust sanctions. Zimbabwean-born, Bredenkamp managed to find favour in the inner circle of both the Ian Smith and Robert Mugabe regimes. He has admitted to having assisted Smith, the prime minister of Rhodesia (now Zimbabwe) in the 1970s, to break international sanctions in order to ensure that the colonial regime remained armed. Despite this history, Bredenkamp was able to form a relationship with Mugabe as the new head of state, which allegedly included the provision of financial and logistical support to Mugabe's regime.[47] This included a role in the illegal exploitation and plundering of the natural resources of the Democratic Republic of the Congo between 1998 and 2003.[48]

The relationship resulted in Bredenkamp being added to the United States sanctions list,[49] a decision the European Union and Switzerland shortly followed.[50] Bredenkamp's legal team eventually had his name and companies removed from the European lists, but he remained on the US Office of Foreign Assets Control sanctions list at the time of his death in 2020.[51]

In addition to his support of Mugabe, he allegedly supplied arms to both sides during the Iran-Iraq war. Perhaps most importantly for present purposes, he also sought to bust sanctions with the South African apartheid government.[52] Declassified South African military documents show that Armscor agents approached Bredenkamp in 1982 in an attempt to procure 20,000 flamethrowers. He agreed to take part and provided fraudulent end-user certificates in order to bypass the arms embargo.[53] Thankfully, the deal fell through when Belgian authorities unknowingly intervened and halted the transport process. Nonetheless, it remains horrifying to imagine the suffering that could have been caused if flamethrowers had found their way into the hands of a regime that did not value black lives and deployed troops readily to townships during this time.

These connections with the South African military establishment means it is little surprise that Bredenkamp is implicated in the post-apartheid arms deal scandal.

Bredenkamp and BAE

The importance of Bredenkamp to BAE's bid for the South African deal was brought to the attention of South African authorities by their counterparts in the United Kingdom.

In 2006, after a number of unsuccessful or compromised attempts by South African authorities to investigate allegations of corruption in the arms deal, the United Kingdom's Serious Fraud Office (SFO) submitted a request for assistance from South African authorities in its investigation into BAE's conduct in securing the arms deal contract. South African investigators granted the request in January 2007.

In 2008, the favour was returned as the SFO submitted an affidavit based on their investigation to the National Prosecuting Authority to help further the SA investigation into Bredenkamp and other implicated individuals. The SFO provided damning evidence that BAE was paying a cool R1.2 billion (roughly R2.5 billion in current value) to maintain a complex web of agents, intermediaries and offshore companies that operated in the interest of BAE's South African arms deal bid.

The affidavit to the NPA sparked a number of probes into the conduct of BAE and was central to a last-ditch effort by the South African Scorpions unit to enforce accountability for corruption in the deal. This was before the Scorpions was shut down by order of President Kgalema Motlanthe in 2009 and replaced with the comparatively toothless Hawks, who would go on to scrap their arms deal investigation by 2010.

What was particularly notable in the SFO affidavit was the huge sum of money paid to John Bredenkamp.

According to evidence obtained by the SFO, Kayswell Services Limited, a company registered in the notorious tax haven of the British Virgin Islands (BVI) in which Bredenkamp held 60 per cent of the shares, entered into a formal consultancy agreement with BAE in 1994.[54] However, by 1999, the decision was made to channel payments to Kayswell through another BVI-registered company that was owned by BAE and used specifically for the purpose, ensuring secrecy and avoiding scrutiny called Red Diamond Trading Limited. Red Diamond was used by BAE to pay Kayswell approximately R400 million in relation to BAE's South African arms contracts.

These staggeringly high payments were made despite BAE being unable to prove that Bredenkamp and his company had in fact completed any work for them. So why was Bredenkamp paid?

It is important to keep in mind that BAE was awarded these contracts despite concerns about the exorbitant cost of the Gripen and Hawk and their failure to initially meet the full requirement specifications.[55] Were the payments for Bredenkamp's assistance in securing the contract despite these concerns?

BAE's former managing director for Africa and Asia, Allan McDonald, admitted that they paid Bredenkamp for political connectivity. McDonald told the SFO that Bredenkamp suggested identifying key decision makers and offering financial incentives to them for the selection of the Hawk and Gripen contracts.[56] In particular, McDonald claims Bredenkamp and his team had direct access to Chippy Shaik, the Chief of Acquisitions for the arms deal, adding that they had obtained secret information about Shaik.[57] It's worth remembering that Chippy Shaik is the brother of Shabir Shaik, who worked with Jacob Zuma and Thales to secure kickbacks in another part of the corrupt arms deal.

New evidence unearthed during the Seriti Commission – but which the Commission failed to test or consider – linked a 2002 payment from Bredenkamp's network of associates to a Julekha Mohamed. The most likely identity of this person is the Julekha Mohamed who was a lawyer to President Jacob Zuma and co-director of a company with Chippy Shaik.[58] In October 2006 the Financial Intelligence Unit (FIU) in the tiny principality of Liechtenstein sent a note to the National Prosecutor of Liechtenstein. The FIU identified a number of Bredenkamp-linked companies and business partners, namely Kayswell Services, ACT Worldwide, Julien Pelissier, Trevor Wilmans and Walter Hailwax, as suspects for money laundering offences related to their receipt of funds from BAE System's Red Diamond.[59]

The FIU noted that Julien Pelissier – a business partner of Bredenkamp and significant shareholder of Kayswell – had received $661,000 from Kayswell Services and a further $1.6 million from other sources into a Liechtenstein-based account. The FIU further noted that, according to a transaction list from Pelissier's account, he had transferred $258,000 in September 2002 to an account held at UBS in Switzerland. That account was in Julekha Mohamed's name.

Bredenkamp's network of payments reached in many directions. The SFO investigations also determined that he used Jasper Consulting, another one of the many companies within his network of offshore businesses, to make payments to another individual central to the BAE network of agents in South Africa – Fana Hlongwane.

Bredenkamp: Gone but not forgotten

There is a wealth of evidence from different jurisdictions that implicated Bredenkamp in crimes. The failure to pursue tangible accountability for Bredenkamp, from his sanctions-busting activities all the way through to his arms deal escapades, allowed him to continue to grow his wealth and network of influence until his death in 2020. His name remains etched on the Zanu-PF headquarters he helped fund in Harare – and in many other ways in which his dirty dealing impacted the people of Southern Africa.

FOUR
Fana 'Styles' Hlongwane: BAE agent

THE SELECTION OF BAE as South Africa's largest arms deal contractor made very little financial or logistical sense. BAE was neither the cheapest nor the best option in terms of their machinery, with the head of the South African Air Force himself opposed to the deal early on.

Denying any malfeasance, the South African government ultimately justified their decision to select BAE based on the company's offset proposals. The 'offset' obligations were economic benefits, like new jobs and industry, that government and the arms companies promised the public would flow from the deal. Few, if any, ever materialised.

Once BAE had secured the contracts, they needed to ensure that these offset promises were delivered. This is where Fana Hlongwane's role became important.

All the styles money can buy

A former ranking commander of uMkhonto weSizwe (MK) and a former director of South African arms manufacturer Denel, it comes as no surprise that Fana Hlongwane has carved himself a space in the South African defence industry. Having made his millions from numerous business ventures, directorships and lucrative consultancy agreements, the controversial businessman has come to be associated with the flashy playboy lifestyle. Known by the nickname 'Styles',[60] his penchant for Italian fashion, luxury vehicles and lavish parties is well documented. As is his role in arms deal-era corruption.

At the time of the arms deal, Hlongwane was an adviser to defence minister Joe Modise, who was also implicated in allegations of corruption related to BAE's arms deal contracts. Before his death in 2001, Modise was accused of altering procurement processes during the arms deal, specifically to ensure BAE's selection. He was also accused of failing to declare clear conflicts of interest, as companies in which he held shares stood to profit approximately R20 million from contracts related to the fulfilment of BAE's offset obligations.[61]

Hlongwane and BAE managed to keep their relationship relatively well hidden until allegations emerged in November 2008 when the Scorpions raided the properties of Fana Hlongwane, BAE Systems South Africa and other agents. In order to secure the search warrants necessary for the raids to take place, the Scorpions relied heavily on an affidavit from the United Kingdom's SFO.[62] As discussed in the first chapter of this section, the SFO affidavit identified payments of £115 million to a system of agents in South Africa in an effort to secure contracts in the arms deal.

Bagging dodgy European arms company consultancies

In their investigation of BAE's relationship with South Africa, the SFO discovered a number of overt and covert agreements signed between BAE and Fana Hlongwane for the work he had completed relating to the 1999 arms deal. As set out below, Hlongwane is alleged to have used his proximity to key decision makers in the arms acquisition process to influence the outcome in favour of BAE and ensure that processes following the signing of the contracts ran smoothly.

The SFO, during the course of their investigation, had received documents from BAE showing that Hlongwane, through his company Hlongwane Consulting, had entered into a general consultancy agreement with BAE in September 2003. This agreement was backdated to 1 January 2002. Hlongwane was brought on to further BAE's interests with regards to its offset obligations, after they had won the contracts.[63] As the South African government had been warned, the fanciful promises of industrial and economic development that BAE had promised as 'offsets' were proving difficult, if not impossible, to achieve. It was purportedly Hlongwane's role to ensure that these obligations were settled as soon as possible.

This agreement placed Hlongwane on a retainer of R15.5 million per year.[64] But the evidence suggests that Hlongwane received much more than this from BAE. Several large additional payments were made to him from BAE-owned companies for the duration of their agreement. One such payment occurred in 2005; approximately R50 million was paid as a 'settlement' figure to Hlongwane in relation to the work done on BAE's South African Gripen project. Between September 2003 and January 2007, Hlongwane Consulting received payments totalling more than R110 million (that's nearly R270 million in 2022), a staggering sum which BAE has failed to sufficiently justify.[65] These extraordinary payments to a consultant suggests that BAE saw a significant payoff from what Hlongwane could provide.

The payments did not stop there. Hlongwane went on to receive a further R51 million through a consultancy agreement with a South African registered company called SANIP. SANIP was owned by BAE's partner on the Gripen deal, SAAB, and was set up in order to monitor the offset obligations related to the arms deal contracts the two companies had been awarded. SAAB would go on to distance itself from these payments, claiming that BAE had taken over running SANIP on its behalf and that they were unaware of the contract with Hlongwane; this is discussed further below.

While these payments received by Hlongwane may be suspicious, they would only have been illegal if they were made in order to exploit Hlongwane's position as Modise's adviser, or if these payments were made to Hlongwane to be further distributed to other politically connected individuals. This was the exact conclusion that the SFO had come to.[66]

In 2010, new evidence emerged supporting the allegation that onward payments were made relating to the arms deal. It showed that chief of the SANDF at the time of the deal, Siphiwe Nyanda, had received a R4.36 million loan from Hlongwane in 2005 to finance the purchasing of a new house.[67] The loan had been written off in 2009 with evidence that there was little to no attempt at repayment, and the loan payment flowed directly from one of Hlongwane's business accounts. Although both parties deny that this loan constituted a bribe, it clearly constituted a serious conflict of interest at the very least.

In 2011, a Swedish documentary released new evidence after an investigation into BAE's Swedish partner SAAB. It found that SANIP, the SAAB-owned company in South Africa, had entered into a consultancy agreement with Hlongwane in order to assist with the fulfilment of offset obligations. However, they were unable to prove that any meaningful work had actually emerged from this agreement. Despite payment of vast sums of money (the initial R51 million consultancy fee and additional bonuses), neither Hlongwane nor SAAB were able to produce anything more than a two-page BEE report as evidence of their work relationship.

The irresistible inference was that this consultancy agreement was merely a cover to ensure that regular payments could be made to Hlongwane for reasons neither party involved could explain. Responding to the new damning evidence, SAAB publicly distanced itself from BAE, claiming that the UK company had run SANIP on its behalf since 2004 and used the SAAB subsidiary without its knowledge to pay Hlongwane R24 million.[68]

Despite attempts to distance itself from BAE, Hlongwane and SANIP, it later emerged that SAAB had in fact entered into its own consultancy agreement directly with Hlongwane Consulting between October 2003 and October 2004. The agreement paid Hlongwane Consulting €18,000 per month for advice on political, economic and security policy.[69]

Hlongwane's confessional to the cover-up commission

Fana Hlongwane was one of only two people accused of receiving corrupt money from the arms deal to actually appear before the Seriti Commission.[70] However, as was too often the case during the Commission, the examination of Hlongwane's evidence by the

Commission was insufficient to uncover any meaningful information related to his agreements with BAE and SAAB, or his implication in various local and international investigations.

In fact, Hlongwane's testimony before the Commission was entirely untested. He was not asked a single question in cross-examination by any interested parties, nor by any of the Commissioners. This was despite the fact that much of his testimony either directly contradicted substantive evidence gathered by local and international authorities or entirely ignored evidence in which he was implicitly named.

The failure of the Commission to test evidence in any meaningful way is one of the many examples of a clear unwillingness by the Commission to uncover the truth and ensure accountability. It should thus come as no surprise that, in 2019, the North Gauteng High Court set aside the findings of the Commission, ruling that the Commission had fundamentally failed to do its job in finding 'a clear failure [by the Seriti Commission and its judges] to test evidence of key witnesses [and] a refusal to take account of documentary evidence which contained the most serious allegations'.[71]

What should have been an opportunity for the South African public to learn about what had really transpired during and after the signing of the arms deal was actually no more than a blatant whitewash.

Gupta styles: Game goes on

In the absence of any accountability for his role in the arms deal, and as with so many of the arms deal middlemen, Hlongwane has also continued to leverage his political connections and network to his advantage.

His association with the notorious Gupta network is one such connection. It is well reported that Hlongwane had introduced British firm Bell Pottinger to the Gupta enterprise, a relationship which would go on to build a propaganda war machine that fuelled racial tensions in South Africa.[72] Hlongwane had built his relationship with the public relations company during his battle against corruption allegations related to his consultancy agreements with BAE.

Allegations of misconduct linking Hlongwane to the Guptas extend beyond just the loathsome Bell Pottinger. Former Public Service and

Administration Minister Ayanda Dlodlo was found to have contravened Parliament's Disclosure of Ethical Conduct and Member's Interests following a 2015 all-expenses-paid stay at the luxury Oberoi Hotel in Dubai.[73] Dlodlo enjoyed spa massages, room service and car hire all paid for by Fana Hlongwane at this plush pad. Dubai, a central node in the world's modern criminal economy, was also a refuge for the Gupta family. They would famously sponsor junkets for spoilt South African politicians or their kin – such as Jacob Zuma's son Duduzane who was a frequent guest of the Guptas at the Oberoi.[74] While Dlodlo has claimed no knowledge of Gupta links, instead arguing that this was a gift from a family pal, civil society organisation OUTA argues that 'there is clear evidence that the Guptas arranged the booking and consulted with Duduzane Zuma regarding the type of suite they were able to book for her'.[75] The story beyond the reflection of the champagne lifestyle of South Africa's elite is a reminder of how intertwined the relationships are between various criminal elites who may wish to influence politicians. Dlodlo decamped to Washington when she was appointed an alternate executive director at the World Bank on 1 April 2022.

In April 2022, Chief Justice Zondo released the fourth part of the State Capture Commission report into the attempted capture of the National Treasury. A key moment in this timeline was an October 2015 meeting set up by Fana Hlongwane which would bring Hlongwane into a room with Duduzane Zuma, Tony Gupta and former Deputy Finance Minister Mcebisi Jonas. At the meeting Jonas was offered a R600-million bribe by the Gupta brother to work with the family, and by extension against the interest of the state. While Hlongwane and Zuma denied any 'wrongdoing' in the matter, Chief Justice Judge Zondo rejected this as a 'fabrication'.[76] According to Zondo, Jonas 'had no reason to lie about what was discussed at that meeting, whereas Mr Duduzane Zuma and Mr Hlongwane had a reason to lie, because, if they admitted Mr Jonas's evidence, they would implicate not just Mr Tony Gupta in criminal conduct but possibly themselves too.'[77]

The playboy parties on

Hlongwane continues to live a life of luxury. He is rumoured to own a fleet of expensive vehicles, and a string of expensive houses across South

Africa, one of which is located in the affluent Johannesburg suburb of Hyde Park and is dubbed 'The Playboy Mansion'.[78] The Joburg jet-set have largely looked the other way when it comes to uncomfortable truths, rather choosing to embrace a man implicated in serious crimes as one of their very own.

Failure to hold Hlongwane, and others like him, to account has allowed him to continue to expand his network of influence and his own bank balance. The overall lack of accountability for the arms deal has been to the detriment of South Africans. BAE similarly has benefited from this culture of impunity – for, if Fana Hlongwane were ever to have his day in court, there is ample reason to suggest that Britain's biggest arms dealer would be seated beside him as a fellow accused.

FIVE
Siphiwe Nyanda and the BAE corruption bombshell

IT IS NOT OFTEN THAT a juicy story comes to you, rather than having to chase it. SANDF chief General Siphiwe Nyanda produced such a bombshell in 2020. Evidence based on internal documents[79] handed to Open Secrets and shared with partner organisation Shadow World Investigations is tangible proof of a highly questionable relationship between Nyanda and arms fixer Fana Hlongwane.

The evidence shows that Nyanda received money from a Hlongwane company that was paid 'commissions' by British arms mega company BAE Systems as part of the corruption-riddled arms deal.[80] With this smoking gun prosecutors can start to dust off the docket on this network and consider prosecutions. The arms deal was never only about Jacob Zuma and his sweetheart relationship with the French arms company. We now have even more proof that it was rotten to the core and demands accountability.

Among the considerable evidence that has stacked up against arms deal mega-agent Fana Hlongwane is the peculiar business relationship he had with Nyanda. As was noted in the previous chapter, in 2005 Nyanda received a R4.36 million home loan from a company controlled by Hlongwane after Nyanda had left the SANDF, and the loan was written off in 2009 with evidence that there was little to no attempt at repayment, and the loan payment flowed directly from one of

Hlongwane's business accounts.[81] And while both Hlongwane and Nyanda denied bribery, the whole loan business clearly constituted a serious conflict of interest at the very least.

Shortly after Open Secrets published an 'Unaccountable' profile on Hlongwane in 2020, Nyanda approached Open Secrets to discuss the allegations. Nyanda believed that the whole home loan imbroglio had been misunderstood, and he wanted to set the record straight. Fair enough. In fact, Nyanda pointed out, he had actually paid back the loan, illustrating that any claims of conflicts of interest (or worse) were unfounded. To substantiate his claim, Nyanda sent a sheaf of documents that inadvertently revealed important new details about the home loan granted to Nyanda: information that paints the relationship between Nyanda and Hlongwane in a very different, and very damning, light.[82]

But, before we get to that, we have to go a little bit back in time. Get in the Delorean, clock set to 1999.

Hlongwane, BAE Systems and the arms deal

As we've described in considerable detail elsewhere, in December 1999 the government purchased a range of expensive and sophisticated military equipment abroad: the arms deal. The biggest winners in the arms deal were British Aerospace (now BAE Systems) and SAAB. BAE Systems was contracted to supply Hawk fighter trainers, while BAE and SAAB were jointly contracted to deliver the Gripen fighter jet. These highly lucrative contracts were together worth R15.77 billion (valued at about R45 billion today) – more than half the total cost of the arms deal at the time.

BAE Systems has been far from immune from allegations of corruption. In 2008, the Scorpions, in the last flick of their tail, raided the properties of Bredenkamp and Hlongwane. The Scorpions raid was motivated by evidence gathered by the UK's Serious Fraud Office in their probe of BAE Systems' involvement in corruption around the world. The SFO had discovered that BAE Systems had made £115 million in payments to overt and covert 'advisers' to win its arms deal contracts. Bredenkamp and Hlongwane were the two biggest 'advisers' in monetary terms. Through various avenues, Hlongwane was paid over R100 million. The SFO believed that the payments had been made by BAE Systems to Hlongwane for corrupt ends.[83]

The BAE 'tranches'

Hlongwane was supposed to perform a range of services for BAE Systems, but one of the most notable revolved around the tranching arrangement entered into between BAE Systems and the South African government.

The tranching arrangement was, like almost everything in the arms deal, an absurdity wrapped in irrationality and sprinkled with favouritism. During the arms deal negotiation process, the cost and economic implications of the deal were subjected to a macroeconomic review by the Department of Finance that ultimately was contained in what was known as the August 1999 Affordability Report.[84] The review found that the whole arms deal was a significant economic risk that threatened to massively increase unemployment if things went wrong. This was in addition to the 300,000 lives lost due to HIV/AIDS as the country could not afford anti-retroviral medication at the time due to the Mbeki administrations arms deals.

The Affordability Report was particularly concerned about the huge costs of the Hawk and Gripen contracts.[85] There were serious concerns that, if the market responded badly to the announcement of the arms deal, buying the Hawk and Gripens would cause serious economic harm over a considerable period of time, not least because the purchase of the Hawks and Gripens was enabled by huge loans given to the government by Barclays Bank that were only fully repaid at the end of 2020. So, as South Africa continues to struggle through an economic crisis now, we should remind ourselves that we are all *still* paying for the arms deal today.

To try and get around the issue of cost and affordability, BAE Systems proposed a tranching system. Under this system, South Africa would buy the Hawks and Gripens in three separate tranches.[86] South Africa, if it was struggling economically, could decide to halt agreeing to tranches two and three, thus limiting the amount of Hawks and Gripens bought from BAE Systems. Sadly, this system made no sense. Because of the way the tranches were structured, South Africa would basically have no fighter jet capacity if it cancelled tranches two and three. Moreover, BAE Systems had front-loaded the costs so that the jets in tranche one cost more per unit than in tranches two and three.[87]

Despite these problems being loudly pointed out in the Affordability Report, which argued strongly that the deals with BAE and SAAB be halted (not least because South Africa had no pilots to fly the jets), the government went ahead with the plan.[88] For BAE Systems to earn the full income it was hoping for, it needed the government to agree to sign the tranche two and tranche three purchase orders in 2002 and 2004 respectively.

Fighting for the tranches: Nyanda's role and Hlongwane's payday

Nyanda, one of the most well-respected MK commanders in exile, was appointed as the chief of the SANDF on 1 June 1998, a position he held until his retirement on 31 May 2005.[89]

Documents from the arms deal selection process show that Nyanda was involved in at least one key moment, where he signed a recommendation with the acting secretary of defence that had the effect of reducing the number of helicopters South Africa was buying (arguably the only equipment that was actually needed and has actually been used from the arms deal) to accommodate buying the Hawk and Gripens.

And in his position as the chief of the SANDF, he would have almost certainly been directly involved in any decision about whether the government would pursue the second and third tranche options. In response to a question posed by us he indicated in a phone call that such decisions would happen at ministerial level and not involve the SANDF, but this beggars belief. At the very least, the SANDF would have been consulted by the ministry about a decision to proceed and such a recommendation would have had to have passed the desk of Nyanda as chief of the SANDF.

It is here that we find the confluence of financial interest shared between Hlongwane and Nyanda.

Hlongwane, for his part, would make a great deal of money if the South African government agreed to tranche 3. This was to be achieved through two separate contracts.

The first was entered into between Hlongwane Consulting and BAE Systems in September 2003, which paid Hlongwane a £250,000 quarterly retainer. In September 2005, this agreement was amended to allow Hlongwane to be paid a once-off 'ex-gratia' payment of $8 million (R50.4 million at the time) 'in full and final settlement for all additional work regarding Gripen tranche 3'.[90]

The second contract was entered into between Hlongwane Consulting and SANIP in August 2003. SANIP was a joint BAE-SAAB company that was effectively controlled by BAE Systems from about 2003 onwards.[91] According to this agreement, Hlongwane Consulting was to be paid a bonus of R22.5 million 'should the Government not terminate Tranche 3' and should BAE be awarded a particular number of 'credits' for its industrial participation programme with the government, known as offsets (a whole other scandal in its own right).[92] This was in addition to a quarterly retainer of R1,875,000.

Importantly, for matters dealt with below, on 1 June 2004, this agreement was altered so that SANIP contracted directly with Ngwane Aerospace – a company where Hlongwane was the sole director – which would now be paid the retainer of R1,875,000. On 23 August 2006, a contract amendment was agreed to pay Ngwane Aerospace a one-off amount of R1,275,000 related to the offset programme.

Hlongwane thus earned R72.9 million in 2004 and 2005 (equal to R180 million in 2022) from the decision of the government to opt for tranche three: a decision over which Nyanda would have had direct and material influence.

The Nyanda documents

Despite Nyanda's stated intention to clear his name, the documents he sent Open Secrets did the exact opposite. In fact, they show that Nyanda had agreed loans with Hlongwane's companies while he was still employed as chief of the SANDF.[93] This represents a clear unmanageable conflict of interest and the type of benefit that could never have been approved – even by President Thabo Mbeki. We pressed Nyanda on this issue and he responded by email that, 'I was not working for the SANDF then and couldn't have sought their approval or any executive for my actions.'[94] This is of course incorrect. In a follow-up email, Nyanda confirmed to us that his last day of employment in the SANDF was 31 May 2005 – months after the loan was agreed upon.[95]

We also wanted to know why Nyanda didn't approach a commercial bank for this loan, to which he responded: 'Would a commercial bank have given me the loan as quickly as I needed it if at all? Don't executives in private companies ask for loans from their companies?'[96] That may well be the case, but he was also chief of the SANDF at the time.

Nyanda also confirmed in his responses that he began negotiating with Ngwane for the loan as speed was of the essence. Nyanda recalled that 'I stopped my search when I saw the house and began negotiating with Ngwane Aerospace for the loan before the house was taken by anyone else.'[97] But the documents sent by Nyanda shows that Nyanda had started making moves to buy the house by at least January 2005, five months before he stepped down as chief of the SANDF. It is striking that Nyanda, in spite of this admission, still believed that he had done nothing wrong.

One of the key documents is a letter from Christo Stockenstrom, Hlongwane's long-time legal representative, to Nyanda on the letterhead of Stockenstrom's law firm (FSF).[98] The letter is dated 2 March 2005: nearly a full three months prior to Nyanda stepping down as chief of the SANDF. The subject of the letter was a reconciliation of the full bond amount that Ngwane Aerospace was granting to Nyanda.

In total, Ngwane Aerospace was to loan Nyanda R4,364,939.24, which was to be used to cover a range of costs. The biggest cost was the purchase price of Nyanda's new home in Bryanston, Johannesburg, which was recorded as R3.75 million.[99]

Another large cost – R305,416 – was the money that Nyanda had to pay to the law firm Connie Myburgh & Partners Inc to cover the transfer costs related to the purchase. A separate letter from Connie Myburgh & Partners shows that they had sent an invoice to Nyanda for this amount on 27 January 2005.[100] The loan that Ngwane was agreeing to give to Nyanda in March 2005 thus also covered costs that Nyanda had incurred in January 2005 – just over five months *before* Nyanda had left the SANDF.

Two related entries in the bond reconciliation are also intriguing: an amount of R250,000 described as a 'Medical Protector Compensation

Loan' and an amount of R37,500 described as 'Plus 15% Interest Per Annum from 1 March 2004 to 1 March 2005'.[101] A simple calculation shows that the R37,500 was equal to 15% of the R250,000 'Medical Protector Compensation Loan'. Nyanda responded to questions as to what this loan was intended for by stating that, 'It was a private venture of mine which failed. It had nothing to do with government and has nothing to do with any public interest. I had to pay the loan with interest as well as the documents show.'[102]

But did he not have to seek approval from the Ministry of Defence or the executive for a private business venture while employed as chief of the SANDF? Nyanda expanded to say that there was no need for approval. 'This has nothing to do with a public entity.'[103] If this was not declared, it would suggest that at the very least the general was engaged in a serious case of moonlighting while employed in a powerful, well-paid position in the public service.

If this is accurate, it is even more damning: it shows that the amount loaned to Nyanda by Hlongwane included covering costs incurred by Nyanda from at least March 2004. This was over a year before Nyanda stepped down from the SANDF and, most importantly, a month before the government renewed tranche three, which was formally completed in April 2004.

A careful reader would have noticed another important detail: the bond that was given to Nyanda was granted to him by Ngwane Aerospace. As we discussed above, in July 2004, Ngwane Aerospace replaced Hlongwane Consulting as the entity through which Fana Hlongwane would be paid a quarterly retainer of R1,875,000 until August 2006. The company from which Nyanda received his bond was thus the very same company that BAE Systems was making payments to, during and after Nyanda served as chief of the SANDF.

What about the claim that Nyanda repaid the loan? Here, Nyanda's claim is both true and entirely disingenuous. A reconciliation of Nyanda's bond shows that Nyanda made two large payments to pay off a portion of the bond: R659,278 in June 2005 and R2.5 million in January 2006. Nyanda indicated in a response to a question that the source of these funds was from his early retirement package from the SANDF which took time to clear.[104] By April 2007, Nyanda owed R1,668,802.80 on the loan, which, paid over twenty years, would cost R17,255.19 a month.[105]

In April 2007, Nyanda wrote to Janet Collier at Ngwane Defence Group, another Hlongwane company, and where Nyanda was employed as CEO almost immediately after he left the SANDF.[106] As an interesting and revealing aside, Janet Collier was the partner of Bernard Collier. Bernard Collier was previously the man who controlled the day-to-day running of SANIP, and who signed the consultancy agreements between SANIP and Hlongwane Consulting (and later Ngwane Aerospace).

Nyanda instructed Collier to 'please transfer the whole amount of my monthly salary' to Ngwane Aerospace, 'the amount being repayments for my bond'.[107] Nyanda instructed the payments to take place every month for twenty months. A second reconciliation of the bond shows that Nyanda did, indeed, transfer his entire monthly salary – just over R70,000 – until December 2009.

What this meant, in reality, was that Nyanda did repay the bond. But he was repaying Ngwane Aerospace with money paid to him by Ngwane Defence. Nyanda was thus repaying Ngwane Aerospace, which was paid massive consultancy fees by BAE Systems between 2004 and 2006, for a bond he agreed with Fana Hlongwane's company Ngwane Aerospace in March 2005, with money paid to him by Fana Hlongwane's Ngwane Defence.

Did Nyanda see this as worrisome or potentially having criminal implication? Seemingly not. Nyanda responded by email to say that, 'I paid interest. Many executives take very soft loans from their companies... If this is criminal conduct many people would be in jail.'[108]

Nyanda explained away his relationship to the Hlongwane family as being separate and distinct from the arms deal. He bought goods as a young man from the Hlongwane family's shop – and he would in turn eventually take Fana Hlongwane under his wing in the days of exile and struggle. These ties are understandable and not criminal. But they do not excuse a sitting chief of the SANDF negotiating a home loan with an agent of BAE, the company that received the largest ever post-apartheid military procurement contract.

Waiting for a new dawn

As democratic South Africa's first example of state capture, the arms deal enabled the fetid institutional decay that allowed the Gupta family and their accomplices to loot the South African purse. Our liberators were replicating the types of economic crimes at which the apartheid regime had become a world leader.

Twenty years later, almost no one has faced any meaningful accountability for the arms deal. Only Tony Yengeni, imprisoned for less than a year, and Schabir Shaik, released on farcical medical parole, have ever faced jail time. Thales and Zuma, due to face corruption charges next year, have lived merry lives in the interim. This is a situation favoured by global corporations like BAE and Thales and the politicians and middlemen they have enriched. We call it impunity.

Meanwhile, those responsible for investigating South Africa's defining corruption scandal have either been beaten, bloodied and betrayed by political interference at home and abroad, or, in the case of the Hawks and the lamentable Arms Deal Commission led by Justice Seriti, content to whitewash the indefensible.

But, if anything, this story shows that, despite these attempts, the evidence of crimes in the arms deal will never go away. Not until justice is done. The pungent relationships between BAE Systems and Fana Hlongwane, and between Hlongwane and Nyanda, might be a good place to start.

Is there the political will to do so? Siphiwe Nyanda was appointed South Africa's Ambassador to corruption- and war-ravaged Mozambique in 2020 by President Cyril Ramaphosa. It seems the new dawn is still a day away.

SIX

RDM and the NCACC: Profiting from misery in Yemen

YEMEN IS HOME TO THE world's worst humanitarian crisis and is the epicentre of a regionalised civil war. Over the past seven years, thousands of combatants have been killed, and United Nations (UN) reports show extensive evidence that civilians have been deliberately targeted in the brutal conflict. Myriad state and non-state actors, including terrorist groups, have joined the conflict, exacerbating its complexity. Schools, factories and hospitals have been destroyed and a staggering 80 per cent of the population – 24 million people – desperately need humanitarian help.[109] In 2018, it was already estimated that 85,000 children had starved to death since the start of the war.[110] Since 2020, Yemen has to face these horrors with the added burden of the Covid-19 global health pandemic and the further marginalisation of the conflict from world view as much of the global media turned its attention to the Russian invasion of Ukraine.

Dogs of war: Saudi Arabia and the UAE

While the conflict is complex and there is evidence of widespread abuses by all parties, the coalition of forces led by Saudi Arabia and the United

Arab Emirates (UAE) have used their considerable military might to unleash a barrage of attacks on the civilian population. In September 2020, a UN report on the conflict concluded that both Saudi Arabia and the UAE, along with the government of Yemen and secessionist forces, have committed acts that may amount to war crimes. These actions include targeting and murdering civilians, rape and sexual violence, torture and use of child soldiers.[111]

When it comes to targeting civilians and using force indiscriminately, Saudi Arabia and the UAE – and their proxies – have used weaponry sourced from arms companies around the world, including South Africa.[112]

Boom time for South African arms makers

The insatiable demand for weapons has in fact been a boon for the South African arms industry, beset with many woes also as a result of more recent state capture. Saudi Arabia and the UAE have become the most important clients of South Africa's arms companies since 2014, the year the civil war broke out in Yemen. South Africa has exported more than R11-billion worth of arms to these two states since 2010, but over R8 billion of this has come since 2014.[113]

In 2015 and 2016, the first two years of the conflict, nearly half of all South Africa's approved weapons exports were for these two states.[114] In 2019, there was a brief respite from South African complicity in arming these warring parties when a dispute over the terms of the end-user certificate (EUC) delayed the granting of export permits to several countries, including the UAE and Saudi Arabia. The gates of the trade in guns were reopened, we believe, in large part due to massive pressure from the arms companies and their partners in the state. South African authorities bowed to industry pressure and moved swiftly to soften the terms of the EUC, amending it in May 2020.

While we cannot track precisely where each exported gun or bomb ends up, or how it is used, there is increasing evidence that some weapons from South Africa have been used in Yemen.

RDM: Berlin's little backdoor

Many South African companies are profiting from war in Yemen, but one of the primary culprits is Rheinmetall Denel Munition (RDM) – a South African-based arms company, and there is evidence that it was the supplier of mortars used in illegal attacks on civilians in Yemen. RDM is a joint venture between German arms company Rheinmetall Waffe Munition GmbH (which holds a 51 per cent stake) and South African state-owned arms company Denel (with 49 per cent).

It is important to note that RDM through its German majority shareholder – Rheinmetall – faces a ban in Germany against exporting any weapons to Saudi Arabia, in large part due to concerns about human rights violations committed by Saudi Arabia and their partners in Yemen.[115] All roads seemingly lead back to Germany. Ultimately, Rheinmetall Waffe Munition GmbH, and executives in Germany higher up in Rheinmetall's corporate food chain, are effectively responsible for RDM's operations in South Africa and so they too should be held accountable for human rights violations.

A massacre in Hodeidah

In June 2018, Saudi–UAE coalition forces launched an offensive on the Yemeni port city of Hodeidah, held and fortified by Houthi forces since 2014.[116] It would become the biggest battle since the conflict started four years earlier, and more than half a million civilians were trapped inside the city as the battle raged. Over the next months, airstrikes and ground attacks from the Saudi and UAE coalition forces became commonplace, along with counterstrikes by Houthi forces defending the city. Scores of civilians were killed.[117]

On 2 August 2018, another attack targeted Hodeidah's fishing harbour. Ambulances rushed casualties to the nearby Al-Thawra Hospital where a second attack targeted survivors and first responders.[118] Sixty people, including children, were killed in the attacks, and more than one hundred were wounded.[119] Coalition forces have been widely criticised for using 'double-tap attacks' – launching a second strike minutes after the first strike to target emergency responders and other civilians who rush to the initial site. Alaa Thabet, a resident who witnessed the strikes,

NUMBERS AT A GLANCE:

16 MILLION
PEOPLE IN YEMEN DO NOT HAVE ACCESS TO ENOUGH FOOD IN 2021

THE UN BELIEVES SAUDI ARABIA IS USING THIS AS A TACTIC IN THE CONFLICT

18 MILLION
YEMENIS WITH NO ACCESS TO DRINKING WATER IN 2019 & MORE THAN A MILLION WERE IMPACTED BY A CHOLERA OUTBREAK

212+
CIVILIANS KILLED OR INJURED BY SAUDI AIR RAIDS IN 2020
54 OF THOSE KILLED WERE CHILDREN

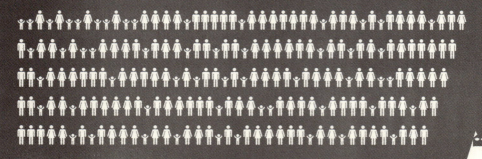

MONEY FOR GUNS
SOUTH AFRICA'S EXPORTS TO THE PARTIES IN THE YEMEN WAR

	Saudi Arabia	United Arab Emirates	All other countries	Proportion of weapons exports going to the UAE and Saudi Arabia
2010	R68 million	R577 million	R7,6 billion	7.8%
2011	R228 million	R279 million	R8,6 billion	5.6%
2012	R279 million	R1.4 billion	R8.9 billion	15.7%
2013	R6 million	R99 million	R3 billion	3.4%
2014	R333 million	R806 million	R1.8 billion	38.2%
2015	R579 million	R574 million	R1.5 billion	42.1%
2016	R411 million	R1.6 billion	R2.1 billion	48.9%
2017	R331 million	R987 million	R2.1 billion	38.3%
2018	R383 million	R1.2 billion	R3.1 billion	33.9%
2019	R575 million	R330 million	R3.1 billion	22.3%
TOTAL	R3.2 billion	R7.8 billion	42 billion	20.8%

(Civil war broke out in Yemen — 2013–2015)

R1.2 BILLION
IN VEHICLES, BOMBS & SHELLS SOLD TO THE UAE IN 2018

R11 BILLION
SOUTH AFRICAN WEAPONS SOLD TO SAUDI ARABIA AND THE UAE BETWEEN 2010 AND 2019

THE VALUE OF MUNITIONS APPROVED BY THE NCACC FOR EXPORT FROM SOUTH AFRICA TO THE TWO MAIN STATES INVOLVED IN THE WAR IN YEMEN

THE PROPORTION OF WEAPONS EXPORTS FROM SOUTH AFRICA BETWEEN 2010 AND 2019 THAT WENT TO THE UAE AND SAUDI ARABIA

20.8%

said 'it seemed as if the warplanes were chasing the casualties and the second batch of strikes killed more than the first... When I went nearer to see the impact, I saw a motorcyclist who had been killed but his hands did not leave the motorcycle. I cannot forget this scene.'[120]

Thabet was not the only person to think that the attacks were from airstrikes. Other initial reports also claimed that the attacks were further Saudi airstrikes, unsurprising given the relentless air bombardment by the Saudi coalition over the previous months in and around Hodeidah.[121] However, a subsequent investigation by the forensic investigative journalist platform Bellingcat showed otherwise. Bellingcat's examination of photographic, video and satellite evidence of the remaining fragments of the munition used, the patterns of damage, and the craters left by the bombs revealed that the attack was in fact from mortars, likely launched by ground forces.[122]

Having worked out that the weapons used in the attacks were mortars, Bellingcat sought to identify their origin. Their investigation led them to RDM:

> The nature of these craters, the damage seen at the harbour and the remnants of munitions found at the scene strongly indicate mortars were used... Mortar bombs produced by Rheinmetall Denel Munition (RDM) appear to have fins with a very similar shape, and display vent holes in the distinctive 4, 5, 4, 5 pattern. However, it was not possible to positively ID a 120mm HE round with this configuration due to augmentation charges obscuring the vent holes. It should be noted that Rheinmetall supply both Saudi Arabia and the UAE with weapon systems, including 120mm mortar systems.[123]

Rheinmetall did not respond to Bellingcat's requests for comment or provide images of examples of its 120mm mortar ammunition.[124] However, when asked by investigators from German weekly news magazine *Stern*, Rheinmetall said it was contractually prevented from commenting on possible projects relating to possible clients.[125]

Perhaps the strongest evidence that Rheinmetall or RDM munitions were used in the massacre at Hodeidah was presented in a January 2019 letter from the UN Panel of Experts on Yemen to the UN's Security Council president. The panel reviewed video and photographic evidence and concluded that while it could not conclusively attribute responsibility for the attacks, '[t]he mortar used for that attack had characteristics of those produced either by Rheinmetall in Germany or by its South African subsidiary Rheinmetall Denel Munition, which reportedly also produces mortar shells in a factory in Saudi Arabia'.[126]

A mortar fires an explosive shell that has a fin to guide it in the air. Like the Bellingcat investigation, the UN panel concluded that the fin assembly (or 'stub') found on the site after the incident had characteristics consistent with the fin assembly of 120mm mortar bombs produced either by Rheinmetall in Germany or by its South African subsidiary Rheinmetall Denel Munition.[127]

Crucially, the expert panel also pointed out that the mortar ammunition in question – 120mm mortar rounds – was produced by a factory in Al-Kharj, Saudi Arabia.[128] That factory was run by RDM. Indeed, in August 2016, Jacob Zuma attended the factory's opening, giving it his presidential blessing. At the time, it was noted that the complex could produce 'military projectiles' including 120mm mortar rounds.[129]

There is thus compelling evidence that RDM was the source of the mortars used in the Hodeidah massacre that cost sixty people their lives and wounded more than a hundred more. However, the link to the factory in Al-Kharj raises a more systemic problem. Rheinmetall and RDM are not only exporting individual weapons systems to Saudi Arabia and the UAE. They are increasingly playing a central role in exporting and setting up entire weapons factories for their customers, regardless of their human rights records.

The NCACC: The arms export watchdog gone AWOL

The obvious question is whether Rheinmetall, and possibly other international companies, may see South Africa as a 'soft touch' jurisdiction – a discreet back door, if you like – from which to export weapons in order to avoid more onerous regulation at home.

This certainly should not be the case. On paper, South Africa has for a generation had a well-constituted, albeit largely dysfunctional, system intended to ensure that dodgy arms deals are not tolerated. Established in 1995 under the presidency of Nelson Mandela, the National Conventional Arms Control Committee (NCACC) consists of a squad of ministers and deputy ministers, and is mandated to stop any weapons exports that could contribute to human rights abuses. Other government departments, including international relations and cooperation, defence and intelligence, also play a role in the Committee's processes.

These officials are meant to scrutinise what weaponry crosses the country's borders to ensure that South Africa does not break domestic and international law, and possibly become complicit in the murder of civilians or other human rights violations. It was precisely South Africa's experience of such trade during apartheid that informed what should be a tough and effective regulatory system, guided and informed by democratic constitutional values.

Open Secrets investigations show that the NCACC is guilty of regulatory failure over an extended period of time. When asked to respond to our questions regarding the war in Yemen, as detailed in this report, the NCACC revealed not only a lackadaisical approach to regulation but an absolute failure to appreciate the seriousness of their task and the magnitude of the consequences. The fact that the NCACC has continued to approve export permits for weapons destined for Saudi Arabia and the UAE when these countries have been publicly implicated over a number of years in war crimes in Yemen is proof of this. The NCACC has, for more than a decade, displayed a profound indifference to the rights of vulnerable civilians who are the target of human rights violations in far-flung corners of the world. They have emulated the indifference displayed by politicians in many of the world's leading arms-exporting nations.

Who benefits from this? The NCACC's weakness is the arms companies' gain. Our evidence shows that arms companies like RDM have taken advantage of weaknesses in the regulatory regime and profited without any regard to resultant human rights abuses.

If the suffering in Yemen is to end, then corporations in countries like South Africa must be prohibited from profiteering in an unjust war. Their enablers in government and regulatory bodies like the NCACC need to ensure that international and domestic laws are applied and these practices ended. Where they fail to do so, the full might of the law must be applied to criminally charge all those complicit in such crimes.

Yemen today is like South Africa once was in the world: a far-off politically complicated land in which human rights violations have become commonplace. South Africa has the responsibility to prevent what the powerful once did to its own people from being revisited on civilians in Yemen. If it fails to do so, it fails the fundamental values of its own struggle for freedom and constitutional democracy.

Stop the war profiteers!

In 2021 Open Secrets published an in-depth investigatory report which details the actions of these Unaccountables, titled, *Profiting from Misery: South Africa's complicity in war crimes in Yemen.*[130] Subsequent to this, Open Secrets, working with the Southern African Litigation Centre and a team of lawyers from Power Singh, Lawyers for Human Rights and a stellar team of Counsel started a legal process to challenge the manner in which the NCACC awards licences to arms companies fuelling conflict in countries such as Yemen. This arduous legal process is the first glimmer of possibility that the NCACC – effectively a rogue regulator – and the arms companies whose actions it empowers are held to account.

3
STATE CAPTURE PROFITEERS

Introduction

THE JUDICIAL COMMISSION of Inquiry into State Capture – popularly known as the Zondo Commission – submitted its final report to President Cyril Ramaphosa on 22 June 2022, just shy of four years on from its first hearings. The Commission sat for over 400 days of hearings and analysed 1.7 million pages of evidence. Its final reports, containing multiple volumes dedicated to different state-owned enterprises (SOEs), have 5,437 pages that implicate 1,438 individuals and entities in state capture. The work of the Commission is now over, but the pursuit of accountability remains in its infancy. With few convictions of big business and high-profile politicians, public belief that state capture and corruption can be disrupted through accountability is dwindling.

Challenging impunity for state capture is vital, not least because of the extraordinary social cost of state capture crimes. Evidence presented to the Commission by Paul Holden from civil society group Shadow World Investigations showed that R57 billion in public funds was spent on contracts tainted by state capture linked to the Gupta racketeering enterprise. This total does not include the billions spent at other sites of state capture not directly linked to the Gupta family. Notably, this includes money lost to systemic corruption at the Passenger Rail Agency of South Africa (Prasa), the subject of several chapters in this section. Moreover, the money spent on corrupt contracts does not begin to approach the true cost of state capture, which conservative estimates put at R500 billion.[1]

The real cost of state capture is evident in unemployment, inequality, rolling blackouts, trains that do not arrive and grants that do not get paid. Public spending on basic services has declined as the government struggles to pay its debts, while fuel and food prices continue to rise. The cost of state capture is most clearly borne by the people who need state funding the most. At every turn, it is the South Africans who were disenfranchised by apartheid who have felt the true burden of corruption. These costs were only exacerbated by the crisis during the Covid-19 pandemic, and undermine the state's capacity to address growing inequality.

Who is responsible for this? This section provides some insight into the individuals and companies that have enabled, participated in and profited from state capture. It focuses on examples at Transnet and Prasa. Crucially, the profiles here show that we should not understand state capture as a simple problem of government corruption. Rather, we need to understand that a network of local and multinational companies looted public funds with the help of complicit politicians, middlemen and SOE board members. Disrupting these networks is a priority, both to challenge impunity and to prevent these crimes and their disastrous consequences from being repeated.

There have been a few important arrests linked to state capture, including those of former Trillian boss Eric Wood and former Transnet chief executive officer Siyabonga Gama over corruption at Transnet. Yet these remain glimmers of hope in an otherwise stark story of unaccountability that has stained South Africa's democracy. The evidence contained in the chapters below has been publicly available for many years. In fact, much of it is drawn from investigations undertaken by or commissioned by the state and law enforcement agencies. It is an indictment on them that, despite this weight of evidence, the individuals and companies discussed in this section remain unaccountable.

ONE

The Chinese Railway Rolling Stock Corporation: China Inc boards the state capture train

STATE-OWNED RAIL COMPANY Transnet was the site of the single largest contract tainted by state capture. The notorious contract to purchase 1064 locomotives for the Transnet fleet was inflated by R16 billion, and was engineered to divert kickbacks to Gupta-linked firms. The final report of the Zondo Commission recommended a number of prosecutions linked to state capture at Transnet. In May 2022, the first major arrests were announced by the National Prosecuting Authority's (NPA) Investigating Directorate. These included former Transnet CEO Siyabonga Gama, Gupta associate Eric Wood and other former Transnet executives.[2] While these are important steps, a key party to the corrupt contracts remains unaccountable: the Chinese state-owned Chinese Railway Rolling Stock Corporation (CRRC). The world's richest rolling stock company, CRRC has never been held to account for its role in state capture, and it is yet to pay back the money it made.

It was May 2014 when Transnet struck a deal to buy 1064 new locomotives for an eye-watering R54.4 billion. This was an escalation of R16 billion from the 'all inclusive' R38.6 billion originally agreed upon. The 1064 locomotives deal was part of a 'Road to Rail' initiative by Transnet. It said that the deal would increase South Africa's rail capacity to the point where the country could boast being the fifth largest rail system in the world by 2019.

But while 'Road to Rail' was meant to bolster the South African economy, it became an opportunity for corrupt networks to loot public funds, and South Africa has suffered as a result. According to Transnet's 2020 annual report, Transnet only had 571 of the new locomotives in operation – effectively operating at 50 per cent capacity. Not surprisingly, Transnet fell short of its own target to move 350.3 million tonnes (Mt) of cargo during the 2018/19 financial year. It only achieved 215.1 Mt in 2019, and continues to struggle to meet its targets in 2022. Given Transnet's vital role in the South African economy's supply chain, these failures have significant negative impacts on growth and employment.[3]

The CRRC: China South Rail (CSR) and China North Rail (CNR)

CRRC is the world's largest manufacturer of rolling stock (locomotives/vehicles) and rail equipment. In 2020, the company reported a workforce of over 165,000 employees operating in 101 countries. CRRC is the result of the 2015 megamerger between China North Rail (CNR) and China South Rail (CSR), at the time the two largest train manufacturers in China. This merger created a behemoth with assets amounting to $65 billion (R956 billion) in 2020.

CRRC was established in 1881 during the Qing dynasty, but state reforms of Chinese state-owned enterprises in 2000 saw CRRC split into CSR and CNR. As detailed later on, Transnet transacted with these two companies (CNR and CSR) before they were again merged as CRRC in 2015. The stated motivation for the re-merger was international competitiveness, as part of China's 'Made in China 2025' initiative. This included strict targets for Chinese companies to compete with their peers on the global market.

CRRC already had A monopoly on China's domestic market, which contributed over 90 per cent to its operational revenue in 2017. However, with shifts in the domestic market and the demanding targets imposed by the state in relation to 'Made in China 2025', foreign expansion was crucial. The dodgy locomotive deals with Transnet show what CRRC – and ultimately its proprietors in the Beijing government – were prepared to do to access new markets.

Setting the tone: The 95 deal and 100 deal

Prior to the 1064 contract, both CNR and CSR were already successful bidders for two Transnet contracts for 95 and 100 locomotives respectively. These procurement processes were riddled with irregularities.

In 2012, Transnet awarded CSR a tender for 95 locomotives valued at R2.7 billion. Transnet executives went out of their way to ensure that CSR won the contract. CSR failed to pay the required fee linked to the tender application and did not meet the required Broad-Based Black Economic Empowerment (B-BBEE) score. These factors should have disqualified CSR. Further, emails from Transnet's then CEO, Brian Molefe, predicted CSR would win the tender before the final decision was made. In addition to these factors, the final deal was R100 million over Transnet's original budget.

After receiving the first payment by Transnet, CSR forwarded 20 per cent – around R80 million – to Century General Trading (CGT), a front company purportedly offering 'consulting services' to CSR. There is no evidence of the purpose of these consulting services or whether they were rendered at all.[4] CGT is listed in the United Arab Emirates (UAE) as trading goods including scrap metal and non-perishables like beans. It became a funnel for probable kickbacks in the Transnet rail deal managed by Ratan Jagati, an associate of the Gupta family.

This method of paying 'consulting fees' to Gupta fronts would become a key means of funnelling money out from Transnet and other SOEs into Gupta hands. In the case of CRRC, the company would acquire 'consulting services' offered by a Gupta-linked shell company and pay them large sums. Firms like CGT and JJ Trading, another Dubai-based shell company, would then send on this money to other Gupta fronts.[5] The use of off-shore firms in secret jurisdictions like the UAE mean that the potential proceeds of crime bleed into global

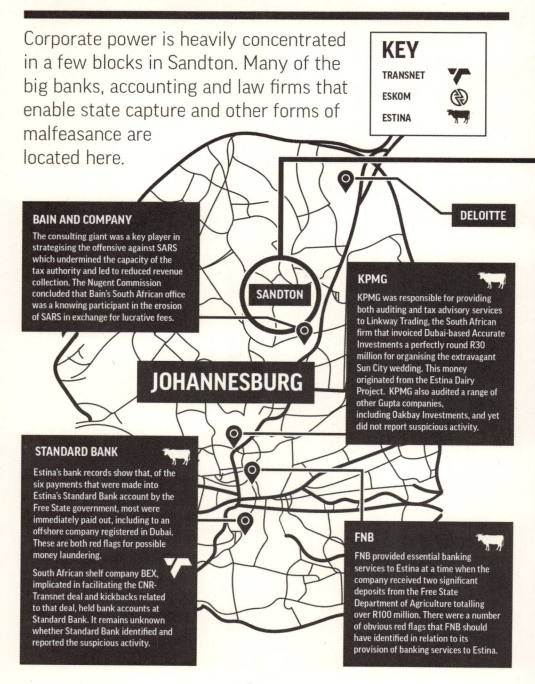

STANDARD CHARTERED

The majority of funds paid to Estina by the Free State Department of Agriculture were transferred out of Estina's banking facilities and into a network of offshore companies controlled by the Gupta enterprise. Standard Chartered and a range of other global banks facilitated these transfers. Standard Chartered closed Gupta linked accounts in 2014, arguably too late. Though this illustrates that monitoring and decisive action by the banks was possible

NEDBANK

Nedbank was party to dubious interest rate swaps organized for Transnet by Regiments. It was estimated in early 2019 that the swaps had cost Transnet over R780 million in additional interest payments to Nedbank.

As Baroda's correspondent bank, Nedbank allowed Baroda to use its infrastructure for all financial transactions. OCCRP has alleged that the nature of the relationship between Nedbank and Baroda enabled both banks to avoid responsibility for identifying and reporting suspicious transactions related to all of these accounts.

JOHANNESBURG STOCK EXCHANGE

RMB PRIVATE BANK

RAND MERCHANT BANK

ENSAFRICA

BOSTON CONSULTING GROUP

SANDTON

BOWMANS

NORTON ROSE FULBRIGHT

OLD MUTUAL

ABSA CORPORATE AND INVESTMENT BANK

EY

WEBBER WENTZEL

HSBC

HSBC was arguably the most important enabler of the looting of Transnet, having handled most of the transactions of the front companies CGT, JJT, Tequesta and Regiments Asia. It failed to act swiftly despite numerous obvious money laundering red flags.

BANK OF BARODA

More than any other local bank, the Bank of Baroda was central to the money-laundering machinations of the Gupta enterprise. In addition to facilitating transactions in and out of Estina's current and fixed deposit accounts, the Bank of Baroda provided loan facilities that were used to create "fake loans" or "loan-backs" as part of the Estina money-laundering network.

Baroda accounts were used extensively to facilitate the purchase of Optimum Coal Mine (OCM) by Tegeta. A forensic investigation concluded that Baroda's conduct violated various legal duties including consistent failure to file suspicious activity reports with the FIC, as well as failure to identify where parties were related.

The Bank of Baroda, like HSBC, facilitated the flow of money between various Gupta front companies linked to the 1064 locomotive deal, allowing kickbacks linked to the deal to be laundered.

McKINSEY AND COMPANY

McKinsey not only entered into an unlawful contract with Eskom, but also played a role in Trillian being paid R565 million, in the absence of any final contract, and with Eskom later admitting that Trillian had done no work for them.

McKinsey and Regiments Capital were transaction advisors on the 1064 locomotive deal. Regiments contributed to rewriting the business case at the last minute to facilitate the escalation of the price. McKinsey has since admitted it had concerns about allegations of impropriety at Regiments in 2014, but did not cease working with them.

money flows where they are hard to track and trace by South African authorities.

This pattern was seen again in CSR's next contract to provide 100 heavy-haul electric locomotives at a cost of R4.8 billion to Transnet. This was close to R1 billion more than initially budgeted by Transnet, despite competitors such as Japanese manufacturer Mitsui offering trains for R1.2 billion less. In short – it was a spectacular rip-off. Like clockwork, after receiving a payment from Transnet, CSR made 'consulting services' payments to JJ Trading FZE, which acted as the conduit for cash in the UAE. As with Century General Trading, JJ Trading FZE was also registered by Ratan Jagati and was described as trading scrap metal and non-perishables.

The 1064 deal

The last (and largest) of the deals between Transnet and CRRC was the 1064 locomotives contract. This was to be the largest purchase of locomotives ever made by Transnet. CNR won the tender to provide 232 diesel locomotives, while CSR was to provide 359 electric locomotives. By 2015, the Guptas had set up an extensive money laundering network in Hong Kong. CSR entered into a contract with Hong Kong-based Tequesta Group Limited, a company registered by Gupta stooge Salim Essa, for 'advisory fees' at a rate of 21 per cent of CSR's earnings from the 1064 contract.[6]

According to agreements uncovered in the #GuptaLeaks investigation, R9 billion in kickbacks (for the 1064, 100 and 95 locomotives deals) were promised to Gupta-linked firms through contract price hikes. Further amaBhungane investigations revealed that R3.7 billion was paid to these Gupta firms.[7] CRRC paid billions in fees to obscure front companies with no discernible services being rendered. Once the front companies received payment, they would distribute funds to a series of further fronts. This is a money-laundering process called 'layering' by which monies are routed via different bank accounts belonging to different shell companies multiple times, thus distancing beneficiaries from the transactions.

In addition to the glaring corruption and the inflation of the 1064 contract by R16 billion to provide space for kickbacks, the trains CRRC ultimately delivered were late and of poor quality. Only 249 of the 359 locomotives have been delivered and these are largely defective and useless prototypes.

Transnet was a significant work stream at the Zondo Commission of Inquiry into State Capture. Comprehensive evidence, along with oral testimony, was presented at the Commission on the 1064 locomotives matter, including by Paul Holden from Shadow World Investigations. In Volume 2 of its final report, the Commission recommended investigation with a view to prosecution of the relevant functionaries of CRRC and the front companies they paid fees to, including Tequesta, CGT and JJ Trading.[8] The Commission suggests that possible charges would include corruption, racketeering and money laundering. This is a recommendation that South African law enforcement should be acting on with urgency.

Although inexplicably delayed, Transnet eventually suspended and applied to overturn the locomotive contracts worth R54 billion. In March 2021, the Special Investigation Unit (SIU) and Transnet applied to court to have the 1064 locomotives contract cancelled due to the many irregularities that beset it. In June 2022, Transnet indicated that it would be putting out a brand new tender for locomotives to fill the gap left by the numerous contracts tainted by state capture.

The freeze begins?

In addition to criminal prosecutions, a vital part of accountability will be to recoup the funds earned by CRRC. At the end of 2020, the South African Reserve Bank (SARB) and South African Revenue Service (SARS) initiated the freezing of a fraction of the funds connected to the 1064 locomotives deal.[9] SARS froze R1.26 billion because of doubts about the veracity of the description CRRC recorded for the funds. SARS also intervened because an initial freeze by the South African Reserve Bank on R4.2 billion was about to expire and the funds returned to CRRC. SARS found that the CRRC companies were paying a fifth of their revenue from Transnet locomotives contracts to Gupta offshore fronts as kickbacks in the form of inflated forex transfers to China from its local subsidiary, CRRC E-Loco Supply. These payments were allegedly recorded by CRRC-E Loco as tax deductible costs of sale.

An order handed down on 8 December 2020 by the high court in Pretoria has ensured R1.5 billion will remain frozen pending a bank guarantee from CRRC for the same amount to SARS. Thus, a total of R2.8 billion will remain preserved while SARS finalises a tax claim against CRRC.

Accountability: On a slow boat to China

It is approaching a decade since Transnet irregularly awarded CRRC what became a multi-billion-rand contract for locomotives. Spending meant to overhaul South African freight rail instead lined the pockets of Gupta-linked front companies offering phantom consulting services. However, state capture at Transnet didn't rely on Jacob Zuma's Gupta network alone. The evidence shows that the CRRC was a central driver and beneficiary of state capture in South Africa. With only a few hundred metres separating the presidential residence and the Chinese embassy in Pretoria, it is inexplicable why China has not been given an ultimatum to clean up this mess. Prosecutions should start in China, which is rule-bound to do so in terms of the United Nations Convention Against Corruption (UNCAC).

If Beijing decides to go soft on their corporations, then we need to see far more concerted action from South African authorities. The actions by the SARB, SARS and the SIU, as well as Transnet's efforts to cancel the contract, are a start. But they are only that. The Zondo Commission has now made unambiguous recommendations for criminal investigation and prosecution against a series of corporations and individuals implicated in the great Transnet heist. The Commission's list includes CRRC executives.

In May 2022, the first major arrests related to Transnet were announced to great excitement. Transnet is clearly one of the top accountability priorities for the NPA, but it is vital that CRRC is part of that agenda. Advocate Shamila Batohi (the National Director of Public Prosecutions) and her colleagues have a constitutional responsibility to uphold the law, regardless of the consequences in Beijing and beyond.

TWO
Prasa: Looted and left for scrap

WHILE STATE CAPTURE AT Transnet has undermined freight rail, mismanagement and corruption at the Passenger Rail Agency of South Africa (Prasa) has wrought destruction on passenger rail in South Africa. The link between corruption and lived experience is nowhere more obvious than the erosion of passenger train services in South Africa. Prasa's service has declined so dramatically over the last decade, the majority of working-class South Africans who once relied on the affordable service have had to turn towards more expensive modes of public transport.

The legacy of spatial apartheid means that most working-class citizens are pushed to the periphery of cities, far away from jobs and other opportunities. Affordable urban commuter rail can play a significant role in reducing these spatial inequalities in the face of other more expensive forms of public transport, but Prasa has failed to provide it. A 2021 National Household Travel Survey (NHTS) estimated that 80 per cent of train users – about 550,000 people – have abandoned their use of rail since 2013.[10]

At the root of this decline is a series of exorbitantly expensive and corrupt contracts that siphoned billions of rands out of the SOE into the hands of politicians and businessmen from 2009–2015. The institutions and individuals who were mandated to ensure the effective functioning of the SOE, which half a million South Africans once relied on to get to work every day, have instead enabled, participated in and covered up systemic corruption at Prasa. It is long past due that they account.

Pipe dreams: The formation of Prasa

Prasa was launched in March 2009. It integrated Metrorail, which operates commuter rail services, Shosholoza Meyl, which operates long-distance regional rail services, and Autopax, which operates coach services.[11] The consolidation was aimed at increasing the efficiency of South Africa's rail system and followed a Cabinet decision on 1 December 2004 to 'offer rail passengers integrated services that prioritize customer needs, provide better mobility and accessibility to transport in pursuit of a better life for all'.[12]

This was an ambitious project and required a significant increase in state investment. According to Prasa's first annual report, government funding increased from R800 million in 2007 to around R5 billion in the 2008/2009 financial year. South Africa was also preparing to host the FIFA World Cup in 2010, and the government wanted to ensure that the public transport system could cope with the influx of passengers and show off an efficient public transport system to the world.[13]

Central to this mission was a series of mega-projects, which were set to modernise South African rail infrastructure and service. This included a significant upgrade of Prasa's locomotive fleet, upgrading station and train security and the installation of high-end technological services at certain stations.[14] Although many of these upgrades were not completed by the time of the World Cup in 2010, the government continued to significantly increase funding to Prasa for the modernisation of rail infrastructure and the upgrade of passenger fleets.[15]

An uphill battle for justice and accountability

In 2015, Public Protector Thuli Madonsela released a report into allegations of corruption and maladministration at Prasa, titled 'Derailed: A Report on an Investigation into Allegations of Maladministration Relating to Financial Mismanagement, Tender

Irregularities and Appointment Irregularities Against the Passenger Rail Agency of South Africa (PRASA)'. The basis of the report was thirty-seven complaints laid by the South African Transport and Allied Workers Union (SATAWU) in 2012 which alleged serious maladministration, flouting of the procurement process, nepotism and whistleblower victimisation.[16]

'Derailed' found evidence of systemic mismanagement and maladministration within the procurement process and supply chain management at every level of Prasa – from the board and CEO to low-level officials within the procurement process.[17] However, some of the allegations had to be deferred for further investigation because the Public Protector's office had struggled to both access documents requested from Prasa's management and verify their authenticity. Some did not have dates or were unsigned. This remained a problem when the Zondo Commission was hearing evidence of corruption at Prasa.

In addition to further investigations, Madonsela called on Prasa's board to take disciplinary action against a number of officials implicated in maladministration. Significantly, she also instructed the board, together with the National Treasury to 'Commission … a forensic investigation into all Prasa contracts above R10 million since 2012 and take measures to address any findings regarding systemic administrative deficiencies allowing ongoing maladministration'.[18]

In 2014, a year prior to the release of 'Derailed', a new board had been appointed to Prasa. Metrorail's service was in serious decline at the time, and the SOE had just reported an accumulated loss of R4.4 billion from 2010/2012.[19] Popo Molefe took up the position of board chairperson. CEO Lucky Montana was released by the new board in July 2015[20] amidst a resurgence of allegations of widespread maladministration at the SOE detailed by the 2015 Auditor General's Draft Final Management Report.[21]

After the release of 'Derailed' later that year, the new board acted quickly to try to stem the tide of irregular expenditure and cancelled dodgy contracts. Several executives implicated in corruption were dismissed. Then in February 2016 the National Treasury, in compliance with Madonsela's recommendations, commissioned investigations into

216 contracts awarded by Prasa between 2012 and 2015. Of these 216 contracts worth around R15 billion, only thirteen were found to be above board.[22]

This revealed a staggering level of corruption and maladministration at Prasa. The investigations showed that Prasa had been captured by private interests determined to drain the coffers of the already faltering rail agency. The investigations and subsequent court cases to set aside several contracts implicated a series of businesspeople, including Makhensa Mabunda,[23] Mario Ferreira and Roy Moodley, all of whose businesses secured lucrative tenders from Prasa from 2009–2014.[24] The reports indicate that these private interests were protected and enabled within Prasa, namely by the ex-CEO Lucky Montana and the board under the chairmanship of Sfiso Buthelezi.[25] Some of these stories are told in the next chapters in this section.

On the basis of these findings, Prasa's board laid about forty criminal charges with the Directorate for Priority Crimes Investigation (DPCI/Hawks) and took two large contracts – the Siyangena and Swifambo contracts – to court to have them cancelled.[26] These had cost Prasa over R4.5 billion rand and were riddled with serious irregularities. The board also commissioned private law firm Werksmans to investigate tenders, which were not within the scope of the Treasury investigations.

However, the Molefe board faced major pushback from senior figures in the ANC, both within the Parliamentary Standing Committee on Transport and from Minister of Transport Dipuo Peters. This pushback attempted to bury the forensic reports from the public eye and stop the Werksmans investigations commissioned by the board, according to Molefe's testimony at the Zondo Commission.[27]

The forensic reports became public only in late 2017 when whistleblowers within Prasa leaked them to commuter activist group #UniteBehind; this leak became known as the #Prasaleaks. #UniteBehind viewed the failure to release the reports as an effort to cover up the extent of the rot at Prasa.[28] They shared the documents with *GroundUp News*, a community news organisation for further investigation and dissemination to the public.

Ultimately, it was a network of corrupt businessmen, civil servants and politicians that sanctioned and participated in the looting of the state-owned enterprise. Many powerful businessmen still enjoy the fruits of dodgy contracts – many of them incomplete or dramatically overpriced – while politicians who either obstructed justice or actively participated in corruption continue to get recycled into new cushy positions in government.

While the following chapters discuss the companies and businessmen implicated in these stories, this chapter discusses the key public institutions and politicians who were complicit in the capture of Prasa.

The ministers of transport

Prasa is wholly state owned and reports to the Minister of Transport. The minister is supposed to provide oversight in relation to its mandate to provide efficient and accessible transport to South Africans. The minister is chiefly responsible for appointing the Board of Control (BOC), which is responsible for approving large tenders – alongside the minister – among other oversight roles. Numerous Transport ministers since the formation of Prasa have turned a blind eye to the capture and looting of Prasa. These include Ben Martins, Dipuo Peters and Joe Maswanganyi, all appointed by former president Jacob Zuma.

As indicated previously, Dipuo Peters, who was appointed in 2013, is alleged to have blocked further investigations into corruption commissioned by the Molefe board. Molefe and four other board members were fired unexpectedly by Peters in early 2017. Molefe testified at the Zondo Commission they were fired for 'shaking the tree' with their investigations, which he claimed were viewed as a threat to certain political interests. Molefe took the minister's decision to court and the board was reinstated to finish their term. The high court lambasted the minister, finding that Peters's decision was 'so unreasonable and disproportionate as to be arbitrary and irrational'.[29]

Peters was fired soon after the judgment, and replaced by Joe Maswanganyi. Maswanganyi continued where Peters left off, with Molefe testifying that Maswanganyi put pressure on the board to step down, after the court ordered their reinstatement. Molefe has also accused Maswanganyi of deliberately leaving executive positions vacant to isolate the board and make it dysfunctional until its term expired later in the year.[30] The SOE did not have a permanent board until the end of 2020, nor a CEO until 2021.

While Ben Martins was minister for a year only, he famously met with Tony Gupta, Prasa CEO Lucky Montana and Duduzane Zuma at his home during his short stint as transport minister. Martins has said that the meeting was to ensure that the Guptas would not try to get Montana fired, after hearing rumours that this might happen.[31]

The board

The Board of Control's (BOC) primary responsibility under Prasa's board charter 'is to ensure that PRASA complies with obligations imposed by various laws and regulations that are applicable to PRASA and management of regulatory compliance, such as the PFMA [Public Finance Management Act]'.[32] Significantly, the board also has the power of 'approval of capital expenditure, acquisitions and disposals in excess of the discretionary power delegated to the Chief Executive officer' as well as approving of major contracts.[33]

Sfiso Buthelezi was appointed as Prasa's first BOC chairperson in 2009.[34] Buthelezi is a close ally of Zuma, having served as an advisor to Zuma from 1994–1999 when Zuma was the Member of Executive Council (MEC) for Economic Development in KwaZulu-Natal. In 2017, three years after leaving Prasa, he was shuffled to the position of Deputy Finance Minister when Zuma removed Pravin Gordhan and Mcebisi Jonas in one particularly infamous Cabinet reshuffle.

Buthelezi is alleged to have played a central role alongside Montana in enabling the capture of Prasa by a network of shady businessmen. The forensic investigations into corruption and maladministration at Prasa commissioned by the Treasury, recommended that he and his fellow board members be criminally charged 'for contravening several sections of the Public Finance Management Act (PFMA) in the course of awarding at least 30 contracts' and for 'ignoring all responsibilities in record keeping within the procurement process'.[35] Buthelezi has also been accused of failing to fully disclose his business interests while he was the chair of Prasa's board.[36] Buthelezi has a chapter dedicated to him later in this section.

The CEO

The chief executive officer (CEO) is mandated to lead Prasa, while reporting to the BOC. The CEO has significant decision-making authority. The Public Protector's report,[37] the forensic investigations,[38] as well as court judgments which set aside the Siyangena and Swifambo contracts, all implicate Lucky Montana – Prasa's first CEO – in enabling and participating in the capture of the state-owned railway agency. Analysing the Swifambo contract, the high court found that Montana, alongside a network of corrupt executives within the procurement process, exhibited ruthless leadership and systemic flouting of procurement and supply chain processes, including the bodies that were mandated to provide oversight on tenders and procurement, such as the Bid Evaluation Committee (BEC) and Cross Functional Sourcing Committee (CFSC).[39]

Montana led Prasa with an iron fist, firing anyone who stood in his way. In the high court judgment which set aside the Swifambo contract in 2017, the court highlighted that 'the discovery of corruption was impeded by the tyrannical manner in which PRASA was controlled by Montana'.[40] This was substantiated by Fani Dingiswayo's testimony at the State Capture Commission of Inquiry last year. Dingiswayo, Prasa's former general manager for legal services, testified that Montana 'ruthlessly abused his power' as CEO. He accused Montana of creating parallel structures within Prasa to advance his own interests and said that anyone who dared to challenge Montana's authority, or flag potential tenders as irregular, was pursued by Montana until they left the SOE.[41] Dingiswayo alleges that he was fired on the spot for refusing to sign off on an irregular Prasa contract, and his account was backed up by his boss, fellow Prasa whistleblower Martha Ngoye.[42]

Looted and left for scrap: Commuters suffer the consequences while the bad guys run free

The effect of corruption and maladministration on Prasa's services has been catastrophic. Cape Town's Central line, the busiest line serving the poorest communities, including Khayelitsha, Mitchells Plain, Nyanga and Bonteheuwel, stopped all services in October 2019. Prasa blamed the closure of the line on vandalism and cable theft and only restored a very limited service to the line in February 2021.[43] It will cost billions to repair the damage to the rail infrastructure and the train fleets, which are severely dilapidated and in short supply.[44] Cape Town is just one example of the collapse of rail infrastructure around the country.

To rebuild Prasa and restore its essential service to the public, it is imperative that those who enabled and participated in the looting of Prasa are held accountable. The Hawks and the NPA have been sitting on Prasa-related cases for over five years, with seemingly little to no progress being made, despite having access to extensive forensic reports that document systemic corruption. Unless and until these cases are finalised, Prasa will continue to fall victim to looters who thrive in an environment of unfettered impunity.

THREE

Auswell Mashaba and Vossloh: The middleman and German rail company that derailed Prasa

THE PREVIOUS CHAPTER FOCUSED on the politicians, board members and public institutions that participated in and failed to stop corruption at Prasa. This chapter explores some of the businesspeople and corporations that profited from this corruption. It does so through the lens of one of the more outrageous procurement scandals in the country's history that saw R2.7 billion spent on trains that were too tall for South Africa's railway system.

It is not only intra-city rail that is in disarray in South Africa. Shosholoza Meyl, which runs the long-distance railway services across South Africa, is also in deep trouble. Mainline Passenger Services (MPS), which oversees Shosholoza Meyl, reported a staggering 90 per cent decline in passengers over ten years – from 3.8 million in 2008/2009 to 387,500 in 2018/2019. In 2020, the director-general of the Department of Transport, Alec Moemi, told Parliament that the failure of South Africa's long-distance railway service was because of a major shortfall in available locomotives.[45] The shortfall has meant that Prasa has had to lease old and unreliable locomotives at exorbitant prices, leading to frequent prolonged breakdowns.[46]

The Swifambo Rail Leasing contract, signed by Prasa in 2013, was supposed to provide a much needed injection of modern locomotives to Prasa's aged fleet.[47] At the heart of the contract sat businessman Auswell Mashaba, the director of private company Swifambo Rail Leasing. Mashaba (through Swifambo) acted as the middleman for the contract between Prasa and Vossloh España, a Spanish subsidiary of the German locomotive company Vossloh. Although it was valued at R3.5 billion, Prasa stopped making payments in 2015 after serious allegations of corruption and maladministration at Prasa were outlined by the public protector and auditor general. In 2017, the contract was set aside by the Gauteng high court. But by then over R2.7 billion had been paid into Swifambo's pockets and thirteen over-sized locomotives had touched South African soil.[48]

A carefully tailored tender

Court documents show that, in 2011, Prasa's executive manager of engineering services, Daniel Mthimkhulu, sent a memorandum to Prasa CEO Lucky Montana recommending the upgrade of Prasa's fleet by eighty-eight locomotives at an estimated cost of R5 billion. This was later reduced to seventy locomotives. Later that year, Prasa published requests for proposals after deciding to purchase seventy locomotives, based on the specifications provided by Mthimkhulu.[49]

In terms of standard procurement policy, the specifications should have been designed by the Cross Functional Sourcing Committee (CFSC). Instead, the specifications were drawn up by Mthimkhulu himself. Another red flag was that these specifications were tailored for European locomotives made by Spanish manufacturer Vossloh España, rather than the usual specifications of South African railways. In the 2017 judgment that set aside the contract, the high court found that in 'numerous instances items appeared to have been included in the specifications to ensure Swifambo was awarded more technical points' in the evaluation phase of the tender. An example was that the specifications stipulated the number of engine cylinders as a V12, when in reality the number of cylinders was irrelevant for the tender. Vossloh's locomotives had V12 cylinders.⁵⁰

Mthimkhulu is alleged to have worked closely with Montana in approving a number of irregular contracts. He was later fired from Prasa in 2015 after it was revealed that he did not hold a doctorate from Technische Universitat Munchen and was not a qualified engineer.⁵¹ In 2022, he was convicted of fraud for lying to Prasa about his qualifications.

At various stages throughout the contract, several qualified Prasa employees raised concerns with Mthimkhulu about the technical specifications of Vossloh's locomotives, including Senior Engineer Peter Stow. Transnet Freight Rail also advised Prasa as far back as October 2013 that the Afro 4000 locomotives manufactured by Vossloh exceeded the allowed height for South African railways. They were all ignored.⁵²

Swifambo Rail Leasing: A front for German grifters

Following a public tender briefing session in December 2011, Swifambo Holdings, under the directorship of Mashaba, bought a company called Mafori Finance Vryheid (Pty) in February 2012. Just two months later, Mafori Finance Vryheid submitted a bid for the Prasa locomotives contract, with almost identical specifications to the ones drawn up by Mthimkhulu. In May 2012, Mafori Finance Vryheid changed its name to Swifambo Rail Leasing in an apparent bid to suggest previous involvement in the railway industry, according to the Supreme Court of Appeal (SCA).⁵³

Swifambo's bid was riddled with major irregularities. It did not have a tax clearance certificate, there was no Broad-Based Black Economic Empowerment (B-BBEE) plan for the procurement of goods and services, and it did not comply with any local content requirements as the locomotives were to be manufactured in Spain by Vossloh. Revealingly, Mashaba did not submit any proof that his two-month-old company had any experience in the railway industry.⁵⁴

Despite the serious irregularities in the proposal, the board of Prasa inexplicably approved Swifambo Rail Leasing as the preferred bidder in July 2012, with the contract being concluded in March 2013. Later that year, in July 2013, Swifambo entered into a contract with Vossloh

España, the Spanish subsidiary of the German railway company.[55]

The high court concluded that 'Swifambo under the agreement with Vossloh was merely a token participant that received monetary compensation in exchange for the use of its B-BBEE rating' because that was the only thing that prevented Vossloh from bidding on its own. There was no transfer of skills either, since Swifambo was effectively a shelf company with 'virtually no employees, business customers and supplier'.[56]

Vossloh is one of Europe's leading railway technology and infrastructure companies in what has become a highly competitive global industry. Established in 1883, it listed on the Dusseldorf Stock Exchange in 1990, a time that saw the privatisation of many railway companies, and the rise in competition to access burgeoning global markets.[57] In recent times, Vossloh has shifted its attention from Europe towards developing economies. In a 2011 presentation to investors, Vossloh stated that accessing new markets such as China, Russia, South Africa and Libya was central to the railway company's growth.[58] South Africa was again named as a 'country of relevance' to Vossloh in 2012, the year before Prasa's contract with Swifambo. It was clear that the German railway company had eyes on the South African market, just as Prasa was announcing its intent on undertaking a major modernisation drive of South African railway infrastructure and systems.

What was Vossloh willing to do to make inroads in South Africa? The high court and Supreme Court of Appeal (SCA) concluded that the 'contractual agreement between Swifambo and Vossloh amounts to fronting practice and is a criminal offence under the B-BBEE Act'. To date, no criminal trial has considered Swifambo's or Vossloh's criminal liability in this regard.

It is clear that Swifambo Rail Leasing was never going to do any actual work. Mashaba was a middleman, who was there to buy exorbitantly expensive locomotives from Vossloh, pocketing wads of public funds in the process. Mashaba's only role was to procure locomotives from Vossloh and deliver them to Prasa. This plan was going smoothly until 2015, when a *Rapport* investigation revealed an extraordinary detail: the keenly anticipated Afro 4000 locomotives manufactured by Vossloh were too tall for South African railways. This was after R1.8 billion had already been paid to Vossloh.⁵⁹ This was confirmed in a 2015 report on the Afro 4000 locomotives by South Africa's Railway Safety Regulator (RSR). The RSR concluded that the 'Afro 4000 Series is designed and manufactured to a height of 4140 above rail head [which exceeds] the vehicle structure gauge of height of 3965mm as required by the Transnet Freight Rail maintenance manual'.⁶⁰

This absurd outcome was not simply a logistical error. Rather, it was the result of the blatant manipulation of the tender and procurement processes which bypassed multiple bodies that were supposed to check the locomotives were financially and technically viable for Prasa and South African railways. The high court confirmed that one of the key reasons for wasting money on trains that were too tall was that 'the locomotives acquired under the contract were not evaluated by the committee responsible for the technical evaluation'.⁶¹

Vossloh must also take responsibility here. Vossloh España had inspected Prasa's fleet in 2011 and were responding to an RFP that stipulated the maximum height of the trains. Their legal and engineering teams working on the contract would have been aware of the feedback from numerous Prasa engineers, who had advised that the Afro 4000s were too tall. Vossloh should have reasonably known that the Afro 4000s that they were manufacturing and delivering could not operate on parts of South African railway lines. They decided to proceed with the lucrative contract regardless.

Seven years after the story broke that the trains were too tall, only thirteen out of the seventy over-sized locomotives have touched South African soil. Further, Prasa has only recovered an estimated R63 million. Where did the rest of the money go?

Following the money

In April 2013, Prasa transferred its first payment of approximately R460 million to Swifambo Holdings, the holding company for Swifambo Rail Leasing. This was an irregular payment because Swifambo Rail Leasing was the contracted company, and so should have received the payment. Immediately after the payment was received, Mashaba began shifting large sums to a number of different companies and individuals, few of which had any obvious links to the R3.5 billion contract. These suspicious payments continued until the last tranche of Prasa payments to Swifambo in 2015. These money flows were revealed in a forensic investigation into the money flows of the Swifambo companies undertaken by Ryan Sacks of Horwath Forensics (now Crowe Forensics), after being commissioned by the Hawks in 2015.[62]

Of the R2.7 billion paid by Prasa to Swifambo, the latter paid Vossloh R1.8 billion. This meant that Swifambo retained around R500 million (excluding VAT) surplus – for doing no material work in the contract. At the end of the contract period, Swifambo was still liable to Vossloh for an amount of R462 million. However, Swifambo could not pay Vossloh as Mashaba had 'illicitly expended the money already' – according to the Horwath forensic report.[63]

Mashaba moved significant amounts of these funds to trusts and companies under his control soon after receiving the Prasa money. This included a total of R85 million deposited into Mamorokolo Makolele (MM) Trust, which lists Mashaba and his wife Joyce as trustees. Additionally, around R20 million was diverted into other companies owned by Mashaba, such as A-M Consulting Engineers and AM Investments. In total Mashaba received around R103 million from Swifambo, which was channelled through his different businesses and the MM Trust across multiple payments from 2013–2015.

In 2015, *City Press* reported that Mashaba spent over R50 million on property just days after Swifambo received the first payment from Prasa in 2013.[64] This included R27 million on the luxury AM Lodge in Limpopo, which he paid for in cash. Mashaba's son, Nsovo Mashaba, works as the manager of the lodge,[65] as does his sister, Prudence Mashaba. In 2022, AM Lodge charges R35 000 a night to stay in its luxury villa.

Large amounts of money also flowed from the two Swifambo entities to WKH Landgrebe, an auditing and accounting firm based in Randburg, Johannesburg. The firm received R27.9 million in fifteen different payments from 2013 to 2016 from Swifambo Rail Holdings and Swifambo Rail Leasing. An investigation by the *Daily Maverick*'s investigative unit Scorpio alleged that 'WKH Landgrebe used

R24.5 million it received from Swifambo to secure a 60% shareholding in [private company] Okapi Farming on behalf of Mashaba's MM Trust'. Okapi owns Orange Grove Farm outside Robertson, among other tracts of land.⁶⁶

Makhensa Mabunda: The king of kitchens

Another person allegedly paid by Mashaba was Makhensa Mabunda – a businessman with an apparent taste for very fine kitchens. Mabunda seems to have played an integral role in setting up the contracts between Swifambo and Prasa, and Swifambo and Vossloh España. In court papers, Mashaba alleged that Mabunda approached him about setting up the Swifambo contract and was a close associate of Prasa CEO Lucky Montana.⁶⁷ Mabunda received an estimated R56.6 million from Swifambo.⁶⁸ This included a payment of R5.2 million to Sterlings Living, a company which specialises in upmarket Italian kitchens. This payment was allegedly for the installation of a kitchen in Mabunda's home in the upmarket Waterfall Equestrian Estate in Gauteng.⁶⁹

Mabunda did not only receive payments from Swifambo. Vossloh also made ten payments totalling R88,991,191.39 to Mabunda. These payments were made to his companies Siyaya Rail Infrastructure Solutions Technology (Pty) and S-Investments (Pty) Ltd. The suspicious payments were first identified in the 2017 report by the Compliance and Enforcement Division of the Financial Surveillance Department in the Reserve Bank.⁷⁰

The first six payments were made between December 2011 and September 2013 by Vossloh Kiepe (another Vossloh subsidiary) to Siyaya Rail Infrastructure, and totalled R13.6 million. The timeframe and source of these payments suggest that they could be related to setting up an earlier highly criticised air-conditioning deal between Vossloh Kiepe and Prasa in 2011.⁷¹ Daniel Mthimkhulu had authorised payment of over R25 million for the air-conditioning units, and it was highly criticised by the Democratic Alliance (DA) at the time on the basis that the units were wholly imported and double the price of locally manufactured systems.⁷² The Horwath report found 'significant irregularities surrounding the supply of these air-conditioning units'.⁷³

Mabunda would receive even more from Vossloh in relation to the

Swifambo deal. The second tranche of payments was made by Vossloh España to Mabunda's S-Investments between February 2014 and September 2015, and totalled R75.3 million. These payments were defined vaguely as 'proceeds for Management Consulting Services'.[74] The payments – first publicised by *News24* in 2018[75] – only added fuel to the suspicions that the R3.5 billion locomotive contract was accompanied by kickbacks. Shortly after the exposé, Vossloh confirmed that Mabunda and his company S-Investments were paid around R90 million as an 'independent sales representative' for bringing 'Vossloh España, the supplier, together with its customer Swifambo'.[76] This is a dubious explanation. According to the Horwath report, Vossloh was paying the start-up costs for Swifambo – its 'customer' – in 2011, three years before the payments to Mabunda and before Swifambo had signed a contract with either Prasa or Vossloh España.

Political connections: The Zuma family

The Horwath forensics report also highlights that Mashaba received instructions to make payments totalling at least R86 million to 'political affiliates' connected to the ANC, and Jacob Zuma in particular.[77] This included a minimum of R40 million to Angolan businesswomen Maria da Cruz Gomes through a company called Similex. Gomes is a close friend of Jacob Zuma.[78] Meanwhile, another payment of around R30 million was made to the law firm Nksoi Sabelo, which is under the directorship of George Sabelo. Sabelo is an associate of Edward Zuma and was implicated in corruption and bribery allegations at Petro SA in 2013.[79] Mashaba was told that they were fundraising for the ANC. The Jacob Zuma Foundation also received a donation of R150,000.[80]

Eight years of impunity

The Swifambo contract sent Prasa's long-distance railway service into turmoil but, nearly a decade on, there have been little to no consequences for the parties involved. In July 2022, no prosecutions had been instigated in relation to the Swifambo contract. A glimmer of hope was seen in 2018 when the high court in Pretoria found that the Hawks had failed to conduct and finalise investigations into alleged irregular tenders between Prasa and Swifambo and Siyangena, and compelled them to do so. This case was brought to the courts by Prasa's then board chairperson Popo Molefe and civil society group the Organisation Undoing Tax Abuse (OUTA).[81] It concerned the lack of action by law enforcement after Molefe's board filed more than fifty cases with the Hawks in 2015 and 2016 after finding evidence of systemic corruption at the parastatal.

Mashaba also managed to dodge an appearance at the Zondo Commission. In February 2021, Mashaba's lawyers sent a letter to the Commission stating that he 'does not recognise that the summons issued against him' is legally binding after being called to testify about his role in the Swifambo contract.[82] Mashaba, taking a page out of Jacob Zuma's state capture playbook, refused to cooperate with the Commission, undermining its vital task. While he did submit a limited affidavit to the Commission wherein he expressed concern about incriminating himself, he never did appear before the Commission. As with many private companies implicated in state capture, Vossloh was never summoned to appear at the Commission and explain themselves, despite being named in evidence.

It also remains unclear how much of the money lost to this contract will be recovered from Vossloh. In 2021, the *Sunday Times* reported that Prasa and Swifambo's liquidators have all but abandoned any attempt to get the R1.87 billion lost to Europe from the tall-trains contract.[83] The report revealed that Prasa and Swifambo's liquidators were seeking a commercial settlement agreement with Stadler Rail for the locomotives that were never delivered. Stadler Rail is the Swiss railway company which took control of Vossloh España in late 2015. A settlement takes us no closer to accountability for Vossloh, like so many of the corporations implicated in state capture. A failure to pursue full accountability will only maintain the environment of corporate impunity that allowed state capture to flourish.

In 2019, a group of activists from #UniteBehind protested outside the German consulate in Cape Town, calling for the prosecution of international companies that have benefited from state capture. #UniteBehind singled out Vossloh and called on the consulate to take action against the German multinational railway company for its role in the unlawful contract.⁸⁴ In December 2019, Deputy German Ambassador, Dr Rudiger Lotz, replied to #UniteBehind that the embassy 'fully share your concern about state capture' and had 'forwarded your complaints to the Foreign Ministry in Berlin'.⁸⁵ However, Lotz added it was up to South Africa's criminal justice system to take the initiative with the case, which had not been done.⁸⁶

FOUR
Roy Moodley: The owner of Prasa?

IN MARCH 2020, the evidence leader of the Prasa stream at the Zondo Commission – Advocate Vas Soni – introduced two names alleged to be the principle 'capturers' of Prasa's procurement process. They were Chockalingam 'Roy' Moodley and Makhensa Mabunda.[87] In the previous chapter, we detailed how Mabunda was one of the masterminds behind the Swifambo 'tall-trains' contract alongside German railway giant Vossloh, and how he and his companies benefited handsomely as a result. In this chapter, we turn attention to Roy Moodley, a politically connected businessman whom employees at the state-owned railway company called 'the owner of Prasa'.

Moodley and his companies have been implicated in corruption allegations at SOEs dating back to 2001, when his security company was named in a tender scandal at Telkom. Many years later, a series of forensic reports into Prasa's major contracts conducted by law firm Werksmans, alongside evidence presented to the Zondo Commission, revealed the level of influence that Moodley and his companies wielded over Prasa and how he used this influence to receive lucrative contracts and crush dissent within the parastatal.

Royal security: Two decades of dubious dealings

The first reported allegation against Moodley came in 2001, when one of his companies – Royal Security – was contracted by Telkom.[88] The security company was hired to protect the parastatal's copper network. The *Mail & Guardian* reported that an internal Telkom investigation revealed that Bheki Langa – a top Telkom executive – was involved in irregularly favouring Moodley's security company and authorising irregular payments for work that they did not do. Langa and Moodley were close friends from their time together in the African National Congress (ANC).[89]

Langa resigned, while Telkom reportedly laid fraud charges against Royal Security and cancelled its contract following the corruption probe.[90] However, nine years later, in 2010, another internal probe accused three Telkom officials of 'colluding with security companies who are hired to protect and monitor Telkom's copper cable network'.[91] Royal Security was again one of the implicated companies.

Jacob Zuma: Employee of royal security?

Roy Moodley is often mentioned due to his close association with Jacob Zuma. Indeed, when Thuli Madonsela was drafting the *State of Capture* report, one of the forty-two questions she sent to then President Zuma was about his relationship with Moodley. According to evidence presented to the Zondo Commission by Prasa evidence leader Advocate Soni, Moodley paid a monthly salary of R64,000 to Zuma through Royal Security from 2007 to 2009, stopping a few months into his presidency.[92] The payments totalled R1.5 million, according to the Commission's investigators. One year later, Royal Security started receiving contracts from Prasa; so far it has been paid more than R471 million.[93]

Royal Security's involvement at Prasa was first mentioned in Public Protector Thuli Madonsela's 2015 'Derailed' report. Considering complaints related to then Prasa CEO Lucky Montana improperly awarding tenders, Madonsela declared that the 'appointment of Royal Security was irregular, as its original contract [from 2006] was terminated by Prasa due to its underperformance'.[94] Just like the

Telkom case, Royal Security managed to find a way to benefit from Prasa's procurement process after having a contract terminated.

A series of further forensic investigations followed the 'Derailed' report. A 2016 Werksmans investigation into Prasa's security contracts found major irregularities in the appointment and extension of security companies' contracts from 2010–2016.[95] The investigation revealed that Prasa spent hundreds of millions of rand on irregular security contracts without a proper procurement process. The security companies investigated included Royal Security. It also noted Prasa's 'practice of continuous contract extensions and/or ad-hoc appointments over several years applied to ensure that the security companies continued to supply services to Prasa'.[96] Some contracts were extended for seven years without following any supply chain management (SCM) process or assessment of the technical ability of the security providers, such as Royal Security. Werksmans concluded this was irregular and may have been in contravention of the Public Finance Management Act (PFMA).

The continuous extensions of these security contracts and failure to assess the capability of service providers left 'the security at Prasa's business units and subsidiaries in disarray' and unable to cope with Prasa's daily security issues.[97] At one point, Prasa's Corporate Security had tried to cancel a contract with Royal Security 'for economic reasons'. However, Prasa CEO Lucky Montana intervened and instructed Prasa's head of Security, Jama Matakata, to keep the contract running.[98]

The most expensive customer-service training in the world?

Royal Security is not the only company connected to Moodley that received lucrative contracts from Prasa. Another 2017 Werksmans report found that at least five companies associated with Moodley received contracts from Prasa.[99] Although Moodley is not a current director at all of these companies, his sons Mageshrepren and Selvan, along with other close associates, are at the helm.

Testimony to the Zondo Commission by Fani Dingiswayo, Prasa's former General Manager of Legal Services, and Tiro Holele, a Prasa executive, alleged that Moodley's contracts were viewed as 'untouchable' by Prasa employees.[100] Holele and Dingiswayo detailed a longstanding dispute concerning Prasa contracts with a Moodley-linked company called Prodigy Business Services. The Companies and Intellectual Property Commission's (CIPC) records show that Moodley was a director of the company but resigned in 2012.[101]

Dingiswayo testified that in early 2015 he received a contract between Prasa and Prodigy from Prasa's supply chain management (SCM) team. The contract, originating in 2010, was for 'customer service' training for Prasa employees, as part of Prasa's 'My Station Programme'. The contract had lapsed, but Prodigy had not trained the set number of employees and were requesting Dingiswayo to finalise the extended scope of the work, which was needed before payment could be made.[102] Prodigy said they had been continuing with the training despite the contract having lapsed, and wanted to be paid.

Dingiswayo requested the contract's SCM file, which would have the original supporting documents for the contract. When he started digging, he became suspicious. The foundation of the contract was a letter from one of the directors of Prodigy, Nerishni Shunmugam, addressed to CEO Lucky Montana, which stated that Prodigy had a grant for the training from the Sector Education and Training Authority (SETA). Shunmugam said that if Prasa paid Prodigy for the training, they could claim it back from the SETA grant.[103] Lucky Montana then instructed Prasa's procurement team to engage Prodigy on confinement – a closed tender process – because they were the 'only people who are accredited' to do this type of customer training, according to Dingiswayo's testimony.[104]

The first contract was signed at a cost of R10.8 million for the training of 300 learners through learnerships, which Dingiswayo said was Prodigy's way of 'getting its foot in the door'.[105] The Prodigy contract, like the Royal Security contract, used the tried-and-tested modus operandi for bypassing the procurement process at Prasa – especially when Montana was CEO. It established an initial contract or partnership – often on confinement – which was then used as a basis for continuous contract extensions and mysterious 'addendums' or annexures, dramatically increasing the cost and bypassing any competitive procurement process.

The extensions of the Prodigy contract – also done on confinement

– entailed a five-day customer service training programme that would train 3000 employees. It would run from September 2011 to 31 March 2014 at a cost of R82 million. The training – which was pitched at a high school-level qualification and ran for five days – cost R24 000 per learner. Dingiswayo told the Commission he thought this was the 'most expensive customer service training in the world'.[106]

Dingiswayo raised his concerns with SCM that the confinement application was unwarranted and that it was far too expensive. He refused to be involved. Montana emailed Dingiswayo in 2015 denying there was anything wrong with the Prodigy contracts and accused Dingiswayo of being part of 'a much bigger agenda ... targeting certain contracts'.[107] A week later Dingiswayo was called to Montana's office and summarily fired for 'working against the interest of Prasa' by trying to cancel the tender.[108] The next day Dingiswayo's boss in the legal department, Martha Ngoye, visited Montana to understand the motivation behind Dingiswayo's dismissal. She too was fired immediately for contesting Montana's authority.

One of the top fifteen decision makers in the country?

As discussed in the previous chapters on Prasa, Popo Molefe took over Prasa's board in late 2014 and started a major overhaul of the entity's procurement process. This included taking two mega contracts to court to have them set aside (Siyangena and Swifambo) and launching extensive investigations into corruption and maladministration at Prasa.[109] While Montana left Prasa in 2015 after clashing with Molefe when the first serious cases of corruption were revealed to the public, Moodley's influence at Prasa was not over.

Tiro Holele, the General Manager of Strategy at Prasa, told the Zondo Commission that in 2017 he was called for a meeting with Prodigy by its director Shunmugam, two years after Montana had left. At the time there was an ongoing dispute about the validity of the contract, based on the issues raised by Dingiswayo, and Prodigy was still trying to secure payment despite the contractual irregularities and ongoing court action.[110] Holele testified that he arrived at the meeting expecting to see Shunmugam, but was greeted by Roy Moodley instead. Holele said that

Moodley immediately demanded that Prasa pay Prodigy R24 million. However, as the contract was before the courts at the time, Prasa could not make any payment – which Holele told Moodley.[111]

According to Holele, Moodley then boasted that he was 'one of the 15 decision makers in this country', that 'big changes were coming', and that Holele 'should be on the right side of those changes'.[112] Moodley also allegedly stated that when those changes happen 'the young man will come back' – which Holele assumed was former CEO Lucky Montana. Holele presumed that the 'big changes' might refer to the transport minister or other Cabinet positions. A month later Popo Molefe and his board were sacked by the Minister of Transport Dipuo Peters, who was herself sacked by Zuma and replaced by Joe Maswanganyi.[113] In 2017, Maswanganyi and the Parliamentary Portfolio on Transport led hearings that were more interested in targeting those wanting to expose the corruption at Prasa.[114] The Committee's targets included Popo Molefe, Martha Ngoye and Fani Dingiswayo.

At the Zondo Commision in 2021, Popo Molefe testified that Moodley tried to 'capture' him six times when he was Prasa board chairperson between late 2014 and 2017. The first time allegedly occurred in 2015, when Molefe was invited to a railway exhibition in Berlin by then CEO Montana, soon after Molefe became Prasa chairperson.[115] At this event Molefe noticed how close Moodley appeared to certain executives within Prasa, especially the CEO Montana. After this encounter Molefe asked employees at Prasa about Moodley's involvement at the SOE. He says he was told that 'Prasa is his [Moodley's] farm… you know a farm, when it is harvesting time you come to harvest'.[116]

Molefe testified that, despite warning Moodley to not get too close to management, Moodley continued with his efforts to influence the Prasa chairperson on numerous occasions. This included offering to pay for Molefe's entire family to travel to the US Golf Masters, offering him a seat at the State of the Nation address, and inviting him to his golf event in Durban.[117]

In a combative and rambling display at the Zondo Commission in 2021, Lucky Montana denied he had an improper relationship with Moodley, saying that the testimony and accusations from Molefe, Dingiswayo and Ngoye had 'nothing to do with facts' but rather had to do 'with pursuing an agenda that was the basis for targeting certain contracts'.¹¹⁸ He said that their focus on Moodley was part of this narrative, and insisted that Prodigy was properly appointed and no longer connected to Moodley.

In its final report on Prasa, the Zondo Commission noted that, despite the extensive evidence against him, Moodley chose only to submit an affidavit denying the allegations. He chose not to appear before the Commission and did not apply to cross-examine any witnesses. The Commission concluded that the substance of the testimony of Molefe and Holele on these issues was likely 'true and correct'.¹¹⁹

Prasa's very own tenderpreneur?

While Moodley was allegedly trying to influence Molefe, Werksmans was undertaking major investigations into the main contracts at the SOE on instruction by Molefe's board. Two of these investigations were being used in Prasa's litigation to get the Swifambo Rail Leasing and Siyangena Technologies mega-contracts – worth over R8 billion combined – set aside in court.¹²⁰

Siyangena Technologies was awarded a contract in 2011 to install an integrated security system at select Prasa stations, at an initial cost of R517 million. However, like the Prodigy contract, the Siyangena contract was irregularly extended in 2013 and 2014, with the total cost ballooning to over R4.5 billion. Prasa asked the court to set aside the contract, claiming that it had no fixed budget, bypassed the procurement process and did not obtain board approval. The court agreed in a damning 2020 judgment, finding that Montana pushed a 'not fit for purpose' contract past Prasa's internal controls meant to prevent corruption.¹²¹

Molefe testified at the Zondo Commission that during the Werksmans investigation investigators discovered that Siyangena paid Moodley a whopping R500 million after being awarded the contract. The money was paid to Hail Way Trading, a company of which Moodley is the sole director. Molefe testified that this money was deposited to Hail Way Trading despite it not doing any work relating to the contract or being a shareholder of Siyangena.¹²² Siyangena is co-owned by soccer boss Mario Ferreira. A *News24* article alleges that Ferreira and Moodley are associates, and co-owned two racing horses.¹²³ Another *News24* investigation in 2017 revealed that Prodigy, the same firm that benefited from the dubious customer service training contract, transferred R4.5 million to Hail Way Trading in 2015.[124] Hail Way Trading shares the same registered address as Royal Security, according to CIPC records.

Justice derailed

Moodley and companies linked to him have scored over a billion rand through irregular contracts with Prasa and mysterious middleman payments from other suppliers, like Siyangena. While Moodley's security companies earned millions, Prasa's failure to provide adequate security for its passengers and infrastructure saw a major rise in vandalism, theft, personal robbery and other security-related incidences – from 4123 in 2012/2013 to 6379 in 2016/17, according to the 2016/17 Railway Safety Report. The lack of security resulted in 'increasing theft of overhead cables', which resulted in train delays and the heightened risk of train collisions or derailments.[125]

It has been ten years since many of these contracts were irregularly awarded and, although Prasa laid numerous criminal charges against implicated parties in 2015/2016, there has not been a single criminal prosecution relating to the looting of Prasa, despite extensive evidence. Moodley and his associates have faced little scrutiny by law enforcement despite leaving two decades of corruption allegations in their wake. This serious lack of any accountability creates an environment of impunity where corruption thrives. It is urgent that the Hawks and NPA act.

FIVE
Sfiso Buthelezi: The board chair who derailed Prasa

THE INDIVIDUALS AND companies that have stripped billions in public funds through dubious contracts with Prasa could not have done so without the assistance of senior members of the board and executive. A particularly important character in this story Sfiso Buthelezi, whose six years as Prasa's first board chairperson saw billions looted from the parastatal, some of which is alleged to have gone to the chairperson himself.

Buthelezi was board chairperson from 2009–2014, during Prasa's formative years. In this period, Prasa undertook a significant modernisation programme to procure modern trains and rail infrastructure for millions of commuters.[126] The previous chapters demonstrate how the budget for this programme was captured by a network of companies and businesspeople who systematically bypassed the procurement process. This all occurred under the watch of Buthelezi. This contributed to the rapid breakdown of Prasa's infrastructure and service; forcing over half a million commuters to find more expensive forms of public transport.

Buthelezi is now the chairperson of the Standing Committee on Appropriations in parliament, responsible not just for allocating funding to government departments, including SOEs like Prasa, but also for ensuring compliance with the PFMA and other procurement legislation.[127] Yet, multiple forensic investigations into corruption and maladministration at Prasa accuse Buthelezi of contravening these very laws. It is untenable that he remains in this position of trust and should be removed until a full investigation into all the allegations is complete.

Buthelezi's revolving door between public and private interests

Sfiso Buthelezi joined Umkhonto weSizwe (MK), the armed wing of the ANC, in 1981. He was arrested in 1983 and spent nine years in prison on Robben Island until his release in 1991. After South Africa's 1994 democratic elections, Buthelezi worked for Jacob Zuma while the former president was MEC for economic development in KwaZulu-Natal (KZN).[128]

After spending a few years in senior public-sector roles, Buthelezi joined the private sector after 1999 to become the Chief Operating Officer (COO) of Makana Investment Corporation, an investment vehicle for Makana Trust, a trust for former political prisoners founded by politically connected businessman and former Robben Island prisoner Peter-Paul Ngwenya.[129] Makana Investment Corporation has a number of subsidiaries and shares in a spectrum of companies, including JSE-listed Cadiz Holdings and Sebenza Forwarding and Shipping. Both these companies have been implicated in benefiting from irregular Prasa contracts while Buthelezi was board chair.[130] These accusations come from the 2015 Public Protector's 'Derailed' report, and subsequent forensic investigations into Prasa contracts.

In 2005, Minister of Transport Jeff Radebe appointed Buthelezi to the board of the South African Rail Commuter Corporation (SARCC) – a predecessor to Prasa. SARCC at that time was planning a significant modernisation of South Africa's rail service for the 2010 FIFA World Cup, which required a significant increase in government funding.[131] A major element of this modernisation was the consolidation passenger rail services in South Africa into a single entity: Prasa. Buthelezi was appointed Prasa's first chairperson.

Prasa's board reports directly to the Minister of Transport and is mandated to ensure that Prasa complies with necessary laws and regulations, including the Public Finance Management Act (PFMA).[132]

Prasa's Board Charter also requires all board members to avoid and promptly disclose conflict of interests and duties.[133] Buthelezi was Prasa's longest standing board chairperson, holding the position from 2009 to 2014. In his final chairman statement in Prasa's 2013–2014 annual report, Buthelezi congratulated his board and ex-CEO Lucky Montana for making progress in the modernisation programme and for creating a rail service as a 'priority for our people'.[134]

Public Protector shatters the façade

That 2014 annual report was hiding a sordid reality. Madonsela's 'Derailed' report in 2015 revealed systemic corruption and maladministration at Prasa, where the procurement process was consistently flouted, leading to billions in irregular expenditure under Buthelezi's watch.[135] As discussed in previous chapters, the report also called for a series of additional forensic investigations into all procurement contracts at Prasa worth over R10 million.

The investigations undertaken by Treasury revealed a staggering level of maladministration at Prasa: out of the 216 contracts investigated, worth a combined value of around R15 billion, only thirteen were found to be above board. These contracts were entered into while Buthelezi was chair of the board, and the investigations into thirty of those contracts recommended Buthelezi and his board be criminally charged for contravening the PFMA.[136] When asked about these recommendations, Buthelezi told Open Secrets he was not privy to the Treasury investigations because he had already left Prasa when they were undertaken.

These reports were a scathing indictment of Buthelezi's tenure as Prasa's board chairperson, but even more troubling were allegations that Buthelezi's companies profited from Prasa contracts without him disclosing any conflicts of interest.

Profiting from Prasa?

One of the complaints that formed the basis of 'Derailed' was an allegation that companies linked to Buthelezi irregularly profited from Prasa contracts while he was chairperson. Madonsela investigated

Buthelezi's alleged failure to disclose a conflict of interest involving Makana Investment Corporation, which has a 15 per cent stake in Cadiz, a company that allegedly provided advisory services to Prasa for a major rolling stock contract.[137] Lucky Montana, in defence of Buthelezi, rejected the accusation that Cadiz won any Prasa contracts and provided the Public Protector with an undated declaration form which listed Buthelezi's involvement in Makana and a seemingly misspelt Cadiz as 'Cadaz' Holdings.[138] Buthelezi likewise denied all allegations that he improperly profited from any Prasa contracts.

Makana bought shares in financial services group Cadiz for R41 million in 2004, introducing BEE ownership, according to reporting at the time.[139] Makana's founder, Ngwenya, was nominated as Makana's representative on the Cadiz board, with Buthelezi as his alternate, according to the article. Buthelezi resigned from Cadiz in 2010 but remained a director of Makana until 2016, according to company records.

Madonsela deferred the complaint to be dealt with in a second report because Prasa failed to provide relevant documents 'to verify' Montana's claim that the conflict of interest had been declared. However, the second Prasa report, released in 2019, was completed by Public Protector Busisiwe Mkhwebane after Madonsela's term expired. Mkwebane dismissed almost all of Madonsela's deferred complaints, including against Buthelezi. Railways activist coalition #UniteBehind rejected Mkwebane's Prasa report as a 'whitewash' that protected powerful figures implicated in corruption at Prasa, including Buthelezi and Montana.[140] In July 2022, Mkhewbane was suspended and subject to a parliamentary hearing to assess her fitness to hold office.

Makana Investment Corporation and Cadiz were also implicated in the shady locomotive contracts at Transnet. Both companies formed part of the local consortium that partnered with China North Rail (CRN) in the contracts, which were set up to provide billions in kickbacks to the Guptas, as detailed in the first chapter of this section. A 2018 forensic investigation into the Transnet contracts by Fundudzi noted that Buthelezi was a director of Makana until 2016, meaning that Buthelezi was both a Member of Parliament and director at Makana while the contracts were active.[141] Makana and Cadiz are not the only companies linked to Buthelezi that are alleged to have received profitable government rail contracts.

The Swifambo saga

Buthelezi's Makana Investment Corporation also has a 55 per cent majority stake in Sebenza Forwarding and Shipping, which is alleged to have profited from multiple Prasa contracts without Buthelezi disclosing his interest, most notably in relation to the 2013 Swifambo 'tall trains' contract. The earlier chapters in this section show how Swifambo Rail Leasing, a local front for Spanish railway company Vossloh España, was established to benefit from a massive 2012 Prasa contract worth R3.5 billion for the supply of locomotives. The entire procurement process was rigged to favour Vossloh España's locomotives – and R450 million out of the R2.7 billion paid by Prasa for locomotives, famously too tall for parts of South Africa's railway lines, was lost in a web of shelf companies, multinational corporations and shady political networks.[142]

In July 2012, Prasa's board met to consider the bids for the locomotive contract, with both Buthelezi and Montana in attendance. This is according to former board chairperson Popo Molefe's founding affidavit in Prasa's successful bid to get the contract set aside, and in his evidence to the Zondo Commission. The board approved Swifambo as the preferred bidder for the R3.5 billion contract, just months after the company had been established. This decision was fiercely criticised by Molefe, who said the board's decision to award the mega contract without necessary information was 'astounding'.[143] Non-executive director at Prasa Bridgette Gasa also raised serious concerns to Buthelezi and Montana about Swifambo's ability to fulfil its contractual obligations, according to Molefe. Despite these concerns, the board signed the contract in March 2013.

Buthelezi is implicated in the Swifambo scandal by signing off the deal in violation of his board chairperson duties. He is also, however, implicated through a conflict of interest. Horwath's analysis of Swifambo's bank account revealed that shipping and logistics company Sebenza Forwarding and Shipping received R99 million from Swifambo Rail Leasing. Buthelezi was a director at Sebenza, and he also approved Swifambo's bid as Prasa chairperson in July 2012, according to Horwath.

Buthelezi resigned as a director of Sebenza in 2012 – before

Swifambo paid the R99 million. However, the Horwath report alleges that Buthelezi failed to disclose his interest in Makana Investment Corporation and its majority stake (55 per cent) in Sebenza. The report found that Buthelezi-linked Sebenza is Prasa's 'preferred forwarding and clearing service provider' for imported railway infrastructure.[144] According to company records, Buthelezi remained a director of Makana until 2016, long after Swifambo paid Sebenza and after the too-tall locomotives arrived in South Africa in 2014 and 2015. He was not the only one in his family to profit from the deal.

Inala Shipping, a company owned by Buthelezi's brother Nkanyiso, also profited from the Swifambo contract, according to reporting by *News24* in 2017. This reporting alleged that Swifambo appointed Inala, who in turn appointed Sebenza to handle the customs and clearing for the locomotives. Sebenza confirmed to *News24* that Swifambo had paid it R99 million and that it worked with Inala, but denied Buthelezi's involvement, as did Buthelezi. The R99 million allegedly went to pay VAT and custom fees on behalf of Swifambo, according to Sebenza. Sebenza stated Inala profited around R1.5 million, which it said was the majority of the profit from the deal.[145] However, Horwath investigators found that as per Swifambo's contract with Prasa, the cost of shipping was Prasa's, not Swifambo's. Additionally, Horwath could not find any billing by Swifambo for shipping costs besides one Swifambo statement which detailed R3,988,195 in 'clearance fees'.[146]

The Horwath report was prepared on request by the Hawks, and it made the recommendation to the Hawks that Buthelezi be investigated for his role in the deal, particularly the Prasa chairperson's 'undisclosed relationship with Sebenza'.[147] Yet, after presenting this damning report to investigating officer Major General Khana of the Hawks in 2017, the forensic investigators never heard back and Buthelezi continued in various senior roles in government and as a member of parliament.[148]

The massive Swifambo locomotive contract was not the only contract that Sebenza scored with Prasa. A 2017 *News24* article alleges that Sebenza scored at least two other Prasa contracts before the Swifambo contract.[149] According to this reporting, Sebenza invoiced Prasa for around R42 million in relation to Prasa importing steel tracks from European manufacturer Tata Steel France in 2013. Additionally,

Vossloh Kiepe, Vossloh España's sister company, paid Sebenza R13 million in 2011 in relation to an air-conditioning contract. This heavily criticised contract was discussed in earlier chapters in this section, and was described in the Horwath report as being beset by 'significant irregularities'.[150]

Buthelezi has denied all allegations; stating that he never abused his chairmanship to influence procurement decisions and that he has always adhered to conflict-of-interest policies. He stated that he was a non-executive director at Sebenza, did not influence procurement decisions while on Prasa's board, and that he did not personally benefit from companies involved in the Swifambo contract.[151] Buthelezi, like Montana, defended the Swifambo contract and too-tall locomotives as legitimate. In an affidavit to the Zondo Commission in 2021 in response to Molefe's and Horwath's allegations, Buthelezi criticised Popo Molefe for branding himself a 'State Capture buster'.[152]

However, in a response to the *News24* article, the Ministry of Finance confirmed that Makana had a 55 per cent shareholding in Sebenza, but rejected that Buthelezi profited from any of the Sebenza contracts.[153] The 2017 reporting about Sebenza came just after Buthelezi was appointed Deputy Finance Minister by Jacob Zuma.

This means that from 2012, Buthelezi was still an active director of Makana until 2016, which had a majority shareholding in Prasa's 'preferred clearing and forwarding company' Sebenza. In that period, Buthelezi's board also signed the Swifambo contract and oversaw the delivery of the too-tall locomotives. This challenges Buthelezi's blanket denial that he did not benefit from Prasa contracts.

Rewarded for negligence

Buthelezi departed Prasa in 2014, leaving the parastatal in disarray. Popo Molefe and his new board were left with the mammoth task of cleaning up. But his predecessor faced no investigations or disciplinary processes. In addition, law enforcement has been criticised for a lack of investigations into Buthelezi. Molefe's board lodged dozens of criminal charges in 2015/2016, many in relation to the Swifambo and Siyangena contracts. In a 2017 letter to Hawks head Berning Ntlemeza, Molefe accused the Hawks, and its investigating officer Major General Alfred

Khana, of failing to investigate the charges.[154] Five years later, not a single case has been brought to court.

In response to questions from Open Secrets, Buthelezi declined to comment on whether he had faced any investigations or disciplinary hearing, but did confirm that no criminal charges had been laid against him since the 2016 Treasury investigations became public. 'I suggest that the first question you should pose should be directed to those who were supposed to lay criminal charges against me and the question should be why have they not done so since 2016', he said in an email to Open Secrets.

Despite the serious allegations against him, Buthelezi has been promoted to key government positions since he left Prasa. Buthelezi – who had a history of working alongside Zuma – was admitted as an ANC MP in 2016. One year later, in one of Zuma's infamous Cabinet shuffles, Buthelezi was appointed Deputy Finance Minister alongside Malusi Gigaba as Minister. As Deputy Finance Minister, he chaired the board of the Public Investment Corporation (PIC), responsible for managing nearly R2 trillion.[155] In 2018, Buthelezi was made Deputy Minister of Agriculture, Forestry and Fisheries. In 2019, he was removed from Cabinet and appointed chairperson of the Standing Committee on Appropriations in Parliament. The committee has the vital task of allocating budget funding to government departments, including SOEs such as Prasa.[156] The Committee is also tasked with upholding the PFMA, which Buthelezi is accused of violating in the Treasury and Werksmans investigations.

Civil society have since 2017 called for Buthelezi to be investigated and removed from holding public office because of his history at Prasa.[157] But to date, he remains unmoved and the inaction suggests that he continues to have the blessing of senior individuals within the state and governing party. If the South African Parliament is serious about accountability, then Buthelezi should be removed as chairperson of the Standing Committee on Appropriations to allow for a full public investigation of this matter. Such a process should either clear him of any wrongdoing or recommend his prosecution for his role in the destruction of Prasa.

SIX

Refiloe Mokoena: The attorney on the wrong side of the law

STATE CAPTURE RELIES ON a vast network of actors, many of whom have evaded accountability for their role in derailing state-owned entities. In later chapters of this book, we turn the spotlight on the banks, consulting firms and audit firms that are part of this network. But the network also includes lawyers who have disregarded their ethical and professional duties in service of corrupt networks. Refiloe Mokoena, an attorney who served as a board member at several SOEs and as an acting judge, is one such lawyer implicated in state capture.

The streets of Sandton and Pretoria are lined by gilded buildings housing South Africa's top law firms. Many of these filled their pockets with state capture loot and continue to work as the enablers of economic crime. The fact that these corporate behemoths have gotten away with their crimes talks to both their cunning and the incapacity of the state. To understand the extent of this problem it is helpful to focus on a lawyer who represents a case study of what is wrong with our accountability mechanisms, and how some lawyers seem to be able to act with impunity despite their complicity in crimes that have devastating consequences.

Mokoena has been implicated in wrongdoing during her tenure as a board member at Denel, and in her personal capacity at the South

African Revenue Service (SARS). Notably, during a period when she sat as acting judge in the Free State high court, she was linked to the Free State asbestos tender scandal. In each of these cases, Mokoena has exhibited a blatant disregard for her responsibility as an officer of court, failing to ensure that the law is observed and upheld. It is, therefore, alarming that she remains a practising attorney and director at her law firm, Refiloe Mokoena Attorneys. Aside from her dismissal from SARS, Mokoena has not yet been appropriately held to account for her role in state capture.

Denel's downfall

Mokoena began her career as an attorney in 1990 and has worked at several law firms. She has since held various executive positions and directorships at public entities. Between 2004 and 2007, she worked at the Independent Communications Authority of South Africa (ICASA) on the Complaints and Compliance Committee, and on the Appeal Tribunal at the Broadcasting Complaints Committee of South Africa (BCCSA).[158] She also served as the executive for Corporate Compliance and Regulation at Telkom from 2008.[159]

Mokoena went on to serve on the board of directors of Armscor in 2013 and Denel in 2015.[160] In 2013, then Defence and Military Veterans Minister Nosiviwe Mapisa-Nqakula dismissed Mokoena from her position as Armscor deputy chairperson for her failure to fulfil her duties as a board member. These failures arose from the way in which she and General Moamela Motau, the former Armscor chairperson, mishandled various procurement projects.[161] Given the reasons for Mokoena's dismissal from the Armscor board, it is concerning that she was subsequently appointed as a member of the state-owned arms company Denel's board (also part of the defence sector family of SOEs) in 2015 and that, in a similar manner, she neglected her duties as a board member.

Former Minister of Public Enterprise Lynne Brown, herself the subject of state capture allegations, appointed Mokoena to Denel's board of directors. The notorious 2015 board was integral to the capture and disintegration of Denel, by the Guptas and their allies.[162] Under the board's oversight and through its direct involvement, dodgy procurement processes, corrupt decision-making and general maladministration were rife. In the Zondo Commission's final report, Zondo found that Brown's 2015 appointments deliberately facilitated the capture of Denel by removing a well-functioning and successful board.[163]

The report made searing findings against Brown, Denel's former chairperson Daniel Mantsha, and all of the board members for their role in the decline of Denel. According to the Zondo Commission, the 2015 board should be investigated for its conduct, particularly its suspension of Denel executives Riaz Saloojee, Fikile Mhlontlo and Elizabeth Afrika, who were fired unlawfully because they posed a threat to the Guptas' attempts to capture Denel. The Commission recommended that action be taken against the 2015 board to declare the members as delinquent directors because of their negligence and role in facilitating corrupt decisions at Denel, finding that the board collectively failed to fulfil their fiduciary duties as directors.[164]

The board's actions harmed Denel significantly. It went from relative financial health in 2015 to teetering on the edge of bankruptcy by November 2021 when it owed R900 million to its suppliers and R650 million to employees, some of whom are still unpaid.[165] In February 2022, Finance Minister Enoch Godongwana announced that Denel would receive R3 billion to settle its outstanding payments, but its survival remains uncertain.[166]

Lawyers like Mokoena were directly complicit in Denel's downfall. As a board member, she had the responsibility to ensure that the enterprise and its interests were protected. In her position, she would have been privy to key decisions that the board took, including endorsing improper procurement processes and the unlawful axing of three executives. Yet there is no evidence that she opposed these decisions at any point. Chief Justice Zondo named Mokoena as one of the Denel board members with a strong connection to the Guptas, indicating that she would have indeed played a key role in ensuring that the Guptas' interests were pursued at Denel, which was a common theme in SOEs that were captured by the family.[167] The actions taken by the 2015 board members indicate a clear objective to profit from dodgy deals to the detriment of the state. That Mokoena permitted this is a clear sign that she is not fit to hold the position of director. Yet, company records indicate that she still serves as a director at other entities.

Dollars from Diamond Hill Trading 71

In October 2020, the *Sunday Times* reported that Mokoena, during her time as an acting judge in the Free State high court in 2015, benefited from the dodgy asbestos audit tender during Ace Magashule's tenure as Free State premier. Evidence gathered by investigators at the Zondo Commission shows that Mokoena received $4,000 (roughly R54,000 at the time) towards her daughter's tuition in the United States from Diamond Hill Trading 71. The company was part of a joint venture that received a tender from the Free State government to identify and remove asbestos from low-cost housing. Magashule's office organised the payment after Mokoena met the former premier in July 2015 in Germany.[168] This arrangement occurred whilst Mokoena was a member of the 2015 Denel board.

Emails exchanged between Mokoena and Magashule's office in July 2015 were made available to the Zondo Commission and show that Mokoena wrote to the office for the 'purposes of settling [her] daughter's university account'.[169] In her initial email to the premier's office, she lists the cost of tuition, the date by which the tuition should be paid (before 31 July 2015), as well as the details necessary for the transaction.[170] The first email request Mokoena made on 17 July 2015 occurred prior to her being appointed as acting judge; however, she followed up on the issue of the funds and received them in August 2015, during her time as an acting judge.[171] These emails also show Ignatius Mpambani, owner of Diamond Hill Trading 71, confirming that payment had been made and Mokoena expressing her intense gratitude.[172] Magashule has denied any involvement in the process of awarding the tender or having received any kickbacks.[173] Magashule and his co-accused are currently in court, after being charged with fraud, corruption and money laundering related to this tender. Mpambani was murdered in Sandton in 2017.

Mokoena has denied knowing the source of the funds that paid her daughter's tuition.[174] However, the evidence suggests that her connection to Magashule ensured that she benefited from the corrupt asbestos deal and her emails indicate that she knew that there was a third party involved in paying her daughter's tuition. Money that was allocated for public use instead funded the personal expenses of a relatively well-paid acting judge. According to the Code of Judicial Conduct, it is improper for a judge in acting service to request or receive remuneration or gifts, and in this case funds for personal use, as this would essentially undermine the integrity of her office.[175] Yet, it is precisely these arrangements and disregard for lawful practices that ensured that the state capture network was maintained. This can be seen in Mokoena's role in unlawful conduct at SARS.

Stealing from SARS: Mokoena enables Guptas' capture

Mokoena joined the SARS executive committee as the chief officer for Legal Counsel in May 2017.[176] By this time, Denel was facing major financial issues due to the conduct of the 2015 board, which included Mokoena. Mokoena, alongside others, had been removed from their positions.[177] That she was green-lighted to a top-position at the country's tax collector is a clear indictment of the leadership of SARS under another state capture kingpin – Tom Moyane.

Mokoena joined SARS during Tom Moyane's tenure as SARS Commissioner and the Zondo Commission found that Moyane himself was an integral part of the capture of SARS, through his connections to former President Zuma, consulting giant Bain and Company and the Guptas.[178] These networks are the subject of a later chapter in this book. During this time, Mokoena was part of the executive committee at SARS responsible for making important financial decisions. Mokoena's involvement in corruption while employed as one of its top inhouse lawyers at SARS is extremely significant and forms part of the broader capture at the entity.

During 2016, major banks in South Africa belatedly closed several accounts of Gupta-linked companies, which meant that these companies could not receive VAT refunds to their accounts. According to the findings of the Nugent Commission of Inquiry into SARS, some of these companies subsequently had the VAT refunds paid into third-party accounts.[179] This is in clear violation of South African tax law. One company that received the unlawful payments was Oakbay Investments

(Pty) Ltd, which was one of the Gupta-affiliated companies at the centre of the capture of state-owned enterprises.

Mokoena signed off on VAT refunds, valued at R150 million, for Oakbay into a third-party account. In doing so, Mokoena facilitated an unlawful payment. It is inexplicable that a legal professional in a senior position in the SARS legal department would make a decision in violation of tax laws. Furthermore, even if Mokoena had been uncertain, she authorised the payment against the advice of SARS executives who had the necessary tax and legal knowledge and who had indicated that doing so would be unlawful.[180]

According to the Nugent Commission's findings, Mokoena was told by Moyane to resolve the issue of the payments, and she went ahead and signed off on them. Her actions here speak to the nature of the relationship that the Guptas had with the entity under Moyane's leadership. Judge Nugent noted that what Moyane did at SARS was more than mismanagement, but that he 'arrived without integrity and [subsequently] dismantled the elements of governance one by one'.[181] Mokoena's facilitation of an unlawful payment speaks precisely to the type of erosion that occurred at SARS.

Mokoena was suspended by SARS in October 2018, seven months after Moyane had been suspended by Cyril Ramaphosa. She underwent a disciplinary hearing in 2019, and was subsequently dismissed from SARS in November 2019. The dismissal was upheld by the CCMA.[182]

Time for accountability

Mokoena's dismissal from SARS was necessary, but raises question around what the repercussions are for breaking the law. Mokoena, an attorney tasked with the responsibility of upholding the law, not only failed to do so, but has actively contributed to a much larger culture of corruption in South Africa. Her involvement in different entities and her connections to individuals linked directly to fraud and corruption in the country are a perfect demonstration of how these networks in state capture are maintained, and how often these individuals remain unaccountable. A dismissal from a job is an inadequate consequence when laws have been broken.

Today, Mokoena still runs her own legal practice, Refiloe Mokoena

Attorneys in Johannesburg. Her unwitting clients who read her credentials on LinkedIn and elsewhere would understandably think this is a lawyer with significant experience who can be trusted to act with integrity. The evidence suggests the contrary.

Mokoena has repeatedly exhibited a disregard for her duties both as a board member and a legal practitioner. As a board member, it was her responsibility to ensure that the board of directors acted in a manner that was in the best interests of the entity, but her complicity enabled the 2015 board to run Denel into the ground. As an admitted attorney and acting judge, her role was to not only uphold the law to the highest degree herself, but to ensure that those who break the law are held to account and she failed on both counts. It is therefore crucial that Refiloe Mokoena should be investigated by law enforcement agencies and held to account for her actions in enabling corruption in her various positions. Further, the Legal Practice Council (LPC) should investigate and consider a disciplinary process against Mokoena for her conduct as a legal practitioner, as there is no indication in public records that a complaint has been laid against her to the LPC. Finally, the Judicial Services Commission must investigate the allegations of improper gifts received by Mokoena and urgently consider submitting these for investigation by its Tribunal.

At the time of writing, none of this has happened. If the most obvious cases of professional failure by the likes of Refiloe Mokoena go unpunished, it sends a message to the profession that such practice is acceptable. For the rule of law to be maintained, legal professionals like Mokoena need to be held to account as well as all enablers in suits drinking lattes in their corporate offices who profited from state capture crimes.

4
WELFARE PROFITEERS

Introduction

IN 2022, SOUTH AFRICA'S official unemployment rate hovered around 35 per cent. The expanded definition, which includes those who have given up looking for work, reached as high as 45 per cent. Research by the World Bank and International Labour Organization (ILO) shows that this is one of the highest unemployment rates in the world. There are a number of serious economic and social consequences that result from this, but an important one is that nearly one third of the population relies on social grants provided by the state. When taking into consideration the 10 million people who qualified for the special R350 Covid Social Relief of Distress (SRD) grant introduced in 2020, that figure rises to nearly half of all South Africans. For millions of South Africans, social grants are essential to ensuring their constitutional right to social security is realised.

Several private companies have viewed the country's social grant system as a means of making profit, regardless of the consequences for grant recipients. The South African Social Security Agency (SASSA) has failed to protect beneficiaries from these companies, making them vulnerable to unscrupulous practices. The story that defined these failures was the unlawful contract entered into between SASSA and Net1 subsidiary Cash Paymaster Services (CPS). SASSA unlawfully awarded a contract to CPS that allowed the company to wholly control the payment of social grants. This control allowed a host of Net1 subsidiaries to make a fortune from social grant recipients. The strategies they used, detailed in a chapter in this section, included deducting money from social grants for financial products that grant recipients had no knowledge of. As this book went to print, CPS had not paid back the profits it made from the contract (upwards of R500 million) despite an order by the Constitutional Court to do so. Meanwhile, new companies on the scene are vying to become SASSA's new private partners in the world of social grants.

For those South Africans who do have formal employment, many rely on a private pension fund to ensure that they and their families will have access to money to support them in their retirement or upon their death. While many economists in South Africa berate the public for a poor savings culture, it is arguably a far greater scandal that, in 2022, R47 billion in private pension benefits was owed to nearly 5 million people but remained unpaid. The causes for this scandal are numerous but it ultimately represents a fundamental failure by state regulators and private pension fund administrators over several decades.

While the issue of unpaid pension benefits represents a systemic problem in the industry, one story reveals how the industry has been structured to benefit its dominant corporations while leaving pensioners and pension fund members in the dark. This story is that of the multiple failures that led to the mass cancellation of pension funds when many still had assets and members to pay out. Open Secrets' investigation into this 'cancellations project' is told in this section. While continued pressure by civil society has led to some progress in this regard over the last two years, fund administrators responsible for the cancellations have never been held accountable, and the broader scandal of unpaid benefits remains.

The story of abuses in the social grant system and private pension fund industry has many differences. Both case studies, however, tell a stark story of private profiteers and weak state regulators that dominate a system to the great detriment of the people who should benefit from that system. The stakes could not be higher. Ensuring accountability, as well as more transparent and equitable pension and social grant systems, is paramount.

ONE
Liberty: Profit over pensioners

MORE THAN 16 MILLION South Africans contribute to a pension fund, most of which are run by financial behemoths like Liberty. They do so in the hope of a decent dignified life in retirement, and to ensure their dependants will be paid if they die. While the South African public is castigated for not saving enough for retirement, the reality is that nearly R50 billion in 'unpaid benefits' are owed to nearly five million people. It is also true that while private fund administrators insist they are doing all that they can to trace beneficiaries, those fund administrators and asset managers can profit from this money.

The 5 million people owed their benefits include pensioners inside and outside South Africa, workers who have moved or lost their jobs, as well as children and spouses who are eligible for benefits. Many do not know that they are owed, how much they are owed, or how to go about claiming their benefits. Many do know they are owed but face a labyrinthine and opaque system that makes accessing their pensions unnecessarily difficult. In a context of pervasive poverty and high inequality, it is unacceptable that private companies profit from the billions owed to vulnerable South Africans.

Liberty and the cancellations project

The 'unpaid benefits' – legally owed to pensioners or fund members but still unpaid – are found in places such as pension funds, provident funds and insurance policies. The story of unlawfully cancelled pension funds is just one part of the broader scandal of unpaid benefits. But it is an important part of understanding the incestuous relationship between the regulator, who should act in the public interest, and financial service providers.

Between 2007 and 2013, the Financial Services Board (FSB) – the precursor to today's Financial Sector Conduct Authority (FSCA) cancelled the registrations of 6757 pension and provident funds. An investigation undertaken by audit firm KPMG examined a sample of over 500 funds that were cancelled. It estimated that up to 98 per cent of the cancellations that took place may have occurred when the regulator had insufficient information to carry them out – making them unlawful.[1] Subsequent investigations have shown that this number may be too high. However, it is common cause that, very often, the information that was submitted to the regulator – by private pension fund administrators like Liberty – was incorrect.[2] This led to the cancellation of funds, which still had assets and members to pay out. Insurance giant Liberty administered 80 per cent of the cancelled funds and was a prime culprit in providing incorrect information that led to the cancellation of these funds.[3]

Many actors in the pensions industry are implicated in contributing to this problem and failing to fulfil their legal duties. Liberty argues that the more than R100 million identified so far that they owe to members of funds that they had cancelled incorrectly is small compared to the industry-wide issue. It is true, of course, that this is a small part of the R47-billion issue of unpaid benefits. But while R100 million may be small fry to a multi-billion-rand company, it is not a small matter to the individual pension fund members who gave up a portion of their income for years, and yet have still not been paid their benefits. Moreover, the story of how pension funds were cancelled is emblematic of systemic problems in the industry.

Cancelling the registration of a pension fund means that it can no longer carry out its usual activities and fulfil its duties to members.

Once cancelled, it cannot pay the fund members their pension benefits. For this reason, the law requires that the registrar have enough evidence in its possession to conclude that the fund no longer has any assets or members to pay before the fund is cancelled.

However, between 2007 and 2013 the regulator at the FSB cancelled thousands of funds without having adequate or accurate information. An important reason for this is that, in this period, the registrar Dube Tshidi appointed single individuals to be sole trustees and authorised representatives (which was unlawful) of over 4000 funds, instead of requiring proper boards to be formed. In most cases, employees of fund administrators like Liberty were chosen to fulfil this role. In many instances, those individuals then submitted the names of hundreds of funds in bulk to the registrar to be cancelled. The problem was that those individuals had often failed to thoroughly check the fund records to work out whether the fund still had members to pay.

Liberty has since admitted that it has discovered at least 130 funds that it had cancelled in this way. These funds owe over R100 million to around 3000 people. There could still be more undiscovered errors given the sheer speed at which the cancellations were carried out. For example, Chantal Hugo (a Liberty employee) was appointed as sole trustee for over 900 pension funds and submitted them all for cancellation in less than two years.

Liberty points to poor records and inconsistent asset registers for its errors, partly as a result of their purchase of other fund administration businesses in the early 2000s. Patchy records are certainly part of the problem. However, Michelle Mitchley, a whistleblower who worked at Liberty on this cancellation project, has reported that she and other staff raised the alarm about errors in the process, but these were ignored. Liberty employees found discrepancies and errors in financial records, but when they reported the errors, they often discovered that the funds had already been cancelled, sometimes when they still had assets. When Mitchley raised concerns about the errors, she was criticised for slowing down the process.

This insistence on speed over caution defined Liberty's approach to cancellations. Liberty contracted boutique consultancy, K2B, to assist them with preparing and submitting funds for cancellation. To incentivise speedy cancellation, Liberty's contract with K2B provided for special bonuses to be paid if they reached certain targets for cancelling funds within a certain time.[4] An investigation by KPMG, at Liberty's request, found that Liberty had 'insufficient oversight of their contractors (K2B)'.[5]

The prioritisation of Liberty's internal targets and K2B's profit failed the legislative requirements that govern how fund administrators behave and seek to protect pensioners. Most importantly, administrators are required to exercise the 'utmost care', keep proper records, and avoid any and all conflicts of interest. Submitting hundreds of pension funds for cancellation when they still had assets and members represents a failure to fulfil these legal duties. Moreover, while Liberty may have inherited poor records when they bought other businesses, it was their legal duty to do what was possible to fix these records.

Fees, fees, fees: Who profits?

Liberty and other fund administrators profit immensely for their role in administering pension funds. On top of basic administration fees, most charge an 'asset-based administration fee', which goes up as the value of the assets goes up. Such fees are deducted from investment earnings. Secondly, asset managers charge their own asset management fees. While the administrators and the asset managers are separate, it does often occur that funds administered by one company choose to invest 'in-house' – for example, many funds administered by Liberty chose to have their assets invested with StanLib (a Liberty subsidiary).

Arguably, the potential of fee income was part of Liberty's motivation to aggressively expand its share of the pension market at the turn of the century. It insisted on buying only 'full service' funds that gave them control of administration services, asset management and risk cover.[6] All of those services generate fee income as well. Incidentally, it was also these purchases that put Liberty in the position of administering funds with poor records, which they give as a reason for many of their mistakes in the cancellations process.

But herein lies the central conflict of interest in the pensions industry. Unpaid benefits, whether they sit in old forgotten investment portfolios, or new specialised 'unclaimed benefits funds', continue to provide an opportunity for fee income and profit for fund administrators and asset managers. When funds were cancelled in error during the cancellations project, beneficiaries could not be paid, but the fee income for the administrators and asset managers continued.

In this context, the public relies on the industry regulator to hold administrators to account and thoroughly investigate how these errors occurred and whether any of these actors benefited unduly. They have the power to compel such actors to hand over records and other information that private corporations will not provide to investigators like us or other civil society organisation like the Unpaid Benefits Campaign (UBC). However, this has not occurred. Responding to questions from Open Secrets and the South African History Archive (SAHA) in 2019, the Financial Sector Conduct Authority confirmed that 'there have been no internal investigations undertaken by the FSCA into the conduct of Liberty Corporate in relation to the Financial Services Board's pensions cancellation project'.[7]

Liberty is just one administrator implicated in errors during the cancellations project. Large questions also linger about the conduct of Alexander Forbes. Yet, the extent of Liberty's involvement in the cancellations, and their own admission of errors, coupled with the FSCA's failure to investigate their conduct, makes them an important case study in the failures in the industry and the complacency of regulators.

Progress made, but accountability deferred

There is no single simple explanation for the failure to ensure that pensioners and their dependants are paid what they are owed. The private fund administrators, the employers and the regulators have collectively failed to build transparent and accountable structures for the management of pension funds. Instead, a system of perverse incentives flourishes. The enormous profit generated both by and for financial services corporations seems to weigh the balance in their favour and against the human rights of pension fund members and the protection they are owed by the state regulator.

In the course of Open Secrets' investigation, we corresponded with the FSCA on its efforts to ensure funds were reinstated and beneficiaries paid. Following this correspondence, in early 2019, the FSCA for the first time directed all fund administrators to investigate their conduct in cancelling funds. Importantly, it also ordered them to approach a court to reinstate funds if and where errors were found.

Out of the 130 funds Liberty had identified as requiring reinstatement, it had applied to court in 2017 to have twenty-five reinstated. It was only after this direction by the FSCA and correspondence by Open Secrets that there was further action in this regard. Liberty made a further court application in 2021, and it was only in 2022 that Liberty finally applied to the court to reinstate the last of the 130 funds it had identified as being cancelled unlawfully.

These are important steps to rectifying what went wrong in the cancellations project, but a significant struggle remains. With unpaid benefits increasing every year, the need for accountability and sweeping reform to the industry is obvious and urgent. Justice for millions of pensioners and their dependants depends on it.

TWO
Captured regulator?: The FSCA and Dube Tshidi

THE PREVIOUS CHAPTER discussed how private pension fund administrators like Liberty acted with haste to cancel thousands of pension funds, even when many still had assets owed to beneficiaries. These fund administrators worked closely with the Financial Services Board (FSB) as the regulator. In fact, it was the FSB and its longstanding head Dube Tshidi who effected the cancellations. When the public needed effective regulation, the FSB and Dube Tshidi failed them.

FSCA's public interest mandate

The Financial Sector Conduct Authority (FSCA) succeeded the FSB and came into operation as South Africa's regulator of financial corporations in April 2018. Its success is vital for public interest, and it quickly found itself at the centre of much controversy and public pressure related to high-profile cases involving alleged major cases of economic crime. Its early investigations, signs of green shoots at the FSCA, included its investigation of Markus Jooste's alleged insider trading at Steinhoff and its public raid of Sekunjalo Investment Holdings, the controversial company linked to Iqbal Survé.

NUMBERS AT A GLANCE:

R47 b

44% OF SOUTH AFRICANS OVER 65 LIVE IN POVERTY

R10 BILLION IN DEDICATED UNCLAIMED BENEFITS FUNDS

illion+ IN UNPAID BENEFITS

16 million+ SOUTH AFRICANS BELONG TO A PENSION FUND

4 million+ PEOPLE OWED UNPAID BENEFITS

6757 DORMANT PENSION FUNDS CANCELLED IN THE CANCELLATIONS PROJECT

The FSCA was also immediately faced with a legal battle against Public Protector Busisiwe Mkhwebane, who made adverse findings regarding the conduct of Dube Tshidi in a separate matter regarding the appointment of curators to pension funds.[8] The Pretoria high court later sided with the FSCA, and set aside the Public Protector's report on that matter. These apparently partisan attacks on the regulator unfortunately made it easy to lose sight of a defining scandal of the FSCA's predecessor, the FSB, and its then chief executive, Dube Tshidi. Tshidi and the FSB oversaw the cancellation of thousands of pension funds, many in error, putting many vulnerable pensioners at risk. They have never been held to account for these failures.

The failure to thoroughly investigate and address these failures, or to hold the FSCA's leadership accountable, haunts an institution that plays a crucial role guarding the public interest. The transition from the FSB to the FSCA is part of Treasury's much-touted 'twin-peaks' approach to financial sector regulation, which includes the FSCA as a dedicated 'market conduct regulator' to hold corporations accountable for their conduct. The success of the FSCA is essential in ensuring accountability for corporations that abuse their power for profit. Yet, this will require a fundamental break from its predecessor's haphazard approach to regulation.

Tshidi cuts corners

Between 2007 and 2013, the Financial Services Board (FSB – now the FSCA) and its CEO and registrar of Pension Funds, Tshidi, oversaw the cancellation of the registrations of 6757 pension funds. It did so with the active assistance of large private fund administrators like Liberty and Alexander Forbes. The process was riddled with systemic errors and unlawful conduct, leading to (at least) hundreds of funds being cancelled in error. The errors meant that the funds were left with hundreds of millions in assets and members, but unable to pay these members out. When Rosemary Hunter, then deputy executive officer for pension funds at the FSB, blew the whistle on the glaring deficiencies in the 'cancellations project', Tshidi and the FSB board, led by Abel Sithole, tried to push her out in a disgraceful manner, which smacks of cover-up.[9] Subsequently Tshidi and Sithole opposed litigation by Hunter that attempted to compel a full investigation of all funds cancelled in the course of the project.

For the duration of the cancellations project, Tshidi appointed employees of private fund administrators like Liberty to be 'sole trustees' or 'authorised representatives' of dormant pension funds in order to ensure their cancellation. These appointments were often unlawful and beyond Tshidi's powers; he should have ensured the funds had fully functioning boards to make sure they were wound up properly. These single trustees were often solely responsible for many hundreds of funds. As discussed in the previous chapter, one Liberty employee was the sole trustee of over 900 funds, which were all eventually cancelled. It appears that the fund administrators were happy enough to go along with the process despite its unlawfulness.

The law is unambiguous on the requirements for cancelling the registration of a pension fund. It required Tshidi to be satisfied that a fund had 'ceased to exist' before ordering its cancellation. This means that Tshidi needed the sole trustees he had appointed to provide him with enough information to show that the fund had no more assets or members before he proceeded with the cancellations. An investigation by KPMG in 2015 concluded that in the sample of 510 cancelled funds, Tshidi did not have sufficient information for the purposes of cancellation for a staggering 98 per cent.[10] It is thus not surprising that firms like Liberty have since admitted that they had more than one hundred funds holding over R100 million cancelled in error.[11]

As discussed in the previous chapter, it was only in 2022 that Liberty made an application to court to rectify these cancellations. The company has never had to account for any fee income and other profits they might have gained from controlling the assets while the funds were cancelled.

This was not a regulator who acted in the public interest. Rather, this was a case of the regulator prioritising the interests of the private fund administrators over pensioners and ordinary fund members. They chose a process that was quick and easy for the companies and turned a blind eye when those companies cut corners, regardless of the harm caused.

Tshidi rewarded

Following these series of errors, Dube Tshidi not only remained an executive of the FSCA but was rewarded handsomely from the public purse. In 2017/18, he had the highest base salary of any executive at a public body at R5.6 million. After further – somewhat inexplicable – bonuses of R1.7 million, he took home a handsome sum of R7.3 million.[12] This is the equivalent of R20,000 per day. For perspective, a South African earning the new national minimum wage would have to work for 174 years to earn what Dube Tshidi earned in one year.

Given the failure of the FSCA and Tshidi to act in the interest of indigent pensioners, it is hard to fathom how either Parliament or the National Treasury allowed such poor performance to be rewarded with such a salary.

The leadership of the FSB in large part became the 'Transitional Management Committee' of the FSCA on 1 April 2018. This included Dube Tshidi and Abel Sithole. At this time, Treasury indicated that a hiring process would ensure that a new Commissioner and Deputy Commissioner would be appointed within six months, before the end of 2018. In April 2019, Open Secrets wrote to then Minister of Finance, Tito Mboweni, to ask why the process was already six months delayed, and to express concern that those implicated in wrongdoing in the cancellations project – including Tshidi – remained in the transitional leadership team of the FSCA. The letter also urged the minister to ensure that the appointment of these positions was a completely public and transparent process.

Despite several follow-up letters, Open Secrets never received any substantive response from Tito Mboweni's office, despite promises to do so. In August 2020, with the process still not completed, Tshidi was appointed as the acting commissioner of the FSCA, the most powerful position at the regulator. He acted in that position until his retirement at the end of 2020. It was only in April 2021 that permanent new leadership was finally appointed to the FSCA, when Unathi Kamlana was appointed commissioner.

While the appointment of a permanent commissioner was welcome, particularly after protracted delays that point to a disturbing disregard for this vital financial regulatory position, the process was unfortunately not open to the public and did not allow meaningful public participation. This points to serious institutional issues between National Treasury and the FSCA, which will hopefully be remedied in future appointments.

The urgent need for a strong FSCA

The South African public needs a financial sector conduct regulator that will stand up to the powerful and hold them accountable for wrongdoing and abuse. The FSCA's pursuit of cases against individuals like Markus Jooste and Iqbal Survé should be encouraged despite those who push back because of a political agenda. An intrusive and energetic regulator will always be the target of this kind of partisan attack.

Yet, it is important that the FSCA shows equal rigour in investigating the conduct of the large financial sector corporations that dominate South Africa's financial sector. It is these corporations whose conduct affects millions of people. Nowhere is this more obvious than in the pensions industry, where millions rely on private companies to handle their money responsibly. Yet, the FSB's deference to private players in this industry was an important factor leading to systemic errors in the pension fund cancellations project. Senior leaders like Tshidi should have been held accountable for failing to adequately regulate the wealthy and powerful.

The mere introduction of the 'twin-peaks' model and promises of more intrusive regulation of financial corporations is not enough. It is also essential that the FSCA cracks down on the culture of impunity for financial sector actors. While the FSCA has been more energetic in its efforts to rectify the cancellations project in the last two years, it still faces a stern test in ensuring the industry-wide problem of unpaid benefits is resolved to the benefit of pension fund beneficiaries. The capture of regulators like the FSCA by corporate players is commonplace around the world, and we must guard against this. South Africa needs an independent, fearless and transparent FSCA that pursues accountability for powerful corporations without fear, favour or deference to those companies' interests.

THREE
Net1 and CPS: Welfare profiteers

BETWEEN 2012 AND 2018, South Africa's social grant payment system, designed by Net1 subsidiary Cash Paymaster Services (CPS), showed how social welfare can be used by private actors for profiteering through the sale of financial products.[13] Despite court orders that the contract was unlawful, and that CPS must pay back any profits made from it, this has not happened. Further, newly rebranded Net1 – now Lesaka – continues to profit from selling financial products to social grant recipients. Its privileged access to this market can be traced back to the original unlawful contract between SASSA and CPS.

More than 30 per cent of people in South Africa rely on a social grant to survive and in some instances to support their families. Since the introduction of the R350 per month Social Relief of Distress (SRD) grant in response to the social and economic crises brought on by the Covid-19 pandemic, this has increased to nearly 50 per cent. South Africa's social welfare system, though inadequate, is thus of paramount importance to supporting millions of people.

Unfortunately, the number of grant recipients has also made the social welfare system an attractive target for profiteers in the private sector. Together with mismanagement by SASSA, this has made millions of people vulnerable to predatory financial practices. The chair of the Digital Frontiers Institute, David Porteous, warned in 2006, that '[t]he regular cash flow of grant recipients may also make them an attractive target for lenders who may use irresponsible marketing techniques to lead to unsustainable indebtedness'.[14] This continues to be a real risk in South Africa.

SASSA's unlawful CPS contract

CPS has a long history with South Africa's social development administration, dating back to paying grants in rural provinces in the 1980s, when it was owned by First National Bank (FNB). It continued to do this after being purchased by Net1 in the 1990s.[15] As a result, when SASSA announced that it wanted to consolidate grant payments under one company, CPS emerged as the clear favourite because of its experience paying grants in relatively remote areas.

SASSA contracted CPS, in 2012, to distribute grants nationwide. At the time, this was the second largest government contract ever issued, after the infamously corrupt arms deal in 1999. The contract empowered CPS to embark on a massive enrolment drive, collecting the personal information of around 17 million beneficiaries and opening bank accounts for 10 million recipients.[16] This would prove essential to allowing other Net1 subsidiaries to profit from the sale of financial products to grant recipients.

Despite the size of the contract in terms of value and public importance, it was declared unlawful by the Constitutional Court in 2013 after it was challenged by ABSA subsidiary AllPay.[17] The process was deemed unlawful because SASSA changed the wording in the request for proposals at the very last minute, resulting in CPS being the only company that could win the contract.[18] Originally, the requirement for biometric verification was only 'preferred', but this was changed to being 'mandatory' at the last minute.

AllPay and CPS both had the capacity to verify recipient biometrics during enrolment, but SASSA now specified that they wanted a service provider to be able to do biometric 'proof of life' checks every month. CPS claimed to have the capacity to verify grantees via fingerprint or voice biometrics each month, though the latter never worked and was stopped. The Constitutional Court ruled that this last-minute change reduced the number of viable bids to one and precluded a proper comparison of costs.[19]

Despite these contractual irregularities, the Constitutional Court recognised that grant recipients had to be paid and that an order jeopardising this would not be just. As a result, it allowed CPS to continue acting in terms of the contract to ensure grant recipients were paid. Private companies like CPS securing contracts with state institutions that cannot afford for the terms of the agreement to not be effectively executed is critical in understanding how Net1 and CPS continued to unabashedly profiteer from an unlawful contract. It is a systemic oversight in both procurement and regulatory frameworks that must be scrutinised.

CPS and Net1 opportunistically exploited the absolute necessity of social grants being paid. Over the next years, the Net1 group of companies would make a mint from their access to and control of the grants payment system, at great cost to many beneficiaries.

Net1 subsidiaries flog financial products to grant recipients

From the very start of the contract, SASSA knew CPS's business model included making additional profits by selling financial products and services to grantees.[20] These products included loans (Moneyline), funeral insurance (Smartlife), airtime and electricity (uManje Mobile), and payments (EasyPay). All these companies were subsidiaries of Net1.

The reason this was so profitable was because Net1 and its subsidiaries had unrestricted access to South African grant recipients, both in person and via their electronic data. CPS was allowed to build a system for grant recipients, separate from the National Payment System (NPS), which is the South African banking standard. Governed by the Reserve Bank, the NPS is the clearinghouse for all payments and settlements between banks. Net1 created a parallel banking system, which could be linked to the NPS but was not directly part of the NPS, giving it significant control over the bank accounts of grant recipients beyond official oversight.[21]

Net1 could thus make grant payments, sell financial products and extract repayments for those products without bearing any risk.[22] Grant recipients could not default on their debts, because Net1 controlled the entire financial flow from the National Treasury into individual bank accounts and could debit those accounts early and automatically. A *Financial Mail* feature article written by Black Sash chronicled the stories of three grant recipients who experienced these unsolicited deductions without their consent.

Maolaotse Grace Bonokwane needed to fight for a refund upon discovering deductions from her bank account for airtime purchases affiliated with a number belonging to neither herself nor anyone in her family.[23] Pension grant recipient Sipho Bani had deductions off his account for a loan he never received due to inadequate information capturing, and many more grant recipients had deductions made on their grant payments for a 1Life funeral policy they never took out.[24]

Net1 made more money on these 'financial inclusion' products than from grant distribution between 2015 and 2017.[25] It is difficult to estimate the exact cost to grantees of Net1's control of the data. However, Black Sash conducted quarterly surveys with grant recipients at pay points.[26] Between October and November 2016, 25.5 per cent of recipients surveyed nationally said that money was deducted from their grants without consent. In some 'hot spots', like Khayelitsha, around 50 per cent of recipients said that they experienced deductions without consent.[27]

This process was so profitable that companies like Moneyline did not market their loans to low-income consumers in general but to social grant recipients specifically. Investigative journalist Craig McKune, then at *amaBhungane*, demonstrated how Net1's financial statements were very explicit about how it targeted grant recipients. In fact, Net1 had two microlending businesses: one that was accessible to anyone and another that was only for grantees (Moneyline). The former business was unprofitable because of the high default rate on loans, but the latter was very profitable because grant recipients were prevented from defaulting on loans.

As Net1 put it, '[W]e consider [social grant-based] lending [to be] less risky than traditional microfinance loans because the grants are distributed to these lenders by us.'[28] Social grantees could not default because Net1 had monopoly control over the entire grant payment process. CPS ensured that any debits owed to Net1 subsidiaries were paid early and automatically before grantees received their money.[29]

As a result, Net1 bore none of the risk of a typical microfinance business when lending to grant recipients. In addition, the South African government guaranteed grants. There was no risk at all that the debts would go unpaid. Yet even though the risk of non-payment was nearly zero, interest rates on social grant-based credit were significant. Net1's CEO Serge Belamant often said that his products were the cheapest available, partly because Moneyline's official interest rates were 0 per cent per month.[30] But the costs of credit were hidden in service fees that could be as high as 5.33 per cent per month (on a six-month loan of R1000). This was within the law and the limits set by the National Credit Regulator,[31] but it amounted to an effective interest rate of 32 per cent on such a loan.[32]

In this way the company was not only profiting from an unlawful contract but doing so through unscrupulous conduct that risked the sustained livelihood of grant recipients. CPS has always denied that there was anything wrong with this, arguing that it was simply applying an early debit order, like most banks do. However, that does not take into account that CPS was in charge of both the payment of the grant and the deduction. It was not at arm's length from participants in the transaction. It demands the question: at what point will the extensive profiteering off vulnerable communities be seen as unjust?

Net1 pivots to EasyPay and plays the long game

Throughout CPS's contract with SASSA, Net1 and CPS were looking ahead. They created another product exclusively geared towards grantees: the EasyPay account, which would ensure that CPS had continued access to grantees' bank accounts if and when the contract with SASSA ended. The EasyPay account ultimately gave Net1 more control over grantee banking beyond SASSA's purview.

Net1 aggressively marketed EasyPay to grant recipients. Black Sash paralegals found that some people were told that the EasyPay card was the 'new SASSA card'; others were told that credit was 'not allowed on the old SASSA card'; and still others that EasyPay is the cheapest, safest bank account 'for life'.[33] Over 2 million grantees opened

EasyPay accounts without filing the necessary declaration with SASSA to have their grant paid into a new bank account. Through the CPS contract, grantees could 'consent' to new product offerings with their fingerprints. Upon giving 'consent', they were moved out of the CPS banking environment, which had some oversight by SASSA, into a private arrangement with EasyPay.[34]

Net1 was right to plan for a period without the contract with SASSA. As Black Sash, investigative journalists and academics exposed the unlawful contract and dubious deductions, political sentiment turned against Net1. Then Minister of Social Development, Bathabile Dlamini, attempted to amend the Social Assistance Act to stop debit orders on the CPS/Grindrod bank account. Dlamini had been an early champion of CPS and Net1. The Constitutional Court declared her conduct 'reckless and grossly negligent', and Dlamini was convicted of perjury in March 2022 for lying to an inquiry about the social grants crisis.[35]

Yet the strategy of pivoting to EasyPay has worked. In May 2022, Net1 changed its name to Lesaka in an effort to avoid the negative image Net1 had after its conduct in relation to the SASSA contract. Lesaka means 'kraal' in Setswana and Sesotho, and Lesaka says that it has chosen this name because it is committed to communities and seeks to drive 'financial inclusion'. This was the same promise that CPS and Net1 made a decade ago, and the evidence from communities is that little has changed in the business model.

In 2022, the cost-of-living crisis brought about by the Covid-19 pandemic, rocketing fuel and food prices, and chronic unemployment, have left millions of South Africans desperate to access cash and looking for loans wherever they can find them. Reporting by *GroundUp* in June 2022 revealed that hundreds of thousands of social grants recipients with EasyPay cards queue for grants and then take out loans against these grants from MoneyLine on the same day. In Lesaka's reporting to its US shareholders (it is listed in the US as well as South Africa), it says that its strategy is to grow the number of EasyPay customers so that it can 'cross-sell' financial products such as insurance policies. Sound familiar?

As *GroundUp* concludes, the success of this business model is down to the 'preferential access to this vast market was handed to them "on a plate" when CPS was given the SASSA contract in 2012'.[36]

CPS yet to pay back the money

As mentioned, South African courts have never settled the issue of the automatic deductions discussed above. However, four years after the Constitutional Court declared the CPS contract unlawful, in 2017, the court made a new order directing CPS to pay back the profits it made in terms of the unlawful contract. SASSA claims that this is over R500 million. This was a significant victory that entrenched the principle that companies should not profit from unlawful contracts.

Yet despite the order, CPS has engaged in a drawn-out fight against repayment. When it first filed its audited financial records with the court in terms of the court order, the records were contested by numerous parties, including Treasury and the accountants hired by SASSA. A report by RAiN Chartered Accountants concluded that CPS had overstated numerous expenses, and that it may have understated its profits by as much as R843 million.[37] RAiN also expressed concerns that more information was needed to determine if CPS had engaged in unlawful profit shifting. Civil society organisation Freedom Under Law approached the Constitutional Court in 2021 alleging that CPS was under-declaring the profits made in terms of the contract by R800 million.[38]

As a result of these concerns, in April 2021, the court again ordered CPS to completely open its records to an independent auditor to determine the profits it must pay back.[39] CPS has been in liquidation since 2020, and its provisional liquidators asked the court to delay enforcing this order. Their application was again denied by the Constitutional Court in February 2022. It is now more than a decade since CPS was first unlawfully awarded the contract by SASSA, and five years since it was directed to repay its profits.

Net1 and CPS blaze a trail

The conduct of Net1 and its subsidiaries in relation to social grant beneficiaries is a stark warning about how private actors can profiteer from the social welfare system in South Africa. In 2021, Open Secrets reported on how new companies were moving into the social grants system and partnering with SASSA to build digital systems for social grant applications. GovChat, a small South African technology firm part-owned by listed tech company Capital Appreciation, is an important example.

GovChat has so far offered its digital services to SASSA for free. However, Capital Appreciation is on record saying that it is constantly looking at ways to monetise GovChat's work on social grants. In a radio interview in 2021, Capital Appreciation CEO Bradly Sacks stated that while GovChat does intend to make money and charge for its services, the SRD grant process was done out of true altruism.[40] But perhaps the offerings of free services are a way to get a foot in the door. At the moment, GovChat helps SASSA with grant applications, but Capital Appreciation is eyeing what CPS and Net1 used to control: the payments system. In response to the *Financial Mail*'s questions to them about the Open Secrets investigative report – *Digital Profiteers: Who profits next from social grants?*, Sacks said that while the investment was about 'giving back' to the country, he also admitted that there were commercial opportunities for Capital Appreciation.[41] In particular he added 'GovChat could evolve to a mechanism of grant distribution, and payments is very much in our DNA'.[42]

It may well be that SASSA is already considering this due to the state's inability to create a functioning grants payments system. In June 2022, a massive technical outage at Postbank meant that the majority of people owed the R350 SRD grant were unable to collect it. In this context, SASSA may well look to turn to another private service provider to manage the grant payment system.

While it may seem a necessary or even attractive step to take, the story of Net1 and CPS revealed that SASSA fundamentally failed to protect grant beneficiaries from private companies seeking ever greater profit margins. The still unsuccessful efforts to ensure repayment of these profits from CPS also show how difficult it is to achieve accountability. One of the key lessons from the story of CPS and Net1 is that SASSA quickly found that it had placed grant recipients into a financially exploited position with a private company that monopolised the grant system to serve its benefit. It is paramount that this is not repeated, and that grant recipients never have to contend with welfare profiteers again.

5

BAD BANKERS

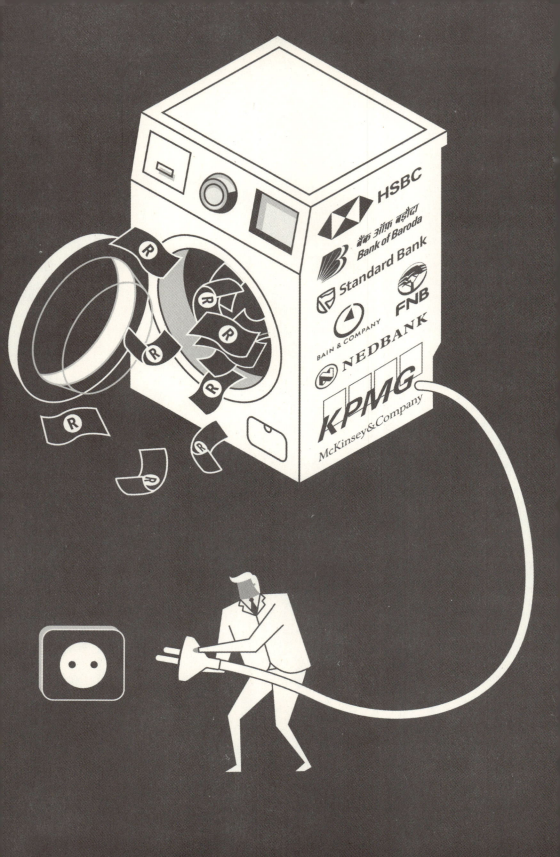

Introduction

CORRUPTION AND THE BANKING sector are inextricably linked. Corrupt politicians and dodgy corporations, just like those engaged in organised crime and drug trafficking, want to enjoy the proceeds of their crimes. Their illicitly obtained cash is useless unless it can be integrated into the global financial system in a way that obscures its illicit origin and makes it appear legitimate. This is where banks come in. Banks are legally required to create and enforce anti-money laundering systems to know their customers and identify suspicious activities, yet it is often profitable for them not to act in the face of suspicious activities. The ease with which the Gupta family siphoned billions of rand in the proceeds of state capture through local and international banks shows that this system is broken.

In February 2020, Open Secrets and Shadow World Investigations jointly submitted detailed information to the Zondo Commission in the form of an investigative report, *The Enablers: The Banks, Accountants and Lawyers that Cashed in on State Capture*. The report argued that to understand the Gupta racketeering enterprise, the Commission needed to scrutinise the conduct of banks, law firms, accounting firms and other professionals that facilitated state capture and failed to perform their lawful duties. It warned that '[a] failure to interrogate, fully and energetically, the private enablers of state capture would leave the work of the Commission incomplete; it would also undermine ongoing efforts not only to understand state capture, but to rebuild institutions and systems in ways that guard against similar abuse in the future.'[1]

Inexplicably, a full and energetic interrogation of these private actors, and particularly the banking sector, was largely missing from the Commission's work. The CEOs of South Africa's private banks were allowed to testify to the unlawful political pressure they faced when they belatedly closed Gupta-linked accounts in 2016. Yet, those CEOs were never compelled to answer questions from the Commission on why, for several years before the closures, the banks happily facilitated numerous obviously dubious transactions that allowed the Guptas to launder the proceeds of state capture crimes. International banking giant HSBC, a key player in the Guptas' laundering network, was never called to testify.

South Africa's experience mirrors that of many other African states. Aside from the state capture-linked stories that are told in this section, we also explore the role of Russian and Swiss banks in enabling Mozambique's largest ever corruption scandal that has left the country heavily indebted, and has had devastating costs for people in Mozambique.

There remains an important gap in the public discussion about the role of banks in state capture and economic crimes. This contributes to continued impunity for the banking sector. Banks should have to answer publicly for their role in secreting away illicit money through the banking system to offshore jurisdictions, beyond the reach of local authorities. They must also be held to account if they have failed to fulfil the requirements of the law. If this does not happen, we will have set the scene for the next generation of criminal networks to use the same system to fleece ordinary people.

ONE
Nedbank and the Bank of Baroda: Banking on state capture

Nedbank, like all banks that appeared before the Zondo Commission, preferred to present itself as a victim of state capture. Nedbank's chief executive, Mike Brown, appeared at the Zondo Commission along with other bank executives in 2018 to testify to political pressure placed on the banks by Cabinet to keep the Gupta accounts open. All South Africa's banks were at pains to tell the Commission that they retain the right to close the accounts of any client, and that they constantly undertake rigorous due diligence on their clients and their accounts.

What Brown did not discuss, and the Commission never publicly probed, was Nedbank's long-running relationship with the Bank of Baroda and how this continued long after it had closed its own Gupta-linked accounts.

Baroda: A state capture bank

The Indian state-owned Bank of Baroda was central to much of the money laundering for the Gupta criminal enterprise. The bank facilitated multiple suspicious transactions that even the bank's employees flagged as questionable.[2] These transactions often appeared to be cases of 'round-tripping' whereby large sums of money would be transferred between companies owned by the Guptas or their associated companies. Round-tripping is a common money laundering tool. The transfers themselves were often inter-company loans – usually with no clear commercial or legal purpose (and sometimes even in the absence of a loan agreement) – and thus apparently done to obscure the origin of money and the real purpose of the transaction. The Organised Crime and Corruption Reporting Project (OCCRP) identified a total of 231 transactions between companies owned or controlled by the Guptas where 'inter-company loan' was stated as the reason for the transfer. These transactions amounted to R4.5 billion.[3]

Many of these transactions were linked to the now infamous sale of Optimum Coal Mine to Gupta-linked firm Tegeta in 2016. The bank fundamentally failed to conduct the lawful due diligence required of it in this case. These violations included a consistent failure to file suspicious activity reports with the Financial Intelligence Centre (FIC). In addition, Bank of Baroda had failed to identify where parties were related, to verify the source of funds being received, and to identify each party to a transaction. They also failed to identify other risk factors like the fact that Salim Essa, a key Gupta ally, was a shareholder in nearly all the companies involved in the transactions.[4] In 2022, Optimum Coal Mine is the subject of a fierce legal battle, with the state seeking to have it forfeited on the basis that it was purchased with the proceeds of crime.

It was these serious violations of Financial Intelligence Centre Act (FICA) and the know-your-client rules that led the FIC to impose an R11 million fine on Bank of Baroda before the bank closed its South African operation entirely.[5] The small fine is indicative of a systemic problem in the regulation of banks, namely, low fines that are disproportionate to the legal transgressions and public cost in question.

The Bank of Baroda was also vital to the creation of elaborate loan-back systems that were used to launder funds linked to the Estina Vrede Dairy Project. Along with First National Bank (FNB) and Standard Bank, Bank of Baroda provided a range of other banking facilities to Estina as the small company diverted provincial government funds meant for a rural dairy farm into the accounts of Gupta front companies based in Dubai. This is discussed in a later chapter.

Crucially, evidence gathered in a joint investigation by journalists at OCCRP and *The Hindu* suggest that junior officials at the Bank of Baroda did flag many of the suspicious transactions linked to this and other transactions. Documents cited in their investigation showed that suspicious activity reports required by FICA were generated daily. Yet senior executives at the bank reportedly stepped in to quash them, ensuring that the suspicious transactions were at least in part hidden from the regulators.[6] This suggests a premeditated intention to assist in covering up suspicious transactions, rather than a mere compliance failure.

Open Secrets and Shadow World Investigations (SWI) also presented evidence to the Zondo Commission in 2020 that showed employees of Bank of Baroda's Johannesburg branch received benefits directly from the Gupta enterprise. These included in particular arrangements for a Cape Town holiday, and assistance with obtaining visas and other familial matters. Bank of Baroda's conduct in relation to Gupta companies should be viewed with these private benefits in mind.

Nedbank facilitates the facilitators

The information above has led many to paint Bank of Baroda as the central 'enabler' in the Gupta enterprise. This overlooks one important fact – because the Bank of Baroda was a foreign bank, it required a South African sponsor bank in order to operate. Enter Nedbank. One of the 'Big Four' South African banks, Nedbank controls over R1 trillion in assets.[7] It is a corporate giant and its executives have been publicly vocal about the continuing costs of state capture, particularly the harm done to SOEs. They have been less frank about their role in the system they call state capture.

As a foreign bank, Bank of Baroda could not clear transactions on its own; rather Nedbank cleared those transactions and relied on 'clearing accounts' to do so. This is typical of correspondent banking.[8] As Baroda's correspondent bank, Nedbank allowed Baroda to use its infrastructure for all financial transactions. Investigators at the OCCRP alleged that the nature of the relationship between Nedbank and Baroda enabled both banks to avoid responsibility for identifying and reporting suspicious transactions related to all of these accounts.[9]

FICA requires banks to know their customers and verify their identity, as well as to do upfront and ongoing due diligence on these clients and their transactions. Crucially, banks must use this information to identify and report suspicious transactions to the FIC. This system is crucial to stop the banking system being used for money laundering and to facilitate other crimes. According to the OCCRP, the Baroda–Nedbank system worked in such a way that neither bank had access to all the information they may have needed to exercise the due diligence demanded by FICA. Nedbank did not have sufficient information to conduct due diligence on transactions that occurred between Bank of Baroda accounts, as they did not have full access to the details of these transactions. At the same time, Baroda did not have access to information about the origin of money transfers to Baroda accounts that came from external banks.[10]

If these gaps in information are an inevitable result of a correspondent banking relationship of this nature, then there is clearly a significant deficiency in the Anti-Money Laundering legal framework. Nedbank should have been compelled to answer to whether they saw nothing wrong with such a system, and whether their compliance department ever reported any concerns about it, given their due diligence obligations in terms of the law.

Nonetheless, the gaps in knowledge seemed to have enabled dubious transactions. Tegeta's purchase of Optimum is a good example. The transaction involved Eskom making a late-night and highly irregular decision to prepay Tegeta for coal to give them the capital they needed to complete the purchase of Optimum. Nearly R600 million was paid for this purpose into a Tegeta account with FNB. From there, a total of R800 million was transferred to a Tegeta account with Bank of Baroda the next day.[11] Baroda could thus claim that they did not have full access to information about the accounts held at FNB, while Nedbank could claim that they had insufficient knowledge about how the money was transferred between different Baroda accounts once there, or how the money was used for collateral or inter-company loans for the purpose of laundering money.

Nedbank's conduct with regard to their relationship with Baroda should be scrutinised for another reason too. Along with the other big

South African banks, Nedbank closed its own Gupta-linked accounts in 2016, citing corruption and money-laundering concerns. The Zondo Commission has confirmed that, as a result, the bank came under unlawful pressure from senior ANC officials, including Mosebenzi Zwane and other Cabinet ministers, in an attempt to protect the Guptas.[12]

In the circumstances, it is curious, even inexplicable, that Nedbank decided to continue acting as Baroda's correspondent bank. Nedbank only terminated this relationship in 2018,[13] long after widespread reporting had indicated that Baroda's South African business was dominated by Gupta companies.[14] In fact, the bank was still engaged in this relationship in 2017 when CEO Mike Brown was bemoaning the state of SOEs and failures of governance, and publicly offering to help new President Cyril Ramaphosa.[15]

When asked about this after Open Secrets first wrote about the relationship in 2018, Nedbank simply said that it had 'fulfilled its regulatory and reporting obligations in assessing the risks of being the Bank of Baroda's clearing bank and ... that the Bank of Baroda, as a regulated entity in the South African banking system, was responsible for its own clients.'[16]

As journalists and investigators, there was little else we could do to extract more information from a bank like Nedbank. That is why we recommended that the Zondo Commission use the powers available to it to obtain this information and summon the bank's executives to appear before it and answer these kinds of important questions. As stated, this never happened, and will be remembered as one of the most significant gaps in the work of the Commission.

Nedbank Transnet's interest-rate swaps

The story of Transnet's purchase of 1064 locomotives is one of the most notorious instances of extracting rent from large-scale capital expenditure from an SOE. As discussed in earlier chapters of this book, the contract cost was escalated by R16 billion and billions were paid to the Gupta networks as kickbacks – after being siphoned through front companies in Dubai and Hong Kong.

Another side to this story is the payoffs associated with the loans obtained by Transnet to pay for the deal. For the 1064 locomotive deal,

Gupta-linked Regiments Capital facilitated and arranged a R12 billion syndicated loan for Transnet from a consortium of banks. Nedbank was one of the banks party to the loan; it contributed R3 billion. Negotiations with the banks started in August 2014, and the contract was signed on 1 December 2015 with an agreement to pay floating (market-based) exchange rates.

According to testimony to the Zondo Commission, it was just two days later, on 3 December, when the head of Transnet's Treasury, Phetolo Ramosebudi (also the brother of a trader at Regiments Capital), recommended that the interest rate be swapped to a fixed rate. This was a deviation from usual Transnet procedure. It also made no sense that a decision was made to revise the terms of a loan, with the accompanying costs, only days after signing the original agreement on 1 December 2015.[17]

The very next day – 4 December 2015 – Regiments stepped in and executed an 'interest-rate swap' for R4.5 billion of the R12 billion loan. In March 2016, Regiments conducted a second interest-rate swap for the remaining R7.5 billion.[18] An interest-rate swap agreement occurs when a company with a market-based or 'floating' interest rate wants to make more predictable loan repayments. To do so, it agrees to pay a higher fixed interest rate by signing a contract with a third party, which would usually be a bank or other financial services company willing to take on the risk and swap its floating rate for a fixed interest rate.

On both occasions, the bank that agreed to the interest rate swap was Nedbank. For the first swap in December 2015, instead of paying the (then) floating rate of 9.1 per cent, Transnet was required to pay an interest rate of 11.15 per cent. The total rate paid went up to 11.83 per cent because Regiments' fees were included or 'folded in' to the deal. The rate for the second swap on 1 March 2016 was even higher at 12.27 per cent.[19] The deal generated significant profits for Nedbank and Regiments. In the first swap, Nedbank made R28.2 million as a cut of the fees, and in the second more than R46 million. Regiments earned R162 and R335 million from these deals respectively.[20] By February 2019, it was estimated that the swaps had cost Transnet over R780 million in additional interest payments to Nedbank – for these two swaps alone.[21]

Nedbank has defended their participation in the swaps as standard business practice, claiming that there was 'nothing untoward' about the deal. However, there are a range of factors that cast serious doubt on this denial. First, a whistleblower who spoke to OCCRP indicated that Nedbank was the only bank willing to undertake the swaps. This was because other banks found the sudden shift from Transnet's internal treasury department to an unknown external consultant inexplicable.[22] Not only was the sudden role of Regiments a surprise, but those familiar with these financial markets described the proposed rates and fees as 'excessive', 'a rip-off', 'laughable', 'unimaginable' and 'an end game to extract ludicrous fees'.[23]

Transnet's new executives testified to the Zondo Commission that the second swap in March 2015 was undertaken at rates significantly higher than the market rate because of the need to fold in Regiments' fees and the fact that the deal was done without a competitive bidding process.[24] Nedbank were not cross-examined on this evidence at the Commission.

The final fact that casts doubt on Nedbank's role in the deal is that Nedbank's compliance department wrote to Phetolo Ramosebudi in mid-March 2016 to request that Transnet confirm that they were satisfied with the value and pricing of the swap even though it was priced significantly higher than the market rate at the time.[25] This request seemed to be an effort to obtain consent for transactions that had taken place months before.

Still waiting for answers

It is imperative that Nedbank and other implicated banks are held to account for their role in state capture. The Zondo Commission was in a unique position to begin this process, but, despite being armed with detailed evidence, the Commission never summoned Nedbank's executives to appear before it and respond to questions regarding their relationship with the Bank of Baroda and their role in the Transnet interest-rate swaps.

This was a missed opportunity, but not the end of the story. The NPA's Investigating Directorate is dedicated to investigating and prosecuting state capture crimes. It and other state entities must use the evidence that was before the commission to determine whether the bank and any of its executives or employees should face criminal action.

TWO
HSBC: The world's oldest cartel

IF TRANSNET WAS A golden goose for the Gupta family and their associates, then global banking giant HSBC played the role of tending their illicit nest eggs. State capture required a global financial machinery, and HSBC was an important bank in this network. In earlier chapters, we told the story of how billions of rands in kickbacks, dressed up in the language of 'advisory service fees', were paid to firms owned and controlled by the Gupta family. Most of these payments went into HSBC bank accounts of these firms in the notorious secrecy jurisdictions of the UAE and Hong Kong, and then rapidly distributed into hundreds of other accounts, many belonging to other front companies. The Gupta network relied on HSBC, a global banking giant, to both hold the accounts and facilitate the payments. The bank did so in the face of overwhelming red flags and evidence that the transactions were suspicious.

This is not the first time that HSBC has been implicated in the facilitation of organised crime and grand corruption for the sake of profit. Arguably, its conduct in enabling state capture in South Africa is a continuation of a pattern of behaviour where HSBC has accepted fines as a cost of doing business. It is long overdue that the impunity HSBC has enjoyed comes to an end.

A cartel bank?

The success of the Netflix series *Narco*s, and several docuseries it has spawned, has led to a romaticisation of figures such as Pablo Escobar and El Chapo.[26] However, left out from the depictions of the extravagant and violent lives led by these figures are the bankers who help move dirty drug money into the legitimate economy, the enablers without whom the drug trade would not be profitable. It is also important to not lose sight of the tremendous violence meted out to the people of Colombia and Mexico by vicious drug cartels who, alongside their enablers like HSBC, profit from the 'nightmare trade' and its associated human rights abuses which include beheadings, kidnapping, torture, gender-based violence and the bribery of officials.[27]

Exemplifying HSBC's role in the drug trade is a United States government Deferred Prosecution Agreement that confirmed that between 2006 and 2010 the Sinaloa Cartel headquartered in Mexico and the Norte del Valle Cartel in Colombia used HSBC to launder proceeds from their drug trade. This is a highly lucrative trade and, according to an estimate by the US Justice Department in 2012, the Mexican and Colombian cartels were making between $18 billion and $39 billion each year from drug sales in the US alone.[28]

It was clear that HSBC had failed to uphold Anti-Money Laundering (AML)/Know Your Customer (KYC) banking standards, and thus facilitated the laundering of criminal proceeds. Yet there was also evidence that HSBC's Mexico offices willingly participated in criminality. HSBC Mexican branches are said to have 'widened tellers' windows' to allow bigger boxes of cash to be pushed across the counters'.[29] In the reporting on this matter, many would soon draw the link between this and the Opium Wars in which HSBC's founder, Thomas Sutherland, and its first board chairman, Thomas Dent, participated in and profited from the freight industry and the opium trade.[30] HSBC is a bank with a sordid history, referred to by some as the 'world's oldest drug cartel'.[31] All this should be born in mind when considering how HSBC facilitated the flow of funds looted by the Gupta enterprise from the South African public purse.

Banking state capture

The R54 billion procurement of 1064 locomotives by state-owned freight rail company Transnet remains one of the most brazen examples of state capture. In the first chapter on state capture profiteers, we argued that Chinese railway company CRRC must be held to account for its role in the single largest contract tainted by state capture. This is because China South Rail (CSR) entered into contracts with Gupta front companies to pay them 'consulting fees' that were in effect nothing more than kickbacks. In that chapter, we discussed how two such companies – Century General Trading (CGT) and JJ Trading (JJT) – were both registered on the same day in the UAE, a popular tax haven, by Gupta associate Ratan Jagati. The companies had no digital footprint but were listed as traders of scrap metal, rice and beans.[32]

HSBC provided banking facilities to both CGT and JJT. In fact, the bank did flag suspicious transactions that had flowed between CGT and JJT and other shell companies, but three years too late. By the time the alarm was raised, CSR had already paid JJT and CGT R1.6 billion of the intended R5.3 billion – and the #GuptaLeaks show substantial evidence of this flowing into the Guptas' offshore accounts.[33]

In 2014, however, CGT and JJT's contract with CSR was succeeded by a similar consulting contract with two different companies – Tequesta Group Limited and Regiments Asia. Tequesta and Regiments Asia's CEO was Salim Essa, a man who has been widely referred to as a 'Gupta lieutenant'.[34] The companies were registered by Essa in Hong Kong, on the same day, 20 June 2014. Essa did this with the assistance of Stephen MS Lai, a chartered accountant based out of Hong Kong and London who specialises in selling tailored corporate entities in Hong Kong and other secrecy jurisdictions.

The company formation documents for Regiments Asia and Tequesta Group Limited make it clear that both companies were formed by Lai's business. As stated above, they show the companies were registered on the same day – 20 June 2014 – and had Salim Essa listed as a director. In addition, the company secretary for both companies is listed as PAMM Corporate Secretary Limited. The email address provided for PAMM Corporate Secretary Limited was a'bbylai@onlinecompanyregister.com. The email address server is the same as the address of Stephen MS Lai's website. Moreover, the physical address provided for PAMM is identical to the Hong Kong physical address listed on Lai's website.

In 2017, the Organised Crime and Corruption Reporting Project (OCCRP) obtained documents and banking data that showed that around R1.3 billion was paid out by China South Rail (CSR) in over forty transactions to HSBC accounts held by Tequesta and Regiments Asia.[35] CSR's payments to Tequesta and Regiments Asia accounted for 90 per cent of the credits to these accounts. Yet these funds did not remain in these two companies' bank accounts for long. More than $100 million was transferred from Regiments Asia to two dozen companies, mostly via HSBC, with other banks in Johannesburg, Dubai and the USA playing a part in the movement of money.[36]

Noting the very narrow period of activity in these bank accounts, and the tendency for large sums to be deposited and immediately moved on, the OCCRP concluded that these companies were shell corporations used at least in part for the purposes of money laundering.[37] These payments by Regiments Asia were all made between late 2014 and February 2017 – the bulk of these transfers occurring in February 2017.

All the evidence in the public domain suggests that HSBC should have swiftly identified that the Tequesta and Regiments Asia accounts required monitoring, investigation and, ultimately, suspension. This would have ensured they were complying with their Know Your Customer (KYC) and Anti-Money Laundering (AML) obligations.

The following factors are the most important evidence of this:

1. At the time they were registered, Tequesta and Regiments Asia had no discernible infrastructure or capacity to provide services. Yet, within months of their formation, they were receiving millions of dollars in payments, purportedly for 'advisory services'.
2. By mid-2015, Essa was already being written about in the South African media related to his dubious activities at Eskom, and by mid-2016 had been clearly linked to the Gupta network and the corruption at Transnet.
3. The payments into the accounts were clearly labelled as emanating from CSR or its sister companies, all owned by the Chinese state. These were the only sources of income for these accounts. A sceptical enquirer, as banks should be, would want to know what sort

HSBC: The world's oldest cartel

of legitimate business, newly formed without any infrastructure, receives such large payments from four related state entities, without receiving any income from any other parties.

4. The moneys deposited by CSR were dissipated almost immediately after they were paid, leaving no operating capital. Receiving large deposits that are immediately dispersed is a discernible red flag for money laundering.
5. A large number of the payments made from the Tequesta and Regiments Asia accounts were made into accounts owned by shelf companies in Hong Kong that, our investigation shows, had been formed in 2014 or 2015. This is exactly the same time that Tequesta and Regiments Asia were registered.
6. A large number of the onward payments were made to garment, textile and furniture manufacturers based in mainland China. Neither Tequesta nor Regiments Asia had the infrastructure or business intent to trade in wholesale merchandise. Certainly, they recorded no income from such a trade. These industries, however, are often used in money laundering schemes as they have significant turnover and an export focus.
7. Finally, it is noteworthy that HSBC had, previously, acted in relation to Gupta-linked accounts on the basis of what it deemed suspicious activity. According to a statement released by the HSBC in November 2017, it felt compelled to close a number of front companies linked to the Guptas in 2014.[38]

Given all of these factors, it seems clear that by the time HSBC Hong Kong was providing banking facilities to Tequesta and Regiments Asia, it was widely known that Salim Essa was closely linked to, and alleged to be a frontman for, the Gupta brothers. It is thus inexplicable that no attempt was made to shut these accounts or, at the very least, investigate and establish what connections the Tequesta and Regiments Asia accounts had with the Gupta family or other South African corruption scandals.

HSBC's response to these investigations has been to deny any knowledge of the scheme and play down their role. Responding to the OCCRP, their response read, 'HSBC simply has no desire to do any

Gupta-related business. To the best of our knowledge, HSBC previously exited, is in the process of exiting, or never had a banking relationship with Tequesta, Regiments ... [and persons such as] Mr. Salim Essa ... or other members of the Gupta family, and other Gupta-related entities we have become aware of through the media or otherwise.'[39]

Velvet accountability

In total HSBC has paid over $6 billion in fines since the year 2000.[40] When it entered into a Deferred Prosecution Agreement with the US Department of Justice in 2012, it paid $1.9 billion and agreed to be monitored by US regulators.[41] Yet, unabated, HSBC has continued to pay fines for AML failures and other failures to comply with their legal duties, as seen by the over forty fines listed on Violation Tracker, a wide-ranging database on corporate misconduct.[42]

While the $1.9 billion fine was the largest paid by a bank at the time and although it sounds significant, it amounted to less than a month of HSBC's profits. It represented what many have come to see as 'velvet accountability' for the banking sector. Even when there is significant evidence of egregious law breaking, authorities decline criminal charges, do not prosecute any executives or employees in their personal capacity, and rely on settlement agreements and penalties that have little impact on super wealthy banks.[43] Velvet accountability leads to impunity and, as seen with HSBC's conduct in the state capture story, unaccountable actors are doomed to repeat the same patterns.

In 2021, a redacted internal HSBC report was published by the Zondo Commission on its website. The report showed that while HSBC was trying to figure out its exposure to the Gupta family, it stumbled upon a much larger money laundering network using HSBC accounts. While tracing funds linked to Gupta-related companies in Hong Kong, the bank's own investigators uncovered what they suspected was a professional money-laundering network 'involving 92 HSBC Hong Kong accounts that received $4.2 billion worth of payments between 2014 and 2017'.[44] It appeared at the time that, despite discovering this, the bank did not pass on the information to monitors appointed in terms of the Deferred Prosecution Agreement with US authorities. In December 2021, United Kingdom authorities levied a further $84 million fine for glaring weaknesses in HSBC's AML systems.

The inescapable conclusion is that banks like HSBC have priced fines into their business model. HSBC has enjoyed the 'too big to fail, too big to jail' privilege enjoyed by global banking giants for decades. While its conduct in enabling state capture is simply the latest in a litany of scandals it has faced, South African authorities can and must challenge the bank on its conduct in this regard, and set a precedent that can contribute to ending the impunity for the banks that enable crimes around the world.

THREE
Estina's banks: FNB and Standard Bank

THE INFAMOUS ESTINA Vrede Dairy Project was supposed to direct public funds to 'empower' indigent Free State farmers and develop local agriculture. Instead, almost all the money was looted to benefit the Gupta enterprise. It remains one of the most iniquitous thefts of the state capture era. In addition to the politicians and Gupta family responsible for this heist, prominent South African banks, Standard Bank and FNB, played an important role in facilitating suspicious payments that were integral to the Estina scandal.

A Gupta project from start to finish

In February 2013 Ace Magashule, then Free State premier and former ANC secretary general, used his State of the Province address to make a major announcement: The Free State government would be setting up a 'state-of-the-art' dairy farm in the town of Vrede.[45] Two months later, Gupta family and friends, along with South Africa's political, economic and media elite, gathered at Sun City to celebrate the wedding of Vega Gupta and Aakash Jahajgarhia. The lavish event prompted one of the first big Gupta-linked scandals when it emerged that guests had been allowed to land at Waterkloof airport, a military installation.

But the wedding involved an even bigger scandal: Funds from Magashule's vaunted dairy project, instead of benefiting local farmers,

The Unaccountables

were laundered into the pockets of Gupta companies to meet the costs of that Sun City wedding. Audit firm KPMG was centrally involved in assisting the Gupta enterprise to launder stolen Estina funds via the books of the Gupta company Linkway, using the costs of the Sun City wedding to do so.[46] We tell this story in more detail in the next section of this book.

Subsequent investigations of the project by the Public Protector and National Treasury, together with analysis of the #GuptaLeaks, reveal that the Estina Vrede Dairy Project was, from start to finish, a Gupta-driven project, established to benefit the Gupta enterprise and loot Free State government funds. An analysis of banking records and other documentation by Shadow World Investigations has revealed that most of the R280.2 million paid to Estina by the Free State government was transferred into accounts owned or controlled by the Gupta enterprise.

As with most state capture schemes, the Gupta network needed to launder the money they extracted. To summarise how this worked: Once deposits from the Free State Department of Agriculture were received in Estina's accounts with Standard Bank and FNB, they were extensively 'washed' through local accounts. This was done through popular money-laundering tools including 'round-tripping' or 'loan-backs'. Once reintegrated in Estina's Standard Bank or FNB accounts, the money would be transferred to Gateway Limited in Dubai, and then further moved between offshore accounts. Finally, the funds were either sent to pay Gupta bills abroad, deposited into Gupta-controlled *hawala* accounts, or, more notably, transferred into the accounts of South African Gupta companies such as Linkway Trading and Oakbay.

This laundering served two purposes. The first was to make it incredibly difficult for authorities to follow the money, potentially confounding a criminal investigation. This worked: the Asset Forfeiture Unit's failed attempt to seize funds related to the Estina project in 2018 was partly a result of its failure to understand fully the sophisticated banking methods used. The second reason was even more cynical – to create the appearance that Estina was securing other sources of investment for the project. The circular laundering systems recycled Estina money multiple times through multiple accounts, allowing for the fabrication of a fraud. It appeared that money additional to the Free

State funds was being paid into the account when this was not the case.

The evidence that follows shows that the banks that held these accounts either did not do enough to identify the conspicuous red flags related to these transactions or, if they did, they and their regulators failed to act.

Standard Bank

Estina was a small private company with no agricultural experience, headed by Kamal Vasram, the sole director of the company. Vasram had no farming experience: The #GuptaLeaks show that he worked as an IT salesperson; then, for much of the life of the Estina project, he worked full-time as a salesperson at Toshiba. The only thing that appears to have counted in Vasram's favour was his connection to the Gupta enterprise.[47] Standard Bank provided banking facilities to both Estina and Vasram.

Between 11 June 2012 and 25 July 2014, Estina received R174 million from the Free State Department of Agriculture in six payments to its Standard Bank account. After this, the funds were subject to the extensive laundering process outlined previously. The evidence suggests that Standard Bank might have missed at least three red flags of possible money laundering that should have been identified.

The first was that, often, the deposits made into Standard Bank accounts by the Free State government were almost immediately transferred onto external beneficiaries. This is usually a major red flag, as legitimate operating businesses tend to keep funds in their accounts in order to transact day-to-day business. Bank records show that, of the six payments that were made into Estina's Standard Bank account by the Free State government, only two deposits were left untouched for more than a week. In one case, the immediate transfer of funds was combined with inexplicable 'smurfing' activity: on 26 April 2013, when Estina was paid R30 million by the Free State government, this full amount was immediately transferred to Estina's Bank of Baroda account in six transfers each equalling R5 million.

The second red flag was that Estina made a number of large and unexplained payments to a single offshore company registered in Dubai – Gateway Limited. Transacting with offshore entities in this way is often a major concern in money laundering.[48] Documents from the #GuptaLeaks, when read against Estina's bank statements, show that Estina transferred $8,348,000 into Gateway's Standard Chartered account. If Standard Bank was proactively monitoring the Estina account, it surely must have wondered why Estina, an agricultural firm reliant on government grants, was transferring large amounts of operating capital, in round amounts, to an offshore company that had no online or public profile.

The final red flag was that for a substantial period of time during which Estina operated its Standard Bank account, it was already widely reported in the media that there were concerns with the Vrede Dairy project. By June 2013, amaBhungane had dug deep into the project, detailing compelling evidence of suspicious activity.[49] Early the following year, it emerged that National Treasury had initiated an investigation into the project, and that a Free State official had testified that the project was linked to Mosebenzi Zwane. In September 2022, Zwane was arrested and charged with fraud and corruption linked to the Estina scandal. Estina's Standard Bank account was, during this entire time, receiving payments from the Free State Department of Agriculture and making a range of suspicious outbound payments. It is hard to see how, if Estina's accounts were being proactively monitored, Standard Bank could not have picked up these warning signs.

Red flags should also have been raised concerning the personal account of Vasram, which was used to facilitate various loan-backs that laundered Estina funds. Documents from court proceedings involving the Gupta enterprise have shown that Vasram received multiple payments from either Oakbay or Aerohaven, and immediately transferred these on to Estina's Standard Bank account. Through this method, Vasram's Standard Bank account received and immediately paid out R33.5 million between October 2012 and December 2013. Aerohaven and Oakbay were both publicly and undeniably part of the Guptas' stable of companies. Surely a proactive Standard Bank must have wondered why an IT salesperson, who was working full-time as a sales consultant, was handling large sums of money paid by Gupta companies, which were then immediately transferred to a dairy farm in the Free State.

We use the term 'proactive' because this is how Standard Bank described its due diligence process to the Zondo Commission. On 12 March 2019, Ian Sinton, a member of Standard Bank's legal department, appeared at the Zondo Commission.[50] In that testimony, Sinton acknowledged that anti-money laundering laws placed a legal duty on the bank not only to ensure they were not knowingly aiding corrupt activity, but also created a positive duty to investigate suspicions of wrongdoing.[51] Sinton assured the Commission that:

> We monitor all of our clients' activities on an ongoing basis and where we have reason to believe quite apart from what is reported on the Financial Intelligence Centre where conduct appears to us to be suspicious we will investigate and if we think that conduct is such as it will expose us to contravention of any of these acts we typically prefer to terminate the relationship, rather than face the risk of prosecution ourselves.[52]

The evidence above illustrates that Estina's bank accounts at Standard Bank should have been subject to rigorous scrutiny by the bank. At a bare minimum, this would have required filing suspicious transaction reports (STRs) with the Financial Intelligence Centre (FIC). Section 29 of the FIC Act requires South African banks to report any transaction to the FIC when it has or is about to receive the proceeds of a crime, which have no apparent lawful or legitimate purpose, and which have facilitated the transfer of unlawful proceeds.[53]

It is not known whether Standard Bank made any suspicious activity reports in relation to money-laundering activities linked to Estina and the Vrede Dairy Project. Shadow World Investigations asked the bank whether it conducted due diligence on these clients, if it enquired into the source and rationale of the deposits into Estina's accounts, and whether it reported any suspicious activity reports to the FIC related to these accounts. Standard Bank responded thus:

> Standard Bank has complied with its regulatory responsibilities and has engaged where applicable and appropriate with the relevant authorities and/or Commission of Inquiry within the ambit of the

NUMBERS AT A GLANCE:

R100

R16 billion
THE ESCALATION IN COST ON THE TRANSNET 1064 LOCOMOTIVE DEAL, TO FACILITATE KICKBACKS

R20 billion
IRREGULAR EXPENDITURE AT POWER UTILITY ESKOM BETWEEN 2012 AND 2018

R600 million
IRREGULAR PRE-PAYMENT BY ESKOM TO TEGETA TO ENABLE THE PURCHASE OF OPTIMUM COAL MINE

50%
THE PROPORTION OF SOUTH AFRICANS WHO LIVE IN POVERTY...
HAVING LESS THAN R1227 PER MONTH

US$2 TRILLION THE MONEY LAUNDERED IN THE GLOBAL FINANCIAL SYSTEM EVERY YEAR

98% THE PROPORTION OF LARGE CORPORATIONS ON THE UK AND US STOCK EXCHANGES AUDITED BY THE 'BIG FOUR' ACCOUNTING FIRMS

billion

THE DECLINE IN SOUTH AFRICAN TAX REVENUE FOLLOWING THE ATTACK ON SARS, FACILITATED BY BAIN & COMPANY

 R288 million / 82% OF THE PUBLIC FUNDS SPENT ON THE ESTINA DAIRY PROJECT WENT TO GUPTA-CONTROLLED COMPANIES IN DUBAI AND SOUTH AFRICA

R1 billion PER YEAR

THE VALUE OF THE CONTRACT BETWEEN ESKOM AND MCKINSEY. GUPTA-LINKED TRILLIAN WAS TO RECEIVE 30% OF THIS, DESPITE THERE BEING NO SIGNED CONTRACT IN PLACE.

law. The Code of Banking Practice prohibits Standard Bank from divulging any confidential information relating to its clients to third parties.[54]

When Sinton appeared before the Commission, he made no disclosure of any suspicious activity reports, also citing confidentiality. The final report of the Zondo Commission did not reference this either. Regardless, Sinton assured the public in his testimony that beyond basic reporting requirements, Standard Bank was proactive and as such monitored all clients 'on an ongoing basis' in order to ensure it was not assisting any unlawful activity.[55] Yet, this assurance of proactive monitoring and action sits at odds with the evidence regarding the red flags linked to Estina's accounts with Standard Bank.

First National Bank (FNB)

First National Bank (FNB) also held Estina accounts that received two significant deposits from the Free State Department of Agriculture. These payments included a deposit of R60 million on 8 May 2015, as well as a deposit of just over R46 million on 5 May 2016. Estina also utilised an FNB call account that was used as a stopping-off point for Estina funds. Bank statements for Estina's FNB business account indicate that this account remained active until at least April 2017, although the last major transaction (R215,000 paid to a little known South African company called Pwe Trading), which also constituted the last of the distribution of funds from the Department of Agriculture, took place on 31 October 2016.

Like all the 'Big Four' banks, FNB appeared before the Commission in September 2018 to testify about why they had closed Gupta-linked accounts in 2016. These discussions were limited to the bank's allegations that there had been an attempt by certain political factions to put pressure on them regarding the closure of these accounts. The bank also stressed the right of the bank to end relationships with clients on the basis of 'perceived illegality', which creates a negative association, regardless of whether actual criminal activity took place.[56]

Yet, just like Standard Bank, there were a number of obvious red flags that FNB should have identified in relation to its provision of banking services to Estina. The first was that by the time Estina started making regular use of its FNB facility, it was publicly confirmed in April 2015 in the Free State legislature that Estina's role in the Vrede Dairy Project had been cancelled in August of the year before.[57] Later that year, in August 2015, it was publicly confirmed that this cancellation was due to irregularities in the awarding of the Estina contract discovered by National Treasury. The cancellation of Estina's part of the deal in 2015, due to irregularities, should have raised an alarm at the bank about their possible complicity in any criminal activity by continuing to permit these transactions.

The second red flag related to how funds were dissipated from the FNB account. Estina's FNB bank records indicate that deposits by the Free State government were paid out to secondary accounts almost immediately after the initial deposits. The first payment received from the Free State Department of Agriculture was on 8 May 2015 (valued at R60 million). On 13 May 2015, five days later, Estina transferred R59.75 million into an FNB account, the ownership of which remains unclear. From there, the funds were transferred into an FNB Money Market account, which started paying money into and out of Estina's FNB account on 28 May 2015. FNB, as the supplier of these accounts, had sight of how these transactions flowed.

The final red flag related to the recipients of money paid out by FNB. In total, of the R106 million that was paid into Estina's FNB account by the Free State government in 2015 and 2016, over R85 million was paid out to Gateway Limited. The payments to Gateway Limited in 2016, drawn from the final tranche of money paid to Estina by the Free State government, were not even subject to any proper laundering. After the Free State government paid R46 million into Estina's FNB account on 5 May 2016, Estina transferred R40,737,452 directly to Gateway Limited. This amount was made up of four payments made between 9 and 18 May 2016. The dispersal of the 5 May 2016 payment was additionally remarkable in that it took place five months after ABSA had terminated its Gupta-linked accounts in December 2015.

Shadow World Investigations put these issues to FNB in September

2019, asking whether FNB had conducted due diligence on Estina, the source and rationale of the payments into Estina's accounts, and whether FNB had filed any suspicious activity reports with the FIC. FNB responded:

> Due to client confidentiality, FNB cannot comment on specific bank accounts. In instances where the bank is required to comply with external legal or judicial processes, the bank will adhere to such requests.[58]

Like Standard Bank, FNB's response was disappointing. It certainly does not answer any of the queries raised, or put to bed doubts about whether the bank met its legal obligations.

Time for banks to account

Those who stole hundreds of millions of rand from poor farmers in the Free State did not only need to capture a minister and corrupt a provincial government department. They needed South African and global banks to move their money. In this case, the conduct of Standard Bank and FNB, along with their answers to our questions, leaves many questions unanswered about whether the banks met their obligations under FICA. Unfortunately, despite being urged to do so, the Zondo Commission never summoned the CEOs of the banks to explain why they provided banking facilities to Estina despite obvious red flags.

However, the Commission's final report did concede that there was extensive money laundering of state capture proceeds, and that South Africa's money laundering monitoring system had failed. It recommended that the FIC urgently investigates whether South African banks complied with the FICA with regard to state capture laundering, what action the FIC took pursuant to any suspicious activity reports that were submitted by banks, and in turn whether law enforcement acted on anything passed to them by the FIC. Such an investigation, coupled with action by law enforcement authorities, is long overdue but an essential and urgent next step in assuring accountability for banks implicated in state capture.

FOUR
Credit Suisse and VTB Capital: Enablers of mega looting in Mozambique

THE PEOPLE OF MOZAMBIQUE have been battered in recent years by devastating cyclones, an armed insurgency and the global Covid-19 pandemic. The backdrop to this is a state battling the latest wave of state capture. This involves a coterie of corrupt politicians. However, two global banks were key enablers of the deal. The first is a bank nestled on the shores of placid Lake Zurich, Credit Suisse, and the other is the investment arm of a Russian bank previously dubbed 'Putin's piggy bank', VTB Capital.

In 2016, fourteen donors and the International Monetary Fund (IMF) stopped all lending to Mozambique. This followed the revelation of $2.2 billion in secret 'tuna bond' loans undertaken by the Mozambican state from two banks – Credit Suisse and VTB Capital, majority owned by the Russian state.[59] The result was an economic crisis in Mozambique, which saw the national currency plummet in value by 70 per cent and the GDP growth rate fall from 6.7 per cent to 3.8 per cent.[60]

The scandal has prompted a series of lawsuits in the UK, the United States, Mozambique and South Africa against the politicians and private sector actors involved in the secret loans. In 2019, three senior Credit Suisse bankers – Andrew Pearse, Detelina Subeva and Surjan Singh – pled guilty in the United States to conspiracy to violate US anti-bribery laws and to commit money laundering and securities fraud.[61] Could it be that only three bankers are responsible? Mozambican, British and US authorities believe that Credit Suisse should also be held to account for this fraud, and Russian Bank VTB Capital has also escaped accountability so far.

Mozambique's ability to respond to myriad social challenges is severely hampered by another crisis – its colossal debt. This debt is largely the product of a profiteering corrupt state, powerful global banks like Credit Suisse and VTB, as well as shipping companies, unscrupulous middlemen and predatory hedge funds. The victims are Mozambique's people, pushed further into austerity to pay off an odious debt, conceived between corrupt local elites and global banks.

Mozambique's security services go to sea

The background to the crisis is Mozambique's 'tuna bond' loans issued in 2013, purportedly to fund three new state-owned companies as part of a project to create a tuna fishing fleet and other maritime infrastructure. In reality much of this money would be spent on maritime security and defence equipment, and the companies were all projects of Mozambique's security services, the Serviço de Informação e Segurança do Estado (SISE). The three companies were Ematum (tuna fishing company), ProIndicus (maritime security) and Mozambique Asset Management (MAM) (maritime repair and maintenance). MAM's $535 million loan was arranged by Russian state bank VTB and ProIndicus borrowed $622 million from Credit Suisse for its maritime security projects.[62]

Mozambique does need to protect its maritime resources. It has a 2700-kilometre coastline and is rich in fish and shellfish which are vulnerable to illegal and unregulated fishing, a major security concern for most African countries.[63] Mozambique also has vast and lucrative reserves of offshore natural gas. With oil and gas prices soaring at the time, the Mozambican government gave the assurance that it was able to repay the debt and provided guaranteed bonds bought by Credit Suisse and VTB.[64]

Yet none of the projects embarked upon would capitalise on Mozambique's resource wealth; rather, the schemes were used to generate kickbacks for politicians and bankers at the expense of Mozambicans. Within the Mozambican government, the project was coordinated by former president Armando Guebuza (president from 2005–2015), then finance minister, Manuel Chang, and senior state security official, António Carlos do Rosário.[65] Contrary to all of the evidence, they maintain that the secret loans were undertaken for the protection of the country and benefit of the people. This despite the fact that the equipment delivered is of no value and mounting evidence that their network of cronies received an estimated $200 million in kickbacks.

In order to conceal the existence of the new companies and the extent of the country's debt,[66] the Mozambican government insisted that the loans be kept strictly secret. The loans for MAM and ProIndicus were not approved by Parliament, the Council of Ministers, the Central Bank and the Attorney General – despite this being a legal requirement.[67] The money for the loans did not even reach Mozambique. Rather, the banks paid the money directly into the accounts of Abu Dhabi-based shipbuilder, Privinvest, the sole contractor for all three contracts. This violated Mozambique's constitution and public finance laws.

There was further evidence of corruption. An independent audit by US business intelligence firm Kroll showed that Privinvest severely inflated the prices of the vessels secured through the deal.[68] Privinvest quoted $22 million for the vessels, but they were found to be worth no more than $2 million by Kroll. Moreover, once delivered it was clear that the vessels would need a major refit if they were to catch tuna efficiently. Industry experts also found the feasibility studies on the Ematum and ProIndicus projects to be worthless, while it is unclear whether one was ever conducted for MAM.[69]

In 2016, IMF president Christine Lagarde described these loans as 'clearly concealing corruption'.[70] The IMF, a primary lender to Mozambique, was only informed about the loan to Ematum, and not of the loans to ProIndicus and MAM. The revelation of the latter loans would lead the IMF to cut off Mozambique's access to credit in 2016. However, the IMF is not without blame. It had been privately warned about a second loan by a 'Frelimo figure'.[71] Further, financial surveillance is a key aspect of the work that the IMF does and the Mozambican government had a history of hiding loans in order to circumvent the requirements of the IMF.[72] It is hard to see why the IMF was caught by surprise by this scandal, if it was indeed fulfilling its due diligence requirements.

Credit Suisse: 'Clearly concealing corruption'?

Despite the obvious irregularities, Credit Suisse paid all the fees to Privinvest, even before delivery of any equipment. Chris Parry of the UK's Royal Navy explains that building an effective maritime security operation from scratch requires years, if not decades, of support from experienced operators. Of ProIndicus, Parry says: 'No maritime security professional would want to be involved in such a shabby scheme. I don't believe I have ever seen such a flimsy case for that scale of loan. Credit Suisse clearly did not do their homework.'[73]

The loans were irregular not just in the secretive nature in which they came about, but it has since come to light that Privinvest was using three Credit Suisse bankers to coordinate kickbacks for themselves and Mozambican politicians. According to the testimony of Credit Suisse bankers, Andrew Pearse and Surjan Singh were paid $45 million and $5.7 million respectively, to arrange lower fees on the Credit Suisse loan for the Mozambique tuna fishing project.[74] According to Pearse, Privinvest also helped him set up his own boutique finance firm with another banker at Credit Suisse, Detelina Subeva, with whom he was romantically involved.[75] In return for these favours, the bankers were to ensure that Credit Suisse would continue to finance the tuna fishing project, which would in turn benefit Privinvest.

Credit Suisse's conduct requires further probing as evidence suggests the bank was aware that Mozambique would be unable to repay this costly loan. According to the Kroll report, the loan agreement was revised four times, escalating costs from an initial $366 million to $616 million.[76] Credit Suisse included a number of pre-conditions on the ProIndicus loan, including approval by Mozambique's Administrative Tribunal (audit court) and informing the IMF about the guarantee. These were not fulfilled but there appear to be no records at the bank explaining why these conditions fell away; Kroll could only find a note saying the conditions had been 'overcome'. Furthermore, the ProIndicus guarantee states that the government would report to Credit Suisse on its finances, including budget, debt strategy and documents provided to the IMF. Kroll found no evidence that this occurred.

According to Joseph Hanlon, an expert in Mozambican political economy, 'Credit Suisse initially imposed conditions which would have made the loans impossible... The conditions were then "overcome". How this happened was never explained to Kroll – but Credit Suisse closed its eyes to the illegitimacy of the debt.'[77]

The precarious situation that Mozambique finds itself in has led the current administration to take Credit Suisse to the UK high court and demand that it foregoes repayment of the $622 million ProIndicus loan because, it argues, the bank failed in its compliance process before granting the loan.[78] The evidence suggests that Credit Suisse did not conduct due diligence when providing the loans. A key question that must be answered is why the bank did not ensure that the loans met parliamentary approval. This would have been part of the due diligence requirements of the bank before issuing the loan. That the bank did not question the lack of legal approval points at best to gross negligence and at worst to knowingly facilitating corruption. This serious failure of internal controls cannot be reduced to the misconduct of a few rogue employees.

Credit Suisse's role in this scandal is tantamount to loan pushing. According to Hanlon, loan pushing 'happens when the banks have too much capital and push developing countries to take loans they do not need and cannot repay. It was outrageous and clearly the liability of Credit Suisse'.[79] Loan pushing is also an element of predatory lending which is the practice of a creditor pushing a loan or bond on a borrower who cannot afford to pay back the loan. According to research by the Committee for the Abolition of Illegitimate Debt (CADTM) and the Kroll report, the fishing enterprise was expected to generate $200 million a year, however the loan repayment was $260 million a year. The most grave consequence of this scandal is the mortgaging of the country's assets in the event of default. Default in this case was guaranteed.

VTB Capital: A taste for risky business

VTB Capital is the London-based investment arm of the Russian VTB Group. Headquartered in Moscow, the VTB Group's majority shareholder is the Russian state and it provides financial services through a suite of more than twenty subsidiaries, which include financial companies and credit institutions. One subsidiary, VTB Bank, has been referred to as 'Putin's piggy bank',[80] and was allegedly the planned financier of Donald Trumps failed venture, the Moscow Trump Tower project.[81] An indication of the bank's political connections is that its chairman, Andrei Kostin, is a Soviet diplomat and close ally of Russian president Vladimir Putin. Following the Russian annexation of Crimea in 2014, VTB Bank and Kostin were placed on the US and EU sanctions list due to their close affiliation with the Russian state.[82] In September 2016, both VTB Bank and VTB Capital were fined $5 million by the US Commodity Futures Trading Commission for 'executing fictitious and non-competitive block trades in Russian Rouble/U.S. dollar futures contracts'.[83]

According to VTB Capital's chief executive, Alexei Yakovitsky, VTB's competitive edge lies in its ability to do risky business, especially with African governments. In an interview with Euromoney, Yakovitsky stated, 'We know that Africa is one of the riskiest regions in the world... Our competitive edge is that we are an emerging market bank and we are prepared to do business other banks won't do. That increases our pricing power and we are able to charge for the increased risk.'[84]

According to Kroll investigators, VTB Capital did in fact charge higher interest rates for the MAM loan than the interest rates for the Ematum and the ProIndicus loans.[85] Beyond that, the case for the loans was flimsy and there were several other suspicious or unsubstantiated payments involving Privinvest and Credit Suisse bankers. These should have raised red flags at VTB, but were ignored. As detailed above, the loans in question did not meet the legal requirements in Mozambique, nor were subject to any proper feasibility requirements. That VTB Capital and Credit Suisse proceeded with the loans despite this and the lack of compliance with Mozambican law reveals either woeful ineptitude or a willingness to cash in on dubious loans.

Kickbacks

Numerous bankers and middlemen made a mint from these secretive loans. The $45 million paid to Andrew Pearse, the senior Credit Suisse banker, is discussed earlier. Documents obtained by Kroll and the US Department of Justice show that Pearse was one of three beneficial owners of a company called Palomar. The other two were Iskandar Safa and his brother Akram Safa.[86] Palomar became a company of the Privinvest Group.

Palomar was an integral player in the 'tuna bond' loans. It helped organise loans and disburse payments between Privinvest, the banks and Mozambican officials. Documents obtained by Kroll show that Palomar arranged the loan between VTB Capital and MAM. According to the Kroll report, MAM borrowed approximately $535 million from VTB Capital between May and June 2014. This money was then sent on to Privinvest through a correspondent bank in New York. It appears that this money only reached Mozambique indirectly as bribe payments. Accounting statements from Privinvest's CFO, Najib Allam, indicate that Privinvest made bribe and kickback payments to Mozambican officials using the money obtained from VTB Capital. These kickbacks included $5 million to former Minister of Finance Manuel Chang and $13 million to António Carlos do Rosário.[87]

While testifying in his trial, in a New York court in 2019, Pearse stated that the VTB Capital executive in charge of the deal, Makram Abboud, also received $2 million in kickbacks from Privinvest.[88] In the same proceedings, Privinvest executive Jean Boustani's lawyers stated that paying bribes was the 'cost of doing business' in Mozambique. However, Privinvest denied making payments to VTB's Abboud.

VTB Capital has vehemently denied Pearse's allegations, stating that their internal investigation found that there was no impropriety by Abboud or any other VTB staff. VTB's press office responded that they were 'surprised to hear the claim in U.S. federal court by a convicted fraudster'.[89]

The alleged $2 million bribe to Abboud is not the only suspicious payment related to the VTB loan. According to Kroll's audit, $40.8 million was paid to VTB Capital from Palomar's bank account. The report found that '[t]he only evidence provided in support of this payment is an undated letter from MAM to Palomar in which Person A references an agreement between MAM and the Contractor to make this payment. Kroll was not provided with a copy of this agreement and it is not currently clear why the Contractor agreed to pay USD 40.8 million due from MAM to VTB Capital, or why the payment was made by Palomar.'[90]

An odious debt

Remarkably, in light of this evidence, it is VTB that brought a lawsuit *against* the Mozambican state in British courts to enforce repayment of the loan. Despite a ruling of Mozambique's Constitutional Court that the loan was unlawful, and VTB's own failings, VTB Capital initiated proceedings against MAM and the Mozambican government in 2020 for missing repayments on the loan.[91] As of 2019, MAM and Mozambique owed VTB Capital $817.5 million. The case could entrench a dangerous precedent whereby a poor country and its people are held ransom by a bank for an 'odious debt' incurred against the interests of its people and without their consent.

Mozambique's Constitutional Court set aside the loans after an application by Mozambican civil society. The coordinator of the Mozambique Budget Monitoring Forum, Adriano Nuvunga, said: 'The debts are not owed by the people of Mozambique, so we should not have to repay them. International action is needed to prevent loans being given in secret in future.'[92] Reacting to reports that Russian state bank VTB had filed the case against Mozambique and MAM in the UK high court, Sarah-Jayne Clifton, Director of Jubilee Debt Campaign, said: 'It is outrageous that UK authorities have so far taken no action against the London banks behind these secret, odious loans… The law should be changed here to make it clear that for a debt to be enforceable against a government, it must have been publicly disclosed when the loan was given.'[93]

The fallout and human cost

Mozambique is in no position to pay back the loans to Credit Suisse and VTB. It has already defaulted on part of the $2.2 billion in loans

Credit Suisse and VTB Capital: Enablers of mega looting in Mozambique

related to the tuna fishing project. A coalition of twenty civil society groups, the Mozambique Budget Monitoring Forum (FMO), has sought to declare the secret loans illegal. Despite the FMO winning a case in Mozambique's Constitutional Court, to have the Ematum loan declared illegal, Mozambique's government is still repaying the loan.

Moreover, since 2020 the country has been ravaged by two cyclones and an insurgency in the north of the country which has deepened poverty and suffering in Mozambique. More than 200,000 Mozambicans have been displaced by the conflict and 700,000 Mozambicans need humanitarian assistance. Seventy per cent of Mozambicans live in poverty, and it is ranked 181st out of 189 nations on the UN's Human Development Index.[94] Mozambicans desperately need aid and, unlike in previous years, the IMF is encouraging social spending in the face of Covid-19. However, Mozambique's debt makes this almost impossible as austerity measures have been put in place in the country to finance its burdensome loan payments. Instead of more pain for the people of Mozambique, VTB Capital, Credit Suisse and the other corporations complicit in the corrupt loans should have to account for their role in a scheme that has left destruction in its wake.

6
FAILING AUDITORS

Introduction

THE 'BIG FOUR' AUDIT FIRMS – Deloitte, EY, KPMG and PwC – all play a systemic role in economic crimes and corruption. The evidence from around the world suggests that these firms have prioritised profit over their professional duties and the law. In July 2020, Open Secrets published the *Corporations and Economic Crime Report (CECR) Volume 2: The Auditors*,[1] which draws on information from Open Secrets' investigations and publicly available information to illustrate the crisis faced by the auditing industry and how this impacts the public. The report also formed the basis of an Open Secrets submission to Parliament's Standing Committee on Finance regarding the Auditing Profession Amendment Bill. That submission supported strengthening the law and tools available to the Independent Regulatory Board for Auditors (IRBA) to hold errant auditors to account.

Auditors are supposed to provide an essential check on abuse in both the private and public sectors. When an auditor signs off on financial statements, they provide an independent assurance to the public that the financial reports presented by an entity's management fairly reflect the actual financial position of that entity. The perceived credibility of a Big Four audit firm adds to the weight that the public places in its findings. This is why an audit fulfils a crucial social utility and public good. It is also why the public cost of audit failure is so high. This is true whether the audit failure occurs in connection with a listed corporation or a state-owned enterprise. There are examples of both in this section.

Audit failure in South Africa reflects a global crisis. In 2019, the UK regulator, the Financial Reporting Council (FRC), reported that none of the Big Four firms had surpassed the 90 per cent target that classifies audits as good quality.[2] One of the reasons for declining audit quality is the long-term relationships that auditors build with their clients. In most economies, the Big Four are the only auditing firms large enough to audit big multi-national corporations and state-owned enterprises. This leads to extremely high market concentration. In South Africa, 96 per cent of the companies on the JSE are audited by one of the Big Four, and many of these relationships are long-standing. Though the mandatory rotation of auditors has been introduced to South African law to address this, the rotation will still take place within a very small pool.

An additional issue that generates serious conflicts of interest is that many large private firms employ the Big Four as consultants as well. The dual role of the Big Four as consultants and auditors results in an 'independence conundrum'. That is, the commercially lucrative consultancy services can compromise the credibility of the auditing side of the firm. A notable decline in the quality of audits performed by the Big Four suggests that the Big Four are failing to strike and maintain the balance between auditing and consulting.[3]

The public cost of audit failure is immense. It has resulted in job losses, the failure of several large corporations, and vast losses for pensioners and other investors. Audit failure at South African Airways (SAA), Steinhoff, Tongaat Hulett and African Bank are South African examples of a global phenomenon. Former EY client Lehman Brothers' collapse was seen as the catalyst in the sub-prime mortgage scandal that precipitated the 2008 global financial crisis.[4] The financial contagion led to extensive job losses, an economic downturn and enforced austerity across the globe. Yet accountability and sanctions for auditors who are either complicit or fail in their professional duties have lagged far behind.

When auditors fail to perform their professional duties, the ripple effects have serious deleterious effects. It is imperative that regulators and prosecutorial authorities recognise the social cost of audit failure and hold failing auditors publicly accountable. Moreover, any sanctions imposed should reflect the real cost of the audit failure, and act as a deterrent to the same conduct in the future.

ONE
Deloot

DELOITTE DOES NOT ONLY know that the public looks to it for assurance, it actively trades on this as its business model. Celebrating its 175th year of operations in 2020, Deloitte stated the following on its website: 'We're not trusted because we've existed for 175 years. We've existed for 175 years because we're trustworthy. That's why clients choose Deloitte.'[5]

But in the past eight years alone, globally and locally, Deloitte has been implicated in audit failure, corporate malfeasance and allegations linked to state capture. Despite this, there has been little accountability for the firm or its employees.

Fraudulent irregularities

'Accounting irregularities' is the euphemism used to whitewash corporate malfeasance and fraud. The news of the frauds perpetrated at both Steinhoff and Tongaat Hulett started with announcements that 'irregularities' had been discovered. It has since been established that both companies were the victims of systemic and long-running fraud by senior management.

At Steinhoff, CEO Markus Jooste and his friends engaged in transactions aimed at enriching themselves while defrauding the company and its shareholders.[6] To do so, they used a global web of companies, including notorious tax havens like the British Virgin

Islands. A forensic investigation by PwC revealed that for at least a decade 'a small group of Steinhoff Group former executives and other non-Steinhoff executives, led by a senior management executive, structured and implemented ... fictitious and/or irregular transactions' to misrepresent profit by over R100 billion.[7]

At Tongaat Hulett, senior executives, including CEO of fifteen years Peter Straude, are accused of making numerous incorrect and likely fraudulent misrepresentations in the financial statements. The alleged fraud ranged from misstating the value of assets; incorrectly listing expenses as assets; declaring income from the sale of land that had not yet been sold; and then, failing to declare it when some of those deals fell through.[8] In December 2019, Tongaat confirmed that the 'undesirable' practices led to the 2018 financial statements being wrong to the tune of nearly R12 billion and that the company's assets were overstated by R10 billion.[9]

In both cases there was a catastrophic failure of corporate governance, but the public harm was also significant. 948 pension funds in South Africa were invested in or exposed to Steinhoff. As a result of the fraud, the company lost 98 per cent of its value in just two years – and most of this happened in just twenty-four hours in September 2017. The Government Employees Pension Fund (GEPF), which provides for civil servants in their retirement, alone lost over R21 billion.[10] Those invested in Tongaat saw similar destruction of value.

It is a searing indictment of the capacity and political will of South Africa's investigative agencies and National Prosecuting Authority (NPA) that executives like Jooste have not yet been formally charged with crimes ranging from fraud to insider trading. Rather the NPA and the Hawks seem to be relying on Steinhoff and the private sector to finance its investigation – in 2021, accepting R30 million from Steinhoff to be paid to PwC who conducted the forensic investigation into this matter.[11]

But, just where were the auditors?

See no evil, report no evil

Aside from being sites of looting and fraud, Steinhoff and Tongaat Hulett have something else in common. Their auditor was Deloitte.

Steinhoff has been described by at least one director as 'in effect just a giant Ponzi scheme'.[12] So how did Deloitte's auditors not spot what was going on? Deloitte was the company's external auditor from the time the company listed in 1998. Every year for twenty years, Deloitte stated that Steinhoff's financial statements 'fairly present, in all material respects, the financial position of the company'.[13] Until 2017, they were apparently oblivious to the billion-rand hole in the company's finances. When they finally did refuse to sign off the statements in November 2017, it was too late.

In 2018, Deloitte accepted the need for an investigation by the Independent Regulatory Board for Auditors (IRBA) but said that they remained 'confident in their conduct' at Steinhoff.[14] Deloitte defends itself on the basis that they flagged concerns about the 2017 accounts. Yet, this was only after a criminal investigation related to possible fraud had commenced in Germany.

Their other defence, popular amongst the Big Four when implicated in audit failure, is that it is not the auditor's job to look for fraud, and that they rely on the honesty of the executive management. In their view, the public is expecting too much. This is the so-called 'expectations gap'. This argument is dangerous because it contains truth and yet is disingenuous in this context.

External auditors are not tasked with looking for fraud. However, the profession is based on a duty to show 'professional scepticism' – defined broadly as 'an attitude that includes a questioning mind, being alert to conditions which may indicate possible misstatement due to error or fraud, and a critical assessment of audit evidence'.[15] If an auditor's professional scepticism leads them to identify any misstatement, fraud or other crime, they are legally bound to report it. Moreover, if an auditor is uncritically signing off on what management says, it is hard to see what value they deliver at all.

It is not enough for Deloitte to say that finding fraud was not its job. The public is right to demand answers as to whether its auditors used a questioning mind, were alert to conditions indicating possible misstatement, and critically examined evidence they were provided with. It is difficult to believe that Deloitte did all of these things and yet failed to identify any of the widespread fraud and misstatement at both Steinhoff and Tongaat.

Deloitte was Steinhoff's auditor for two decades. It was Tongaat's auditor for more than fifteen years as well. This kind of entrenched relationship inherently undermines the independence that an auditor is supposed to exercise. Deloitte's long running work for these firms means they should have had an even greater insight into the company and how it operated. The only upside to this is that it should have made it easier to identify patterns of strange transactions in both cases. This did not happen.

Will there be accountability?

There are serious questions about the quality of Deloitte's work at Steinhoff and Tongaat. However, we cannot say with certainty precisely what the auditors knew, and for how long. Both Steinhoff and Tongaat have refused to release the full forensic reports (both compiled by PwC at incredible cost) that expose the extent of the rot. In 2022, Steinhoff was ordered by the Western Cape high court to release the full 7000-page report to the *Financial Mail* and amaBhungane who had applied to the court, following Steinhoff's refusal to comply with a Promotion of Access to Information Act (PAIA) request.[16] Steinhoff is seeking to appeal this judgment.

Given the public cost of these corporate crimes and the public interest in truth and accountability, it is important that the findings of these reports are made public and that the relevant authorities act on this information.

In the absence of this information, the public relies on the IRBA to investigate and hold the firms to account. But the reality has been disappointing. While Treasury and the IRBA are in the process of increasing the regulator's powers of investigation and sanction, the IRBA still faces incredibly well-resourced firms who throw money at the best legal teams to fight their cases.

Consultants at the trough

Fees from the Big Four's consulting work now make up around

two-thirds of their income.[17] While they should ensure that these commercially lucrative consultancy services do not compromise the credibility of the auditing side of the firms, the evidence suggests that they have repeatedly failed to strike this balance. Further, their consulting work has often been linked to dubious contracts with state entities.

In the chapter on McKinsey & Company in this book, we tell the story of how the consulting giant made R1 billion from an unlawful contract with Eskom. It also partnered with Gupta-linked Trillian, which was paid R700 million by Eskom despite no contract being in place and no work being done. McKinsey later admitted to overcharging Eskom and paid back the R1 billion. It also cut its ties with Trillian and told Eskom that the partnership would not continue.[18]

It was around this time that Deloitte started engaging Eskom on consulting work. In June and September 2016, Eskom procured the services of Deloitte's 'CFO [Chief Financial Officer] Transition Laboratory', which aims to train CFOs entering the position.[19] Deloitte was appointed by Eskom CFO Anoj Singh and senior executive Prish Govender.[20]

The way Deloitte secured these contracts was suspicious for several reasons. For one, Deloitte submitted proposals before the tender process was opened (such unsolicited bids to SOEs were common in the state capture period). The CFO tender – much like other suspicious tenders in which Anoj Singh participated when he was at Transnet – was a closed bidding process, used when there is an urgent need for services. It remains unclear why the CFO training was urgent.[21] Deloitte also used 'off-the-record briefings' with Eskom to submit proposals. Eskom management later alleged this made the process uncompetitive, untransparent and inequitable.[22]

Further digging by investigators at amaBhungane showed that Deloitte was already conducting extensive work for Eskom on unsolicited bids 'at risk' (another common state capture feature), meaning the company would not be paid unless a formal contract was concluded. This meant that forty-two Deloitte staffers, including senior partners and at least one director, were working full time for five months without a contract to guarantee payment.[23] When a tender process was finally opened, Deloitte was granted these contracts despite their proposals being up to five times more expensive than their competitors. This constituted a clear violation of the Preferential Procurement Policy Framework Act (PPPFA).[24]

Responding to questions by journalists from amaBhungane, Deloitte Consulting's managing director for Africa, Thiru Pillay, said:

> I do feel we were led down a path by Eskom, and we tried to cooperate and do the best that we could... The world is in a very different place today. When you look at what was happening in 2016; our environment is very, very different... Was our intent to go and defraud and exploit Eskom? Definitely not.[25]

The Public Finance Management Act (PFMA) has been in existence since 1999, so it is not clear what the relevance of the 2016 'environment' has on this matter.

In October 2019, Eskom made a court application to recover funds from Deloitte linked to these contracts. Eskom described the R207 million tenders as 'pure corruption'.[26] However, Eskom and Deloitte would soon reach an out-of-court settlement. Deloitte agreed to pay back R150 million, keeping over R57 million earned between April 2016 and September 2017.

In a joint statement, Deloitte and Eskom agreed their respective investigations showed no evidence of state capture or corruption. It stated that Eskom did benefit from Deloitte's work and that Deloitte should be paid for this. All that was conceded was that there were 'technical irregularities' within the procurement process, and that Deloitte Consulting accepted that it participated in this irregular procurement process.[27]

Just as in the case of Steinhoff and Tongaat, detailed findings of these 'investigations' have not been made public, nor is it clear if external investigators were consulted. This makes it difficult to understand the basis on which Eskom has abandoned its allegation of 'pure corruption'.[28]

Deloitte has since confirmed that both Thiru Pillay and Shamal Sivasanker resigned in the wake of the Eskom revelations. The firm has said that the two senior directors 'have acknowledged that the events related to the Eskom matter occurred on their watch. They have taken leadership accountability and have withdrawn from the Firm.'[29]

This is the extent of accountability in so many cases where powerful private firms are implicated. Directors and partners quietly exit their firms and, if the public is lucky, some of the illegitimate fees are paid back, but there is little meaningful accountability for those responsible. It's a set-up that ensures the cycle of impunity remains unbroken. Inadequately regulated, these professionals continue to benefit from dubious but lucrative financial and consulting services to the state.

A reckoning for Deloitte?

In its 2019 'Transparency Report', Deloitte says that it has embarked on a 'journey of self-reflection as a firm' as a result of its work at Steinhoff, Tongaat Hulett, African Bank and Eskom. However, despite acknowledging what it calls 'gaps' in its processes, and committing to 'self-correct', Deloitte does not acknowledge any wrongdoing; adding that 'none of our internal investigations have found evidence of any unethical behaviour, corruption or state capture on the part of the firm or the partners leading the above-mentioned client engagements'.[30]

In sum, nothing to see here, move on.

Given the cost to the public of the implosions of Steinhoff, Tongaat and African Bank, as well as state capture at Eskom, this reflection is inadequate. It is essential that the IRBA and the NPA act as required by the law and conduct rigorous investigations into Deloitte's conduct in these cases. Where there is wrongdoing found, the penalties should be significant enough to provide justice to the public and harsh enough to deter this pattern of wrongdoing.

Deloitte and its peers cannot be trusted to 'self-correct'. Only full accountability can change their 'irregular' conduct.

TWO
EY and those fishy $2.2 billion scams

ERNST & YOUNG (EY) IS NO stranger to corporate scandal or audit failure. Hot on the heels of their dubious role as auditors and consultants at the now defunct Lehman Brothers,[31] EY is again facing another credibility crisis. The firm is embroiled in one of Germany's biggest financial frauds since the end of the Second World War, namely Wirecard. On 25 June, fintech company Wirecard collapsed when it was unable to confirm the existence of €1.9 billion ($2.2 billion) in cash.[32] Yet for ten years up until this moment, EY consistently approved Wirecard's financial statements and accounts. This despite many reports from short-sellers and journalists questioning the company's third-party acquiring (TPA) businesses in Asia. These TPAs were at the heart of the missing (non-existent) €1.9 billion.

In a scathing report following an investigation by the German parliament, EY is said to have missed serious errors in Wirecard's accounts, raising questions about its due diligence and its ability to apply the auditing principle of professional scepticism. According to the report, EY failed to spot fraud risks, did not implement professional guidelines and, in an outrageous departure from basic auditing practice, EY relied on verbal assurances from executives rather than original documentation.[33] The fraudulent accounting practices at Wirecard and the machismo of its CEO, former KPMG auditor, Markus Braun, and its CFO, Jan Marsalek (alleged Russian intelligence affiliate and arms dealer), have led to the scam being referred to as Germany's Enron.

Several EY Germany partners are under investigation by prosecutors in Germany and by the audit oversight body Apas. EY is also facing what the *Financial Times* describes as an 'avalanche of lawsuits' and class actions by Wirecard investors who lost billions on their investments.[34]

Given the questions in Germany about EY's unquestioning audits, it is perhaps prudent to ask questions of the mysterious role of EY's auditing and consulting arms in Mozambique's own massive $2.2 billion fraud – the tuna bond scandal.

Tuna bonds

In the bankers section, we explained the role that Credit Suisse and VTB Capital played in the provision of dubios loans to stateowned companies created by Mozambique's government in 2013 to fund a tuna fishing fleet and maritime infrastructure. The loans for $2.2 billion were used to divert funds to the state's intelligence agency, the Serviço de Informação e Segurança do Estado (SISE), and to the inner circle of former president Armando Guebuza. The Mozambican people saw no benefits.

Credit Suisse financed the $622 million loan for ProIndicus, the supposed maritime security company. VTB Capital financed the $535 million for Mozambique Asset Management (MAM), which was for maritime repair and maintenance services. The $850 million Ematum loan was financed jointly by VTB Capital and Credit Suisse. Of these three loans, only the Ematum loan was disclosed to the Mozambican public and the government's other creditors, though it amounted to 6 per cent of Mozambique's GDP at the time. Aided by the banks, Ematum securitised the loans and sliced them up into bonds and sold them to international investors, earning the nickname 'tuna bonds'. The further two loans for MAM and ProIndicus were kept secret, making them illegal.[35]

All three loans were state guaranteed; if the companies defaulted, the state and by extension the Mozambican people were on the hook to repay them. When the companies did default in 2016, the full scale of the loans was revealed and Mozambique was plunged into an economic crisis. The economic catastrophe was not just due to the secretive nature of the loans, but because the limited maritime security and tuna fleets provided were of no value.

Though the Ematum loan was the only loan disclosed, Ematum proved to be full of financial irregularities and lies at the centre of questions about a missing $500 million. Investigators and prosecutors in Mozambique allege that this money was embezzled by shipping company Privinvest, former president Armando Guebuza and his inner circle, including his son Ndambi Guebuza, head of SISE, António Carlos do Rosário, and the Minister of Finance, Manuel Chang. Manuel Chang has been imprisoned in South Africa since 2018, where lawyers have been haggling over the decision to extradite him to the United States or Mozambique.[36]

In 2017 lawyers from the UK branch of the firm Kroll were hired by the Swedish embassy in Mozambique on the request of the Mozambique Public Prosecutor to undertake an independent forensic audit into the financial state of Ematum, ProIndicus and MAM. The investigation concluded that VTB Capital and Credit Suisse had failed to perform their due diligence requirements and should not have financed the loans because Mozambique's loans are required by law to be approved by Parliament, the Council of Ministers, the Central Bank or the Attorney General.[37] Moreover, feasibility studies of the projects found the Ematum and ProIndicus projects to be worthless, while it is unclear whether one was conducted for MAM at all.[38] In 2019, the Ematum loan was also declared illegal by the Constitutional Court of Mozambique.

The dubious nature of these loans to three state-owned companies does not only implicate the banks. It also demands questions of other professionals who were involved in these deals. The first question is, where were the auditors?

Auditors and consultants

EY was contracted by the Mozambican state to conduct a statutory audit of Ematum's financial statements for the years 2013 and 2014.[39] However, this was not their only role. In 2016, when it was clear the government was about to default on the loan repayments, EY and Mozambique's state-owned development bank Banco Nacional de Investimento (BNI) were paid $17.3 million to advise on the tuna bonds debt structuring.[40]

EY's dual role as both auditor of Ematum and as an advisor on the bond restructuring raises serious questions over its role in the scandal and how conflicts of interest in the audit profession undermine audit quality and may facilitate corruption. EY's role as Ematum's independent auditor meant it had the legal responsibility to take a balanced and fair view of the financial health of Ematum and, if warranted, raise the alarm over any potential corruption risks. Yet, despite Ematum's financial statements exhibiting several major corruption red flags and being littered with irregularities, EY had a strong incentive to keep quiet because it was at the same time jostling to offer lucrative consultancy services to the same client, in this case the Mozambican government.

This conflict of interest gets to the heart of the problem in audit firms' business model and provides another case study in why all jurisdictions should prohibit audit firms from offering consultancy services to the same client.

EY's 2013 and 2014 Ematum audits

In the absence of reliable financial information from Ematum's management, Kroll's forensic audit was based on information provided to it by EY.[41] Kroll's report uncovered highly irregular and suspicious business practices, undisclosed bank accounts and several other corruption red flags that auditors are required to inspect further during their audits.[42]

For example, in February and August 2014 Credit Suisse sent two interest payment request notices to Ematum for a total of $51.8 million.[43] During the course of its investigation, Kroll identified a previously undisclosed Ematum bank account at Mozambican bank Moza Banco that received the funds from a bank account connected to SISE (Mozambique's intelligence services), which were then used to pay Credit Suisse directly.[44]

Then in March 2015, while EY was undertaking its 2014 Ematum audit, Ematum's directors sent an audit representation letter to EY claiming that the shipbuilder Privinvest had in fact paid $51.7 million to Credit Suisse (as well as $1.2 million to 'another entity')[45] on Ematum's behalf to cover the interest payments. Two days later, EY finalised Ematum's 2014 statements and recorded a liability of $53 million.[46] Kroll's forensic audit, however, found that these figures did not match the banking records for the corresponding transactions and concludes that the representations on the letter sent to EY are 'incorrect'.[47] Neither Ematum nor Privinvest have been available to provide any evidence for an agreement in relation to this amount.

In his testimony before a New York Court, former Credit Suisse banker Andrew Pearse confirmed that this audit representation letter was designed to deceive EY auditors and convince them that the source of interest payments on loans came from Privinvest instead of Ematum. This was because the Mozambique Ministry of Finance was hiding the existence of these interest payments from the Mozambican parliament, despite this being unlawful.

Although there may have been an intention to deceive EY, serious questions remain as to whether EY adequately checked banking records during its audit and whether it acted with the appropriate levels of professional scepticism that may have identified the source of the illegal interest payments. After all, checking bank statements is auditing 101.

There were other inconsistencies picked up by Kroll's forensic audit. Ematum's income in 2013 was recorded as $3,049,084 but only $14,268 of this came from fishing revenues with the $3 million coming from an unexplained loan from Ematum's supplier, Logistics International, in September 2013.[48] A further $1.2 million from the same supplier was sent to Ematum in December 2014. Yet Kroll noted that the corresponding supply contracts made no mention of such amounts for operational expenses.[49] However, the audited statements signed off by EY refer to the payments as being '…provided by the supplier of the vessels to support the company's current expenses during the initial stage of its business'.[50]

Despite the almost non-existent revenue, Ematum's audited statements for 2013 and 2014 identify significant 'foreign exchange losses' as a major contributing factor to Ematum recording overall losses for those years. In 2013 foreign exchange losses of $13.5 million were reported which contributed to an overall accounting loss of $10.7 million.[51] The following year, Ematum recorded a foreign exchange loss of $13.9 million which contributed to an overall loss of $25.5 million.[52] Overall, in the years EY audited the accounts, Ematum recorded $27.4 in total foreign exchange losses.

Shoddy record-keeping by Ematum

It is important that EY clarifies to the Mozambican public the reason why it did not sign off on Ematum's later accounts (after it had signed off on the 2013 and 2014 statements), given the questions surrounding the records kept by Ematum. Kroll's report directly queries the validity of invoices passed to EY's audit partners, which it concludes do not correspond to the supply contracts and contain only limited information on the value of the vessels purchased.[53] The Ematum supply contract examined by Kroll (worth $635,582,800) ran to just one page, and other invoices supplied to Kroll amounted to just $538,248,000. With the support of an independent expert, Kroll estimates that the price discrepancy between the prices of the assets as stated in the invoices provided to Ematum by the contractor, and the prices estimated by Kroll's independent expert amount to $647,478,000.[54] Kroll concluded that without the proper documentation the differences remain unexplained.[55]

The lack of detail on the invoices and general standard of bookkeeping with relation to the transactions is, according to Kroll, a potential breach of Article 42 of Mozambican law[56] as well as Article 150 for failing to have care with regard to their due diligence obligations to keep accurate documentation 'in the interests of the company, taking into account the interests of the partners and its employees'.[57] In addition, the fact that EY was not able to finish its 2015 and 2016 audits due to a lack of documentation means that Ematum directors were in breach of their obligations (Article 415) to engage an independent auditor.[58]

EY's Ematum consultancy

Kroll's report confirms that the Mozambique Ministry of Finance paid a total of $31.4 million in fees to twelve parties in relation to the April 2016 Ematum debt restructuring.[59] The largest amount

($17.3 million) was paid to a consortium of Banco Nacional de Investimento Mozambique (BNI Mozambique) and EY as the 'local advisor to the government'.[60]

Kroll obtained an undated copy of the mandate letter naming the consortium as an advisor to the Ministry of Finance for the restructuring of the Ematum loan. The document sets out that the consortium's fee was performance based and depended on the amount of debt raised, the number of notes exchanged and the amount of equity raised.[61]

Andrew Pearse from Credit Suisse claims that Mr Matola was the representative of BNI Mozambique along with Mr Come from EY. According to his LinkedIn page, Tomás Matola is the president of BNI and was at the time of this contract. Local analysts claim in practice BNI demonstrates its worth as Mozambique's main development bank by 'hunting commissions' by providing assistance to government institutions searching for loans on the international financial markets.

According to the Mozambican government proceedings launched at the UK high court, EY prepared a five-year business plan for Ematum in September 2015 claiming that with appropriate support from the Mozambican government and with changes to its revenue and debt obligation, Ematum's business was 'viable'. It is unclear how EY could consider Ematum, which was just months from a default on its loans and had no tuna fleet or revenues, could have possibly been a viable business. How did EY's consultants come to this conclusion? Were they placing profit over their professional duties, securing the business of advising the government at the expense of their professional duties?

These are some of the many questions that remain about EY's role in Mozambique, though the firm has remained silent on their role in the tuna bonds scheme.

Holding the audit firms to account

While Mozambique and US prosecutors drag the politicians, bankers and shipping magnets throughout the legal systems of the US, UK and Mozambique, EY has largely avoided scrutiny, remains silent and is, to date, unaccountable for its role in this scandal.

This is one of the reasons that Spotlight on Corruption – a UK-based non-profit organisation working on anti-corruption – is pushing for accountability for EY's repeated misconduct. In late 2020, Spotlight wrote to the UK's Crown Commercial Service asking it to review whether EY should be banned from bidding on public contracts for three years. In its response, the UK government claims that despite a UK high court judge finding that EY had engaged in 'professional misconduct' in the UK, and despite a litany of egregious misconduct in other jurisdictions, it still does not meet the threshold to be debarred.[62]

As a result, the search for accountability for audit failure continues. Firms like EY have a strong monopoly on public contracts and face little consequence for poor behaviour and misconduct. Until governments take a tougher line with the audit firms, we will continue to see them signing off on the accounts of companies involved in corruption and other forms of misconduct.

THREE

KPMG: At the heart of state capture

THE COSTS OF CONTEMPORARY state capture in South Africa have been disastrous. Taking into account the money lost directly to corruption, low or non-existent economic growth, lost jobs, and an explosion of public debt and borrowing costs, estimates range from the conservative R500 billion to R1.5 trillion.[63] The austerity measures enforced to appease credit ratings agencies have hit vulnerable South Africans the hardest. This was the case even before the devastation wrought by the Covid-19 pandemic, which has also disproportionately harmed the poor.

But when it comes to state capture, not even the upper bound estimates can fully cover the consequences of the destruction of institutional independence and capacity throughout the state, including crucial institutions like the South African Revenue Service (SARS).

As Open Secrets and Shadow World Investigations submitted to the Zondo Commission, banks, law firms, consultancies and the Big Four audit firms were key enablers of the state capture project, and are also responsible for the associated harms of state capture.[64] This is nowhere more clear than in the case of KPMG.

After apologising for its role in enabling some of the most egregious state capture corruption, KPMG committed to appearing before the Zondo Commission in early 2019. This never happened, and KPMG's leadership have still not had to answer the difficult questions of clarifying its role in state capture.

A rogue investigation

KPMG's role in state capture first garnered public attention in relation to the infamous KPMG 'rogue unit' report it completed in 2015 at the behest of then SARS Commissioner Tom Moyane.

In 2007, a special investigative and enforcement unit was created within SARS by a joint agreement between SARS and what was then the National Intelligence Agency (now the State Security Agency).[65] SARS obtained three legal opinions at the time on the legality of the unit – all gave the green light to proceed. Two months after his appointment as SARS commissioner by Jacob Zuma in September 2014, Tom Moyane enlisted KPMG to conduct a forensic investigation into allegations of a covert unit at SARS that was allegedly spying on Zuma and Julius Malema, the leader of the EFF.[66]

Given the importance of the issue in the public interest and in safeguarding the integrity of SARS, South Africans expected that a leading forensic firm would undertake a thorough and careful investigation. This was not the case.

The KPMG report found that the unit was breaking the law and was thus 'rogue in nature'.[67] However, the report had striking similarities to earlier investigations by Advocate Muzi Sikhakhane and the law firm Mashiane Moodley and Monama (MMM), which had been commissioned by former acting head of SARS Ivan Pillay. A later examination revealed that KPMG had plagiarised sections of the MMM report, including even grammatical and spelling errors – it was literally a copy-and-paste exercise.[68]

Roy Waligora, head of KPMG forensics, led an internal investigation into the report. Waligora found that the lead auditor on the KPMG report had been 'unprofessional and lazy', leading to an inaccurate report.[69] Advocate Dumisa Ntsebeza, who chaired the SAICA inquiry into the saga, went further and concluded that the KPMG auditor's conduct had been 'an act of absolute dishonesty'.[70] KPMG later admitted that there had been no internal partner review of the investigation, calling this 'substandard' quality control.[71] Ntsebeza's report found that there was a prima facie case that KPMG staff had violated SAICA's professional code of ethics.

KPMG's report, alongside those of Sikhakhane and MMM, was used to justify the dismissal of around fifty senior officials at SARS, and investigations into Ivan Pillay, Pravin Gordhan and Johann van Loggerenberg. This, coupled with a coordinated restructuring of SARS by Moyane and management consultant Bain and Co., had an undoubtedly negative effect on SARS's capacity to generate revenue. In the first quarter of 2017 alone, the agency failed to meet its revenue target by R13 billion, and rebuilding the institution continues today.[72] KPMG would eventually retract the report and apologise to those affected. In 2020, all criminal charges against former SARS officials were withdrawn by the NPA.

This was not the last time KPMG would be linked to state capture. It also played a critical role in one of the most audacious and iniquitous state capture stories to date.[73]

The Gupta cash cow

Billed by then KPMG CEO Moses Kgosana as 'an event of the millennium', the 2013 wedding of Vega Gupta and Aakash Jahajgarhia at Sun City cost South African taxpayers R30 million.[74] The lavish wedding and the arrival of some guests through the Waterkloof Air Force Base catalysed a number of investigations by Treasury and the Public Protector, which first revealed a vast state capture network of Gupta enterprises.[75]

It emerged later that the wedding was connected to another scandal: the Vrede Dairy Project, a project where public money that was intended to benefit local dairy farmers in the Free State had instead been laundered into the pockets of Gupta companies and to meet the costs of the Sun City wedding.

The Vrede Dairy Project was a project between the Free State government and B-BBEE company, Estina. It was meant to establish a productive dairy farm near the town of Vrede that would create local jobs and opportunity.[76]

The #GuptaLeaks revealed that the project, from its conception, was set up to loot the Free State agriculture department. KPMG was centrally involved in assisting the Gupta enterprise to launder stolen Estina funds onto the books of Linkway Trading, a Gupta company.

THE AUDIT RAP SHEET:

96% of all companies listed on the JSE are audited by one of the Big Four, which have become some of the biggest companies in the world. Yet they are all implicated in scandals in South Africa and around the world.

- PwC acted as auditor and consultants for Sonangol, the Angolan government owned oil company which was used by Isabel dos Santos to secret away billions from the Angolan fiscus through a network of 400 shell companies.
- In 2014, PwC was found to have negotiated over 500 deals with tax authorities in Luxembourg which allowed companies to pay tax at a rate below 1%.
- In 2007, PwC was fined $225 million for failing to flag an overstated profit of $5.8 billion at US firm Tyco. This fraud ultimately cost investors an estimated $10 billion.
- PwC failed to identify major misstatements while the external auditors at SAA. PwC and its partner, Nkonki, earned R19 million for their work at SAA, but were only fined R200 000 for failing to disclose SAA's non-compliance with legislation.

- In 2013, a Deloitte document was leaked. It encouraged investors to use Mauritius to escape taxes, as part of a package to reduce the tax burden of its wealthy clients at the expense of African states.
- Deloitte failed to report suspicious activities and fraud at both Steinhoff and Tongaat Hulett. The Steinhoff fraud resulted in an overnight loss of R120 billion, to the detriment of 948 pension funds. The Government Employees Pension Fund (GEPF) alone lost over R21 billion. Tongaat's 'accounting irregularities' meant that the company's assets were overstated by R10 billion.
- Deloitte's audit of African Bank failed spectacularly in 2014. Deloitte missed red flags in the overstated future cash flow predictions for the Bank and ignored the red flags raised in their own internal reports.
- Deloitte earned R207 million in fees for an Eskom tender based on an irregular contract. In March 2020, Deloitte agreed to pay back R150 million, which allowed them to keep over R57 million earned between April 2016 and September 2017.

Sometimes, all of the Big Four are implicated in a single scandal. Each of the Big Four acted as external auditors for Danske Bank at some point between 2010-2014. This was the period in which the bank was used to launder 200 billion euros for organised criminals and authoritarian governments in Eastern Europe. They all gave unqualified audits.

- EY paid $123 million to US regulators in 2013 after admitting that, between 1999 and 2004, its senior partners had been involved in developing, marketing and defending tax avoidance schemes to dodge taxes worth $2 billion.
- EY acted as auditors and consultants for Lehman Brothers and did not raise red flags over questionable accounting practices at the bank nor act on a whistle-blower's report. The fraudulent practices led to Lehman's collapse in 2008, viewed as one of major catalysts of the Great Recession.
- In April 2020, a UK court ordered EY to pay $11 million to Amjad Rihan, a former EY partner. Rihan was forced to resign after exposing money-laundering and compliance failures by EY client, Kaloti, the largest gold refinery in the United Arab Emirates.

- KPMG was fined $456 million (nearly R10 billion) in 2005 for 'tax-shelter fraud'. Between 1996 and 2003, it concocted transactions for wealthy individuals and filed false and fraudulent tax returns that claimed phoney tax-breaks. The scheme cost the US fiscus $11 billion (over R200 billion).
- KPMG auditor, Sipho Malaba, failed to raise any red flags in VBS statements and provided a falsified regulatory audit opinion. VBS's failure had catastrophic consequences for its poorest depositors, stokvels, and municipalities.
- In 2015, KPMG produced the erroneous and fictitious 'rogue unit report' for SARS. This report was used to fire over 50 senior SARS officials and it was a contributory factor in diminishing SARS' capacity.
- KPMG provided tax-advisory services to and audited Linkway Trading, a Gupta shell company. Linkway was used to launder money from the Estina Dairy Farm. KPMG earned R40 million rand for its work.

KPMG provided both auditing and tax advisory services to Linkway Trading, the South African firm that invoiced Dubai-based Accurate Investments R30 million for organising the extravagant wedding.[77] Accurate Investments was one of four offshore companies in the Gupta's UAE-based 'laundromat'.

Linkway Trading was 53 per cent owned by Islandsite Investments, which was also owned by the Gupta family. Linkway drew up an invoice addressed to Accurate Investments on 31 July 2013 that provided a detailed breakdown of costs related to the wedding.[78]

Jacques Wessels, then an auditor partner at KPMG, managed Linkway's accounts. His work failed several standards for the auditing profession. Firstly, the Gupta wedding raised obvious red flags: for example, Linkway was registered as a construction company, yet had taken an odd foray into wedding planning. Secondly, the R30 million invoice accounted for 55 per cent of Linkway's 2013 revenue.[79] Thirdly, both firms had the same beneficial ownership and so should have been classified as related parties.

The 'oversights' for these transactions in financial statements indicate that the company was using them for the purpose of tax evasion – which KPMG allowed.[80] To add insult to injury, Linkway's 2014 annual financial report stated a R7 million loss on the wedding as a 'cost of sales', a misstatement aimed to evade taxes.

A competent auditor should have been able to pick these up, and one did. A junior auditor at KPMG voiced concerns to Wessels that the wedding expenses had nothing to do with Linkway's real business. However, these concerns were brushed aside. One possible reason the junior auditor was shut down was the close relationship between senior KPMG partners and the Gupta family. Despite what would appear as an overt conflict of interest, which the IRBA later criticised, senior KPMG partners attended the wedding – including Jacques Wessels, who led the Linkway account, and CEO Moses Kgosana, who attended with his wife and subsequently wrote a gushing thank-you email to Atul Gupta.[81]

The Independent Regulatory Board for Auditors (IRBA) investigated the case, and in March 2019 made a ruling striking Wessels off the auditor's register, ordering him to pay part of the IRBA's legal costs, and instructing that Wessel's name, KPMG's name and the findings were made fully publicly available.[82]

While arrests have been made of key officials and Gupta associates involved in the Estina Dairy Farm matter in late 2021, KPMG auditors are not amongst those who have been arrested.

The venal VBS heist: Where were the auditors?

VBS was set up as a building society in 1982 in what was then the Venda Bantustan and became a mutual bank in 1992. By the time of its implosion, it served tens of thousands of depositors in Limpopo, including many poor and working-class people. It was placed under curatorship as a result of a liquidity crisis in March 2018. The bank could not be saved because it had been looted into insolvency.

An independent report, commissioned by the South African Reserve Bank and authored by senior advocate Terry Motau, found that fifty-three individuals and other entities had benefited from VBS money to the tune of just under R2 billion.[83] In November 2019, the bank's liquidator announced that R800 million more than initially thought was stolen – making the total as much as R2.7 billion.[84] The deposits of everyday South Africans had been looted by bank executives to pay for luxury cars, multiple properties and various personal vanity projects.[85]

This was an unsophisticated heist. Not only was money looted straight out of the bank's cash reserves, but payments were made to obviously related parties without the necessary reporting. This required VBS to publish fraudulent misrepresentations in their 2017 annual statements and their monthly regulatory reports to the Registrar of Banks.[86] Yet, the annual financial statements were signed off as an accurate representation by KPMG.

In March 2018, the Minister of Finance placed VBS under curatorship. The appointed curator immediately found that the bank could not confirm the existence of nearly R1 billion in cash deposits. He also flagged deficiencies in the management of the financial systems, as well as fraudulent transactions between VBS and related parties. He could not understand how a senior KPMG auditor had signed off the financial statements without reporting a single transaction to the IRBA or raising any other red flags.[87] The annual financial statements had to be withdrawn as they were completely inaccurate.

It turned out that this was not a case of an auditor being hoodwinked by its client. KPMG's lead auditor on the VBS account, Sipho Malaba, is alleged to have covered up the crimes. Motau's report concludes that Malaba 'gave an unqualified audit opinion in circumstances where he knew the financial statements were misstated. He also gave a regulatory audit opinion which he knew to be false.'[88] In plain words, Malaba lied.

It is estimated that Malaba received up to R34 million in exchange for assisting in the cover-up at VBS.[89] This was done predominantly through loan facilities that were extended to Malaba's companies and to himself in his personal capacity. This included loans for three luxury vehicles through VBS's special financial scheme for employees and shareholders, for which Malaba did not qualify.[90] The loans turned into gifts as Malaba would invariably reverse the debit orders, and VBS would not follow up to pursue repayment.

As was the case for KPMG's failures at Linkway Trading, one junior auditor did in fact spot trouble at VBS. Zondi Nduli soon learned that silence was the order of the day, even if the irregularities could not be explained. A third-year audit clerk at KPMG, Nduli found a R700 million overstatement in the financial statements.[91] When Nduli asked VBS to provide documents to explain this, the bank's officials were, of course, unable to. Sipho Malaba, the senior auditor, was called in to clean up the situation.

Testifying under the promise of immunity, Nduli told Motau that, when he saw the audit signed off by Malaba, he realised that no further work had been done to clarify the glaring problem he had seen in the cash accounts.[92] Confused and worried that he would be implicated in wrongdoing, he admits to going back and deliberately altering his original audit note to say that 'specific procedures were performed by the Partner and CEO respectively'.[93] Nduli also testified that he spoke about his concerns with both his counselling partner and counselling manager at KPMG, but received 'little assistance from them'.[94]

As is apparent from this account, there was a team of KPMG auditors working on the VBS financial statements in 2017. There may have been a rogue auditor, but there was also a collective failure to exercise the professional scepticism and accountability that is required of auditors.

It is encouraging that the NPA has decided to pursue a criminal prosecution of Sipho Malaba. Yet this is still not enough; KPMG's failure to exercise independence and professional scrutiny is indicative of an industry riven with structural problems and deficiencies in governance that will continue to produce major conflicts of interest. Without effective sanction for the firms themselves, they will reoffend.

The rot lies deep

Since the full extent of KPMG's role in these crimes has emerged, the firm has spent a lot of time apologising to South Africans and the institutions they harmed. They also agreed to pay back R23 million in fees from SARS and pledged to donate the R40 million it earned in fees from Gupta-linked entities.[95] It is unclear how these meagre offers are supposed to provide restitution for the dairy farmers, or for the billions lost in tax revenue and the near-collapse of several state institutions. KPMG should face far larger fines for its conduct.

This is why it remains essential that KPMG as a firm, and its executives, former and current, are held accountable by law enforcement and the NPA, who should pursue cases against all those at KPMG who broke the law. While KPMG assures the public that is has self-corrected, only full accountability will change the calculus for how it conducts itself in the future.

FOUR
PwC and Nkonki asleep in the cockpit of SAA

FOR MORE THAN A DECADE, South African Airways (SAA) has been a drain on an already strained public purse, while systemic corruption and mismanagement has hollowed out the state-owned airline. Public ire has rightly been directed at Dudu Myeni and other directors who oversaw the long-term decline of SAA. Yet, what of the auditors who cashed in on contracts while turning a blind eye to malfeasance?

Counting the cost of the destruction of SAA

Corruption and mismanagement at SAA have cost SAA employees and the broader public dearly. The state has spent more than R50 billion on bailouts to SAA since 2008. Treasury told Parliament bluntly in 2021 that 'the value from this contribution has not been seen'.[96] Many of the recent bailouts have been made in the context of a reduction in spending on essential public services. Early in 2021, the government passed an austerity budget that demanded real-term cuts to spending on healthcare and social assistance.[97] It later announced that it could not afford to continue the R350 Covid-19 Social Relief of Distress grant, while admitting that this would inevitably lead to increased hunger for many South Africans. Despite this, there was still R10.5 billion to be found to bailout SAA.

SAA's employees have been deserted and deeply affected by the collapse of the airline. After the entity was placed under business rescue, it was announced that around two-thirds of all employees – 2700 people – would be retrenched.[98] Both the retrenched employees and those still working at SAA engaged in a long-running battle to be paid overdue salaries and retrenchment packages, with a settlement with SAA's pilots only being finalised after many months. Many employees lost their homes and savings due to the failure to pay them what was owed.[99]

While government fails to rescue the people and employees of SAA, SAA has been given many lifelines. In June 2021, just months after SAA emerged from 18 months under business rescue, the government controversially announced that it was finally selling a 51 per cent stake in SAA to private buyers. The Takatso Consortium, consisting of Harith General Partners and Global Airways, paid just R3 billion for the majority stake, enough for the airline to operate for one to three years while they seek to make it profitable.[100] Despite that apparent sale (the final deal was still not finalised when the book went to print), there remains uncertainty around the airline's long-term viability, with further investment needed. Crucially, the state also remains on the hook for all 'legacy issues', including the airline's debt and ongoing settlement negotiations with pilots and other staff, many of whom have gone unpaid for years.

The rot starts at the top

By far the most important variable in SAA's collapse was a systematic breakdown of internal and external controls on transparent and lawful procurement systems at the airline. This was condoned and overseen by executive management, and the central character in this regard was Duduzile Myeni. Myeni sat on SAA's board from 2009 to 2017 and was either an acting or permanent chair of the board between 2012 and 2017.

In 2020, in response to an application by civil society organisation OUTA and the South African Airways Pilots Association (SAAPA), the high court declared Myeni a delinquent director and ordered that she could never again hold a directorship. The court agreed that Myeni had engaged in dishonest conduct at SAA that amounted to a wilful and grossly negligent breach of her fiduciary duties as a director.[101]

Myeni unilaterally and deliberately undermined two crucial SAA contracts, one with Emirates and the other with Airbus, lying to the contracting partners and the Minister of Finance in the process and completely disregarding the provisions of South Africa's public procurement and governance law – the Public Finance Management Act (PFMA). The court held that Myeni was a 'director gone rogue' whose conduct had done 'immense harm to SAA and the country'.[102]

Under this leadership, it is little surprise that disregard for procurement law and internal controls became the norm. In 2021, the Special Investigating Unit (SIU) indicated that it was undertaking forensic investigations into a range of allegations of corruption at SAA. In its report to Parliament, it said that investigations into more than one hundred procurement contracts had revealed 'inflated pricing; fronting; conflicts of interest on the part of SAA staff; fictitious vendors; fictitious work orders; fictitious bank accounts; overpayments; non-delivery; non-performance and no value for money'.[103] In its May 2022 report to the Portfolio Committee on Justice and Correctional Services, the SIU indicated that they had identified for investigation nine matters related to SAA from Part 1 of the findings of the Zondo Commission.[104]

So where were the auditors?

One of the most important tasks of an auditor is to identify the highest risk areas for the entity they are auditing. In the case of SAA, the nature of its business meant that most of its annual budget was spent on procurement – nearly R25 billion per year.[105] Any deficiencies and malfeasance in the procurement process – such as the inflated pricing, overpayment and non-delivery identified by the SIU – posed a very high and material risk to the business. This fact should have been flagged and resulted in greater scrutiny by both SAA's internal and external auditors, but this did not happen.

PwC and Nkonki jointly took over the external audit function at SAA from Deloitte in 2012 and remained the auditors until the Auditor General (AG) took over the function in 2017 when the airline was in crisis. Their appointment as auditors from 2013 to 2016 was itself irregular expenditure by SAA as it did not follow any proper procurement process.[106]

Their period as the external auditors coincided almost precisely with Myeni's time as the permanent chairperson of the board, and the malfeasance that took place under her watch. Despite this, the auditors signed off SAA's financial statements without qualification or concern every year during this period. They did not report any failures to comply with procurement law or raise any red flags about SAA's internal controls or their financial statements.

When the AG took over the audit function in 2017, it quickly became apparent that these clean audit opinions were the result of very serious audit failures. The AG issued a qualified opinion on the 2017 SAA financial statements. This is done when there are material misstatements in the financial statements, or the entity has not provided the auditors with enough evidence. In this case, SAA had misrepresented its financial position by including assets whose existence could not be verified, misreporting inventory and the costs of maintenance, and failing to properly account for the impairment of assets.[107] The AG concluded that the previous auditors had failed to identify eight major misstatements and that SAA's board was clearly in breach of several requirements in the PFMA.[108] This included that the SAA group 'did not establish adequate controls to maintain complete records of irregular expenditure' despite this being a requirement of the PFMA.[109]

These errors from the auditors are difficult to explain. From 2014 to 2016, the PwC auditor responsible for the SAA audit was Pule Mothibe, a director at the firm since 2002. The Nkonki auditor on the SAA audit from 2014 to 2016 was Thuto Masasa. Masasa was also a partner at Nkonki and was the head of audit from 2016 until it closed in 2018. Both Mothibe and Masasa came with a wealth of audit experience and enjoyed senior roles at their firms, which makes their errors even more inexplicable.

When he appeared at the Zondo Commission, it was put to Mothibe that this conduct constituted a dereliction of duty, but he insisted on calling it an 'omission'.[110] Mothibe admitted that they had identified the failures to comply with the PFMA and alerted the audit committee but was forced to admit that they should have reported these failures in the annual report. Mothibe told Judge Zondo that this had been an 'error in judgment'.[111] It is hard to reconcile such an error with Mothibe's decades of experience and senior position at PwC.

Subsequent investigations by the Independent Regulatory Board for Auditors (the IRBA) have confirmed that these serious auditing errors were evident in 2014, 2015 and 2016. Mothibe and Masasa settled these matters by consent order, the most common way such complaints are dealt with at the IRBA. Nonetheless, the IRBA confirmed that Mothibe and Masasa had, in every audit from 2014 to 2016, 'failed to disclose material non-compliance with legislation', failed to report on serious internal control deficiencies within SAA, and 'failed to obtain sufficient appropriate audit evidence relating to … irregular expenditure and fruitless and wasteful expenditure'.[112] The investigation also found additional audit failures in the 2016 financial year, including a failure to document their work and a failure to show the required 'professional scepticism' expected of an auditor.[113]

They knew, but said nothing

It is particularly disturbing that the audit failures in the SAA case occurred, not due to the executive management pulling the wool over the auditors' eyes, but rather due to the auditors failing to report irregularities that were conspicuous and known to them. As indicated, Mothibe admitted to the Zondo Commission that they were aware of SAA's failure to comply with the PFMA but made an 'error' in not disclosing this in their audit report.

The same is true for their failure, as determined by the IRBA, to report the glaring internal control deficiencies within SAA's governance systems. In its 2011 audit, SAA's previous auditor, Deloitte, stated that they had observed serious 'control deficiencies', particularly with regards to procurement and contract management.[114] Because of this, they could not establish that the company was compliant with the PFMA.

In the *Corporations and Economic Crime Report (CECR) Volume 2: The Auditors*, Open Secrets explained how these internal problems must have been known to the new auditors from PwC and Nkonki. In 2014, SAA obtained an independent review of their internal audit function by a company called Outsourced Risk and Compliance Assessment (ORCA). The findings revealed a completely inadequate and chaotic internal audit system. Amongst the most serious findings were that many of the audit notes were handwritten and never digitised, that audit papers were often unsigned and not dated, and that audit papers were not archived properly and could be accessed and changed without people's knowledge.[115]

These findings were presented to SAA's audit and risk committee and the chief audit executive admitted that the audit working papers were completely inadequate in 2011, 2012, 2013 and 2014, which caused him to go back and re-write scattered handwritten papers.[116] As the external auditors, PwC and Nkonki would have taken part in this meeting or at least received the full details of it, and thus must have been aware of these problems. Despite this, none of the audit reports from 2014 to 2016 ever reported any concerns about the state of the internal audit processes.

Auditors get a slap on the wrist, and the public picks up the tab

The consequences of repeated audit failure over several years were serious. The state kept bailing out the airline with public funds, and creditors kept on lending, while glaring errors in the financial statements and continued failures to comply with the law were ignored by the auditors and excluded from their reports.

The auditors' settlement agreements with the IRBA included an agreement to pay fines. Despite the serious and repeated errors, each auditor received less than R1 million in total fines for all errors (the paltry maximum fine possible at the time). In contrast, it is estimated that PwC and Nkonki received up to R90 million in fees from their work at SAA.[117] It is hard to see how the firms can justify the retention of any of these fees given the quality of their work at SAA.

The Zondo Commission's final report found that 'PWC was either not equipped to assess, or was just not particularly concerned about, the peculiar requirements and obligations attendant on a public entity and ensuring that irregularities that contravened the PFMA and other procurement legislation were carefully investigated and reported on'.[118] In light of these findings surely it would have been appropriate for the fees PwC earned to be paid back and used to pay the salaries of SAA employees left stranded when the airline was placed into business rescue.

Apart from the inadequate fines, there have been no other consequences for the auditors or their firms. In fact, because the matters were settled by consent order, the IRBA's quarterly newsletter published just half a page on the entire case. It confirmed that the auditors in question were found guilty on four charges and explained what the charges were. The report did not even indicate which firms the auditors belong to, nor that the entity was indeed SAA. There was also no attempt to provide a detailed explanation of the IRBA's investigation or why the failures occurred.[119] The entire approach is indicative of a desire to protect the reputations of auditors and audit firms, rather than the public, from the costs of audit failure.

It is this kind of soft touch regulation that allowed PwC to go on record afterwards to say that while it was disappointed about the audit, the findings did not indicate any kind of 'ethical breach' in the audit failure. As pointed out by journalist Ann Crotty, this seems to reflect a view within PwC that a persistent failure to do a job for which the firm is paid lucrative fees does not have ethical implications.[120] Indeed, that appears to be the view of most audit firms, banks and other corporations implicated in enabling or participating in state capture and corruption in exchange for lucrative fees.[121]

Real accountability – for all

The public is still eager to see genuine accountability for those implicated in state capture, as well as the return of illicit proceeds from corrupt and tainted contracts. There are important green shoots in this regard when we consider the arrests and corruption charges instituted against key individuals and officials alleged to have played a role in the Guptas' Estina Dairy Farm heist and the looting of Transnet. Yet, accountability will be incomplete without a proper reckoning for the corporate enablers of this era of state capture.

We cannot leave corporate accountability to soft touch regulators and sweetheart settlements. Instead, proper punitive and remedial measures that will discourage recurrence of the same conduct are essential. The full repayment of all fees and interest thereon is just the start. There must also be real justice, meted out without fear or favour, to corporations and their executives alike.

FIVE
IRBA: Soft touch audit regulator in turmoil?

THE 'BIG FOUR' AUDIT FIRMS are regularly implicated in audit failures at both listed private companies and public entities. These failures have devastating public costs; just ask the pensioners and investors who lost R200 billion when Steinhoff collapsed, or the South Africans who are being asked to fork out more money to bail out South African Airways (SAA). The Independent Regulatory Board of Auditors (IRBA) is the regulator tasked with holding auditors to account in cases of misconduct, unlawful or unethical behaviour, yet the IRBA have repeatedly failed to live up to this task.

The evidence shows that IRBA does not have sufficient powers to be an effective regulator. It has also often failed to use the powers it does have to effectively deter unlawful conduct by registered auditors.

IRBA: Failing to fulfil a crucial mandate

Auditors are among the professionals who fail to fulfil their professional and legal duties, and there is evidence that many have been knowingly or negligently complicit in serious economic crimes. Even when their conduct has not been criminal, they have failed to fulfil the public's legitimate expectation that auditors be independent and exercise professional scepticism when signing off on financial statements, rather than uncritically deferring to management. This is not IRBA's fault alone, of course. However, it must answer to the public as one of several regulators in the financial sector that have failed to adequately ensure ethical and lawful conduct in the profession it regulates.

On its website, the IRBA states that its mandate is to contribute to 'an ethical, value-driven financial sector that encourages investment, creates confidence in the financial markets and promotes sound practices'.[122] Despite this, on the rare occasion that auditors have been hauled before the IRBA, a slap on the wrist behind closed doors has been the usual outcome. A crucial way in which the IRBA is supposed to fulfil its mandate of building an ethical financial sector that creates public confidence is by 'monitoring registered auditors' compliance with professional standards', and 'investigating and taking appropriate action against registered auditors in respect of improper conduct'. Where it fails to do so, a key deterrent against improper and unethical conduct is lost, and public trust is further eroded.

Too slow, secretive and toothless?

While the IRBA has the power to make life very difficult for smaller independent registered auditors, it is less equipped to ensure swift and appropriate accountability for the extremely wealthy and powerful Big Four firms.

When a Big Four firm decides to dig its heels in and fight disciplinary action, it can result in disciplinary processes dragging on for years, long after the events took place. Such battles become highly legalistic, and the question of whether the auditor has fulfilled their ethical duties is often lost. A good example of this is the IRBA's long disciplinary proceedings against partners at Deloitte for failures at African Bank, which crashed spectacularly in 2014. The IRBA charged the Deloitte partners with misconduct, alleging that they missed red flags in the financial statements that massively overstated future cash flow predictions for the bank, and ignored the red flags raised in their own internal reports.[123] The IRBA called it an 'auditing disaster'.[124]

While investors in African Bank lost out dramatically when the bank failed in 2014, it was nearly four years until the IRBA actually instituted disciplinary proceedings for misconduct against two Deloitte partners in March 2018. Deloitte vigorously defended the proceedings at every step, including alleging that the IRBA's witnesses lied. Only in December 2020 was the matter concluded, to the dissatisfaction of the IRBA.

The IRBA's disciplinary committee found the auditor in charge of the African Bank accounts, Mgcinisihlalo Jordan, guilty of only five of the ten charges. He was fined R800,000 in total and given a suspended suspension (IRBA had argued for deregistration), meaning that the IRBA suspended its decision to suspend Jordan. Deloitte was also ordered to cover half the IRBA's costs for the investigation which amounted to R31.2 million.[125] In its statement on the matter, the IRBA expressed dismay that their own process had resulted in such 'soft' or lenient sanctions.[126]

Such legal battles are also very expensive for the IRBA. In its 2019 annual report, it noted that its expenses linked to disciplinary proceedings had gone up nearly R15 million due to 'an increase in high profile cases'.[127] These expenses will likely continue to rise as it grapples with the fallout from state capture, and its need to litigate against Steinhoff to access the PwC forensic report into the collapse of Steinhoff, that the latter is refusing to release.

Even when a disciplinary matter does get wrapped up quickly, the IRBA does not have the necessary punitive powers to deter repeated misconduct. It has also not shown the necessary commitment to transparency and openness that would build public trust in its processes.

A good example of this is the IRBA's findings against PwC and Nkonki in relation to some of their audit work at SAA. The disciplinary committee in that case concluded that PwC and Nkonki's auditors 'did not appropriately respond to the risk related to procurement in terms of the requirements of international standards on auditing [and] failed to disclose noncompliance with legislation regarding procurement in the joint audit'. The auditors were given the maximum fine for each charge – a paltry R200,000 – with the total fines being less than R1 million.

While this finding seems encouraging, the fine is just a rap across the knuckles compared to the R90 million that PwC and Nkonki were paid for their work at SAA. Since then, PwC has abandoned its earlier protests and announced that they have 'used the opportunity to effect the necessary remediation as important lessons are learnt'. Yet again, the cost of PwC's education was paid by South African taxpayers who bear the brunt of SAA's failures, while the firm's partners pocket their proceeds.

Given the repeated bailouts of SAA by the South African taxpayer, and the vast procurement budget of the airline, one would expect that, despite the limited fine, the IRBA would have made the effort to publicly condemn such significant audit failure. However, the IRBA refused to publish the names of PwC and Nkonki in relation to this matter. The only reason the public knows that these firms were guilty of misconduct is because of a determined investigation by the *Financial Mail*.[128]

This has been an unfortunate pattern in the disciplinary work of the IRBA. Auditors are rarely named in the quarterly newsletter that details the regulator's investigations and findings. It has often appeared that the IRBA's desire to protect its members overshadows its responsibility 'to enhance performance, accountability and public confidence', which should include informing the public about dodgy auditors.

IRBA's previous CEO, Bernard Agulhas, agreed that the punitive power of the IRBA was completely inadequate. Speaking on action taken against the KPMG auditors who were complicit in the looting of VBS Mutual Bank, Agulhas said:

> The limits to sanctions are up to R200 000 per charge. The public has expressed its dissatisfaction and termed it a slap on the wrist. We agree. The amount is far too low and so the act amendments currently underway include an important change which will allow the Minister of Finance to set the upper limit to sanctions from time to time. This will allow the IRBA to apply sanctions which are more appropriate to the scale of the negligence.[129]

Leadership crisis scuppers new opportunities

Despite the myriad issues outlined above, there were positive signs in the last few years that the IRBA and Treasury recognised that the audit industry faced a crisis. Changes were needed to bolster the regulators' investigative and enforcement capacity, and to ensure the independence of auditors from their clients. The first step towards the latter was the decision to make the rotation of auditors mandatory, to avoid the cosy situation at a company like Naspers who had PwC as their 'independent' auditor for more than 105 years.

Attempts to increase investigative and enforcement capacity at the IRBA was introduced via the Auditing Profession Amendment Bill. The Bill grants IRBA the power to issue a warrant, to 'enter and search premises and to subpoena persons with information required for an investigation or disciplinary process', as well as creating a duty to disclose information.[130] It also allows for higher sanctions which may serve as greater deterrents. Finally, the Bill introduces greater independence on the IRBA's board by preventing registered auditors from being appointed, to avoid the usual revolving door where the audit regulatory board is staffed by former members of the Big Four firms. As was the case in terms of mandatory audit rotation, the Big Four firms have pushed back hard against many of the Bill's changes.

In a submission to Parliament's Standing Committee on Finance, Open Secrets expressed support for many of these proposed amendments.[131] However, it's clear that they can only partly address the issues facing the audit industry. For one, more systemic changes are required to safeguard audit independence – including the permanent separation of audit and consulting and the creation of audit-only firms.

As this book went to print, the IRBA and Treasury invited public comment on proposed new maximum fines for auditors found guilty of misconduct. The proposed new limits are between R5 million and R10 million for individual auditors, and between R15 million and R25 million for audit firms, with the amount depending on whether there is an admission of guilt. While these new fines are a significant improvement on R200,000, they still do not begin to match either the fees earned through audit work, nor the often extraordinary cost of audit failure. Open Secrets has suggested that there should be no maximum fine in law, and that the regulator should have greater discretion in imposing fines that take these other factors into consideration.

The other factor at play is that the new powers and independence of the IRBA will mean little if the regulator does not energetically use them to ensure accountability and acts independently of the industry it regulates. In the CECR report, we also called on the IRBA to commit to improving its own transparency and information sharing, including always publishing the names of individual auditors and their firms found to have engaged in misconduct.

The current reality sits in contrast to that. In February 2021, the IRBA's CEO, Jenitha John, tendered her resignation due to concerns voiced by civil society organisations like OUTA and Open Secrets, about John's work as the non-executive director who headed Tongaat Hulett's audit committee for nine years up to May 2019. The decision to appoint her in the first place was rather perplexing as her non-executive directorship at Tongaat was during the period in which Tongaat's management were presenting completely inaccurate accounts and Deloitte's auditors were signing them off. The IRBA is currently investigating Deloitte's conduct at Tongaat.

Essentially, John would have had to lead an organisation tasked with investigating the Deloitte auditors that reported to her as head of the audit committee at Tongaat. Civil society organisations such as OUTA have pointed out that this presents serious conflicts of interest and should have disqualified John's appointment by the outgoing board of the IRBA.

Responding to concerns raised, then finance minister, Tito Mboweni, who himself inexplicably delayed the appointment of the new board of the IRBA, announced that he would meet with the new board to discuss the appointment, and to discuss a review of the decision to appoint John. However, because of his delay, John started her work at the regulator with no board in place and the talk of a review of her appointment hanging over her. Employees at the IRBA described these first days to the *Financial Mail* as 'chaos'.[132]

In a letter seen by Open Secrets, one board member submitted their resignation to the minister, citing turmoil and alleging that the board became entirely dysfunctional due to disagreement on whether John's appointment was appropriate. The *Financial Mail* reported on this letter and the internal discord at the IRBA.[133] They also reported new information that suggests that John may have done more than previously reported to flag accounting irregularities and stand up to management long before the Tongaat scandal broke.[134]

However, even if this is true and John is not personally culpable for wrongdoing at Tongaat, public perception of possible conflicts of interest would have continued and tainted IRBA's investigations and findings in this matter.

Urgency is required

Despite many of the IRBA's shortcomings, it is the regulatory body that South Africans are looking to to ensure accountability from those audit firms that have been complicit in economic and corporate crimes. Possible audit failures at Steinhoff, Tongaat Hulett, EOH and SAA, that cost pensioners and the wider public billions of rand, are just some of the matters on its plate. But if it is to face off against the power of the Big Four firms, it cannot do so while compromised or distracted by internal discord and poor decision making by its board. The IRBA needs to get to work holding the auditing giants to account.

7
CONSPIRING CONSULTANTS

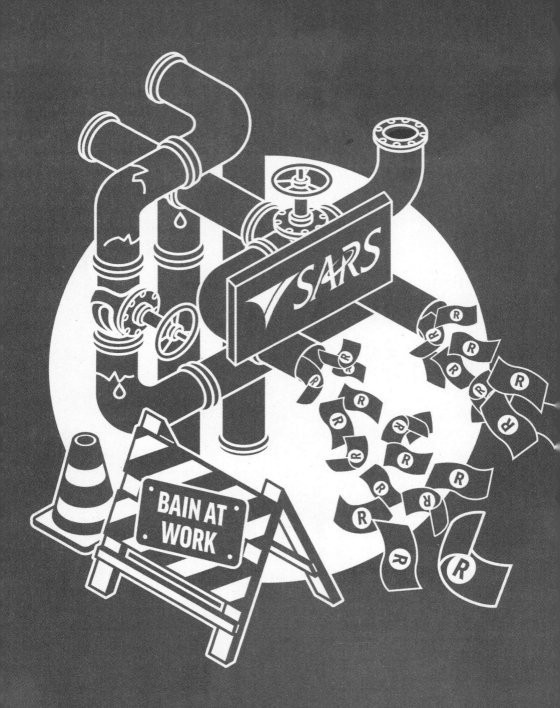

Introduction

They take no credit and they accept no blame. The 'management consulting' industry is an opaque industry with a suitably vague name. Exactly what management consultants do is often hard to decipher, but the names of the United States-based firms McKinsey & Company, Bain & Company and the Boston Consulting Group (BCG) are well known. They are the 'Big Three' of management consulting, also known as MBB. While the 'Big Four' audit firms discussed in the previous chapters increasingly compete for consulting work, MBB remain major players in the global consulting industry. And while the industry may tell you that the 'Big Three' owe their notoriety to their history, prestige, revenue and expertise, they have also become synonymous with scandal, grand corruption and reputation laundering for human rights abusers and kleptocrats.

In South Africa, Bain and McKinsey have been implicated as essential enablers of the state capture network; and, in Angola, BCG was involved in state capture of another kind by the Dos Santos family. Their work – and damage – in Southern Africa spanned a variety of industries; in Angola it was minerals and oil, in South Africa freight rail, revenue services, airlines and energy. The common themes running through the stories in this chapter, regardless of the country or industry in question, are the catastrophic human cost that was left in the wake of the consultants' work, and the manner in which they have failed to fully account for their role.

US academic Duff McDonald has written extensively on consulting firms, and on McKinsey in particular. He argues that consultancies like McKinsey have, since the 20th century, been instrumental in cultivating and shaping the 'abstract, white-collar nature of modern business'[1] – a white-collar nature of modern business that is as American as apple pie. While the giants of accounting and auditing discussed in the previous section trace many of their roots to Britain, management consultancy is deeply American, emerging from US academia's focus on the fields of management studies and scientific management. While McKinsey is seen as the pioneer of the field, all of the 'Big Three' were founded in America, though they now command offices around the world, including South Africa.

McKinsey not only dominates the industry in terms of revenue, it has been instrumental in exporting a culture of doing business. Consultants provide advisory services on management, strategy, human resources, IT, operations and finance. They do this all behind a veil of secrecy. This is at least in part due to the complex relationship between consultants and their clients, where secrecy and obfuscation of the precise responsibilities of each party is in the interests of both.[2] This is true when management consultants work for other companies in the private sector, but also when they take on work for governments and state-owned enterprises, as they have done during state capture in South Africa.

Operating behind a veil of secrecy is a particularly dangerous business model as more and more governments are engaging consultants in public work without the knowledge of the public. These consultants are not held to the same standards as public servants, and it is accepted that they serve the bottom line, even when they are contracted on projects to provide vital public services.

Whether they are peddling opiods for Big Pharma in the United States, working for kleptocratic regimes in Southern Africa, or working with authoritarian regimes like Saudi Arabia, these management consultants have shown that they will continue to prioritise profit over all else.

ONE
McKinsey: Profit over principle

MCKINSEY & COMPANY is the largest of the so-called 'Big Three' management consulting firms. McKinsey, or 'The Firm' as it is referred to by its consultants, is a global army of 30,000 consultants operating in over 130 cities across sixty-six countries.[3] The firm has a total annual global revenue estimated at over $10.6 billion in 2021.[4] McKinsey's client list includes both top corporations and governments with poor human rights records, including China, Ukraine's ousted president Viktor Yanukovych and state-owned entities in Saudi Arabia.[5] McKinsey resolutely maintains that it makes a positive contribution in these countries.[6]

McKinsey can boldly make this claim due to a central (and controversial) aspect of management consulting – the industry's opacity. In this vein, on 25 February 2020, Open Secrets received a letter from McKinsey requesting corrections for alleged 'errors' in 'The Enablers' and related coverage in the *Financial Mail*.[7] While we have made some additions to our report, on the whole, McKinsey's meandering seven-page response reflects a refusal of the firm to fully accept responsibility for its role in state capture and the related economic and social costs. Rather, they lay blame at the foot of unscrupulous public sector actors and inefficient SOEs.

They seek to deflect evidence that in its contracts with Gupta associates, Regiments Capital and Trillian Capital Management, McKinsey were delinquent in their duties in the pursuit of lucrative consulting fees. The evidence shows that McKinsey were essential enablers of gross corruption at Transnet and Eskom, which was confirmed in the findings of Part II and Part IV of the State Capture Commission report released in 2022.

Transnet: Dubious escalations make room for kickbacks

McKinsey began working for state-owned rail agency Transnet in 2005. While it does not reveal exactly what this work entailed, its website advertises its work in South Africa's public sector as 'advising on industrial development issues in specific industry sectors, such as energy and mining' as well as 'advising state-owned enterprises on how to improve operations and delivery of services'.[8]

In 2012, when Transnet began the process of its fleet recapitalisation, McKinsey was contracted to work on the business case. However, because McKinsey is a multinational company, it is required by the Supplier Development Programme (SDP) to partner with a B-BBEE business partner who receives a 30 per cent stake in profits.[9]

Anoj Singh, then Transnet CFO and Gupta associate implicated in corruption at both Eskom and Transnet, suggested Regiments Capital to McKinsey.[10] In August 2012, McKinsey signed a R35.2 million contract with Transnet and Regiments Capital became its partner on Transnet's procurement of 1064 locomotives. The 1064 locomotive transactions have since been shown to be riddled with corruption and kickbacks, and this all started with the writing of the business case.[11]

McKinsey and Regiments were tasked with validating the 'business case' for the 1064 locomotives. This process led to the splitting of the tender between four suppliers, and crucially also an unsubstantiated escalation in costs. The State Capture Commission's final report, as well as the Fundudzi report commissioned by National Treasury to look into corruption at Transnet and Eskom, confirmed that Regiments assisted Transnet in rewriting the business case to justify a R16 billion escalation in cost, from an estimated R38.6 billion to R54.5 billion.[12]

This R16 billion was then paid as kickbacks and laundered through the HSBC bank accounts of front companies in Hong Kong and Dubai. This story is told in more detail in the Bad Bankers section on HSBC.

The Fundudzi investigation concluded that Regiments altered the business case at the last minute to misrepresent the R38.6 billion as excluding 'the potential effects from forex hedging, forex escalation and other price escalations'.[13] This provided the reason for Brian Molefe and Anoj Singh to present an adjusted contract cost of R54.5 billion to the board in May 2014. Rewriting the business case was an essential step that Molefe and others at Transnet used to allow for the payment of commissions and bribes worth 21 per cent of the total contract value.[14]

The State Capture Commission found that the original business case was approved on 7 March 2012, then only changed again on 25 April 2013 once McKinsey had been appointed as transaction advisor.[15] McKinsey was not involved in the last-minute rewrite of the business case, and confirmed to investigators that Regiments did know that the R38.6 billion was an all-inclusive figure. However, they continued to work with Regiments Capital until 2016. During the period in which McKinsey and Regiments were partnered, particularly 2012–2015, Regiments Capital and McKinsey were paid millions in fees and 'reimbursements' by Transnet without any proper documentation.[16]

Though McKinsey had appeared reluctant to accept responsibility when it responded to our investigative reports in February 2020, in May 2021 they made a somewhat about turn and settled with Transnet following months of heavily publicised State Capture Commission testimony about their conduct. They agreed to pay only R870 million (Transnet had been seeking R1.2 billion) as according to McKinsey they were not paying back the fees based on 'legal obligation' but 'principle'.[17]

The issue of payments being made without a proper legal basis arose again with regard to McKinsey's work at Eskom.

The contract that never was: Eskom, McKinsey and Trillian

At the end of 2015, McKinsey entered into a contract with Eskom with the purported goal of developing internal project management and engineering capacity.[18] However, the contract was not subject to a bid procedure, contrary to basic public procurement requirements. The contract had the potential to earn McKinsey R9 billion by its conclusion and was the firm's biggest ever contract in Africa. Despite objections by some at the firm, the contract was supported by several of McKinsey's senior partners globally.[19]

At McKinsey's South African office, the project was led by Vikas Sagar with assistance by Alexander Weiss. Sagar has been described as a popular McKinsey partner.[20] Sagar and Salim Essa – the hand behind countless firms in the Gupta enterprise – had attempted to partner on several projects before McKinsey's deal with Eskom. In 2014, Sagar asked a McKinsey expert for an opinion on the viability of a uranium and gold mine in South Africa. Sagar subsequently forwarded this opinion to Essa.[21]

Apart from the lack of competitive bidding, the Eskom–McKinsey contract should for a number of reasons have immediately raised concern within Eskom management. One was that McKinsey proposed a 'no fee, at risk contract', in which they agreed to forgo payment if they failed to deliver the project's benefits. On the flip side, if they did deliver these strategies, they stood to receive a massive cut of their client's upside. While in theory this could look like McKinsey was accepting the project risk, 'in practice, it allows consultancies [like McKinsey] to earn billions in fees as a cut of savings that may never be realised'.[22]

This is because the consultant also calculates the saving they have achieved, often using dubious baseline estimates to calculate their own achievements. In the case of McKinsey and Eskom, a review by fellow consultants Oliver Wyman and risk-management firm Marsh found that McKinsey and their new partner Trillian had used highly questionable ways of calculating Eskom's 'savings', including 'charging double the market rate for coal contract negotiations' and using 'baselines ... that could exaggerate effects achieved'.[23] When asked about this, McKinsey's global head admitted that they had overcharged Eskom and needed to implement stricter controls which would include 'real recognition that there has to be clarity on what performance means'.[24]

This type of at-risk contract also required special permissions from Treasury as Treasury requires SOE consultants to be paid fixed hourly rates. Eskom's compliance department and legal counsel informed Edwin Mabelane (Eskom's head of procurement) that the expenditure would be irregular should the requisite permissions not be sought.[25] Eskom's management ignored the warnings and Treasury was informed of the contract after the fact.

The Parliamentary Portfolio Committee on Public Enterprises that heard evidence on the deal made an important observation: It should have been obvious to McKinsey that the deal was deficient and unlawful. The committee concluded that 'it is highly improbable that a company as sophisticated as McKinsey could, in good faith, have acted on the assumption that a contract based on a sole sourcing arrangement and on the applicable remuneration structure was lawful'.[26]

At Eskom, Trillian was McKinsey's chosen B-BBEE partner, just as it had partnered with Regiments Capital for their work at Transnet. McKinsey's agreement with Trillian envisaged McKinsey paying the latter 30 per cent of its R1-billion-a-year contract with Eskom.[27] However, although a contract between McKinsey and Trillian had been prepared and then edited, it had never actually been signed: No contract was concluded. Despite this, on 9 February 2016, McKinsey partner Vikas Sagar sent a letter to Eskom indicating that McKinsey had subcontracted Trillian, and authorising Eskom to pay Trillian directly.[28]

This letter by McKinsey's Vikas Sagar was used as part of the justification by Eskom's management to pay Trillian R700 million, even though Trillian had no contact with Eskom. It was also used by Eric Wood in attempts to obtain payment from Eskom.

Denials

In its letter to Open Secrets, McKinsey argues that Sagar's letter did not result in the illicit payment to Trillian as illustrated by a Gauteng high court ruling in June 2019. It is true that this was not the only reason, and that Eskom proceeded to pay Trillian after McKinsey informed them that their relationship with Trillian was over. Nonetheless, the evidence still shows that McKinsey's conduct was central to these dubious payments:

1. McKinsey partner Sagar wrote the letter, knowing that no contract existed between Eskom and Trillian.

2. A parliamentary inquiry into the matter concluded that 'McKinsey worked as the de facto legitimising vehicle for Trillian's access to Eskom work and payment'.[29]
3. Whistleblower and the former CEO of Trillian, Ms Bianca Goodson, made it clear in her testimony to Parliament that McKinsey never expected Trillian to actually do any work to get paid. She states that McKinsey senior partners told her to 'just take your 30 per cent and go'. The parliamentary report attributes this statement to Lorenz Jüngling, a McKinsey partner.
4. Due to allegations of impropriety, then Trillian chairperson Tokyo Sexwale initiated an investigation led by Advocate Geoff Budlender SC into the nature of the contract or agreements between Eskom, McKinsey and Trillian. Both Trillian and McKinsey declined to cooperate fully with Budlender's investigation. Crucially, McKinsey repeatedly falsely denied working with Trillian.[30]
5. The report compiled by Advocate Budlender also confirms that Eric Wood used Vikas Sagar's letter to justify Eskom paying Trillian R565 million, in the absence of any contract.
6. Whistleblower Bianca Goodson also provided documentary proof that for the three months that she was the CEO of Trillian Management Consulting (TMC), she engaged extensively with McKinsey on the Eskom and Trillian contract.[31]
7. It was only after the release of Budlender's public findings that McKinsey began divulging the extent of their dealings with Trillian, by which time Sagar had left McKinsey.
8. McKinsey entered into a contract with Trillian before they had completed the requisite beneficial ownership 'due diligence' checks.[32] Despite this, 'work' between these two companies commenced in September 2015 and continued until March 2016.

Thus, by the time McKinsey terminated its relationship with Trillian, Trillian had already been paid more than half a billion rand for work they had not performed. The nature of this consultancy, and why McKinsey was also paid a R1 billion (including over R90 million in interest) fee, is still unclear.

Following the North Gauteng high court judgment, McKinsey agreed to return R902 million to Eskom. It later paid back nearly R100 million more in interest on that sum. McKinsey's senior partner at the time, Kevin Sneader, also apologised for its relationship with Trillian, saying McKinsey was 'not careful enough about who we associated with'. He added that 'we are embarrassed by these failings, and we apologise to the people of South Africa, our clients, our colleagues and our alumni, who rightly expect more of our firm.'[33]

Such apologies ring hollow in the absence of hard accountability. Sagar nor any other McKinsey partner has faced proper accountability for their role in the calamities at Eskom and Transnet. McKinsey's statement on its repayment of Transnet and SAA's fees stated: 'The settlement is made without any admission of liability or wrongdoing on the part of McKinsey or its employees.'[34] Despite this settlement resulting from the State Capture Commission's work, McKinsey's statement does not use the words state capture, they merely refer to the State Capture Commission as 'the commission' or 'the Judicial Commission of Inquiry'.[35] They take no credit, and they accept no blame.

Saudi Arabia

Such an ethos reflects McKinsey's global strategy. In its February 2020 letter to Open Secrets, McKinsey also challenged the issue of a document prepared by McKinsey that had been used by Saudi Arabia to track dissidents, following the murder of *Washington Post* journalist, Jamal Khashoggi.[36] The *New York Times* article we cited had since posted a retraction that the document was only meant for McKinsey's internal use, not the Saudi authorities. McKinsey, however, has yet to reveal how this document was shared with its Saudi clients. We have thus written to ask that they provide us with the unredacted copy of the report of the internal investigation[37] they said they would be undertaking[38] and reveal how an internal McKinsey document was used to facilitate human rights abuses.

A threat to democracy

The increasingly prominent role of unaccountable management consultants in decisions with massive public impact speaks to a fundamental risk to democracy. The *New York Times* coverage of McKinsey's role in corruption in South Africa noted that the role of consultants in these spheres 'underscores the risks that arise as governments increasingly turn over responsibilities to consultants who operate mostly in secret, with little or no public accountability'.[39]

It is important to challenge the management consultancy doctrine of no credit and no blame. This veil of secrecy allows those motivated by profit over principle to have deleterious effects on democracy.

In September 2022, as this book was going to print, the NPA announced that it was indicting McKinsey on charges of fraud and corruption related to state capture at Transnet. McKinsey has said that the charges are baseless and pointed to it paying back the fees as sufficient accountability. A successful prosecution would be an important precedent for holding consulting firms to account.

TWO
Bain & Company: The 'KGB of consulting'

THE EROSION OF THE SOUTH African Revenue Service (SARS) reduced the financial resources available to the state to tackle vital social issues, including the fallout from the Covid-19 pandemic. Bain & Company (Bain) helped destroy SARS, which led to consistent failures to collect revenue over a number of years. Bain, working with a network of corrupt politicians and bureaucrats, has enabled the pillaging of the country's future.

To get a better sense of this global consulting firm, we need to understand its origins. Bain is a global management consulting firm headquartered in Boston in the United States. Founded in 1973, Bain today has over 12,000 employees in sixty-five offices in forty countries.[40] Despite being the newest and smallest of the 'Big Three', it still enjoyed an estimated revenue of $4.1 billion in 2021 (more than R60 billion).[41] Like its competitors, Bain has a diverse client list that includes the world's top corporations, state-owned enterprises and governments.

Bain opened its South African office in Johannesburg in 1997.[42] Today, Bain & Company Africa runs offices in Johannesburg and Lagos, Nigeria, and proudly claims to have 'collectively completed more than 350 projects throughout sub-Saharan Africa'.[43] One of these was at the heart of state capture and contributed to gutting SARS.

'Relationship consulting': Main man Massone doing things the Bain way

Since the 1980s, Bain has been dubbed the 'KGB of consulting' due to its notoriously secretive modus operandi.[44] Bain's business is built on 'relationship consulting', which demands close ties developed with clients, typically among the powerful in business and politics.[45] This approach is evidenced by the firm's conduct at SARS, which left South Africa's tax agency a hollowed-out shell. Bain reportedly raked in about R164 million in fees from the havoc it wreaked at SARS.[46]

Prior to its destructive reign at SARS, Bain had been trying to secure lucrative public sector contracts for some time. A door was finally opened by Ambrobrite (Pty) Ltd and its two directors, prominent entertainment industry businessman Dumakude (Duma) Ndlovu and Mpumelelo Ngema, a close friend of Jacob Zuma's.[47]

Ambrobrite was registered as an events, communications and project management company. Its connection with Bain began as an informal relationship between Vittorio Massone, then managing partner of Bain South Africa, Ndlovu and Ngema. The relationship was formalised in November 2013 when Bain entered into a business development and stakeholder management contract with Ambrobrite (Pty) Ltd, which ran from 1 November 2013 to December 2016.[48] According to the contract, Bain would pay Ambrobrite a monthly retainer fee of R100,000, and R200,000 in instances where Ambrobrite 'exceeds expectations'.[49] The contract explicitly states the purpose of the relationship as that which will, 'drive commercial success for Bain & Company SA in the Government and State-Owned Enterprises sector'.[50]

In other words, Bain paid Ambrobrite's two showman owners, Ndlovu and Ngema, a minimum of R100,000 every month for almost four years to be introduced to various figures in the public sector – at least R4.8 million over the period. When taken in context, and one considers the R255 million Bain earned in the public sector (Telkom tender and fees from SARS), the almost R5 million paid by Bain & Co to gain access to the public sector is clearly a well-calculated cost. This meagre 'introduction fee' ensured high returns on investment for the consultancy firm.

The relationship was a hit. It facilitated Bain's connection with prominent figures in the public sector, chief among which included key architects of contemporary state capture, former president Jacob Zuma and SARS commissioner Tom Moyane.

Evidence shows that Massone first encountered Jacob Zuma on 11 August 2012.[51] Dumakude Ndlovu was also present at this meeting. It was here that Massone presented a brainchild of Bain – Project Phoenix.[52] Bain was ready to enter the lucrative public sector consultancy game and it had set its sights on the part state-owned telecommunications company Telkom, as a start.

Within a year, Bain – with little public sector experience in South Africa – had secured a dubious R91.1 million contract with Telkom. This is according to multiple media reports that first broke back in 2014, including reports in *Bloomberg* and *Business Day*.[53] Telkom hired Bain without any formal proposals and there is no record of Bain bidding for the work. It seems that Bain applied its classic strategy of 'relationship consulting' to bag the Telkom contract.[54] It was a strategy it would later deploy to gain access to lucrative work at SARS.

SARS and the Bain brain drain

Vittorio Massone first met Tom Moyane at the Bain office in Melrose Arch, Johannesburg, in October 2013. It was the first of several meetings, between October 2013 and August 2014, in which Moyane would receive 'CEO coaching' from Bain. At the time, Moyane had just been ousted as commissioner of Correctional Services in September 2013, and had been appointed as an adviser to the State Information Technology Agency (Sita).[55] To appreciate Moyane's chequered public service career, it is worth recalling that in January 2019 the Zondo Commission heard evidence that he was a direct beneficiary of bribes by private prisons company Bosasa – at the time of his employment as chief of the country's prison services.[56]

It was during Bain's 'CEO coaching sessions' in May 2014 that Moyane was presented with a document it had authored, titled 'TM First 100 Days'.[57] It set out the changes Moyane was expected to implement once he became the new head of SARS. That same month, Zuma was elected to his second and final term as president. Four months later, in September 2014, Zuma announced Moyane's appointment as commissioner of SARS.[58] Massone, aided by his unique consultancy crystal ball, had thus discussed Moyane's first 100 days at SARS at a meeting four months prior to the president appointing Moyane as commissioner of SARS.

When Moyane took office, he made quick work of appointing his old CEO coach Bain to conduct a review of the operating model at SARS. The Commission of Inquiry into SARS (led by Judge Nugent, and also known as the Nugent Commission) – which was established in 2018 and was tasked with investigating the demise of the tax agency – found that the appointment of Bain had been a foregone conclusion once Moyane was in office. In fact, Bain was so confident of the deal that it already had preselected teams ready to assist the new tax commissioner.[59] Once again, either Bain was crystal ball gazing, or it found an inside track into procurement processes at SARS.

Once appointed, Bain's review of the SARS operating model was rushed and woefully inadequate. The consultants conducted a meagre 33 interviews with SARS employees over six rushed days and failed to consult a single senior official involved in the modernisation of SARS. In other words, Bain made little effort to understand the basic structures and facts about the institution. It was ticking the boxes and in so doing, it failed to substantively interrogate whether it was necessary to restructure SARS at all. Restructuring seems to have been a foregone conclusion.

Despite a clearly inadequate review, Bain proceeded to make a proposal that would effectively gut the capacity of SARS to track, trace and tax the wealth of the very rich and the very corrupt (often the same people, and corporations). As a first step, Bain recommended the culling of numerous key staff at SARS. In addition to a skills culling exercise, Bain recommended SARS overhaul its structure and introduce four new divisions.

Moyane pressed for a fifth structure, which was added. A key part of the restructuring saw the divisions that oversaw corporate tax and individual tax merged into a single division named Business and Individual Tax (BAIT), which reported to the commissioner.[60] Jonas Makwakwa was appointed chief operations officer (COO) of the SARS

BAIT unit, prior to which he had been SARS audit group executive. As the COO of BAIT, Makwakwa was in an extremely powerful position, in which he had operational control over all taxpayer (corporate and individual) affairs.[61]

Makwakwa worked close to and along with Bain, as Tom Moyane's right-hand man, to execute the Bain plan and Moyane's recommended changes that proved to be so detrimental to SARS.[62]

In March 2018, after twenty-two years at the tax agency, Makwakwa resigned. He left following a great deal of controversy. It had become clear that Makwakwa had been engaged in a litany of suspicious activity, chief among which included using his position to advance romantic interests,[63] being on the receiving end of suspicious payments for a number of years, stuffing cash into ATMs and unlawfully dishing out confidential SARS information.[64]

All of these 'shenanigans' must be seen within the context of state capture. Jacob Zuma and his allies needed the keys to SARS, which proved harder to capture than the intelligence and the criminal justice system. Bain's restructuring of SARS provided the unfettered access, for the likes of Zuma and Moyane, to an essential state institution that was repurposed for the political and private gain of Bain and Moyane alike.

The findings of the Nugent Commission neatly sum up who would benefit from this assault on the integrity of SARS: '[w]e think what occurred can fairly be described as a premeditated offensive against SARS … Mr Moyane's interest was to take control of SARS. Bain's interest was to make money.'[65]

In other words, according to a judicial commission of inquiry, Bain contributed to the gutting of SARS, and the implosion of South Africa's public finance, which contributed to the suffering of millions for one reason only: profit.

Bain: Destruction in their wake

Until Moyane and Bain got their teeth into SARS, it had been deemed a 'model state institution'. In the final report of the Commission of Inquiry into SARS, Judge Nugent noted that 'SARS was on a trajectory that had earned it accolades domestically and abroad'.[66]

Its success was vital to the country given that it faced the Herculean task of collecting revenue to enable South Africa's democratic government to deliver on its promises and fulfil its constitutional duties. A well-governed, resourced and effective SARS is vital in the guarantee of crucial rights, such as the right to social security and, ultimately, to strengthening democracy.

It is clear that Bain did not only have a negative effect on SARS's capacity to collect revenue, but that it undid years of significant gains made by the tax agency.[67] The restructuring at SARS spearheaded by Bain & Co led to enormous and rapidly escalating shortfalls in tax revenue collection.

Evidence presented to the Nugent Commission revealed that in the period after Moyane took over at SARS and contracted Bain, the service consistently failed to meet its revenue targets. The shortfall for 2014/15 was R7.3 billion; for 2015/16 R11.3 billion, and for 2016/2017 R30.7 billion.[68] In 2018, the tax revenue shortfall at SARS contributed to the first VAT hike since democracy, disproportionately affecting the most vulnerable in our society. All this is the legacy of Tom Moyane and his CEO coaches at Bain during its foray into public sector consultancy.

How has Bain responded to these accusations? In December 2018 it issued what could be described as a half-hearted apology for its role in the destruction of SARS.[69] This followed the release of the final report of the Nugent Commission. However, true to form of all great management consultancies, Bain failed to take full responsibility, but admitted that the firm should have been aware that Tom Moyane 'was pushing a personal political agenda'.

Bain, in an attempt to square its debt with South Africa, paid back the money it earned from its work at SARS with interest, which amounted to R217 million. However, considering the damage Bain caused at SARS and to the wellbeing of South Africa's people, its tab would be much larger when calculating the social damage it and other enablers have incurred. Its tab, therefore, remains unsettled.

Bain's apology is described as half-hearted precisely because it continues to evade responsibility and paints what the consultancy did at SARS as a mistake, a misguided error of judgement as it were, which could have been avoided if they had done the due diligence.

Bain's man in South Africa, Vittorio Massone, disappeared to Italy under the guise of a medical emergency after one short appearance at the Nugent Commission, never to be seen again under South African skies.[70] This former member of the Council at Business Leadership South Africa, according to his website on which he flashes his smiles and airbrushes over his role in the destruction of SARS, is now vice-chairman of Italian management consultancy Alkemy, which is listed on the Italian bourse.

True to form, Bain remains unaccountable

In 2019, Bain hired business ethics expert Athol Williams in an attempt to reform its tainted public image in South Africa. With a wealth of experience in the field of business ethics and as a previous partner of the consultancy, Williams was brought in as a fixer at Bain, supposedly to review the company's processes and ethical standards in the wake of its complicity in state capture.[71] However, a mere six months later, Williams resigned his plum posting and publicly accused the firm of not being transparent with him and the Nugent Commission.

Williams claims that Bain was transparent with neither him nor the Nugent Commission about the role it played in enabling state capture in South Africa. Williams has also blown the whistle on an offer by Bain to pay his relocation fees to the United Kingdom (presumably to keep him far away from South African corruption investigators) and threatened him with legal action. Williams has reportedly described his life as a living hell, thanks to Bain.[72]

Bain has vehemently denied that it was not transparent with Williams about the internal investigation it conducted and denied withholding any information from him. Bain has also rejected the allegation by Williams that it has made any attempts to 'coerce him or influence him through monetary levers or otherwise'.[73]

Considering the notorious modus operandi of global auditing and consulting firms and the treatment of whistleblowers who speak out against private sector enablers of state capture and corporate crimes, such intimidation by Bain, if indeed true, is unsurprising. Turning on a powerful corporation such as Bain and the big consultancy cash, which buys one's silence, comes with personal consequences.

Bain has also neither been honest with the people of South Africa nor has it fully disclosed the extent of its role in state capture. Despite what seems to be considerable pushback on the part of Bain, Williams made it clear that he was 'prepared to spill the beans at the Zondo Commission' and in March 2021 Williams appeared at the Zondo Commission.

In Part 1 of the final Zondo Commission report, Judge Zondo dedicated an entire section of the report to the destruction of SARS, critiquing the needless and destructive infiltration of SARS using Bain's consultancy services. It is not enough that Bain merely pays back fees when the costs of their destruction are so deep. Given their role at SARS, Bain should face prosecution. Little changes when corporations are left to self-correct – only legal accountability will change a culture of practice embedded in companies such as Bain.

Days before this book went to print, National Treasury announced that Bain would be banned from any public tenders in South Africa for a period of ten years, citing its involvement in 'corruption and fraudulent conduct in relation to SARS'. This is welcome news, but it is still essential that the NPA acts and that criminal accountability is pursued.

THREE
BCG Consulting: Consultant to kleptocrats

THE CHAPTERS ABOVE show that McKinsey and Bain have been deeply implicated in several cases linked to state capture and corruption in South Africa: Bain in connection with its work at SARS and McKinsey at multiple sites of capture but most notably at Eskom and Transnet. On the other hand, the final member of the 'Big Three', the Boston Consulting Group (BCG), has not featured in the saga of South African state capture. Yet evidence from Angola and Saudi Arabia reveals that BCG is no stranger to profiting from their relationships with kleptocrats, as well as politicians and companies involved in economic crimes. BCG, like the other two of the Big Three, is well-versed in this business model.

BCG was established in 1963 and has offices in over ninety cities across fifty countries and regions across the world, with operations in Africa, Asia Pacific, Central and South America, Europe, the Middle East and North America.[74] The firm has a large executive committee to manage their operations in different regions, with Rich Lesser serving as its global chair based in New York.[75] The firm set up operations in Johannesburg in 2011, and its website promotes its work in Africa as having a heavy focus on renewable energy and addressing the climate crisis. Yet BCG's global offices also have an extensive list of clients to which it provides tailored advice and business models, including those implicated in corruption and other crimes. Angola's Isabel dos Santos was one of those clients.

Luanda Leaks: Consultant to a kleptocratic dynasty

Isabel dos Santos rose to international fame under the guise of being a 'self-made billionaire' from Angola, enjoying the company of some of the wealthiest celebrities and business moguls in the world and living a life of extreme opulence.[76] According to *Forbes*, Dos Santos was 'once the richest woman in Africa' featuring on both the Forbes Billionaires and Africa's Billionaires lists with an estimated net worth of $1.4 billion as of 2020. However, she was removed from these lists in January 2021 after her assets were frozen, following revelations of the full extent of her role in looting the Angolan state.[77]

Dos Santos was born in Baku, Azerbaijan, and is the eldest child of Russian-born Tatiana Kukanova and former Angolan president José Eduardo dos Santos, who ruled as its dictator from 1979 to 2017.[78] Dos Santos's parents divorced in 1979, and she moved to London with her mother in that same year. After schooling and working in London, she returned to Angola in the late 1990s and immediately began to profit from the nepotism of the Dos Santos dynasty.

Dos Santos senior had seized control over almost all state entities, including Sonangol, the oil company that functioned as the bedrock of the regime and Angolan economy.[79] In the wake of the collapse of world oil prices in 2014, the president issued a decree that called for the restructuring of Angola's oil sector, and invited Wise Intelligence Solutions, a company owned by Isabel dos Santos, to put together a team of consultants to advise on this process.[80] Later, Dos Santos senior appointed his daughter as the director of Sonangol in June 2016 through a presidential decree.

Dos Santos's exploitation of Sonangol, as well as a complex web of corrupt deals and contracts, beginning in 1980 and spanning the entirety of the 2000s, was revealed by the Luanda Leaks. The Luanda Leaks is an investigation by the International Consortium of Investigative Journalists (ICIJ) and thirty-six media partners into Dos Santos and her business empire. The Luanda Leaks exposed the way in which the Dos Santos kleptocracy acquired and moved public funds to offshore jurisdictions, with the help of powerful Western firms, including BCG.[81]

Enter BCG

The deal to modernise Sonangol is where BCG's involvement with Dos Santos becomes clear. According to evidence in the Luanda Leaks,[82] BCG was one of three consulting firms that received millions of dollars in payments from a Dubai firm linked to Dos Santos – Matter Business Solutions – in connection with the corrupt 2017 project to 'modernise' Sonangol. BCG entered into contracts with and received funds from private companies that were fronts for Dos Santos and her connections. These front companies were the tool used by Dos Santos to transform Angola's public funds into her personal fortune, and arguably should have raised red flags at BCG and the other firms that were involved.

BCG was initially brought on board by Wise Intelligence Solutions, Dos Santos's firm, in 2015, when its consultants put forward a plan that outlined ways to revive the state-owned oil company.[83] BCG was hired by Wise and received over $3.5 million to consult on the project.[84] Wise's consulting contract was then transferred to Matter Business Solutions, which was owned by a close friend of Dos Santos, Paula Oliviera. Matter Business Solutions went on to contract with global consulting giants, BCG, PwC and McKinsey.[85]

Documents and bank statements from the investigations further revealed that in total BCG received $31.2 million, while PwC and McKinsey received $21.4 million and $15.4 million respectively in consulting contracts.[86] According to the Luanda Leaks, these payments were actioned by Matter Business Solutions, which was a front for Dos Santos and played a pivotal role in the network that she used to move Angola's public funds into offshore accounts that were linked to her and her late husband Sindika Dokolo.[87] Money was siphoned from Sonangol into Matter Business Solutions, and other companies linked to Dos Santos and her associates, leaving the state entity with little more than $300 in its bank account.[88] This was uncovered after her father ceded the presidency in 2017. After she was fired in 2017, the new Sonangol chair announced that Isabel Dos Santos had approved over $135 million to be spent on consulting fees.[89] But this wasn't the only dodgy project that BCG was involved in that contributed to the economic decline of Angola; it had received a lucrative contract years before they worked for Sonangol.

It was also revealed that BCG, alongside PwC, played a crucial role in maintaining Dos Santos's business dealings, with BCG facilitating the operation of a 'failing jewellery business that was acquired with Angolan public money'.[90] This failing jewellery business was De Grisogono, a Swiss jeweller. Sindika Dokolo and Angola's diamond trading company Sodiam made a $120 million investment into De Grisogono and acquired a controlling stake in the company in 2012.[91] Under this new ownership structure, De Grisogono hired consultants from BCG and placed several of them in top leadership roles. In 2013, the company named a BCG project leader, John Leitão, as its CEO who described BCG's role as 'shadow management', which BCG later disputed.[92] Despite the millions of dollars invested, millions spent on extravagant parties and Sodiam's soaring debt led the already struggling firm to file for bankruptcy in 2020, following the release of Luanda Leaks.[93]

Consulting firms like BCG are able to avoid legal responsibility for this kind of conduct due to them generally having fewer legal requirements to vet their clients. Unlike banks and other financial institutions, whose due diligence requirements have increased since the global financial crisis in 2008, consulting firms are permitted to operate with less scrutiny.[94] Responding to the exposé of their role in Angola, BCG has insisted that it adequately 'reviewed the payment structures and contracts ... to avoid corruption and other risks'. Yet, this response does not account for the fact that it paid money to and received money from companies with opaque ownership structures that were owned by or affiliated with Dos Santos and Dokolo. These individuals were using fronts to loot state-owned entities, with grave consequences for Angolan people, but BCG were content to do business with them. It is notable that BCG retained these business relationships after several global banks had cut ties with Dos Santos due to questions about the sources of her wealth.[95]

Angola's economy is heavily reliant on oil and diamond exports, and the oil crisis of 2014 had a dire impact on the already struggling country, which had emerged from a brutal civil war just over a decade earlier. After the war ended, the government made a commitment that revenues from oil and diamond exports would go towards rebuilding the economy, strengthening infrastructure and civil institutions that had been destroyed in the war. However, Angola today paints a different picture. According to the World Bank, over 32 per cent of Angolan people live in poverty, and underinvestment in key social sectors such as education and healthcare has had disastrous consequences.[96] Contrary to those early promises, funds that could have been used to strengthen education, healthcare, housing and other crucial infrastructure were invested into state entities that were pillaged to line the pockets of Dos Santos, her associates and her consultants.

It was reported in December 2019 that Dos Santos had been sanctioned by the United States 'for her involvement in significant corruption by misappropriating public funds for her personal benefit'.[97] Following the publication of Luanda Leaks, authorities in Angola, Portugal, Malta and the Netherlands announced that they had filed lawsuits against and were investigating her and her companies, many of which ceased operations.[98]

Saudi Arabia: Reputation laundering for human rights abuse

This pattern of providing services to clients with insufficient concern for the possible human cost is also apparent in BCG's relationship with Crown Prince of Saudi Arabia, Mohammed bin Salman (colloquially referred to as MBS). MBS has fostered close relationships with several Western firms, which have been instrumental in strengthening his rise to power. BCG, McKinsey and Booz Allen are the top consulting firms that have provided extensive services to MBS and have continued to cultivate and enjoy beneficial relationships with the kingdom. This despite human rights groups calling on global leaders and corporations to distance themselves from the Saudi government following the brutal state sanctioned murder of Jamal Khashoggi, a Saudi Arabian journalist and critic of the Saudi government.[99]

Saudi Arabia has a notorious reputation for human rights violations that persists to this day, including brutal repression by security forces, the use of torture and executions as punishment, abuse and exploitation of migrant workers, discrimination based on gender and religious grounds, lack of freedom of expression as well as a continued violations of international humanitarian law in the conflict in Yemen.[100] These violations have been rife under Prince Mohammed's leadership, with human rights groups calling for global powers such as the United States to hold him, and other Saudi Arabian officials to account.[101] Whilst the long list of human rights violations are a cause for outrage and condemnation, consulting firms have not been deterred.

BCG's connection to Prince Mohammed goes back to 2015, when he was appointed minister of defence. Following this appointment, BCG was awarded a contract to facilitate the reconstruction and improvement of the ministry's procurement, personnel and finance systems. It was also reported that the managing director of BCG's operations in the Middle East, Joerg Hildebrandt, had cultivated a personal relationship with MBS.[102] In February 2016, consultants from BCG and McKinsey accompanied five representatives from the Saudi royal court to Washington to attend a series of presentations to Gulf experts about MBS's plans to 'remake Saudi life'.[103]

BCG has been instrumental in the development of Saudi Arabia's economic blueprint, called Vision 2030. This ambitious plan aims to reduce the country's dependency on oil revenues and diversify its economy.[104] BCG is also a key advisor to the prince's foundation, Misk, a non-profit organisation that specialises in running programmes focusing on education and entrepreneurship, as well as culture and the creative arts for youth.[105] The firm has helped shape and strengthen significant parts of Prince Mohammed's rule and, while the prospects of modernising Saudi Arabia have been presented as an important way forward for the kingdom by BCG, injustice continues to persist against the people of Saudi Arabia at the hands of its ruler and the consultants on his payroll.

BCG's work for MBS and Saudi Arabia can be described as reputation laundering, that is the work of transforming despots to debutantes by guiding kleptocratic actors through a process of rebranding.[106] While this has traditionally been the stronghold of PR firms like Bell Pottinger, reputation laundering is a growing industry that includes lawyers, accountants, image consults and consultancy firms like the Big Three – BCG, Bain and McKinsey.

BCG has also been implicated in a highly controversial plan to build megacity Neom in the north-western province of Tabuk, on Saudi Arabia's Red Sea coastline.[107] It has been reported that BCG has struck a multimillion-dollar deal in relation to the construction of this city.[108] While it has been claimed that this is 'virgin' territory, much of the region is home to the Huwaitat people, who are being forced to leave the area by Saudi officials to make way for the new city.[109] Abdul Rahim al-Huwaiti, a member of the Huwaitat people and a campaigner against the project, was shot dead by Saudi security forces when he refused to leave his home. Josh Cooper, the deputy director of ALQST, a Saudi human rights watchdog, has said that the firms involved in this contract are complicit in the violence against and the arrests of the Huwaitat people.[110]

BCG walks free

The 'world-class' reputation of consulting firms such as BCG, McKinsey and Bain adds a veneer of respectability which allows clients like MBS and Dos Santos to sanitise their images, making it easier to line their pockets, while simultaneously repressing and impoverishing their people. On the one hand, the legal requirements to vet their clients aren't as stringent as other financial institutions and professional firms, which enables them to avoid accountability when their clients are implicated in corruption or human rights abuses. On the other hand, legal mechanisms do not cover or punish the type of reputation laundering that consulting firms like BCG specialise in, despite the fact that the human cost that results from this is so high.

The glaring involvement of consulting firms with despots and in global money laundering networks, and their impunity, must be challenged. Exposing their work is one way of doing this, but stronger legal frameworks to hold them accountable are also required. While some of the politicians mentioned here have been subjected to a significant amount of scrutiny, and action taken against them in some instances, BCG remains unaccountable.

8
BAD LAWYERS

Introduction

The previous chapters of this book have identified more than thirty individuals and corporations that remain unaccountable despite extensive evidence of their wrongdoing. This section examines a key cause of this impunity; the failure of our prosecuting authority to pursue justice without fear or favour. In particular, the chapters that follow investigate why the National Prosecuting Authority (NPA) has struggled to investigate and prosecute state capture corruption and how officials accused of wrongdoing inside the NPA themselves remain unaccountable.

When Shamila Batohi was appointed National Director of Public Prosecutions (NDPP) in 2018, hope grew that public trust in the NPA could be restored and that those implicated in corruption would be seen in the dock. In the NPA's 2019–2020 annual report, the NDPP noted that prosecutors at the authority had been implicated in state capture allegations and that the NPA was struggling with a dire skills shortage to prosecute grand corruption.[1]

Yet, almost four years after Batohi's appointment, the leadership of the NPA has done little to restore the authority's integrity and has failed to take responsibility for the challenges it continues to face. Data analysed by Africa Criminal Justice Reform (ACJR), a project housed at the University of the Western Cape and the Dullah Omar Institute, shows that from 2014/2015 to 2019/2020, the number of prosecutors employed by the NPA declined by a significant 22 per cent.[2] In the NPA's Asset Forfeiture Unit (AFU), which is responsible for finding and seizing proceeds from crimes, the ACJR found that one in two positions remain vacant. The institute also found 'worrying trends' that the NPA is struggling to prosecute financial crime cases, particularly grand corruption, as it relies on minor offences and guilty pleas to report a high conviction rate.

The Zondo Commission investigated, and heard evidence on, interference in criminal justice agencies, including the NPA. At the commission, the Civil Society Working Group on State Capture, an umbrella organisation of interest groups that challenge state capture, submitted recommendations that called for urgent reforms in the criminal justice sector.[3] However, the commission declined to make findings and recommendations on the NPA in its final report, despite the significance of this institution for ensuring accountability and justice.

As the first chapter in this section shows, interference at the NPA predates the Zuma era. Politicians have meddled in the authority since its creation, notably including long-term efforts by senior ANC politicians to prevent prosecutions of those denied amnesty by the Truth and Reconciliation Commission (TRC). This interference reached new heights under Zuma. Strategic appointments were made to capture this agency for Zuma and his acolytes. As a result of the devastating decisions made by Zuma-favoured appointees, South Africa is still struggling to hold the perpetrators of grand corruption and serious crime to account.

At the NPA, Nomgcobo Jiba became the acting NDPP and made decisions that favoured Zuma's interests. She used her powers to instruct prosecutors who would do her bidding to prosecute cases that ultimately delayed state capture prosecutions. Later, her predecessor, Shaun Abrahams, would follow in Jiba's footsteps to make prosecutorial decision which harmed the reputation of the NPA and led to growing concerns that the authority's independence had become eroded. Zuma's chosen appointees may have long departed from the NPA, but the damage they did remains.

Jiba and Abrahams created bottlenecks in the NPA. These bottlenecks are prosecutors who stand accused of instituting charges against law enforcement officials investigating corruption without sufficient evidence, while unduly delaying important high-profile cases.[4] In the following chapters, Open Secrets identifies the bottlenecks in the NPA and shows how they remain unaccountable. For South Africa's broken law enforcement system to be rehabilitated, these officials need to face investigation and sanction, where necessary. If they do not, then the public perception that compromised officials remain employed at these important agencies will linger, and investigations into state capture cases may never be completed.

ONE
The national postponement authority

OVER THE LAST DECADE, the National Prosecuting Authority (NPA) has become better known for its failure to prosecute than for doing its job, particularly when it comes to high-profile corruption cases involving corporations, politicians and state officials.[5] Questionable decision-making, poor leadership and political interference has collapsed public trust in the NPA. The current leadership at the authority has yet to bring about change to address the wrongdoing that has left it vulnerable to corruption. It is the institution that should define accountability in South Africa, but it has become one of the country's most unaccountable agencies.

When Shamila Batohi became the National Director of Public Prosecutions (NDPP) in December 2018, her arrival promised a disruption of past mistakes and a reckoning for prosecutors accused of wrongdoing by people who had been prosecuted without sufficient evidence to support these cases. These include former KwaZulu-Natal Hawks boss Johan Booysen[6] and former Independent Police Investigative Directorate (IPID) head Robert McBride. A string of Batohi's predecessors – which included then President Jacob Zuma's carefully handpicked NDPPs Nomgcobo Jiba and Shaun Abrahams – had allowed questionable prosecutorial conduct within the authority but had been forced out through inquiries and court action. No NDPP has lasted a full ten-year term in office. Prior to Batohi's arrival, the country had seen six 'permanent' NDPPs since the NPA was established in 1998. An NDPP term is supposed to be ten years. Political meddling has been a defining contributor to the instability within the NPA's leadership.

Batohi was meant to be different. She was meant to be the NDPP who would face corruption fearlessly and return the NPA to a force of integrity that would prioritise justice in the public interest. But as this book goes to print nearly four years after her appointment, the NPA has yet to conclude a single successful state capture-related prosecution under Batohi's watch. In February 2022, Justice Minister Ronald Lamola confirmed the NPA was looking into thirty-seven high-profile corruption cases linked to state capture and that fourteen had been enrolled in court.[7] These matters are being undertaken by the Investigating Directorate (ID), a unit inside the NPA which was established by President Cyril Ramaphosa to deal with state capture cases. But at the end of 2021, the NPA had found itself in further distress as the head of the ID, Hermione Cronje, officially departed.

In December 2021, Batohi addressed journalists on Cronje's departure.[8] Cronje had been in the post just thirty months before she resigned and has since been replaced by NPA advocate Andrea Johnson.[9] The NPA has faced budget cuts and Cronje herself has said that a shortage of skilled staff in the authority has made it difficult to proceed with grand corruption cases.[10] While Batohi acknowledged that the authority has fallen short, her belief is that the NPA is on the right track.

'People in South Africa do not feel safe and they do not believe that justice is being delivered swiftly or broadly enough,' Batohi said in a press briefing in December 2021.[11] 'But please be assured that there is a lot of good things happening,' she added. 'We are making important progress and we hope to demonstrate that together.'

But not enough has changed inside the authority. In the NPA's 2019/2020 annual report, the NDPP admitted that prosecutors within the NPA had been implicated in 'aiding and abetting' state capture corruption and that there was a dire skills shortage to prosecute financial crime cases.[12] Batohi vowed to implement a turnaround strategy to return the NPA's integrity. Yet, in December 2021, Batohi admitted that the NPA is still struggling with a skills shortage.

'The particular complexities of grand corruption require certain specialised skills that we do not have in the NPA,' she said.[13]

Three years after her appointment, Batohi said that investigations against prosecutors implicated in alleged wrongdoing were not complete, stating that they were at an 'advanced stage'.[14] In the meantime, these prosecutors remain employed in senior positions in the NPA despite having acted as bottlenecks to slow down important cases.

While the NPA struggles with allegations of internal wrongdoing and a skills shortage, it has also faced backlash for its delayed progress in prosecuting high-profile corruption cases. Public interest group Accountability Now has threatened legal action against the authority for its failure to authorise state capture-related prosecutions,[15] while Eskom has indicated it would consider private prosecutions if the NPA would not act on the fifty-four state capture cases referred to it by the Special Investigating Unit (SIU) and Bowmans law firm that are linked to corruption at the power utility.[16]

This lacklustre performance in the post-Zuma era illustrates that the NPA's current leadership is failing to rebuild the institution. Ultimately, the NPA's paralysis to make decisions to prosecute state capture crimes is an indication that the destruction wrought by former President Jacob Zuma still lives on inside the authority.

The Zuma authority

The NPA was always vulnerable to political interference. Its first and longest-serving NDPP, Bulelani Ngcuka, was accused of being an apartheid spy by a group of supporters for Jacob Zuma – primarily former intelligence boss Mo Shaik and Mac Maharaj. Ngcuka was the subject of a gruelling public ordeal as his struggle credentials were picked apart by a Judicial Commission of Inquiry. While his name was cleared by the commission, Ngcuka resigned as NDPP in 2004 after six years in office.

This smear campaign coincided with the NPA's investigation into the arms deal, which also implicated Zuma.[17] In 2003, Ngcuka said that the NPA had a prima facie case against Zuma but declined to prosecute on the basis that there was a low prospect of successful prosecution. He faced public outcry and controversy when the statement came to light.

His successor, Vusi Pikoli, also left the NDPP's office after facing controversy. At the time, Pikoli had issued an arrest warrant for then Police Commissioner Jackie Selebi, a close ally of then President Thabo Mbeki. Mbeki appointed an inquiry to consider Pikoli's fitness to hold office, led by Frene Ginwala, after Pikoli had issued the warrant of arrest. Despite the inquiry finding that he was a 'person of unimpeachable integrity',[18] Pikoli nevertheless left the NDPP's office after reaching a R7.5 million settlement with government to vacate the post.[19] Selebi was later convicted on corruption charges.

The arrival of Jacob Zuma in the Presidency accelerated interference at the NPA and posed even greater danger to its integrity. Zuma made significant decisions to appoint officials within the NPA to seemingly stifle the arms deal case building against him. Just seven months after he assumed the Presidency in 2009, Zuma made a bold move, which ignited widespread criticism. He announced that Menzi Simelane, then director general (DG) in the department of justice, was going to replace Mokotedi Mpshe as the NDPP. Mpshe had been in the post for just two years, from 2007 to 2009, when Simelane took over.

At the time, Simelane was embroiled in allegations of serious misconduct after the Ginwala inquiry found that he unduly interfered in the Selebi case during his time as DG in the justice department.[20] A similar finding was made by the Public Service Commission after then Justice Minister Enver Surty asked the commission to investigate Simelane's conduct. Yet, despite the evidence and findings against him, Zuma appointed Simelane to the position of NDPP in 2009 – a decision which was found to be unlawful by the Supreme Court of Appeal in 2011.

Upon entering the office of the NDPP, Simelane abandoned a preservation order to freeze a bank account held by arms deal fixer Fana Hlongwane in Lichtenstein. The decision was contrary to the advice of senior NPA prosecutors and would have significant ramifications for the investigation into the arms deal, which implicated Zuma and a host of powerful politicians and corporations. His predecessor, Mpshe, had also made a decision to drop corruption charges against Zuma and French arms company Thales because of the alleged 'spy tapes' claims. These relate to recorded phone conversations between former Scorpions boss Leonard McCarthy and Ngcuka, who were alleged to have conspired to charge Zuma. Mpshe's decision to drop the charges was later declared irrational by the Supreme Court of Appeal (SCA), which also found that the authenticity of the so-called 'spy tapes' could not be verified and questioned if the tapes had been legally obtained.[21]

A series of similar decisions to seemingly protect Zuma's interests would follow when Nomgcobo Jiba and Shaun Abrahams were NDPPs. Two sources close to the NPA have said they believe that Jiba's arrival in the NDPP seat prompted the true collapse of the NPA. Karen van Rensburg, the NPA's former CEO and current head of administration, told the Zondo Commission in a 2020 affidavit that the NPA was 'utilised and manipulated at the instance of various people'.[22] She listed Jiba and Abrahams among those who 'were involved in state capture'.[23]

As acting NDPP in 2012, Jiba took the decision to authorise a racketeering prosecution in the so-called Cato Manor 'death squad' case. The allegations included that a Hawks unit in KwaZulu-Natal had been involved in extrajudicial killings. Then KZN Hawks boss Johan Booysen was accused number one but denied there was any truth to the allegations. In his affidavit to the Zondo Commission, Booysen described Jiba as being 'at the heart of all the nefarious activities' that led to law enforcement officers who were investigating state capture cases to be targeted for dodgy prosecutions by the NPA.[24]

An internal NPA investigation, conducted by NPA deputy national director of public prosecutions Rodney de Kock in 2019, agreed that there was no basis for Jiba to authorise the racketeering prosecution as no sufficient evidence was found to support the charges.[25] At the time the prosecution was launched, Booysen had been investigating a R60-million corruption case linked to Thoshan Panday, an associate of Edward Zuma, Jacob Zuma's son. The former Hawks boss alleged that the charges against him had been trumped up to stop the Panday investigation,[26] which has since gone to court.

In 2013, Mxolisi Nxasana was appointed NDPP to replace Jiba. He

NUMBERS AT A GLANCE:

5473
PAGES OF EVIDENCE AND FINDINGS HAVE BEEN PUBLISHED BY THE ZONDO COMMISSION

9 YEARS SINCE THE GUPTA PLANE LANDED AT WATERKLOOF AIR FORCE BASE

52%
THE VACANCY RATE AT THE DIRECTORATE FOR PRIORITY CRIME INVESTIGATION (THE HAWKS)

HAWKS
DIRECTORATE FOR PRIORITY CRIME INVESTIGATION

22%
THE DECLINE IN THE NUMBER OF PROSECUTORS EMPLOYED BY THE NATIONAL PROSECUTING AUTHORITY (NPA) BETWEEN 2014 AND 2019:

86
INVESTIGATIONS HAVE BEEN DECLARED BY THE INVESTIGATING DIRECTORATE OF THE NPA

THE NUMBER OF STATE CAPTURE CONVICTIONS: 0

7 YEARS HAVE PASSED SINCE THE HAWKS BEGAN INVESTIGATIONS INTO CORRUPTION AT PRASA

THE NUMBER OF STATE CAPTURE MATTERS HAVE BEEN ENROLLED IN COURT: **21**

ACCUSED PERSONS HAVE APPEARED IN COURT ON ALLEGED STATE CAPTURE CRIMES: **65**

110 THE NUMBER OF CASES ESKOM HAS REFERRED TO POLICE SINCE 2018

60 THE NUMBER OF ESKOM CASES REFERRED TO THE NPA BY THE SIU later accepted a R17 million retirement pay-out to leave the office of the NDPP in 2015, which was declared unlawful by the Pretoria high court in 2017. At the time, Nxasana had been unwilling to appeal a Durban high court judgment, which had set aside all charges against Booysen and found that Jiba had no sufficient evidence on which to authorise the racketeering charges.[27]

The State Capture Commission heard testimony from Terrence Joubert, an NPA risk specialist in Durban, that there had been a possible plot to oust Nxasana from office. Joubert had surreptitiously recorded a phone conversation where his colleague, police Colonel Welcome Mhlongo, had discussed finding information to connect Nxasana to a murder.[28] According to Joubert, Mhlongo had said Jiba was the best candidate for the NDPP job. Mhlongo has denied the allegations.

Dodgy prosecutorial decisions

Inside the NPA, Jiba also instructed a group of prosecutors who proved willing to prosecute the Booysen case without sufficient evidence. Booysen challenged the charges against him in the Durban high court and, in 2014, Judge Trevor Gorven found that there had not been sufficient evidence to prosecute Booysen. The internal NPA investigation led by Rodney de Kock also found there was insufficient evidence to prosecute Booysen on racketeering charges.

The NPA's prosecution policy states that a decision to prosecute should only be taken in cases where there is sufficient evidence to support a reasonable prospect of a successful prosecution.[29] The NDPP makes this decision, but relies on memorandums summarising the evidence made by the prosecutors. In this case, prosecutors who worked on the Booysen case failed in their duty to ensure that there was enough evidence to prosecute Booysen. The policy also directs prosecutors to consider whether the evidence they gather is reliable and admissible.[30] In the Booysen matter, the De Kock report[31] and the Durban high court judgment held that evidence from various witnesses was either unreliable or inadmissible, rendering it insufficient to support the NPA's case on racketeering charges. Significantly, the De Kock report found that prosecutors had also failed to conduct a proper and complete investigation into the racketeering charges before the prosecution went ahead.

Despite prosecutors in the case failing to produce viable evidence, a memorandum was prepared for Jiba by certain prosecutors on the case to motivate for prosecution. In the end, Jiba made the decision to prosecute. She later faced fraud and perjury charges for authorising the Booysen prosecution without sufficient evidence, and for misrepresenting the evidence she had at the time she made the decision to the Pretoria high court. The fraud and perjury charges were dropped by then NDPP Shaun Abrahams in 2015. Civil society organisation Freedom Under Law challenged this decision in court, and in 2017 the Pretoria high court set aside Abrahams's decision to drop the charges, saying his reasons were 'wrong in law'. The NPA, however, has still not taken a decision on the matter.

In March 2022, right-wing group Afriforum accused the NPA of 'unreasonable delays' in the case against Jiba.[32] Afriforum had previously threatened court action to compel the NPA to make a decision and give effect to the court order. According to Afriforum, the NPA responded, saying the matter had been delegated to the ID, that was finalising its investigation before a decision could be taken by the NDPP. Open Secrets has seen internal NPA documents from 2021 which indicate the NPA has considered re-opening fraud and perjury charges against Jiba.[33] Ultimately, however, it has taken almost five years for the NPA to decide on whether to charge Jiba.

After the case against Booysen was discredited, Jiba was removed from her post as NDPP and was appointed Deputy National Director of Public Prosecutions. She faced a commission of inquiry into her fitness to hold office – chaired by Justice Yvonne Mokgoro – which found that she was unfit for the job and recommended her removal.

When Zuma appointed Shaun Abrahams as NDPP in 2015, some of the prosecutors who had worked on the Booysen case were promoted to greater heights. Abrahams took the decision to charge former Finance Minister Pravin Gordhan with fraud in relation to a pension pay-out agreement he sgined off for former SARS Commissioner Ivan Pillay's early retirement. Abrahams also authorised prosecutions against former Hawks national boss Anwa Dramat and Gauteng former Hawks head Shadrack Sibiya for the alleged illegal rendition of five Zimbabwean nationals. Each of these cases were alleged to have ulterior motives for prosecution, which the prosecutors denied at the Zondo Commission. During his term as Finance Minister from 2015 to 2017, Gordhan became a vocal opponent of Zuma, condemning state capture, while Dramat and Sibiya had been investigating state funding of upgrades to Zuma's private Nkandla residence, and kidnapping and murder charges against former crime intelligence boss Richard Mdluli, a known Zuma ally.[34] The charges against Gordhan were dropped after the NPA said there was no criminal intent in the matter, while charges against Sibiya and Dramat were provisionally withdrawn after the two made representations to the NPA.

Each of these cases, under Abrahams's watch, was moved to the Priority Crimes Litigation Unit (PCLU). In a further affidavit submitted to the Zondo Commission last year, Van Rensburg explained that the PCLU was established by presidential proclamation to prosecute matters generally involving crimes against the state, the state's international obligations and crimes against state security.[35] Although the presidential proclamation allowed the PCLU to investigate and prosecute 'such other priority crimes' as determined by the NDPP, Abrahams's predecessors had confined the investigations and prosecutions of the PCLU to matters such as high treason, the Non-Proliferation of Weapons of Mass Destruction Act, the Nuclear Energy Act and the Protection of Constitutional Democracy Against Terrorist and Related Activities Act and other related cases.[36]

However, once Abrahams came into office, he directed cases to the PCLU which were no longer aimed at the investigation and prosecution of these crimes. Rather, the unit pursued the McBride matter, the SARS 'rogue unit' investigations, the Booysen case and the Nkandla investigation. Van Rensburg explained that there are restrictions on what 'other priority crimes' could be referred to the PCLU, namely they must be of utmost importance and that they had to apply to categories of crimes, rather than individual cases.[37] 'Abrahams' referral of most of the "matters" did not meet any one of these standards,' Van Rensburg submitted to the Zondo Commission.[38]

The work of Jiba and Abrahams was to create an NPA that made decisions for the benefit of Zuma, and which eroded the authority's ability to act in the interests of justice. Under Batohi's leadership, despite promises that justice will finally prevail, the NPA seems to be struggling to address the legacy left by her predecessors. While Jiba and Abrahams have denied that their prosecution decisions were politically motivated, neither appeared before the Zondo Commission to respond to the allegations made against them there.

Time for decisions

In the Zuma era, the NPA became known for making absurd and damaging prosecutorial decisions. Successive NDPPs stopped prosecutions of grand corruption, while pursuing politically motivated cases where there was no evidence. There has been one significant change since Batohi had been appointed by Ramaphosa: The prosecuting authority is now known for making very few decisions.

In the four years since Batohi has been boss, relatively few high-profile state capture cases have been launched, and no successful state capture prosecutions have been completed. Evidence has existed of the auditors, banks, individuals and politicians who enabled state capture, long before the Zondo Commission began, but the NPA has yet to successfully prosecute even one person linked to these corruption allegations. In addition, despite Batohi confirming that she is aware of the allegations against prosecutors who have been accused of wrongdoing, these prosecutors remain employed at the NPA.[39]

The NPA's current failure to make strong decisions, and to prosecute fearlessly – as it is guided to do by the Constitution and the NPA Act – means that it has yet to free itself from the destruction paved by Zuma and his cronies who captured the NDPP seat. This is a crisis that not only affects the integrity of the NPA, but also the rights of South Africans to access justice through the agency that is tasked with safeguarding the law through prosecutorial accountability. It is time for Batohi to deliver on the promises she made in 2019. Deal decisively with corruption and incompetence inside the NPA, and put the crooks in jail.

TWO
Andrew Chauke: Joburg's king of public prosecutions

IN DOWNTOWN JOHANNESBURG, in the midst of the city centre bustle, the NPA's building – known as Innes Chamber – is covered by windows shaped like honeycomb. The building has undergone extensive restoration to return to its former glory,[40] but, deep in its interior, the NPA is grappling to clean up its image. A key reason is the failure of the NPA to act against its own prosecutors who stand accused of prosecuting officials without necessary evidence, and delaying important cases. Among the most senior prosecutors implicated is Andrew Chauke, the NPA's head of public prosecutions in Johannesburg.

As the Director of Public Prosecutions (DPP) in Joburg, Chauke makes decisions on prosecutions that are heard in the Johannesburg high court. These include decisions on state capture cases in the South Gauteng region – such as those linked to the Passenger Rail Agency of South Africa (Prasa) – which are assigned to the DPP's office in collaboration with the Investigating Directorate. Chauke has been the Joburg DPP since 2011. His position is appointed by the President,[41] who has the power to remove him. Chauke maintains he has made responsible decisions,[42] despite facing criticism over his handling of various high-profile cases. His role in the ten-year delay to prosecute former Gauteng Health MEC Brian Hlongwa's R1.2 billion corruption case has been closely scrutinised. Court documents filed by the NPA also raise concerns about his decision-making involving a case of alleged torture against a former senior Hawks official in the North West, Major-General Jan Mabula. In addition, Chauke was a member of the prosecution team who brought the debunked racketeering case against former KwaZulu-Natal Hawks boss Johan Booysen.

Open Secrets sent detailed questions on each of these cases to Chauke in June 2022. NPA regional communications manager Phindi Mjonondwane responded on Chauke's behalf via email.[43] She confirmed that the prosecuting authority is investigating the prosecutors, including Chauke, who had worked on the Booysen case. 'The NPA instituted internal proceedings regarding the role played by the DPP and the prosecutors in this matter and it is prudent to wait for the finalisation of such internal processes,' Mjonondwane said.

The confirmation that Chauke is being investigated by the NPA is an indication that there are serious concerns within the authority over Chauke's conduct. He may face a presidential inquiry into his fitness to hold office if he is found guilty of misconduct. Yet, the Joburg DPP had not been placed on precautionary suspension pending the outcome of the investigation at the time of writing. Instead, he remains seated as the Johannesburg prosecutions boss, where he retains authority over high-profile cases.

The Booysen charges

The previous chapter highlighted the erosion of the NPA in the Zuma era and how the prosecution of former KZN Hawks head Johan Booysen led to declined public trust in the prosecuting authority. Then acting NDPP Nomgcobo Jiba had authorised racketeering and murder charges against Booysen and several other police officers in 2012. At the time, Booysen had been investigating a corruption case which had alleged links to Jacob Zuma's son, Edward. The Durban high court set aside Jiba's decision to prosecute Booysen in 2015, finding there was not sufficient evidence to support the racketeering charges.[44] However, the charges were re-instated in 2016 by then NDPP Shaun Abrahams after the NPA ostensibly found further evidence to support the case. The NPA's own investigation in 2019, undertaken by Rodney de Kock, again found that there had been insufficient evidence and recommended the case be dropped. In 2019, Batohi withdrew the charges in accordance with De Kock's recommendation.[45]

When Jiba first authorised the Booysen prosecution, she assigned a group of prosecutors – including Chauke – to the case.[46] Details from the De Kock report significantly note that Chauke attempted to have the indictment signed without handing over a prosecution memorandum – a document which summarises the evidence in the case and which is required before the indictment can be signed. In June 2012, Chauke and KZN prosecutions boss Simphiwe Mlotshwa clashed via email over the indictment. Chauke, in emails sent by his assistant, insisted that Mlotshwa sign the indictment, while Mlotshwa refused without a prosecution memorandum that detailed the evidence to support the charges.[47] Chauke never sent the memorandum. At the Zondo Commission, he blamed his assistant for the oversight, ignoring the fact that he had the ultimate responsibility to ensure the report was shared with Mlotshwa.[48]

In an affidavit submitted to the Zondo Commission in 2021, Chauke also denied that he had detailed knowledge of the Booysen-related evidence on which the charges were brought. He claimed that he would not have been able to comment on the success of the prosecution as he had not studied the dockets. He distanced himself as only being a 'co-ordinator' on the case who was not responsible for final decisions that were made.[49]

However, the De Kock report contradicts Chauke's claim that he was unaware of the evidence in the case. Between 2012 and 2014, Chauke received four documents that dealt with evidence from the prosecution team, indicating he was aware of some evidence in the case. The Mokgoro Inquiry – a 2019 presidential inquiry which investigated allegations of wrongdoing against Jiba and former senior NPA prosecutor Lawrence Mrwebi – also made findings which contradict Chauke's claims.[50] According to the Mokgoro report, Chauke was responsible for signing and submitting a memorandum in 2012 for the charges against Booysen to be authorised. The application will have contained details of evidence in the case.

The Mokgoro Inquiry also casts doubt on Chauke's role as merely a distanced supervisor, stating that prosecutors had been reporting to him on their daily operations and he signed the 2012 prosecution memorandum on the case. This signifies that he was involved in important details of the case, beyond merely coordinating staff members.

Despite all these findings, the NPA's Mjonondwane reaffirmed to Open Secrets that Chauke's role on the case was 'limited to that of a coordinator at the behest of his then senior, Adv Nomgcobo Jiba'. In response to questions about Chauke's knowledge of the evidence in the case and his reasons for encouraging Mlotshwa to sign the indictment without a prosecution memorandum, Mjonondwane said that the NPA was dealing with these matters internally.

The findings of the Mokgoro Inquiry and the De Kock report are significant because all prosecutors are bound by the NPA's Prosecution Policy, which states that there must be sufficient evidence and a reasonable prospect of a successful prosecution for a case to proceed.[51] In the Booysen case, the Durban high court in 2015 and the De Kock report in 2019 found that neither of these requirements were met. While Chauke was not the lead prosecutor on the case and was not responsible for making the decision to prosecute, he still had a duty as a prosecutor to abide by the NPA's Prosecution Policy.

Chauke's role in questionable prosecutions is not limited to the Booysen case. Recently, Chauke has upset the NPA over his delay to prosecute former North West SAPS Deputy Commissioner Major-General Jan Mabula, who stands accused of authorising and overseeing the kidnapping and torture of detainees in police custody. Mabula was also the lead investigator in the Booysen case.

The Mabula case

In a throwback to the violent and vicious apartheid-style abuses by the Security Branch, Mabula faces charges of kidnapping, assault and extortion along with seven of his colleagues in a case dating back to 2006.[52] Open Secrets has seen a 2018 indictment, where Mabula faces charges of assault to do grievous bodily harm and kidnapping in relation to the alleged torture in detention of Paul Kgoedi, a suspect in a case Mabula's team had been investigating.[53]

Senior officials in the NPA have criticised Chauke's handling of the case, which includes an agreement he made with the accused's lawyers that would add significant delays. Correspondence between BDK Attorneys, who represent the policemen, and Chauke confirm that the parties agreed to postpone the case pending a review from the NDPP. In an email, dated 10 June 2019, Chauke told BDK Attorneys that the indictment would 'not be served on the accused pending your application for review by the office of the NDPP as well as your intended application to the high court'.[54] One year later, in 2020, *News24* reported that Chauke had provisionally withdrawn the summonses against Mabula and his co-accused, pending the finalisation of the indictment and a review of the case as requested by the policemen's lawyers.[55] The concern officials within the NPA raised about the deal was that it would add significant delays to the case.

In November 2020, Rodney de Kock reportedly blasted Chauke's decision in court papers submitted to the Johannesburg high court, stating that Chauke had acted 'contrary to the instructions you received from this [the National Deputy Director of Public Prosecution's] office'.[56] De Kock also pointed out the crushing effect such an agreement would have. 'This would bring the wheels of justice to a dramatic halt and would hold the NPA to ransom for many years to come,' De Kock reportedly submitted in an affidavit before the court.[57]

Mjonondwane said in an email to Open Secrets that Chauke's decision to enter into an agreement with BDK may be reviewed by the NDPP's office. The NPA communications manager added that Chauke believed the agreement was a sound decision. 'The DPP was of the view that it was only rational to give the accused the opportunity to exhaust recourse mechanisms to avert any details that would be of hindrance to the trial,' Mjonondwane said.

Mabula and his co-accused appeared in the Johannesburg high court in May 2022 as trial proceedings began.[58] The lengthy delay, however, is an injustice for which Chauke should be held to account.

Hlongwa and the R1.2 billion corruption scandal

Chauke has also faced criticism over his handling of a case which involves another former high-profile official: Brian Hlongwa. The ten-year delay to prosecute the former Gauteng Health MEC has been widely documented in media coverage. Hlongwa faces allegations of tender corruption amounting to a staggering R1.2 billion in a case that dates back to 2006.[59] The Hlongwa case was at the heart of capture involving healthcare investment advisory firm Regiments Health in the years that preceded its partner company, Regiments Capital, becoming a key player in state capture.

The Special Investigating Unit (SIU) first handed the matter over to the Anti-Corruption Task Team (ACTT) – an inter-ministerial unit that includes members of the NPA and the Hawks – in 2011. The SIU's investigation revealed that the Gauteng Health Department had awarded corrupt tenders for the establishment of an internal project management unit in 2007.[60] According to the SIU, Regiments Health director Niven Pillay had paid R1 million towards the purchase of Hlongwa's R7-million home in Bryanston, Johannesburg, while 3P Consulting boss Richard Payne, who is widely implicated in the scandal, paid a further R1.6 million.[61] This is just one example of how Hlongwa benefited from irregularly awarding the tender to 3P and Regiments Health.

Chauke's office has been working with the NPA's Specialised Commercial Crime Unit on the Hlongwa prosecution. According to NPA documents from 2019, officials inside the NPA were struggling to understand the delays in the case. An NPA report on the case in 2019 stated that 'The [matter] is to date still to be enrolled and it is not clear as to what has been the cause of the delay'. A separate memorandum on the cases, dated 4 June 2019, stated that a forensic auditor contracted to help investigate the financial details of the case in 2011 had still not delivered their findings in 2013. The memorandum said that 'the charges could not be finalised' without the forensic report, which meant that the NDPP could not authorise the prosecution. Eventually, the auditor submitted a report in November 2013, but it was incomplete, insufficient and could not be used as expert evidence in court, according to the NPA memorandum.

In November 2014, another forensic audit specialist was contracted to produce an expert investigative report. However, due to delays in handing over necessary evidence, a breakdown of communication with police and a time lapse in the contract, the new forensic auditor was unable to deliver the report in a reasonable time. Significantly, the NPA memorandum mentioned that Chauke only escalated concerns in February 2016 to request that the NDPP intervene to help finalise the case. This means Chauke waited a significant period of time before he took serious action to stem the delays. Eventually, in August 2018, the new forensic auditor submitted the report. The NPA memorandum stated that the new report was still 'incomplete', however.

In the course of this time, warrants of arrest had been authorised for the arrests of Hlongwa and others in the case. However, in a strange turn of events, the NPA memorandum stated that 'after the matter was discussed with the DPP, Adv. Chauke, and the ACTT [Anti-Corruption Task Team], an instruction was issued for the warrants of arrest to be cancelled for everyone except Richard Payne'. According to the Criminal Procedure Act, only the authority which authorised the arrest warrant – such as a magistrate – can revoke it. Unless a warrant is revoked, it must be acted upon and executed.

Hlongwa finally appeared in the Johannesburg magistrate's court in December 2021 on charges related to violating the Prevention of Organised Crime Act – ten years after the case landed with the NPA.[62] Mjonondwane stated that the delays in the case could not be solely attributed to Chauke's office, saying that the case had been moved to the Priority Crimes Litigation Unit, before it was returned to Chauke's office in 2019. 'There were no undue delays from the prosecution team and or the DPP,' Mjonondwane said. Regarding any role Chauke potentially held in the decision for the warrants of arrest to be cancelled, Mjonondwane said: 'This relates to internal matters which are subject to internal processes.'

Many of these cases which have been on Chauke's desk for a number of years have yet to be finalised. Mjonondwane has said that no in-depth comment can be made on these cases, because they are still ongoing. In the meantime, Chauke has not faced any serious consequence for his role in these delays, but there is some indication that the NPA has considered holding him accountable for the Booysen prosecution.

Time for justice

The NPA's confirmation that it is conducting an internal investigation into Chauke indicates that there are serious concerns about his conduct as the Joburg DPP. Despite these concerns, Chauke remains Joburg's public prosecutions boss. In that position, he continues to make important decisions that impact on which prosecutions are pursued and how they are conducted. These include decisions on state capture cases, where there is an urgent need for prosecutions and convictions to hold perpetrators of corruption to account.

There is arguably enough in Chauke's track record for the prosecuting authority to place him on precautionary suspension pending the outcome of its investigation. If its own investigation suggests Chauke is guilty of misconduct, it is imperative that the NPA also request that the Presidency appoint a commission of inquiry into Chauke's fitness to occupy the important office he holds.

THREE

Sello Maema: The NPA's deputy prosecutions boss in the North West

A KEY CAUSE OF THE CRISIS in public confidence in the NPA is the fact that prosecutors instituted and pursued prosecutions – without sufficient evidence – against officials who investigated state capture-linked cases. Sello Maema is one the prosecutor inside the NPA who led three of the authority's most questionable cases when it was under the leadership of Nomgcobo Jiba and later Shaun Abrahams.

Maema is the current Deputy Director of Public Prosecutions in the North West, and his prosecutions history dates to 1995. He led the prosecutions on three high-profile cases that weakened public confidence in the NPA. They include the racketeering charges against former KwaZulu-Natal Hawks boss Johan Booysen, the fraud case against former Independent Police Investigative Directorate head Robert McBride and the prosecution of former SARS officials falsely implicated in the alleged 'rogue unit' case. The 'rogue unit' case involved allegations that former SARS officials Ivan Pillay, Johann van Loggerenberg and Andries Janse van Rensburg had operated an illegal clandestine unit in SARS that bugged the NPA's offices.

Each of these cases have since been discredited, but Maema has not faced any consequences for his role in these prosecutions. Open Secrets sent detailed questions to Maema regarding the allegations against him in each case. He responded by saying he could not provide answers to the questions without the approval of NDPP Shamila Batohi. 'Section 41(6) of the NPA Act 32 of 1998 requires written authorisation from the National Director before disclosure of any information that came to your knowledge in the performance of your functions, l have no such authorization & cannot do so, until there is authorization, l cannot assist you,'[63] Maema said.

The NPA confirmed to Open Secrets in June 2022 that Maema – along with Andrew Chauke, whose role in delaying high-profile cases is discussed in the previous chapter – is the subject of an internal NPA investigation for his role in the Booysen case, but he has not been placed on precautionary suspension pending the outcome of the investigation. Instead, he remains the NPA's second-in-command in the North West, despite a track record of questionable decisions which have had grave consequences.

The failed Booysen prosecution

Maema played a key role in the Booysen prosecution as the lead prosecutor on the case.[64] The prosecution involved charges of racketeering and extrajudicial killings laid against Booysen and several other police officers in KwaZulu-Natal. At the time that the charges against Booysen were authorised, the KZN Hawks boss was investigating a R60 million corruption case against Thoshan Panday, a dubious businessman linked to Jacob Zuma's son, Edward.[65] The prosecution against Booysen delayed the Panday investigation, but in 2020 Panday was finally charged with corruption, money laundering, fraud and racketeering, signifying that the Hawks investigation under Booysen was important.

The prosecution was discredited by the Durban high court and an internal NPA investigation, both finding that there was insufficient evidence to support it. The NPA's investigation by Rodney de Kock reported that Maema was involved in the daily operations of the case and had access to the evidence.[66] His role in preparing a prosecution memorandum for then NDPP Shaun Abrahams has come under scrutiny. The prosecution memorandum is an important document prosecutors prepare for the NDPP that explains the evidence in the case. The NDPP uses this document to decide if there is enough evidence to authorise a prosecution.

On 17 August 2015, Maema signed a prosecution memorandum that recorded detailed evidence in the case to motivate Abrahams to approve racketeering charges against Booysen. The memorandum was submitted to Abrahams on 19 August 2015. At the time, however, Abrahams stated that there was insufficient evidence to bring charges against Booysen and instructed the prosecutors to investigate the case further.[67]

A new memorandum was submitted to Abrahams in October 2015, but still dissatisfied, the NDPP instructed Maema and a colleague, Dawood Adam, to interview a witness and former policeman Ari Danikas, who resided in Greece. Danikas's statement was about incidents of police violence that preceded the Booysen charges, but which prosecutors hoped would help prove the Booysen case. Upon returning to South Africa, Maema and Adam verbally briefed Abrahams on the trip and the NDPP approved racketeering charges against Booysen in February 2016.[68]

Both Abrahams and Maema stated that the October 2015 memorandum was amended to include the new evidence. However, the De Kock report found that while the memorandum had been edited, these edits were not of substance, and no new evidence had been introduced to the October 2015 memorandum. This contradicts the claim that Maema found new and sufficient evidence to prosecute Booysen on racketeering charges. 'We are of the view that these changes to the October Memorandum were merely cosmetic changes made to the memorandum based on information and evidence already in possession of the prosecution,' the De Kock report states.[69]

Abrahams stated that the October 2015 memorandum, specifically Maema's inputs into the report and the Danikas statement, were some of the key documents that he relied upon to authorise the racketeering charges against Booysen. However, Maema, in an email to Danikas's lawyer, stated that he was concerned the Greek national had not made full disclosures in his statement and that the South African prosecuting authorities were unconvinced that Danikas's evidence would 'assist the state['s] case in any way'.[70] It is, therefore, clear that Maema knew that Danikas's evidence might not be sufficient to support the charges, yet the statement was still used to ostensibly substantiate the Booysen charges.

According to the De Kock report, Maema made another vital admission in an email dated 24 April 2019: a statement in English from Danikas had never been lawfully obtained. Instead, according to Maema's email, Danikas's signature was 'superimposed' on the English version.[71] In his email, Maema noted that Danikas had refused to sign the English translation because it contained errors, according to the report. Danikas later stated that he had never been requested to sign the English version.[72] The Booysen case had initially been prosecuted in 2012. By 2019, Maema had still not been able to obtain an English statement from Danikas. Later that year, in July, Batohi withdrew charges after the De Kock investigation was completed.

Maema's conduct in obtaining the Danikas evidence alone provides a strong basis for the NPA to investigate him for violating the NPA's Prosecution Policy. The policy states that a prosecutor can only proceed with a case if there is sufficient and admissible evidence, and a reasonable prospect of successful prosecution. Owing in part to Maema's representation of the evidence, Abrahams decided to authorise charges of racketeering against Booysen, saying the Danikas statement was a key piece of new evidence. Yet, details contained in the De Kock report show that Maema would have known that the Danikas statement was incomplete and inadmissible, and, therefore, could not be used to prove the charges.

The NPA, under Shamila Batohi's leadership, has been slow to act in response to allegations of misconduct involving Maema. The NPA's leadership has been in place for almost four years, but it has yet to finalise its internal investigation on Maema and other prosecutors involved in the Booysen case. While the NPA conducts its internal investigation, there is a possibility that Maema may face more serious criminal charges over his role in the Booysen case.

The criminal charges

Booysen – the subject of the racketeering charges brought by the NPA – opened a case against Maema with the Hawks in 2016 and referred the matter to the Investigating Directorate (ID) of the NPA in 2019. In his complaint to the Hawks and the ID, Booysen stated that Maema should be charged with fraud for his role in misrepresenting evidence to Abrahams in the prosecution memoranda he signed in August 2015 and October 2015.[73] In 2021, Booysen wrote to the NPA to request feedback on the status of the complaints he had made. To date, it remains unclear if the Hawks or the ID have investigated the complaints.

In an affidavit to the Zondo Commission, Maema stated that he was aware a case had been opened against him, but he had not been approached by any investigating officers and did not know the status of the investigation.[74] Maema's affidavit and Booysen's correspondence with the NPA are clear indications that the NPA is aware a criminal case has been opened against one of their most senior prosecutors in North West. Yet, the prosecuting authority has still not moved to suspend Maema pending an outcome of the investigation, and there is no evidence they have urged the Hawks to investigate the charges.

Johan Booysen submitted an affidavit to the Zondo Commission alleging that a series of prosecutors – including Maema – were 'captured'. In response, lawyers representing these prosecutors submitted a document recording their version of events to the Zondo Commission. The document was submitted after the prosecutors, including Maema, abandoned an application to cross-examine Booysen and instead opted to have their versions read into the record of the commission. The document stated that the Department of Justice was dealing with the Danikas statement at the time the signature may have been superimposed, as it was the Justice Department that had arranged for the statement to be translated from Greek into English. The document read: 'The allegations sought to be imputed to Maema in this regard demonstrate the extent to which Booysen can go in placing untruthful information before the Court.'[75]

In an affidavit submitted to the Zondo Commission, Maema denied Booysen's allegations, saying they were 'without merit' and that there 'still is prima facie evidence' implicating Booysen in the racketeering charges.[76] Maema went on to say that NDPP Batohi's decision to drop the charges against Booysen and his co-accused was 'unlawful', 'irrational' and 'subvert[ed] the rule of law'.[77] He added that Booysen's claim about his role in writing the prosecution memoranda was misleading as several prosecutors and investigators were involved in the process. While Maema confirmed he signed the documents, he said it was only in his capacity as the team leader.[78]

However, Maema is now the subject of an internal NPA investigation for his role in the Booysen saga. The NPA's investigation gives impetus to questions raised over Maema's conduct in the Booysen prosecution. However, despite the concerns raised at the NPA, Maema has not been placed on precautionary suspension and remains in his position as North West DDPP. It is vital that the NPA take action to suspend Maema pending the outcome of the investigation and that Maema is dismissed if he is found guilty of misconduct. Maema's role in prosecutions of the SARS 'rogue unit' and McBride cases give further urgency for the investigations into his conduct to be completed.

The McBride and SARS cases

In 2016, former Independent Police Investigative Directorate (IPID) boss Robert McBride was accused of fraudulently amending a report that cleared senior Hawks officials Anwa Dramat and Shadrack Sibiya of wrongdoing in relation to the alleged illegal rendition of Zimbabwean nationals. He also faced charges of defeating the ends of justice. McBride told the Zondo Commission that there was no basis for the fraud charges against him in relation to his amendments to the IPID report. Maema was the lead prosecutor on the case.

In an affidavit to the state capture inquiry, McBride said, 'I have already expressed my concern that Advocate Sello Maema ("Maema") saw fit to prosecute us in respect of the rendition matter, as I know that there was not a shred of evidence to substantiate his decision to charge us with fraud and defeating the ends of justice (or any other charges).'[79] In 2016, just months after announcing the charges, the NPA announced it was dropping the charges against McBride. At the time, NPA spokesperson Luvuyo Mfaku said that the state could not prove a case of fraud against McBride. Mfaku said, 'The charges have been withdrawn after consultation with witnesses. The state would be unable to prove its case beyond any reasonable doubt'.[80]

The NPA's statement showed the McBride case to be yet another example of a prosecution led by Maema that was not supported by sufficient evidence – a violation of the NPA's Prosecution Policy. Maema, however, told the Zondo Commission that, at the time the decision was taken to prosecute McBride and his co-accused, it had been 'justified'.[81] Maema stated in his affidavit that McBride and his co-accused made changes to the IPID report 'solely with the intention of exonerating Dramat and Sibiya'.[82] This formed a large part of the reason the prosecution went ahead, according to Maema. While Maema maintained in his affidavit to the Zondo Commission that the charges against Dramat and Sibiya were valid, the NPA leadership, in contradiction to Maema's claims, found it necessary to drop the charges five years ago.

The timing of the investigation into the McBride matter is significant as it occurred in a politically charged environment. McBride had been investigating corruption charges against former acting National Police Commissioner Khomotso Phahlane, who had been appointed to the top job by Jacob Zuma in 2015. Dramat and Sibiya had also been working on cases that posed a challenge to Zuma's interests. They had been investigating the case against former crime intelligence boss Richard Mdluli, a Zuma ally, over murder charges related to a 1999 case, and Dramat had taken a decision to investigate upgrades to Zuma's Nkandla homestead. The rendition charges against them were brought in this context, and McBride's amended report posed a challenge to the charges that appeared to be trumped up to push Dramat and Sibiya out of the Hawks.

In addition to the Booysen and McBride cases, Maema was also the lead prosecutor on the SARS 'rogue unit' case, in which SARS officials Ivan Pillay, Johann van Loggerenberg and Andries Janse van Rensburg were accused of operating an illegal clandestine unit in SARS that bugged the NPA's offices. The tax officials were members of the enforcement department at SARS – namely, the High Risk Investigation Unit – which had powers to investigate tax compliance of wealthy, high-profile and politically connected individuals, as well as those linked to organised crime and industries like tobacco. Former

SARS Commissioner Tom Moyane had 'ordered the disbandment of the High Risk Investigation Unit, and the termination of surveillance of those who were under investigation by the unit,' according to the first interim report of the Nugent Commission – a presidential commission of inquiry which investigated wrongdoing at SARS in 2018.[83]

Moyane's efforts to disband the unit indicate that it was part of concerted efforts to undermine SARS. Reports of the 'rogue unit' emerged soon after Tom Moyane became SARS commissioner. As discussed in the section of this book dealing with consultants, the Zondo Commission found that Moyane colluded with consulting firm Bain & Company and Zuma to dismantle SARS. The charges against the SARS officials have since been debunked, and in 2020, Batohi announced she was dropping the case against the trio after they had made representations to the NPA. The *Sunday Times*, that carried stories about the 'rogue unit', have since apologised and admitted that the stories were false.

While Maema defended the case as legitimate at the Zondo Commission, NPA spokesperson Bulelwa Makeke confirmed, in 2020, that an internal NPA panel had reviewed the case and found the evidence would not support a reasonable prospect of a successful prosecution.[84] Makeke said, 'After a careful assessment of the evidence and other relevant material, the unanimous conclusion of the panel in respect of all counts, is that there are no reasonable prospects of a successful prosecution.'[85]

The SARS and McBride matters were important cases that defined a loss of public trust in the NPA as speculation mounted that these cases were pursued for ulterior motives. In both cases, the NPA has admitted that the evidence did not support the charges which Maema attempted to bring against the accused, who at the time were investigating important corruption cases. There is little doubt that these prosecutions have had dire consequences for those who attempted to investigate and prosecute corruption. Booysen and McBride are no longer employed by their former agencies, and many of the important cases they were working on have taken years to reach court. Both Panday and Phahlane are facing charges in court in connection with allegations of impropriety that Booysen and McBride had been investigating. But these cases have faced delays because of the now debunked and dropped charges against McBride and Booysen.

Holding Maema to account

The persistent attempts to push for the prosecution of Booysen, McBride and the SARS officials indicate that Maema may have abused his role as a senior prosecutor, and he should be fully investigated for repeatedly prosecuting cases without sufficient evidence. The NPA's internal investigation must determine if Maema violated the authority's Prosecution Policy. In addition, it should urge the Hawks to investigate the case opened by Booysen to determine if Maema violated the law by fraudulently misrepresenting evidence to Abrahams.

While these investigations take place, Maema should be placed on precautionary suspension from his office as DDPP in the North West until it is clear he is fit to remain in office. It is unclear why the NPA has not yet taken such steps, when it is in the urgent interests of justice for it to employ reliable and credible prosecutors.

We have not forgotten

YOU HAVE NOW MET some of the politicians, CEOs, arms dealers, mega corporations, accountants and lawyers, whom we call the Unaccountables. Their conduct spans a wide range: from unambiguous criminality, to complicity in the schemes of others and, in some instances the failure to do their jobs to hold others unaccountable. Yet, they are unified in a shared desire – that their role in illicit activity be forgotten. Whether you are a senior politician or the CEO of a global consulting firm, the response to evidence of involvement in economic crimes is often the same: deny, obfuscate and delay. They hope that the passing of time, new scandals and weak law enforcement will guarantee them impunity. This is why the tagline of Open Secrets's Unaccountables investigations is: 'We have not forgotten.' It is a reminder to those who remain unaccountable that the public has the evidence of what they've done, and that efforts to challenge their impunity will continue. We believe that there is power in continuing to expose the role of the powerful in corruption and economic crimes that impact millions of people.

If you have read all thirty-five investigations in this book, you will likely be angry as you read this conclusion, but you should not feel hopeless. While this book is a testament to impunity and a fundamental failure to achieve substantive justice, it also points to the routes to accountability and justice. These remain possible. Indeed, they are essential. We cannot build a more just society nor fair democracy without challenging the powerful and holding them to account for their crimes. While the individual chapters in this book included recommendations for how these actors can be held accountable, they also helped reveal the bigger patterns of changes and reforms that are urgently needed to build a culture of accountability, rather than impunity.

Rebuild independent law enforcement to prosecute now!

We believe it is essential to start where this book ends, that is, to address the long-term failure to build a fierce and independent National Prosecuting Authority (NPA). The NPA has been subject to relentless political interference since its inception, which has led to long periods of instability, and periods where the authority acted in the interests of those accused of economic crime. It is paramount that the new leadership of the NPA acts swiftly to rid the institution of those who are accused of wrongdoing, or failing to do their jobs. It must also act swiftly to prosecute all individuals and companies implicated in economic crimes, including state capture. Only these actions will rebuild public trust in the institution whose job is to serve the public.

While the NPA faces this task, it is essential that government offers adequate support. This includes urgent reforms at the police to ensure that they are able to contribute to the work of the NPA, rather than being an obstacle to accountability. Further, continued pressure to cut budgets of the NPA and other law enforcement agencies are counter-productive and harmful. It is ironic that these pressures are the result of entrenched corruption that has looted the state and led to soaring public debt. Yet, the failure of law enforcement agencies to track and recover those looted funds is hindered by the failure to ensure that those agencies have the skills and resources required to do this work. Investing in these agencies is the only way to ensure their ability to deliver accountability and recover stolen assets in the long term.

Reform the law

While strengthening law enforcement is essential, many of the chapters in this book also reveal the gaps in the law, particularly when it comes to holding larger corporations to account. These gaps exist at a domestic and international level. For example, the crimes of state capture simply would not have been possible without South Africa's lax laws on beneficial ownership, which still allow shell companies to be set up and operate with the true owners hidden from sight. A bill introducing a beneficial ownership registry to South African law is before Parliament in 2022, and it is essential that the final version of this law is strong and entrenches public accessibility to this information. Further, it is clear that South Africa's anti-money laundering laws and their enforcement is completely inadequate. This has allowed for those engaged in economic and other crimes to launder the proceeds of those crimes through South Africa's financial sector, either without detection, or without sanction.[1] It has also meant that South Africa's banks have joined their global peers as key nodes in the movement of illicit money. It is imperative that stricter laws and monitoring are introduced urgently in order to stop this.

Yet, changes at home will not be enough. The crimes discussed in this book, from apartheid sanctions busting to contemporary state capture, all have global dimensions. In particular, they were enabled by professionals, politicians and corporations in the secrecy jurisdictions of the world. Apartheid's bankers sat in Luxembourg, while the Gupta network predominantly relied on banks and front companies in the secrecy centres of London, Dubai and Hong Kong. The reality is that private lawyers, consultants, accountants and bankers have co-created a global financial system predicated on secrecy, tax evasion and the absence of accountability. This system is integral not only to grand corruption around the world, but also the larger scandal of illicit financial flows that bleed poorer countries to the benefit of wealthy tax havens. As a result, the system is a key contributor to inequality. The countries that benefit from this system, like the United Arab Emirates, also become the boltholes for fugitives from justice when their schemes come crashing down, as the Guptas have shown.

The South African government should be showing leadership on the international stage to challenge the status quo in this regard. It should be a priority to direct our diplomatic efforts to international legal and other reforms to challenge secrecy. This must including building and improving mechanisms that make it easier to track and recover stolen assets, and to access the information (whether it is bank account data or beneficial ownership information) that is needed to hold individuals and companies to account for their crimes.

Support whistleblowers and investigators

As indicated in the introduction, our writing through much of this book relied heavily on whistleblowers who stood up to wrong-doing and provided vital information to the public that revealed malfeasance. For example, our work on the unlawful cancellation of pension funds would not have been possible without whistleblowers from the financial sector regulator and the companies involved. They paid a heavy price for speaking out about the scandal that they discovered. Similarly, our profiles on state capture all ultimately rely on the extensive information revealed by a number of whistleblowers who undertook great risks to speak out about the extent of the criminality that they witnessed. Similarly, they have faced grave costs for doing so. Too often, whistleblowers are hounded out of work, ostracised by their industries, abandoned by the state and face threats and attacks – legal and otherwise. Some of this can be remedied by strengthening our laws to better protect whistleblowers. But it will take more than that; both the state and private companies will have to change a culture that rewards looking the other way and punishes those who speak out when they see something is wrong.

It is too easy to forget that many of these good people are, or were, employees in the private and public sector, and that they and others represent the best South Africa has to offer. It is easy to forget the millions of ordinary folks who grind away at work on a daily basis in business and the public sector – and do so with integrity. They may not seem like revolutionaries – but their actions remind us that another way – and maybe even another world – is possible. For things to change and people's lives to improve and for our planet to recover from the ravages of war, poverty and climate violence, we have to change the rules of the game, challenge the system and confront the powerful. This will take the work of many and not only of the few, and hence we should stand in solidarity with people who speak out and expose injustice with integrity.

Our investigations are also deeply reliant on the outstanding investigative and analytical work done by investigative journalists, activists and others in civil society. Together, they protect the public's right to truth, and they also provide us with the information we need to hold the powerful to account and shine a light on their conduct. Open Secrets is proud to try and contribute to this work. Yet, it is also a time of great upheaval and uncertainty for journalists and for many in civil society. It is vital that, collectively, we stand up and reject the attacks by the powerful politicians and corporations on those who work to expose them and hold them to account. It is also important that we – wherever we can – support those who do this work by paying for the media we consume when we are able to, and by standing in solidarity with those whose work we so value.

The thirty-five individuals, companies and institutions profiled in this book have up to now escaped substantive justice for their role in economic crimes and other activities that have had significant human cost. Some have enjoyed impunity for forty years, some for twenty, and some have just recently been implicated in their crimes. Regardless, it remains urgent that they are all held to account. It also remains possible to do so, and until then we will continue to investigate and advocate for accountability. Our message to all of those implicated is simple: we have not forgotten. Justice may grind slowly, but it grinds.

Acknowledgements

WE RELY ON PARTNERS to catch the bad guys.

Open Secrets relies on the support of individuals and organisations who provide solidarity, time, skills and funding. We acknowledge all of you. Our work is built on the shoulders of others. Thank you to the individuals and organisations who have funded Open Secrets since 2017; as we do not accept funding from governments or corporations, your assistance has been invaluable. Thank you in particular to the Claude Leon Foundation, Heinrich Boell Foundation for Southern Africa, Joffe Charitable Trust, Luminate, Open Society Foundation for South Africa, Open Society Foundation Human Rights Initiative and Sigrid Rausing Trust.

We are proud that the Daily Maverick made its pages available to publish the first draft of the Unaccountable profiles starting in November 2019. Thanks also to our media lawyer Zanele Mbuyisa for guiding us through minefields.

Small feisty organisations work best with publishers who match our enthusiasm for this work. Thanks to the inspiring team at Jacana, led by Bridget Impey and Maggie Davey.

This book is a labour of a collective effort. The Open Secrets team provides the energy and commitment to go where it's hard. We are a team of lawyers, operations staff, campaigners and investigators working from our office in Community House in Salt River. Sometimes, all it takes is a small group of people, good coffee and an office pooch to open our secrets. Without challenging profit and power, we will not establish truth and ensure justice.

Notes

Challenging impunity: The Unaccountables

1   Henley and Partners, *Africa Wealth Report*, April 2022. Available at: https://www.henleyglobal.com/download/africa-wealth-report-2022, accessed 30 August 2022.
2   Henley and Partners, *Africa Wealth Report*.
3   Aroop Chatterjee, Léo Czajka and Amory Gethin, 'Estimating the distribution of household wealth in South Africa', Southern Centre for Inequality Studies and World Inequality Lab, WID. world Working Paper 2020/06, April 2020.
4   Chatterjee, Czajka and Gethin, 'Estimating the distribution of household wealth in South Africa'.
5   National Treasury, 'Draft Anti-Poverty Strategy', September 2021. Available: https://www.groundup.org.za/media/uploads/documents/abridged_anti-poverty_strategy.pdf, accessed 30 August 2022.

Section 1: Apartheid Profiteers

1   SABC News, 'FW de Klerk's last words to South Africans', 11 November 2021. Available at: https://www.youtube.com/watch?v=snmxTq9rBG0.
2   SABC News, 'FW de Klerk's last words to South Africans', 11 November 2021. Available at: https://www.youtube.com/watch?v=snmxTq9rBG0.
3   Hennie van Vuuren, *Apartheid Guns and Money: A Tale of Profit*, Jacana Media, 2017, pp. 114–118.
4   Jenni Evans, 'He was a very private man, says FW de Klerk's neighbors', *News 24*, 11 November 2021. Available at: https://www.news24.com/news24/southafrica/news/he-was-a-very-private-man-fw-de-klerks-

neighbour-20211111.

5   Evans, 'He was a very private man, says FW de Klerk's neighbors'.
6   Hennie van Vuuren, *Apartheid Guns and Money: A Tale of Profit*, Jacana Media, 2017.
7   Letter from HJ van Wijk to DE Cooper (Barlow Rand), 6 October 1988, University of the Free State, Archive for Contemporary Affairs (PV 734, 4/A/5/1 Vol. 1, 1987–1988, FW de Klerk).
8   Letter from HJ van Wijk to DE Cooper (Barlow Rand), 6 October 1988, University of the Free State, Archive for Contemporary Affairs (PV 734, 4/A/5/1 Vol. 1, 1987–1988, FW de Klerk).
9   Letter from Dr FJ du Plessis (Sanlam) to PW Botha, 2 September 1983, University of the Free State, Archive for Contemporary Affairs (PV 203, A1/2/27, 1983, PW Botha).
10 Letter from PW Botha to Dr FJ du Plessis (Sanlam), 14 September 1983, University of the Free State, Archive for Contemporary Affairs (PV 203, A1/2/27, 1983, PW Botha).
11 Letter from Kent Durr to FW de Klerk, 25 August 1989, University of the Free State, Archive for Contemporary Affairs (PV 734, 4/1/5/2 Vol. 2, 1989–1990, FW de Klerk).
12 Letter from Kent Durr to FW de Klerk, 25 August 1989, University of the Free State, Archive for Contemporary Affairs (PV 734, 4/1/5/2 Vol. 2, 1989–1990, FW de Klerk).
13 Letter from B Lubner (PGSI) to PW Botha, 23 June 1982, University of the Free State, Archive for Contemporary Affairs (PV 203, C3/15/2, 1981–1982, PW Botha).
14 Letter from B Lubner (PGSI) to PW Botha, 23 June 1982, University of the Free State, Archive for Contemporary Affairs (PV 203, C3/15/2, 1981–1982, PW Botha).
15 Letter from B Slome (Tedelex) to PW Botha, 25 June 1984, University of the Free State, Archive for Contemporary Affairs (PV 203, C3/15/3, 1983–1984, PW Botha).
16 Record of Income to the Federale Raad, 20 August 1987, University of the Free State, Archive for Contemporary Affairs (PV 203, PS2/3/4, 1986–1988, PW Botha).
17 Letter from WP Venter (Altech) to FW de Klerk, 22 September 1982, University of the Free State, Archive for Contemporary Affairs (PV 203, C3/15/2, 1981–1982, PW Botha).
18 Minutes of meeting of the National Party Finance Committee of the Transvaal, 17 October 1985, DW Steyn Private Papers.

19 Minutes of meeting of the National Party Finance Committee of the Transvaal, 17 October 1985, DW Steyn Private Papers.
20 Record of Income to the Federale Raad, 20 August 1987, University of the Free State, Archive for Contemporary Affairs (PV 203, PS2/3/4, 1986–1988, PW Botha).
21 Truth and Reconciliation Commission Report, vol. 6, section 2, chapter 5, 'Reparations and the business sector'.
22 Awonke Baba, 'The corruption potential created by absence of political party funding regulation is laid bare by Zondo', *Daly Maverick*, 20 January 2022. Available at: https://www.dailymaverick.co.za/opinionista/2022-01-20-the-corruption-potential-created-by-absence-of-political-party-funding-regulation-is-laid-bare-by-zondo/, accessed 29 August 2022.
23 Andrea Murphy and Isabel Contreras (eds), *The Forbes Global 2000 in 2022*, Forbes, 12 May 2022. Available at: https://www.forbes.com/lists/global2000/?sh=24e3619b5ac0, accessed 29 August 2022.
24 Naspers Profile, *Forbes*, 2022. Available at: https://www.forbes.com/companies/naspers/?sh=1f1d5b067170.
25 Letter from PJ Cillié (Nasionale Pers) to PW Botha, 23 January 1985, University of the Free State, Archive for Contemporary Affairs (PV 203, A1/2/38, 1984 December – 1985 January, PW Botha).
26 Letter from PW Botha to PJ Cillié (Nasionale Pers), 9 October 1981, University of the Free State, Archive for Contemporary Affairs (PV 203, A1/2/14, 1981 October – 1981 November, PW Botha).
27 Letter from PW Botha to PJ Cillié (Nasionale Pers), 9 October 1981, University of the Free State, Archive for Contemporary Affairs (PV 203, A1/2/14, 1981 October – 1981 November, PW Botha).
28 Letter from PW Botha to PJ Cillié (Nasionale Pers), 9 October 1981, University of the Free State, Archive for Contemporary Affairs (PV 203, A1/2/14, 1981 October – 1981 November, PW Botha).
29 Letter from PW Botha to PJ Cillié (Nasionale Pers), 9 October 1981, University of the Free State, Archive for Contemporary Affairs (PV 203, A1/2/14, 1981 October – 1981 November, PW Botha).
30 Minutes, NP of Transvaal Executive Management, Pretoria, 18 October 1984, DW Steyn Private Papers.
31 Correspondence between FW de Klerk and T Vosloo (Nasionale Pers), 17 August – 5 September 1989, University of the Free State, Archive for Contemporary Affairs (PV 734, 4/1/5/2 Vol. 2, 1989–1990, FW de Klerk).
32 Correspondence between FW de Klerk and T Vosloo (Nasionale Pers),

17 August – 5 September 1989, University of the Free State, Archive for Contemporary Affairs (PV 734, 4/1/5/2 Vol. 2, 1989–1990, FW de Klerk).
33   Document on Project RBC Sent from Ton Vosloo (Nasionale Pers) to PW Botha, 25 April 1984, University of the Free State, Archive for Contemporary Affairs (PV 203, B1/6, 1985 June–July, PW Botha).
34   Report on the Awarding of the Contract for Subscription Television, 14 March 1985, University of the Free State, Archive for Contemporary Affairs (PV 203, PS 6/6/3, 1985, PW Botha).
35   Document on Project RBC Sent from Ton Vosloo (Nasionale Pers) to PW Botha, 25 April 1984, University of the Free State, Archive for Contemporary Affairs (PV 203, B1/6, 1985 June–July, PW Botha).
36   Gareth van Zyl, (31 May 2016) 'Naspers market cap hits R1 trillion', Fin24 Tech.
37   Ton Vosloo, *Across Boundries: A life in the media at a time of change*, Jonathan Ball Publishers, 2018.
38   Kerry Dolan and Chase Peterson-Withorn *Forbes Billionaires List – the Richest in 2022*, 2022, Forbes, Available at: https://www.forbes.com/billionaires/, accessed 29 August 2022.
39   John Matisonn, *God, Spies and Lies*, Missing Ink, 2015, p. 305.
40   Anton Harber, Ton Vosloo's book has lessons for today's political journalists who actively take sides, *Daily Maverick*, 8 October 2018, Available at: https://www.dailymaverick.co.za/article/2018-10-08-ton-vosloos-book-has-lessons-for-todays-political-journalists-who-actively-take-sides/, accessed 29 August 2022.
41   Jan Johannes Strydom and Ton Vosloo, *Oupa Jan se boek: Die interneringsjare van Jan Johannes Strydom: gedenkboek by geleentheid van sy 80ste verjaardag op 9 Junie 2000*.
42   Anton Steenkamp, 'Regter se tronkverlede', *Vrye Weekblad*, 17 February 1989.
43   Jan Johannes Strydom and Ton Vosloo, *Oupa Jan se boek: Die interneringsjare van Jan Johannes Strydom: gedenkboek by geleentheid van sy 80ste verjaardag op 9 Junie 2000*, p. 5.
44   Sibusiso Tshabalala, 'What's missing? Naspers' late half-apology for apartheid', *The Journalist*, July 2015. Available at: www.thejournalist.org.za.
45   Karin Brynard, 'The media and the TRC: My individual yes', *Rhodes Journalism Review*, November 1997, p. 33.
46   Jenna Etheridge, 'Naspers apologises for its role in apartheid', *News24*, 25 July 2015, Available: https://www.news24.com/News24/Naspers-apologises-for-its-role-in-apartheid-20150725, accessed 29 August 2022.

47 John Christensen, 'Dirty money flows distort our economy and corrupt democracy', *The Guardian*, 20 May 2007.
48 Swissinfo.ch, 'Swiss lift restrictions on South Africa archives', 20 June 2014, Available at: https://www.swissinfo.ch/eng/apartheid-dealings_swiss-lift-restrictions-on-south-africa-archives/38828730?utm_campaign=teaser-inchannel&utm_source=swissinfoch&utm_medium=display&utm_content=o, accessed 29 August 2022.
49 Available at: www.khulumani.net/khulumani/statements/item/826-joint-pressrelease-us-circuit-court-dismisses-apartheid-litigation.html.
50 Correspondence from the Swiss Department of Foreign Affairs to the Mission in Pretoria, 4 February 1960, Federal Archives of Switzerland (E2200.178#2000/44#41*, 244.0, 8, Sitzverlegung schweizerischer Firmen, 1960–1982).
51 Correspondence to Minister R Kohli, Secretary General of Political Department in Swiss Department of Foreign Affairs, 5 May 1960, Federal Archives of Switzerland (E2200.178#2000/44#41*, 244.0, 8, Sitzverlegung schweizerischer Firmen, 1960–1982).
52 Memorandum on the 'Emergency Agreement for the South African Trust Fund', Sent to the Swiss Embassy in Pretoria, 11 November 1982, Federal Archives of Switzerland (E2200.178#2000/44#41*, 244.0, 8, Sitzverlegung schweizerischer Firmen, 1960–1982).
53 Letter from Francois EP Jeannerat (UBS) to Ambassador CH Bruggmann, Swiss Embassy Pretoria, 9 December 1982, Federal Archives of Switzerland (E2200.178#2000/44#41*, 244.0, 8, Sitzverlegung schweizerischer Firmen, 1960–1982).
54 Interview with Barend du Plessis, Pretoria, 6 June 2016.
55 Interview with Barend du Plessis, Pretoria, 6 June 2016.
56 Noopur Tiwari, 'Switzerland's biggest political party threatens to derail India's plan to get black money data', *The Wire*, 14 August 2017. Available at: https://thewire.in/banking/switzerland-india-black-money-data-swap, accessed 29 August 2022.
57 Van Vuuren, *Apartheid Guns and Money*, p. 160.
58 Terry Gourvish (ed), *Business and Politics in Europe: 1900–1970*, Cambridge University Press, 2003.
59 Van Vuuren, *Apartheid Guns and Money*, p. 160.
60 Clipping from Knack magazine titled 'Protea beklim die berg', 26 October 1977, KADOC, Archief Walter de Bock (Centraal en Zuidelijk Afrika, Zuid-Afrika, 5.06, 1, 1981–1988).
61 Minutes of Eurosa Board Meeting, 14 July 1980, KADOC, Archief

André Vlerick (Diverse engagementen en persoonlijke stukken, Zuid-Afrika, 9.1.1.8, Protea/Eurosa, 1979–1982).

62 Van Vuuren, *Apartheid Guns and Money*, p. 166.
63 Armscor Trimester Report, 2 October 1980, DOD/SANDF (CSF, GP 3, Box 933, HSF 521/4/1/2, Krygkor, 1, 17/04/1979–28/02/1985).
64 Armscor Trimester Report, 2 October 1980, DOD/SANDF (CSF, GP 3, Box 933, HSF 521/4/1/2, Krygkor, 1, 17/04/1979–28/02/1985).
65 Van Vuuren, *Apartheid Guns and Money*, p. 160.
66 Supplementary Statement by Mr Martin Steynberg, 8 April 2006, Open Secrets Collection.
67 Van Vuuren, *Apartheid Guns and Money*, pp. 189–198.
68 Van Vuuren, *Apartheid Guns and Money*, pp. 397–401.
69 Export Invoice for Payment to Be Made to Kredietbank Luxembourg, 25 February 1984, DOD/SANDF (DI, GP 31, Box 4, DBB/SK 311/1/30 Gallery, Ops Zaire: Gallery, 3, 27/02/1984–18/01/1985).
70 Van Vuuren, *Apartheid Guns and Money*, p. 183.
71 LJ van der Westhuizen and JH le Roux, 'Armscor: The Leading Edge', unpublished, University of the Free State, Institute for Contemporary History, 1997.
72 Letter from PW Botha to LW Dekker, 1 June 1979, University of the Free State, Archive for Contemporary Affairs (PV 203, A1/2/2, 1979 July–October, PW Botha).
73 Letter from LW Dekker to PW Botha, 26 July 1979, University of the Free State, Archive for Contemporary Affairs (PV 203, A1/2/2, 1979 July–October, PW Botha).
74 KBL had a representative in South Africa from at least 1978; their 1978 annual report lists KBL representative in Johannesburg as Jurie J Visagie, one of ten offices outside Luxembourg.
75 Telephone conversation, Leendert Dekker, August 2016.
76 Deza Mones and Rehan Ahmad, 'Europe's 50 largest banks by assets 2022', S&P Global Market Intelligence, 13 April 2022, Available at: https://www.spglobal.com/marketintelligence/en/news-insights/latest-news-headlines/europe-s-50-largest-banks-by-assets-2022-69689461, accessed 29 August 2022.
77 OECD Watch, Open Secrets & CALS vs. KBL: Banks violating arms embargo during apartheid South Africa. Available at: https://www.oecdwatch.org/complaint/open-secrets-cals-vs-kbl/, accessed 29 August 2022.
78 Available at: https://www.opensecrets.org.za/what_we_do/using-the-

law/oecd/the-complaint/#amicussubmission, accessed 19 August 2022.
79 https://www.opensecrets.org.za/what_we_do/using-the-law/oecd/.
80 Available at: https://www.opensecrets.org.za/apartheidbanksdocket/, accessed 19 August 2022.
81 *New Statesman and Society*, United Kingdom, 17 June 1994, p. 13.
82 *New Statesman and Society*, United Kingdom, 17 June 1994, p. 13.
83 Interview with Alex Conneely Hughes, Telephonic, 19 November 2019.
84 *Financial Times*, 'Jindal fight puts focus on British steel trader', 16 July 2013, Available at: https://www.ft.com/content/48f6e8be-f60c-11e2-8388-00144feabdc0, accessed 29 August 2020.
85 *Ship2Shore*, 'Down the curtain on Ralph Oppenheimer's activity before an eventual sinking of Stemcor might occur', 23 September 2019, Available at: http://www.ship2shore.it/en/energy/down-the-curtain-on-ralph-oppenheimer-s-activity-before-an-eventual-sinking-of-stemcor-might-occur_50250.htm, accessed 29 August 2022.
86 Stemcor Holdings Limited, 'Stemcor looks to bounce back after a challenging year', *Steel Times International*, July/August 2010. Available at: https://www.steeltimesint.com/content-images/news/Stemcor.pdf, accessed on 4 October 2022.
87 See annual report of Coutinho, Caro & Co Limited (1974) and annual reports of Irene Securities (1974 onwards).
88 Protea International: Return of Allotment of Shares from 28/4/1973 to 30/10/1973 and every Stemcor annual report from 1973 onwards.
89 Anti-Apartheid Movement Report 'UK Companies and Their Subsidiary or Related Companies in South Africa and Namibia', June 1988, Available at: http://www.aluka.org/action/showMetadata?doi=10.5555/AL.SFF.DOCUMENT.aam00025.
90 CCC Annual Reports from year end 1983 to 1987.
91 Stemcor Annual Report (1988) 'Chairman's Statement' pp. 5–7.
92 Vera Beljakova,'Protea sells R45m to South America' *Sunday Times*, 20 January 1980.
93 Beljakova, 'Protea sells R45m to South America'.
94 South African Jewish Review, 'Richard Lurie – Obituary', 8 June 2007. Available at: https://www.sajr.co.za/docs/default-source/pdf/2007/june/june-8-2007.pdf?sfvrsn=2, accessed 29 August 2022.
95 Letter for signature by PW Botha and list of addressee Handwritten notes by Magnus Malan, 1981, University of the Free State, Archive for Contemporary Affairs (PV 203, 6/22/1, 1979, PW Botha).
96 Paul Holden and Hennie van Vuuren, *The Devil in the Detail: How the*

Arms Deal Changed Everything. Jonathan Ball, Cape Town, 2011, p. 194.
97   Ruth First, Jonathan Steele and Christabel Gurney, *The South African Connection: Western Investment in Apartheid*, Maurice Temple Smith, 1972.
98   *Brief Report*, Bad days in bedlam, Vol. 7, Issue 1, 1 January 1978, pp. 52–53. Available at: https://journals.sagepub.com/doi/pdf/10.1080/03064227808532735, accessed 29 August 2022.
99   *Brief Report*, Bad days in bedlam, pp. 52–53.
100 Memorandum from Walter E. Fauntroy to the Congressional Black Caucus, 07 September 1976.
101 Peter Deeley, 'Scandal of the Money-Making Mental Homes', *Observer*, 3 June 1979, p. 6.
102 *Science News*, 'South African Snake Pits: For Blacks Only', Vol. 115, No. 21, 26 May 1979, p. 340
103 Rowena Mayson, '"Just close them down", Margaret Hodge on antisemitism in Labour branches', *The Guardian*, 8 March 2019, https://www.theguardian.com/politics/2019/mar/08/just-close-them-down-margaret-hodge-on-antisemitism-in-labour-branches, accessed 10 October 2022.

Section 2: War Profiteers

1   See https://corruptiontribunal.org.za/.
2   Paul Holden, 'R142 bn bomb: Revisiting the costs of the Arms Deal, twenty years on', *Daily Maverick*, 18 August 2020. Available at: https://www.dailymaverick.co.za/article/2020-08-18-the-r142bn-bomb-revisiting-the-cost-of-the-arms-deal-twenty-years-on/, accessed 1 September 2022.
3   Holden, 'R142 bn bomb: Revisiting the costs of the Arms Deal, twenty years on'.
4   Paul Holden, *The Arms Deal in Your Pocket*, Jonathan Ball Publishers, Cape Town, 2008.
5   Paul Holden and Hennie van Vuuren, *The Devil in the Detail: How the arms deal changed everything*, Jonathan Ball, Cape Town, 2011.
6   *The White Paper on National Defence for the Republic of South Africa*, published 8 May 1996.
7   *The State v Shaik and Others*, 2005, p. 29.
8   Holden, *The Arms Deal in Your Pocket*.
9   Michael Marchant, 'Joining the Dots: The Long Shadow of Economic Crime in South Africa', *Open Secrets*, 2018, p. 15.
10 Stephan Hofstatter, Mzilikazi wa Afrika, Piet Rampedi and André

Jurgens, 'Exposed: How arms dealer Thales bankrolled Zuma', *Sunday Times*, 28 September 2014. Available at: https://www.timeslive.co.za/politics/2014-09-28-exposed-how-arms-dealer-thales-bankrolled-zuma/, accessed 1 September 2022.

11 Nic Andersen, 'Zuma corruption trial: A timeline of how we got to court', *The South African*, 8 June 2018. Available at: https://www.thesouthafrican.com/news/zuma-corruption-trial-timeline-court/, accessed 1 September 2022.

12 Holden, *The Arms Deal in Your Pocket*.

13 Matt Weaver, 'Judge throws out Zuma corruption charges', *The Guardian*, 20 September 2006. Available at: https://www.theguardian.com/world/2006/sep/20/southafrica.matthewweaver, accessed 1 September 2022.

14 Craig Dodds, 'What is really on Zuma "spy tapes"?', *IOL*, 31 August 2014. Available at: https://www.iol.co.za/news/politics/what-is-really-on-zuma-spy-tapes-1743568, accessed 1 September 2022.

15 Greg Nicolson, 'Seriti findings a failure: 'Inexplicable' for commission to ignore evidence of corruption', *Daily Maverick*, 21 August 2019. Available at: https://www.dailymaverick.co.za/article/2019-08-21-seriti-findings-a-failure-inexplicable-for-commission-to-ignore-evidence-of-corruption/, accessed 1 September 2022.

16 *Corruption Watch and Another v Arms Procurement Commission and Others* (81368/2016) [2019] ZAGPPHC 351, p. 39.

17 See https://www.opensecrets.org.za/what_we_do/investigations/the-arms-deal-and-the-seriti-commission/.

18 Franny Rabkin, 'High Court rejects Zuma's application for a permanent stay of prosecution', *Mail & Guardian*, 11 October 2019. Available at: https://mg.co.za/article/2019-10-11-high-court-rejects-zumas-application-for-a-permanent-stay-of-prosecution/, accessed 1 September 2022.

19 Karyn Maughan, 'SCA dismisses Jacob Zuma's bid to appeal ruling in corruption case', *Business Day*, 13 March 2020. Available at: https://www.businesslive.co.za/bd/national/2020-03-13-sca-dismisses-jacob-zumas-bid-to-appeal-ruling-in-corruption-case/, accessed 1 September 2022.

20 Maughan, 'SCA dismisses Jacob Zuma's bid to appeal ruling in corruption case'.

21 Des Erasmus, 'Miracles aside Zuma Arms Deal trial likely to begin in 2023', *Daily Maverick*, 31 July 2022. Available at: https://www.dailymaverick.co.za/article/2022-07-31-miracles-aside-zuma-arms-

deal-trial-is-likely-to-begin-in-2023/.

22 Jamie Doward, 'UK accused of selling arms to Saudi Arabia a year after court ban', *The Guardian*, 21 June 2020. Available at: https://www.theguardian.com/world/2020/jun/21/uk-accused-of-selling-arms-to-saudi-arabia-a-year-after-court-ban, accessed 1 September 2022.

23 Phil Miller, 'Coronavirus cannot stop Britain's war in Yemen', *Daily Maverick*, 22 April 2020. Available at: https://www.dailymaverick.co.za/article/2020-04-22-coronavirus-cannot-stop-britains-war-in-yemen/#gsc.tab=0, accessed 1 September 2022.

24 Andrew Feinstein, You Tube, 4 September 2017. Available at: https://www.youtube.com/watch?v=b5sgqskniWo&t=11s, accessed 1 September 2022.

25 David Leigh and Rob Evans, 'BAE Admits guilt over corrupt arms deals', *The Guardian*, 6 February 2010. Available at: https://www.theguardian.com/world/2010/feb/05/bae-systems-arms-deal-corruption, accessed 1 September 2022.

26 David Leigh and Rob Evans, 'How Blair put pressure on Goldsmith to end BAE investigation', *The Guardian,* 21 December 2007. Available at: https://www.theguardian.com/world/2007/dec/21/bae.tonyblair.

27 https://sites.tufts.edu/corruptarmsdeals/the-south-african-arms-deal/, accessed 1 September 2022.

28 Holden and Van Vuuren, *The Devil in the Detail*, p. 120.

29 Corruption Watch, Evidence for the People's Tribunal on Economic Crime, January 2018. Available at: https://corruptiontribunal.org.za/site/wp-content/uploads/2018/02/1999-Arms-Deal-Submission_CW.pdf, accessed 1 September 2022.

30 Corruption Watch, Evidence for the People's Tribunal on Economic Crime.

31 Holden, *The Arms Deal in Your Pocket*, p. 98.

32 Corruption Watch, Evidence for the People's Tribunal on Economic Crime, para 92.

33 Holden and Van Vuuren, *The Devil in the Detail*, pp. 174–175.

34 Holden, *The Arms Deal in Your Pocket*, p. 22.

35 SIPRI, Available at: https://www.sipri.org/yearbook/2011/01, accessed 1 September 2022.

36 Corruption Watch, Evidence for the People's Tribunal on Economic Crime, para 92.

37 G. Murphy, Affidavit submitted as Annexure JDP-SW12 in the High Court of South Africa (Transvaal Provincial Division) in the matter of

Ex Parte the National Director of Public Prosecutions (applicant) in re: an application for issue of search warrants in terms of Section 29(5) and 29(6) of the National Prosecuting, 2008.

38 Murphy, Affidavit submitted as Annexure JDP-SW12 in the High Court of South Africa (Transvaal Provincial Division).
39 Murphy, Affidavit submitted as Annexure JDP-SW12 in the High Court of South Africa (Transvaal Provincial Division), para 14.
40 DefenceWeb, 'New Evidence of arms deal corruption – report', 3 June 2013. Available at: https://www.defenceweb.co.za/governance/governance-governance/new-evidence-of-arms-deal-corruption-report/, accessed 1 September 2022.
41 Allan McDonald, Fax to Terry Morgan dated 4 September 1998.
42 Allan McDonald, Fax to Terry Morgan dated 4 September 1998.
43 Portia Ndzamela, Fax to Niels Petersen, British Aerospace dated 12 October 1998.
44 Portia Ndzamela, Fax to Niels Petersen, British Aerospace dated 12 October 1998.
45 Corruption Watch, Evidence for the People's Tribunal on Economic Crime, para 92.
46 Holden and Van Vuuren, *The Devil in the Detail*, p. 192.
47 US Treasury, 'John Bredenkamp, Billy Rautenbach, added to the US sanctions list', 25 November 2008. Available at: https://www.politicsweb.co.za/documents/john-bredenkamp-billy-rautenbach-added-to-us-sanct, accessed 1 September 2022.
48 Hennie van Vuuren, *Apartheid Guns and Money: A tale of profit*, Jacana Media, Johannesburg, 2014.
49 Tom Harper, 'Zimbabwean arms dealer sues Foreign Office for freezing assets', *The Independent*, 21 June 2013. Available at: https://www.independent.co.uk/news/uk/crime/zimbabwean-arms-dealer-sues-foreign-office-for-freezing-assets-8669188.html, accessed 1 September 2022.
50 Tribune de Geneve, 'How Geneva lawyers exploit loopholes in the offshore – Translated', *Tribune de Geneve*, 6 April 2016 Available at: https://www.tdg.ch/news/standard/avocats-genevois-exploitent-failles-offshore/story/18863799, accessed 1 September 2022.
51 See: https://sanctionssearch.ofac.treas.gov/Details.aspx?id=1876, accessed 1 September 2022.
52 Van Vuuren, *Apartheid Guns and Money*, p. 426.
53 Van Vuuren, *Apartheid Guns and Money*, pp. 425, 426.

54 Murphy, Affidavit submitted as Annexure JDP-SW12 in the High Court of South Africa (Transvaal Provincial Division)
55 Holden, *The Arms Deal in Your Pocket*.
56 Murphy, Affidavit submitted as Annexure JDP-SW12 in the High Court of South Africa (Transvaal Provincial Division), para 52.
57 Murphy, Affidavit submitted as Annexure JDP-SW12 in the High Court of South Africa (Transvaal Provincial Division), para 52.
58 Corruption Watch, Media Strategy Working Notes, 2018. Available at: https://www.corruptionwatch.org.za/wp-content/uploads/2018/09/Detailed-notes-for-arms-deal-affidavit.pdf, accessed 1 September 2022.
59 Holden and Van Vuuren, *The Devil in the Detail*, p. 192.
60 Niren Tolsi, 'The Zondo Commision's dapper dodger', *New Frame*, 6 December 2019. Available at: https://www.newframe.com/the-zondo-commissions-dapper-dodger/.
61 Andrew Feinstein, 'Letter to the Editor: Sadly, Joe Modise was no angel on the Arms Deal', *Daily Maverick*, 22 August 2017. Available at: https://www.dailymaverick.co.za/article/2017-08-22-letter-to-the-editor-sadly-joe-modise-was-no-angel-on-the-arms-deal/#gsc.tab=0, accessed 1 September 2022.
62 Murphy, Affidavit submitted as Annexure JDP-SW12 in the High Court of South Africa (Transvaal Provincial Division), para 56.
63 Ivor Powell, 'How arms deal man made his million', *IOL*, 17 July 2011. Available at: https://www.iol.co.za/news/politics/how-arms-deal-man-made-his-millions-1100424, accessed 1 September 2022.
64 Holden and Van Vuuren, *The Devil in the Detail*, p. 195.
65 Holden and Van Vuuren, *The Devil in the Detail*, p. 195.
66 Murphy, Affidavit submitted as Annexure JDP-SW12 in the High Court of South Africa (Transvaal Provincial Division), para 56.
67 Sam Sole, 'The house the arms deal bought', *Mail & Guardian*, 3 December 2010. Available at: https://mg.co.za/article/2010-12-03-the-house-arms-deal-bought/, accessed 1 September 2022.
68 Sam Sole, 'BAE's "bribery" channel', *Mail & Guardian*, 24 June 2011. Available at: https://mg.co.za/article/2011-06-24-baes-bribery-channel/, accessed 1 September 2022.
69 Corruption Watch, Evidence for the People's Tribunal on Economic Crime.
70 Corruption Watch, Evidence for the People's Tribunal on Economic Crime.
71 *Corruption Watch and Another v Arms Procurement Commission and Others*,

2019, p. 39.
72   ANCIR, 'How the Guptas' propaganda war machine was built', *Times Live*, 4 September 2017. Available at: https://www.timeslive.co.za/news/south-africa/2017-09-04-how-the-guptas-propaganda-war-machine-was-built/, accessed 1 September 2022.
73   Babalo Ndenze, 'Fana Hlongwane paid for Ayanda Dlodlo's Dubai trip', *EyeWitness News*, 11 March 2018. Available at: https://ewn.co.za/2019/03/11/fana-hlongwane-paid-for-ayanda-dlodlo-s-dubai-trip.
74   Outa, 'The Gupta's, the Oberoi and their guests....', Outa, Undated online. Available at: https://www.outa.co.za/projects/state-capture/gupta-associates/oberio-guests.
75   Outa, 'The Gupta's, the Oberoi and their guests…'.
76   Bernadette Wicks, 'Zondo recommends NPA consider corruption charges against Tony Gupta', *EyeWitness News*, 29 April 2022. Available at: https://ewn.co.za/2022/04/29/zondo-recommends-npa-consider-corruption-charges-against-tony-gupta, accessed 1 September 2022.
77   Wicks, Zondo recommends NPA consider corruption charges against Tony Gupta.
78   Buddy Naidu, 'Arms deals billionaire bachelor', *Sunday Times*, 30 November 2008. Available at: http://www.armsdeal-vpo.co.za/articles13/billionaire.html, accessed 1 September 2022.
79   See https://www.opensecrets.org.za/wp-content/uploads/4.-Nyanda-Homeloan-and-Financial-Documents.pdf, accessed 1 September 2022.
80   See https://www.opensecrets.org.za/wp-content/uploads/4.-Nyanda-Homeloan-and-Financial-Documents.pdf, accessed 1 September 2022.
81   Sole, 'The house the arms deal bought'.
82   See https://www.opensecrets.org.za/wp-content/uploads/4.-Nyanda-Homeloan-and-Financial-Documents.pdf, accessed 1 September 2022.
83   Murphy, Affidavit submitted as Annexure JDP-SW12 in the High Court of South Africa (Transvaal Provincial Division).
84   Affordability of the Defence Strategic Arms, August 1999. Available at: https://www.opensecrets.org.za/wp-content/uploads/5.-Arms-Deal-Affordability-Report.pdf, accessed 1 September 2022.
85   Affordability of the Defence Strategic Arms, August 1999.
86   Holden and Van Vuuren, *The Devil in the Detail*, p. 181
87   Holden and Van Vuuren, *The Devil in the Detail*, p. 181.
88   Affordability of the Defence Strategic Arms, August 1999.
89   See https://www.gov.za/about-government/contact-directory/simphiwe-nyanda-mr, accessed 1 September 2022.

90 Holden and Van Vuuren, *The Devil in the Detail*, p. 195.
91 Holden and Van Vuuren, *The Devil in the Detail*, p. 196.
92 Holden and Van Vuuren, *The Devil in the Detail*, p. 196.
93 See https://www.opensecrets.org.za/wp-content/uploads/4.-Nyanda-Homeloan-and-Financial-Documents.pdf, accessed 1 September 2022.
94 Email from Siphiwe Nyanda to Open Secrets, 23 July 2020.
95 Email from Siphiwe Nyanda to Open Secrets, 28 July 2020.
96 Email from Siphiwe Nyanda to Open Secrets, 23 July 2020.
97 Email from Siphiwe Nyanda to Open Secrets, 23 July 2020.
98 Letter from C. Stockenström to Genl. S. Nyanda, re: Bond Ngwane Aerospace (Pty) Ltd/Genl S Nyanda, 02 March 2020. Available at: https://www.opensecrets.org.za/wp-content/uploads/4.-Nyanda-Homeloan-and-Financial-Documents.pdf, accessed 1 September 2022.
99 Letter from C. Stockenström to Genl. S. Nyanda.
100 Pro-Forma Statement of Account from Connie Myburgh & Partners, 27 January 2005. Available at: https://www.opensecrets.org.za/wp-content/uploads/4.-Nyanda-Homeloan-and-Financial-Documents.pdf, accessed 1 September 2022.
101 Letter from C. Stockenström to Genl. S. Nyanda.
102 Email from Siphiwe Nyanda to Open Secrets, 23 July 2020.
103 Email from Siphiwe Nyanda to Open Secrets, 23 July 2020.
104 Email from Siphiwe Nyanda to Open Secrets, 23 July 2020.
105 Ngwane Aerospace (Pty) Ltd, Schedule of Loan to Gen Nyanda, Undated. Available at: https://www.opensecrets.org.za/wp-content/uploads/4.-Nyanda-Homeloan-and-Financial-Documents.pdf, accessed 1 September 2022.
106 Letter from General (Ret) S. Nyanda to Janet Collier, April 2007. Available at: https://www.opensecrets.org.za/wp-content/uploads/4.-Nyanda-Homeloan-and-Financial-Documents.pdf, accessed 1 September 2022.
107 Letter from General (Ret) S. Nyanda to Janet Collier.
108 Email from Siphiwe Nyanda to Open Secrets, 23 July 2020.
109 United Nations Yemen, 'Yemen: 2019 Humanitarian Needs Overview', United Nations Yemen. Available at: https://yemen.un.org/en/11690-yemen-2019-humanitarian-needs-overview, accessed 4 August 2020.
110 Save the Children, 'Yemen: 85,000 children may have died from starvation since start of war', Press release by the organisation Save the Children, 20 November 2018. Available at: https://www.savethechildren.org/us/about-us/media-and-news/2018-press-releases/yemen-85000-children-may-have-died-from-starvation, accessed 4 August 2020.

111 Group of eminent international and regional experts on Yemen, *Situation of human rights in Yemen including violations and abuses since September 2014*, UN Human Rights Council 45th Session, 28 September 2020.
112 Amnesty International, 'When arms go astray', *Amnesty International*, 6 February 2019. Available at: https://arms-uae.amnesty.org/en/, accessed 31 March 2020.
113 Figures deduced from National Conventional Arms Control Committee annual reports 2010 to 2019.
114 42% in 2015 and 49% in 2016.
115 Timothy Jones, 'Saudi Arabia urges Germany to lift arms export ban', *Deutsche Welle*, 17 February 2020. Available at: https://www.dw.com/en/saudi-arabia-urges-germany-to-lift-arms-export-ban/a-52403302, accessed 31 March 2020.
116 Al Jazeera, 'Dozens killed in Hodeidah attacks after peace talks collapse', *Al Jazeera*, 9 September 2018. Available at: https://www.aljazeera.com/news/2018/9/9/dozens-killed-in-hodeidah-attacks-after-peace-talks-collapse, accessed 14 November 2020.
117 Al Jazeera, 'Dozens killed in Hodeidah attacks after peace talks collapse'.
118 Nick Waters, 'Who attacked the Hodeidah Hospital? Examining allegations the Saudi coalition bombed a hospital in Yemen', *Bellingcat*, 9 August 2018. Available at: https://www.bellingcat.com/news/mena/2018/08/09/attacked-hodeidah-hospital-examining-allegations-saudi-coalition-bombed-hospital-yemen/, accessed 31 March 2020.
119 Middle East Eye and agencies, '60 dead after air strike hits hospital and market in Hodeidah', *Middle East Eye*, 4 August 2018. Available at: https://www.middleeasteye.net/news/60-dead-after-air-strike-hits-hospital-and-market-hodeidah, accessed 6 August 2020.
120 Middle East Eye and agencies, '60 dead after air strike hits hospital and market in Hodeidah'.
121 Middle East Eye and agencies, '60 dead after air strike hits hospital and market in Hodeidah'.
122 Waters, 'Who Attacked the Hodeidah Hospital?'.
123 Waters, 'Who attacked the Hodeidah Hospital?'.
124 Waters, 'Who attacked the Hodeidah Hospital?'.
125 Hans-Martin Tillack, 'Eine Whistleblowerin gegen den Rüstungskonzern Rheinmetall', *Stern*, 4 June 2019. Available at: https://www.stern.de/politik/ausland/rheinmetall--eine-whistleblowerin-gegen-den-ruestungskonzern-8738194.html, accessed 19 May 2020.
126 United Nations, Letter from the Panel of Experts on Yemen addressed to

the President of the Security Council, 25 January 2019, p. 48. Available at: https://www.securitycouncilreport.org/atf/cf/%7B65BFCF9B-6D27-4E9C-8CD3-CF6E4FF96FF9%7D/s_2019_83.pdf, Accessed 9 July 2020.

127   United Nations, Letter from the Panel of Experts on Yemen addressed to the President of the Security Council.

128   United Nations, Letter from the Panel of Experts on Yemen addressed to the President of the Security Council.

129   Saudi Press Agency, 'President of South Africa, Deputy Crown Prince open projectiles factory at Military Industries Corporation, *Saudi Press Agency*, 27 March 2016. Available at: https://www.spa.gov.sa/viewstory.php?lang=en&newsid=1482484, accessed 31 March 2020.

130   Michael Marchant, Zen Mathe, Caryn Dolley, Hennie van Vuuren and Naushina Rahim, *Profiting from Misery: South Africa's complicity in war crimes in Yemen*, Open Secrets, March 2021. Available at: www.opensecrets.org.za

Section 3: State Capture Profiteers

1   Lameez Omarjee, 'Ramaphosa says state capture cost SA more than R500bn, overseas criminals will be brought to book', *News24*, 14 October 2019. Available at: https://www.news24.com/fin24/economy/south-africa/ramaphosa-says-state-capture-cost-sa-more-than-r500bn-overseas-criminals-will-be-brought-to-book-20191014, accessed 30 August 2022.

2   Sarah Smit, 'Former Transnet chief exec Siyabonga Gama, Gupta associate Eric Wood arrested', *Mail & Guardian*, 27 May 2022. Available at: https://mg.co.za/news/2022-05-27-former-transnet-chief-exec-siyabonga-gama-gupta-associate-eric-wood-arrested/, accessed 30 August 2022.

3   Jacques Claassen, 'Transnet crisis emphasise urgency to invest and reinvent', *FInWeek*, 5 September 2021. Available at: https://www.news24.com/fin24/finweek/transnet-crisis-emphasises-urgency-to-invest-and-reinvent-20210902, accessed 30 August 2022.

4   Justice RMM Zondo, 'Judicial Commission of Inquiry into State Capture Report: Part 2, Volume 1: Transnet'. Available at: https://www.statecapture.org.za/site/files/announcements/674/OCR_version_-_State_Capture_Commission_Report_Part_II_Vol_I.pdf, accessed 30 August 2022.

5   Zondo, 'Judicial Commission of Inquiry into State Capture Report: Part

2, Volume 1: Transnet'.
6   Michael Marchant, Mamello Mosiana, Paul Holden and Hennie van Vuuren, 'The Enablers: The Bankers, Accountants and Lawyers that Cashed in on State Capture'. Report submitted to the Zondo Commission of Inquiry into State Capture, Open Secrets & Shadow World Investigations, February 2020.
7   Stefaans Brümmer, 'How the Guptas R9 billion locomotive heist went down', *Daily Maverick*, 1 June 2020. Available at: https://www.dailymaverick.co.za/article/2020-06-01-how-the-guptas-r9bn-locomotive-heist-went-down/, accessed 30 August 2022.
8   Zondo, 'Judicial Commission of Inquiry into State Capture Report: Part 2, Volume 1: Transnet', p. 483.
9   Micah Reddy, 'Update: SARS freezes R2.8 billion from Chinese rail company that paid Gupta kickbacks', *AmaBhungane*, 9 December 2020. Available at: https://amabhungane.org/stories/201209-update-sars-freezes-r2-8-billion-from-chinese-rail-company-that-paid-gupta-kickbacks/, accessed 30 August 2022.
10 Luke Daniel, 'Shock new numbers show SA train service went off the rails – Even before Covid hit', *Business Insider SA*, 6 March 2021. Available at: https://www.businessinsider.co.za/travel-survey-shows-how-sas-train-service-has-gone-off-the-rails-even-before-covid-hit-2021-3, accessed 30 August 2022.
11 Prasa Annual Report (2008/2009). Available at: https://www.prasa.com/Annual%20Reports.html, accessed 30 August 2022.
12 Prasa Annual Report (2012/2013. Available at: https://www.prasa.com/Annual%20Reports.html, accessed 30 August 2022.
13 Prasa Annual Report (2008/2009). Available at: https://www.prasa.com/Annual%20Reports.html, accessed 30 August 2022.
14 Prasa Annual Report (2008/2009). Available at: https://www.prasa.com/Annual%20Reports.html, accessed 30 August 2022.
15 Prasa Annual Report (2010/2011). Available at: https://www.prasa.com/Annual%20Reports.html, accessed 30 August 2022.
16 Public Protector of South Africa, 'Derailed: A Report on an Investigation into Allegations of Maladministration Relating to Financial Mismanagement, Tender Irregularities and Appointment Irregularities Against the Passenger Rail Agency of South Africa (PRASA)', 2015, (xviii), p. 20. Available at: https://www.gov.za/sites/default/files/gcis_document/201508/publicprotectorinvestigationreportno3of201516Prasa24082015a.pdf, accessed 30 August 2022.

17 Public Protector South Africa, 'Derailed', 2015, (xviii), p. 23.
18 Public Protector South Africa, 'Derailed', 2015, (xviii), p. 389.
19 Public Protector South Africa, 'Derailed', 2015, (xviii), p.4.
20 Greg Nicolson, 'Derailed and released: Lucky Montana out of Prasa', *The Daily Maverick*, 17 July 2015. Available at: https://www.dailymaverick.co.za/article/2015-07-17-derailed-released-lucky-montana-out-of-Prasa/, accessed 30 August 2022.
21 Horwath Forensics, 'Passenger Rail Agency of South Africa (PRASA), Swifambo flow of funds analysis (Draft) preliminary report', 20 April 2017, p. 6. Available at: https://www.statecapture.org.za/site/files/documents/411/Day_350_-_SS_24._Sacks,_RM_(Prasa_Bundle_L).pdf, accessed 30 August 2022.
22 UniteBehind, 'UniteBehind Interim Report for the Standing Committee on Public Accounts and Portfolio Committee on Finance on leaked forensic investigations by Treasury of about 200 contracts worth about R15 billion at the Passenger Rail Agency of South Africa', December 2017. Available at: https://unitebehind.org.za/wp-content/uploads/Prasa-leaks-how-state-capture-happened-at-Prasa..pdf, accessed 31 August 2022.
23 ENS forensics 'Executive summary of Siyaya Energy contracts', 2017, p. 4.
24 UniteBehind, 'UniteBehind interim Report'.
25 Deloitte, 'Forensic investigation into the appointment of and payments made to various service providers of the Passenger Rail Agency South Africa (PRASA) Executive summary', 2016, p. 24.
26 UniteBehind, 'UniteBehind Interim Report'.
27 Popo Molefe, State Capture Commission of Inquiry transcript, 29 June 2020, pp. 50–59. Available at: https://www.statecapture.org.za/site/files/transcript/228/29_June_2020_Sessions.pdf, accessed 31 August 2022.
28 UniteBehind, 'UniteBehind interim Report'.
29 *Molefe and others v Minister of Transport* (17748/17) [2017] ZAGPPHC 120 (10 April 2017).
30 Popo Molefe, State Capture Commission of Inquiry transcript, 29 June 2020, pp. 50–59.
31 eNCA, 'Update: Martins confirms meeting with Montana, Guptas', *eNCA*, 31 January 2018.
32 Board Charter of Board of Control of the Passenger Rail Agency of South Africa. Available at: https://www.opensecrets.org.za/wp-content/

uploads/PRASA_Board_Charter.pdf, accessed 31 August 2022.
33 Board Charter of Board of Control of the Passenger Rail Agency of South Africa.
34 UniteBehind, 'UniteBehind Interim Report'.
35 Pauli van Wyk, 'Scorpio: Prasa - Treasury Investigation recommends Sfiso Buthelezi be criminally charged', *Daily Maverick*, 10 June 2017. Available at: https://www.dailymaverick.co.za/article/2017-06-10-scorpio-Prasa-treasury-investigation-recommends-sfiso-buthelezi-be-criminally-charged/#.WjFd2N-WbIU, accessed 31 August 2022.
36 Howarth Forensics, 'Passenger Rail Agency of South Africa (PRASA), Swifambo flow of funds analysis (Draft) preliminary report', 20 April 2017, pp. 97–100.
37 Public Protector South Africa, 'Derailed', (2015), (xviii), p. 42.
38 GroundUp News, 'PRASA leaks', November 2018. Available at: https://www.groundup.org.za/topic/Prasaleaks/#:~:text=Two%20sets%20of%20leaked%20documents,first%20reported%20in%20October%202018, accessed 31 August 2022.
39 *Passenger Rail Agency of South Africa v Swifambo Rail Agency (Pty) Ltd* (2015/42219) [2017] ZAGPJHC.
40 *Passenger Rail Agency of South Africa v Swifambo Rail Agency (Pty) Ltd* (2015/42219) [2017] ZAGPJHC.
41 Fani Dingiswayo, 'State Capture Commission of Inquiry transcript', 2 July 2020, Day 229, pp. 100–103. Available at: https://www.opensecrets.org.za/wp-content/uploads/State_Capture_Inquiry_02_July_2020_Dingiswayo_Transcript.pdf, accessed 31 August 2022.
42 Dingiswayo, 'State Capture Commission of Inquiry transcript', pp. 100–103.
43 Tariro Washinyira, 'Commuters weary of trains as they resume', *GroundUp News*, 18 February 2021. Available at: https://www.groundup.org.za/article/commuters-wary-trains-service-resumes/, accessed 31 August 2022.
44 Luyolo Mkentane, 'Fixing PRASA will cost billions, says board chair', *BusinessLive*, 7 March 2021. Available at: https://www.businesslive.co.za/bd/national/2021-03-07-fixing-Prasa-will-cost-billions-of-rand-says-board-chair/, accessed 31 August 2022.
45 Parliamentary Monitoring Group, 'Parliamentary Committee on Transport', 25 February 2022. Available at: https://pmg.org.za/committee-meeting/29881/, accessed 31 August 2022.
46 Gemma Ritchie, 'Commuters and rail industry feel the pinch as Prasa delays refurbishing trains', amaBhungane, 5 February 2021. Available

at: https://amabhungane.org/stories/210205-commuters-and-rail-industry-feel-the-pinch-as-prasa-delays-refurbishing-trains/, accessed 31 August 2022.

47 Gemma Ritchie, 'Commuters and rail industry feel the pinch as Prasa delays refurnishing trains'.

48 Horwath Forensics, 'Passenger Rail Agency of South Africa (PRASA), Swifambo flow of funds analysis (Draft) preliminary report', 20 April 2017, p. 68.

49 *Passenger Rail Agency of South Africa v Swifambo Rail Agency (Pty) Ltd* (2015/42219) [2017] ZAGPJHC.

50 *Passenger Rail Agency of South Africa v Swifambo Rail Agency (Pty) Ltd* (2015/42219) [2017] ZAGPJHC.

51 *Passenger Rail Agency South Africa v Mthimkhulu* (42056/2015) [2019] ZAGPJHC 416 (26 November 2019).

52 Horwath Forensics, 'Passenger Rail Agency of South Africa (PRASA), Swifambo flow of funds analysis (Draft) preliminary report', 20 April 2017, p.35.

53 *Swifambo Rail Leasing v PRASA* (1030/2017) ZASCA 167 (SCA) (30 November 2018).

54 *Passenger Rail Agency of South Africa v Swifambo Rail Agency (Pty) Ltd* (2015/42219) [2017] ZAGPJHC.

55 *Passenger Rail Agency of South Africa v Swifambo Rail Agency (Pty) Ltd* (2015/42219) [2017] ZAGPJHC.

56 *Passenger Rail Agency of South Africa v Swifambo Rail Agency (Pty) Ltd* (2015/42219) [2017] ZAGPJHC.

57 J.A. Gómez-Ibáñez and G. de Rus (eds), *Competition in the Railway Industry: An International Comparative Analysis*, Edward Elgar Publishing, 2006.

58 Vossloh Group, 'Presentation to investors', 29 March 2012, p. 11. Available at: https://media.vossloh.com/media/dokumente/investor_relations_1/finanzpublikationen/praesentationen/2012/Vossloh_Praesentation_GB_2011_us.pdf, accessed 31 August 2022.

59 Horwath Forensics, 'Passenger Rail Agency of South Africa (PRASA), Swifambo flow of funds analysis (Draft) preliminary report', 20 April 2017.

60 Railway Safety Regulator, 'Afro 4000 Locomotives: Inspection and Verification report', 2015. Available at: https://www.opensecrets.org.za/wp-content/uploads/Railway-Safety-Regulator-report-on-Afro4000-locomotives-2015.pdf, accessed 31 August 2022.

61 *Passenger Rail Agency of South Africa v Swifambo Rail Agency (Pty) Ltd* (2015/42219) [2017] ZAGPJHC.
62 Horwath Forensics, 'Passenger Rail Agency of South Africa (PRASA), Swifambo flow of funds analysis (Draft) preliminary report', 20 April 2017.
63 Horwath Forensics, 'Passenger Rail Agency of South Africa (PRASA), Swifambo flow of funds analysis (Draft) preliminary report', 20 April 2017.
64 Leanne George and Pieter-Louis Myburgh, 'Big property splurge after train tender', *City Press*, 14 December 2015. Available at: https://www.news24.com/citypress/News/big-property-splurge-after-train-tender-20151214, accessed 31 August 2022.
65 Opera News, 'Check Nsovo M lifestyle, who has a baby with SA actress Mrs Gela', December 2020. Available at: https://za.opera.news/za/en/entertainment/fd7497be4598fe125ddd1bb42764d2b8, accessed 31 August 2022.
66 Pieter-Louis Myburgh, 'Gravy trains: R500m from failed Prasa locomotives deal "fraudulently" funnelled to trust, private accounts and properties', *Daily Maverick*, 3 March 2020. Available at: https://www.dailymaverick.co.za/article/2020-03-03-gravy-trains-r500m-from-failed-prasa-locomotives-deal-fraudulently-funnelled-to-trust-private-accounts-and-properties/, accessed 31 August 2022.
67 *Passenger Rail Agency of South Africa v Swifambo Rail Agency (Pty) Ltd* (2015/42219) [2017] ZAGPJHC.
68 Horwath Forensics, 'Passenger Rail Agency of South Africa (PRASA), Swifambo flow of funds analysis (Draft) preliminary report', 20 April 2017, p. 80.
69 Myburgh, 'Gravy trains: R500m from failed Prasa locomotives deal 'fraudulently' funnelled to trust, private accounts and properties'.
70 Horwath Forensics, 'Passenger Rail Agency of South Africa (PRASA), Swifambo flow of funds analysis (Draft) preliminary report', 20 April 2017, p. 111.
71 Horwath Forensics, 'Passenger Rail Agency of South Africa (PRASA), Swifambo flow of funds analysis (Draft) preliminary report', 20 April 2017, p. 111.
72 Donwald Pressly, 'Spanish firm wins tender for Prasa engines', *IOL*, 13 October 2013.
73 Horwath Forensics, 'Passenger Rail Agency of South Africa (PRASA), Swifambo flow of funds analysis (Draft) preliminary report', 20 April

2017, p. 21.

74 Horwath Forensics, 'Passenger Rail Agency of South Africa (PRASA), Swifambo flow of funds analysis (Draft) preliminary report', 20 April 2017, p. 112.

75 Pieter-Louis Myburgh, 'Prasa: European rail companies at odds over payments to Montana's "friend"', *News 24*, 8 February 2018. Available at: https://www.news24.com/news24/SouthAfrica/News/prasa-european-rail-companies-at-odds-over-payments-to-montanas-friend-20180207, accessed 31 August 2022.

76 Myburgh, 'Prasa: European rail companies at odds over payments to Montana's "friend"'.

77 Horwath Forensics, 'Passenger Rail Agency of South Africa (PRASA), Swifambo flow of funds analysis (Draft) preliminary report', 20 April 2017, p. 80.

78 Pieter-Louis Myburgh, 'Exclusive: Prasa locomotives contractor paid ANC fundraisers', *News24*, 10 March 2017. Available at: https://www.news24.com/news24/SouthAfrica/News/exclusive-prasa-locomotives-contractor-paid-anc-fundraisers-20170310, accessed 31 August 2022.

79 Myburgh, 'Exclusive: Prasa locomotives contractor paid ANC fundraisers'.

80 Horwath Forensics, 'Passenger Rail Agency of South Africa (PRASA), Swifambo flow of funds analysis (Draft) preliminary report', 20 April 2017, p.68.

81 Aidan Jones, 'Hawks fail to stop court application', *GroundUp News*, 4 May 2018. Available at: https://www.groundup.org.za/article/hawks-lose-challenge-against-prasa/, accessed 31 August 2022.

82 TimesLive, 'As another witness refuses to testify at the commission, has the flood gates of defiance opened?', *TimesLive*, 24 February 2021. Available at: https://www.timeslive.co.za/politics/2021-02-24-as-another-witness-refuses-to-appear-at-state-capture-inquiry-have-the-floodgates-of-defiance-opened/, accessed 31 August 2022.

83 Thanduxolo Jika, 'Prasa backtracks on tall trains' deal, claims need for locomotives "still remains"', *The Sunday Times*, 13 June 2021. Available at: https://www.timeslive.co.za/sunday-times/news/2021-06-13-prasa-backtracks-on-tall-trains-deal-claims-need-for-locomotives-still-remains/, accessed 31 August 2022.

84 Ashraf Hendricks, 'Activists call on German government to prosecute state capturers', *GroundUp News*, 25 July 2019. Available at: https://www.groundup.org.za/article/activist-call-international-authorities-

prosecute-those-involved-state-capture/, accessed 31 August 2022.

85   Letter from Rudiger Lotz to UniteBehind, 6 December 2019. Available at: https://www.opensecrets.org.za/wp-content/uploads/Letter-from-Deputy-German-Ambassador-to-UniteBehind.pdf, accessed 30 August 2022.

86   Letter from Rudiger Lotz to UniteBehind, 6 December 2019. Available at: https://www.opensecrets.org.za/wp-content/uploads/Letter-from-Deputy-German-Ambassador-to-UniteBehind.pdf, accessed 30 August 2022.

87   Tiro Holele, State Capture Commission of Inquiry Transcript, 11 March 2020, Day 221, p. 7. Available at: https://www.statecapture.org.za/site/files/transcript/222/11_March_2020_Sessions.pdf, accessed 31 August 2022.

88   Mungo Soggot, Stefaans Brummer and David Shapshak, 'Right Royal Scandal Hits Telkom', *The Mail & Guardian*, 20 July 2001. Available at: https://mg.co.za/article/2001-07-20-right-royal-scandal-hits-telkom/, accessed 31 August 2022.

89   Stefaans Brummer and Mungo Soggot, 'Telkom acts on scandal', *Mail & Guardian*, 3 August 2001. Available at: https://mg.co.za/article/2001-08-03-telkom-acts-on-scandal/, accessed 31 August 2022.

90   Mungo Soggot and Stefaans Brummer, 'Telkom severs ties with Royal Security', *Mail & Guardian*, 28 September 2001. Available at: https://mg.co.za/article/2001-09-28-telkom-severs-ties-with-royal-security/, accessed 31 August 2022.

91   Lloyd Gedye, 'Telkom probes corruption scandal', *Mail & Guardian*, 21 May 2010. Available at: https://mg.co.za/article/2010-05-21-telkom-probes-corruption-scandal/, accessed 31 August 2022.

92   Holele, State Capture Commission of Inquiry Transcript, 11 March 2020, Day 221, p. 6.

93   Holele, State Capture Commission of Inquiry Transcript, 11 March 2020, Day 221, p. 6.

94   Public Protector South Africa, 'Derailed', 2015, p. 56.

95   Werksmans Attorneys, 'Report: Passenger Rail Agency of South Africa/Royal Security', 2017, p. 3. Available at: https://www.groundup.org.za/media/uploads/documents/IN%20THE%20MATTER%20OF%20PRASA%20IN%20RE%20ROYAL%20SECURITY%20CC%20REPORT%20%20ANNEXURES.pdf, accessed 31 August 2022.

96   Werksmans Attorneys, 'Report: Passenger Rail Agency of South Africa/Royal Security', p. 16.

97   Werksmans Attorneys, 'Report: Passenger Rail Agency of South Africa/Royal Security' p. 17.

98 Werksmans Attorneys, 'Report: Passenger Rail Agency of South Africa/ Royal Security' p. 16.
99 Werksmans Attorneys, 'Report: Passenger Rail Agency of South Africa // Goldex Engineering // Hailway Trading (PTY) [Trading as Goldex Engineering]', 2017, page 7. Available at: https://www.groundup.org.za/media/uploads/documents/PRASA%20REPORT%20-%20HAIL%20WAY%20-%20GOLDEX%2030%2007%202017%20Final.PDF, accessed 31 August 2022.
100 Martha Nogye, State Capture Commission of Inquiry Transcript, 16 March 2020, Day 224, p. 49. Available at: https://www.statecapture.org.za/site/files/transcript/231/02_July_2020_Sessions.pdf, accessed 31 August 2022.
101 CIPC Records, 'Prodigy Business Enterprises', accessed in 2021.
102 Dingiswayo, 'State Capture Commission of Inquiry transcript', p. 143.
103 Dingiswayo, 'State Capture Commission of Inquiry transcript', p. 146.
104 Dingiswayo, 'State Capture Commission of Inquiry transcript', p. 147.
105 Dingiswayo, 'State Capture Commission of Inquiry transcript', p. 150.
106 Dingiswayo, 'State Capture Commission of Inquiry transcript', p. 161.
107 Dingiswayo, 'State Capture Commission of Inquiry transcript', p. 166.
108 Dingiswayo, 'State Capture Commission of Inquiry transcript', p. 183.
109 UniteBehind, 'UniteBehind interim Report', p. 3.
110 Holele, State Capture Commission of Inquiry Transcript, 11 March 2020, Day 221, p. 49.
111 Holele, State Capture Commission of Inquiry Transcript, 11 March 2020, Day 221, p. 50.
112 Holele, State Capture Commission of Inquiry Transcript, 11 March 2020, Day 221, p. 53.
113 Sam Mkokeli and Mike Cohen, 'Zuma's night of long knives threatens split in the ANC', *Bloomberg*, 30 March 2017. Available at: https://www.bloomberg.com/news/articles/2017-03-30/zuma-fires-gordhan-over-feud-to-control-south-african-finances, accessed 31 August 2022.
114 UniteBehind, 'UniteBehind interim Report', p. 3.
115 Popo Molefe, State Capture Commission of Inquiry Transcript, 12 March 2020, Day 222, p. 95. Available at: https://www.statecapture.org.za/site/files/transcript/223/12_March_2020_Sessions.pdf, accessed 31 August 2022.
116 Molefe, State Capture Commission of Inquiry Transcript, 12 March 2020, Day 222, p. 100.
117 Molefe, State Capture Commission of Inquiry Transcript, 12 March

2020, Day 222, p. 98.
118 Lucky Montana, State Capture Commission of Inquiry Transcript, 20 April 2021, Day 378, p. 126. Available at: https://www.statecapture.org.za/site/files/transcript/393/Day_378_-_2021-04-20.pdf, accessed 31 August 2022.
119 Justice RMM Zondo, 'Judicial Commission of Inquiry into State Capture Report: Volume 5, Part 2, Prasa, p. 761. Available at: https://www.statecapture.org.za/site/files/announcements/668/OCR_version_-_State_Capture_Commission_Report_Part_V_Vol_II_-_SABC,Waterkloof,Prasa.pdf, accessed 31 August 2022.
120 UniteBehind, 'UniteBehind Interim Report', December 2017, p. 3.
121 *Passenger Rail Agency of South Africa vs Siyangena Technologies* (2018/14332) GPHC, 2020.
122 Molefe, State Capture Commission of Inquiry Transcript, 12 March 2020, Day 222, p. 123.
123 *News24*, 'Exclusive: Zuma's friend's R550m bonanza', *News24*, 14 August 2016. Available at: https://www.news24.com/News24/exclusive-zuma-friends-r550m-bonanza-20160814, accessed 31 August 2022.
124 Pieter-Louis Myburgh, 'Exclusive: ANC delegate and Zuma "keeper" Moodley scores Prasa millions', *News24*, 15 December 2017. Available at: https://www.news24.com/news24/SouthAfrica/News/exclusive-anc-delegate-and-zuma-keeper-moodley-scores-prasa-millions-20171215, accessed 31 August 2022.
125 Railway Safety Regular, 'State of Safety Report 2016/2017', p. 42.
126 South African Government News, 'Govt to invest R50bn in rail infrastructure', 19 October 2013. Available at: https://www.sanews.gov.za/south-africa/govt-invest-r50bn-rail-infrastructure, accessed 31 August 2022.
127 Sune' Payne, 'Sfiso Buthelezi to be sworn in as an MP on Monday', *Daily Maverick*, 7 June 2019. Available at: https://www.dailymaverick.co.za/article/2019-06-07-sfiso-buthelezi-to-be-sworn-in-as-an-mp-on-monday/, accessed 31 August 2022.
128 Setumo Stone, 'The man who would be Jonas', *City Press*, 20 March 2016. Available at: https://www.news24.com/citypress/news/the-man-who-would-be-jonas-20160319, accessed 31 August 2022.
129 *Mail & Guardian*, 'BEE partner bags 10% stake in Cadiz', *Mail & Guardian*, 23 March 2004. Available at: https://mg.co.za/article/2004-03-23-bee-partner-bags-10-stake-in-cadiz/, accessed 31 August 2022.
130 Horwath Forensics, 'Passenger Rail Agency of South Africa (PRASA),

Swifambo flow of funds analysis (Draft) preliminary report', 20 April 2017, p. 30.
131 South African Rail Commuter Corporation (SARCC) (2006) '2006/2006 annual report'.
132 Prasa Board of Control charter.
133 Prasa Board of Control charter, p. 8.
134 Prasa 2013/2014 annual report, p. 17.
135 Public Protector South Africa, 'Derailed', 2015.
136 Van Wyk, 'Scorpio: Prasa – Treasury investigations recommends Sfiso Buthelezi be criminally charged'.
137 Public Protector South Africa, 'Derailed', 2015, p. 295.
138 Public Protector South Africa, 'Derailed', 2015, p. 295.
139 *Mail & Guardian*, 'BEE partner bags 10% stake in Cadiz'.
140 UniteBehind, 'Media Statement: #Unitebehind takes Public Protector to Court for Possible Prasa Cover Up', 4 November 2019. Available at: https://unitebehind.org.za/unitebehind-takes-public-protector-to-court-for-possible-prasa-cover-up/, accessed 31 August 2022.
141 Fundudzi, 'National Treasury: Final report forensic investigation into various allegations at Transnet and Eskom', 2018, p. 239. Available at: http://www.treasury.gov.za/comm_media/press/2018/Final%20Report%20-%20Fundudzi%20-%20Eskom%2015112018.pdf, accessed 31 August 2022.
142 Horwath Forensics, 'Passenger Rail Agency of South Africa (PRASA), Swifambo flow of funds analysis (Draft) preliminary report', 20 April 2017, p. 27.
143 Horwath Forensics, 'Passenger Rail Agency of South Africa (PRASA), Swifambo flow of funds analysis (Draft) preliminary report', 20 April 2017, p. 31.
144 Horwath Forensics, 'Passenger Rail Agency of South Africa (PRASA), Swifambo flow of funds analysis (Draft) preliminary report', 20 April 2017, p. 30.
145 Pieter-Louis Myburgh, 'Exclusive: Deputy FinMin scored Prasa tenders as agency chair', *News24*, 5 June 2017. Available at: https://www.news24.com/news24/southafrica/news/exclusive-deputy-finmin-scored-prasa-tenders-as-agency-chair-20170605, accessed 31 August 2022.
146 Horwath Forensics, 'Passenger Rail Agency of South Africa (PRASA), Swifambo flow of funds analysis (Draft) preliminary report', 20 April 2017, p. 99.
147 Horwath Forensics, 'Passenger Rail Agency of South Africa (PRASA),

Swifambo flow of funds analysis (Draft) preliminary report', 20 April 2017, p. 100.
148 Horwath Forensics, 'Ryan Marc Sacks affidavit', 2021, p. 4.
149 Pieter-Louis Myburgh, 'Exclusive: Deputy FinMin scored Prasa tenders as agency chair', *News24*, 5 June 2017. Available at: https://www.news24.com/news24/southafrica/news/exclusive-deputy-finmin-scored-prasa-tenders-as-agency-chair-20170605, accessed 31 August 2022.
150 Horwath Forensics, 'Passenger Rail Agency of South Africa (PRASA), Swifambo flow of funds analysis (Draft) preliminary report', 20 April 2017, p. 21.
151 Ministry of Finance, 'Media Statement: Deputy Minister Sfiso Buthelezi was never conflicted in Prasa tenders', 6 June 2017. Available at: https://www.opensecrets.org.za/wp-content/uploads/Buthelezi-Finance-Ministery-defence.pdf, accessed 31 August 2022.
152 Commission of Inquiry into State Capture Transcript, 15 July 2021, Day 422. Available at: https://www.statecapture.org.za/site/files/transcript/441/Day_422_-_2021-07-15.pdf, accessed 31 August 2022.
153 Ministry of Finance, 'Media Statement: Deputy Minister Sfiso Buthelezi was never conflicted in Prasa tenders', 6 June 2017.
154 Popo Molefe, 'Prasa investigations', Letter to Berning Ntlemeza, 13 February 2017. Available at: https://www.forensicsforjustice.org/wp-content/uploads/2017/07/Letter-Popo-Molefe-to-Ntlemeza-2017-02-13.pdf, accessed 31 August 2022.
155 Paul Herman, 'Former Prasa board chair Sfiso Buthelezi named deputy finance minister', *News24*, 31 March 2017. Available at: https://www.news24.com/news24/southafrica/news/former-prasa-board-chairperson-sfiso-buthelezi-named-deputy-finance-minister-20170331, accessed 31 August 2022.
156 Sune' Payne, 'Sfiso Buthelezi to be sworn in as an MP on Monday', *Daily Maverick*, 7 June 2019. Available at: https://www.dailymaverick.co.za/article/2019-06-07-sfiso-buthelezi-to-be-sworn-in-as-an-mp-on-monday/, accessed 31 August 2022.
157 Justin Brown, 'Concerns over appointment process for new head of Parliamentary Budget Office', *GroundUp*, 13 October 2020. Available at: https://www.groundup.org.za/article/concerns-over-appointment-process-new-head-parliamentary-budget-office/, accessed 31 August 2022.
158 ICASA, 'Complaints and Compliance Committee: Monitoring and Complaints Unit of the Independent Communications Authority

of South Africa vs. Ilitha Community Radio', 13 December 2007. Available at: https://www.icasa.org.za/uploads/files/ICASA-vs-Ilitha-Community-Radio-Judgment-14-2007.pdf, accessed 31 August 2022.
159 SARS, 'South African Revenue Service Annual Report, 2017–2018', 2018. Available at: https://www.sars.gov.za/wp-content/uploads/Enterprise/AnnualReports/SARS-AR-23-Annual-Report-2017-2018.pdf., accessed 31 August 2022.
160 CIPC Records, 'Refiloe Mokoena', March 2022.
161 *Minister of Defence and Military Veterans v Motau and Others (CCT 133/13) [2014] ZACC 18; 2014 (8) BCLR 930 (CC); 2014 (5) SA 69 (CC)* (10 June 2014), para 8.
162 OUTA, 'No room to hide: A president caught in the act', 28 June 2017. Available at: https://www.sars.gov.za/wp-content/uploads/Enterprise/AnnualReports/SARS-AR-23-Annual-Report-2017-2018.pdf., accessed 31 August 2022..
163 Justice RMM Zondo, 'Judicial Commission of Inquiry into State Capture Report: Part 2, Volume 2: Denel', 2022, p. 620, para. 408. Available at: https://www.sars.gov.za/wp-content/uploads/Enterprise/AnnualReports/SARS-AR-23-Annual-Report-2017-2018.pdf, accessed 31 August 2022.
164 Justice RMM Zondo, 'Judicial Commission of Inquiry into State Capture Report: Part 2, Volume 2: Denel', 2022, p. 626, para 421.
165 Guy Martin, 'More money for SANDF, Denel in medium term budget', *DefenceWeb*, 11 November 2021. Available at: https://www.defenceweb.co.za/featured/more-money-for-sandf-denel-in-medium-term-budget/, accessed 31 August 2022.
166 Lameez Omarjee, ' "Tough love": Treasury snubs SAA, but Denel and Saria score', *News24*, 23 February 2022. Available at: https://www.news24.com/fin24/economy/budget-2022-tough-love-treasury-snubs-saa-but-denel-and-sasria-score-20220223, accessed 31 August 2022.
167 Justice RMM Zondo, 'Judicial Commission of Inquiry into State Capture Report: Part 2, Volume 2: Denel', 2022, p. 67, para 193.3.
168 Mawande AmaShabalala, 'Gupta ally Refiloe Mokoena shared in asbestos loot via Ace Magashule', *TimesLive*, 4 October 2020. Available at: https://www.timeslive.co.za/sunday-times/news/2020-10-04-gupta-ally-refiloe-mokoena-shared-in-asbestos-loot-via-ace-magashule/, accessed 31 August 2022.
169 'Witness Statement & Annexure: Mxolisi Dukwana', Commission of Inquiry into State Capture, 28 August 2019, pp. 113–117. Available at:

Notes

https://www.statecapture.org.za/site/files/documents/199/X_5._Second_Affidavit_for_Dukoana.pdf, accessed 31 August 2022.
170 'Witness Statement & Annexure: Mxolisi Dukwana', pp. 113–117.
171 AmaShabalala, 'Gupta ally Refiloe Mokoena shared in asbestos loot via Ace Magashule'.
172 'Witness Statement & Annexure: Mxolisi Dukwana', pp. 113–117.
173 Karyn Maughan, 'Ace Magashule's challenge to his corruption prosecution exposes its weaknesses', *News24*, 23 February 2022. Available at: https://www.news24.com/news24/columnists/karynmaughan/karyn-maughan-ace-magashules-challenge-to-his-corruption-prosecution-exposes-its-weaknesses-20220223, accessed 31 August 2022.
174 AmaShabalala, 'Gupta ally Refiloe Mokoena shared in asbestos loot via Ace Magashule'.
175 Code of Judicial Conduct in Government Gazette 35802, 18 October 2012.
176 SARS, 'South African Revenue Service Annual Report, 2017–2018', 2018.
177 Denel, 'Denel Annual Report 2017/2018', 2018. Available at: http://admin.denel.co.za/uploads/29a2543d6eec1dfc373dd0b17c7f37e0.pdf, accessed 31 August 2022.
178 Justice RMM Zondo, 'Judicial Commission of Inquiry into State Capture Report: Part 1, Volume 3: South African Revenue Services (SARS) and Public Procurement in South Africa', 2022. Available at: https://www.statecapture.org.za/site/files/announcements/673/OCR_version_-_State_Capture_Commission_Report_Part_1_Vol_I.pdf, accessed 31 August 2022.
179 Judge Nugent, Commission Of Inquiry Into Tax Administration and Governance By SARS, Final Report, 2018, p. 125, para 8. Available at: http://www.inqcomm.co.za/Docs/media/SARS%20Commission%20Final%20Report.pdf, accessed 31 August 2022.
180 SARS, 'SARS's dismissal of former Chief Legal Officer Refiloe Mokoena is fair', 15 June 2021. Available at: https://www.sars.gov.za/media-release/sarss-dismissal-of-former-chief-legal-officer-refiloe-mokoena-is-fair/, accessed 31 August 2022.
181 Judge Nugent, Commission Of Inquiry Into Tax Administration and Governance By SARS, Final Report, p. 4, para 5.
182 Lameez Omarjee, 'CCMA dismisses claim of SARS's Chief Legal Officer axed over R150m Gupta VAT refunds', *News24*, 15 June 2021.

https://www.news24.com/fin24/companies/financial-services/ccma-dismisses-claim-of-sarss-chief-legal-officer-axed-over-r150m-gupta-vat-refunds-20210615, accessed 31 August 2022.

Section 4: Welfare Profiteers

1. KPMG, 'Forensic investigation into cancelled pension funds', Volume 1: Report on Factual Determinations, 20 October 2015.
2. Chantal Hugo Founding Affidavit, *Liberty Group Limited v The Registrar of Pension Funds*, 2017.
3. Jonathan Mort, 'First Inspection Report', submitted to FSB, 7 June 2016.
4. Contract between Liberty Group Limited and Biggs, Kleingeld and Bekker Pty. Ltd., December 2012.
5. Jonathan Mort, 'First Inspection Report', submitted to FSB, 7 June 2016.
6. Personal Finance, 'Legal wrangle continues as inquiry into Fedsure ends', *Personal Finance*, 26 April 2003.
7. Letter from the FSCA to SAHA, 23 January 2019.
8. Tim Cohen, 'Public Protector tears into Financial Services Board and former boss Dube Tshidi, vindicating EFF's Julius Malema', *Daily Maverick*, 3 April 2019. Available at: https://www.dailymaverick.co.za/article/2019-04-03-public-protector-tears-into-financial-services-board-and-former-boss-dube-tshidi-vindicating-effs-julius-malema/, accessed 31 August 2022.
9. Open Secrets, *The Bottom Line: Who Profits from Unpaid Pensions?*, 2019.
10. KPMG, 'Forensic Investigation into Cancelled Pension Funds', Volume 1: Report on Factual Determinations, 20 October 2015.
11. Chantal Hugo Founding Affidavit, *Liberty Group Limited v The Registrar of Pension Funds*, 2017.
12. Jon Allsop, 'Top public officials earn more than the President', GroundUp, 27 March 2019. Available at: https://www.groundup.org.za/article/top-public-officials-earn-more-president/, accessed 31 August 2022.
13. Eric Torkelson, 'Collateral damages: Cash transfer and debt transfer in South Africa', *World Development* (2020), p. 126.
14. David Porteous, 'Scoping report on the payment of social transfers through the financial system'. *Bankable Frontier Associates*. London, UK: Department for International Development, 2006, p. 23; Torkelson, 'Collateral damages', p. 126.
15. Keith Breckenridge, *Biometric State*, Cambridge University Press, 2014.

16 While there are 17.6 million beneficiaries, there are only 10 million recipients, because some recipients receive grants for multiple beneficiaries, eg, mothers with multiple children.
17 J. Froneman, *Allpay Consolidated Investment Holdings (Pty) Ltd and Others v Chief Executive Officer of the South African Social Security Agency and Others.* Constitutional Court, Johannesburg, 29 November 2013.
18 Erin Torkelson, 'Deductions from social grants', *GroundUp*, 3 March.
19 *Allpay Consolidated Investment Holdings (Pty) Ltd and Others v Chief Executive Officer of the South African Social Security Agency and Others* (CCT 48/13) [2013] ZACC 42; Torkelson, 'Collateral damages', p. 126.
20 Robyn Foley and Mark Swilling, 'How one word can change the game: Case study of state capture and the South African Social Security Agency', 2018; Net1 Annual Report, Net1 UEPS Technologies, 2018; Torkelson, 'Collateral damages', p. 126.
21 Torkelson, 'Collateral damages', p. 126.
22 Torkelson, 'Collateral damages', p. 126.
23 Lynette Maart and Angi Richardsson, 'Hands off our grants', *Financial Mail*, 19 May 2022. Available at: https://www.businesslive.co.za/fm/features/2022-05-19-hands-off-our-grants/, accessed 31 August 2022.
24 Maart and Richardsson, 'Hands off our grants'.
25 Adapted from H. Kotzé, Chairman's letter, Net1 UEPS Technologies Annual report 2018, cited in Torkelson, 'Collateral damages', p. 126.
26 Black Sash, 'Community-based monitoring: SASSA paypoints: October 2016 – November 2016', 2016, cited in Torkelson, 'Collateral damages', p. 126.
27 Poster created by the Black Sash based on a survey conducted by the Social Justice Coalition at a SASSA Pay Point in Khayelitsha between October and November 2016. Over 50 per cent of participants said they had money deducted from their grants without their consent. Complete survey data is available at the Black Sash website: https://cbm.blacksash.org.za/survey-types/sassa-paypoint-citizen.
28 Craig McKune, 'Serge Belamant, SASSA, and the war chest of poor people', AmaBhungane, 16 March 2017. Available at: https://mg.co.za/article/2017-03-16-serge-belamant-sassa-and-the-war-chest-of-poor-people/, accessed 31 August 2022.
29 Erin Torkelson, 'Collateral damages', p. 126.
30 Alec Hogg, 'Net1's Serge Belamant: Business is ugly. Disrupt at your reputational peril', *BizNews*, 9 August 2016. Available at: https://

	www.biznews.com/entrepreneur/2016/08/09/net1s-serge-belamant-business-is-ugly-disrupt-at-your-reputational-peril, accessed 31 August 2022.
31	The NCR allows interest rates of 5 per cent per month on short-term, unsecured credit (under 6 months), as well as initiation fees up to 15 per cent of the value of the loan, and service fees of R50 per month.
32	Torkelson, 'Collateral damages', p. 126.
33	Torkelson, 'Collateral damages', p.126; Black Sash, 'Community based monitoring: SASSA paypoints'.
34	Torkelson, 'Collateral damages', p. 126.
35	Lee-Ann Bruce, 'Former Minister Bathabile Dlamini found guilty of perjury', Centre for Applied Legal Studies, 10 March 2022.
36	Mosima Rafapa, 'Desperate for money, social grant recipients borrow from a surprising source', *GroundUp*, 10 June 2022. Available at: https://www.groundup.org.za/article/people-on-social-grants-live-by-borrowing/, accessed 30 August 2022.
37	Zoë Postman, 'Cash Paymaster Services may have to pay SASSA R1 billion', *GroundUp*, 6 February 2020. Available at: https://www.groundup.org.za/article/cash-paymaster-services-might-have-pay-sassa-r1-billion/, accessed 31 August 2022.
38	Tania Broughton, 'Concourt hammers unlawful social grants company', *GroundUp*, 14 February 2022. Available at: https://www.moneyweb.co.za/news/south-africa/concourt-hammers-unlawful-social-grants-company/, accessed 31 August 2022.
39	Emsie Ferreria, 'ConCourt orders CPS to file all records relating to its illicit profits', *Mail & Guardian*, 1 April 2021. Available at: https://mg.co.za/news/2021-04-01-concourt-orders-cps-to-file-all-records-relating-to-its-illicit-profits/, accessed 31 August 2022.
40	Hot102.7FM, 'Capital Appreciation bats away Govchat concerns as Open Secrets asks some searching questions', 30 November 2021. Available at: https://iono.fm/e/1132191, accessed 31 August 2022.
41	Open Secrets, 'Digital Profiteers: Who Profits Next From Social Grants?', November 2022. Available at: https://www.opensecrets.org.za/digital_profiteers/, accessed 30 August 2022.
42	Rob Rose, 'Inside SA's welfare-industrial complex', *Financial Mail*, 25 November 2021. Available at: https://www.businesslive.co.za/fm/features/cover-story/2021-11-25-inside-sas-welfare-industrial-complex/, accessed 30 August 2022.

Notes

Section 5: Bad Bankers

1. Michael Marchant, Mamello Mosiana, Paul Holden and Hennie van Vuuren, 'The Enablers: The Bankers, Accountants and Lawyers that Cashed in on State Capture', Report submitted to the Zondo Commission of Inquiry into State Capture, Open Secrets and Shadow World Investigations, 2020.
2. Khadija Sharife and Josy Joseph, 'India's Bank of Baroda played a key role in South Africa's Gupta scandal', Organised Crime and Corruption Reporting Project, 27 February 2018. Available at: https://www.occrp.org/en/investigations/7696-india-s-bank-of-baroda-played-a-key-role-in-south-africa-s-gupta-scandal, accessed 31 August 2022.
3. Sharife and Joseph, 'India's Bank of Baroda played a key role in South Africa's Gupta scandal'.
4. Ryk van Niekerk and Warren Thomson, 'FIC fines Bank of Baroda for flouting anti-corruption laws', *Moneyweb*, 4 September 2017. Available at: https://www.moneyweb.co.za/news/companies-and-deals/fic-fines-bank-of-baroda-for-flouting-anti-corruption-laws/, accessed 31 August 2022.
5. Van Niekerk and Thomson, 'FIC fines Bank of Baroda for flouting anti-corruption laws'.
6. Sharife and Joseph, 'India's Bank of Baroda played a key role in South Africa's Gupta scandal'.
7. Nedbank Group, 'Group at a Glance', December 2018.
8. Nico Gous, 'Nedbank says no more to Bank of Baroda', *Business Day*, 28 February 2018. Available at: https://www.businesslive.co.za/bd/companies/financial-services/2018-02-28-nedbank-says-no-more-to-bank-of-baroda/, accessed 31 August 2022.
9. Sharife and Joseph, 'India's Bank of Baroda played a key role in South Africa's Gupta scandal'.
10. Sharife and Joseph, 'India's Bank of Baroda played a key role in South Africa's Gupta scandal'.
11. Van Niekerk and Thomson, 'FIC fines Bank of Baroda for flouting anti-corruption laws'.
12. Statement by Michael Brown to the Commission of Inquiry into State Capture, 29 August 2018. Available at: https://www.sastatecapture.org.za/site/files/documents/14/Statement-_Nedbank.pdf, accessed 31 August 2022.
13. Gous, 'Nedbank says no more to Bank of Baroda.

14 Sharife and Joseph, 'India's Bank of Baroda played a key role in South Africa's Gupta scandal'.

15 *Fin24*, I'm at your disposal, Nedbank CEO tells Ramaphosa in open letter, 19 December 2017.

16 Tebogo Tshwane, 'Banks called out over Gupta Heists, *Mail & Guardian*, 16 November 2018. Available at: https://mg.co.za/article/2018-11-16-00-banks-called-out-over-gupta-heists/, accessed 30 August 2022.

17 Mohammed Mahomedy, Acting Chief Financial Officer of Transnet, Statement to the Zondo Commission of Inquiry, 16 April 2019. Available at: https://www.statecapture.org.za/site/files/documents/108/BB_3._MS_Mahomedy_-_Statement_&_Annexure_Part_1.pdf, accessed 31 August 2022.

18 Mohammed Mahomedy, Acting Chief Financial Officer of Transnet, Statement to the Zondo Commission of Inquiry, 16 April 2019, para 5.65.

19 Mohammed Mahomedy, Acting Chief Financial Officer of Transnet, Statement to the Zondo Commission of Inquiry, 16 April 2019, para 5.66.

20 Khadija Sharife and Josy Joseph, 'India's Bank of Baroda Played a Key Role in South Africa's Gupta Scandal', Organised Crime and Corruption Reporting Project.

21 Sipho Masondo, 'Nedbank pockets more than R780 million from Transnet', *City Press*, 12 May 2019. Available at: https://www.news24.com/citypress/business/nedbank-pockets-r780m-from-transnet-20190512, accessed 31 August 2022.

22 Khadija Sharife, 'Guptas, Nedbank skilfully extract money from South African state firm', Organised Crime and Corruption Reporting Project, 3 November 2017. Available at: https://www.occrp.org/en/investigations/7215-guptas-nedbank-skillfully-extract-money-from-south-african-state-firm, accessed 31 August 2022.

23 Sharife, 'Guptas, Nedbank skilfully extract money from South African state firm'.

24 Mohammed Mahomedy, Acting Chief Financial Officer of Transnet, Statement to the Zondo Commission of Inquiry, 16th April 2019, para 5.6.16.6.

25 Mohammed Mahomedy, Acting Chief Financial Officer of Transnet, Statement to the Zondo Commission of Inquiry, 16 April 2019, para 5.67.

26 Delmar Tarrago, 'Glamorizing the nightmare trade', *The Common Reader*, 13 November 2017.

27   Tom Dart, 'Families of Americans killed by Mexican cartels sue HSBC for laundering billions', *The Guardian*, 2016. Available at: https://www.theguardian.com/business/2016/feb/11/families-of-americans-killed-by-mexican-cartels-sue-hsbc, accessed 31 August 2022.
28   Patrick Radden Keefe, 'Cocaine Incorporated', *New York Times Magazine*, 15 June 2012.
29   Deferred Prosecution Agreement between United States Department of Justice, Criminal Division, Asset Forfeiture and Money Laundering Section, the United States Attorney's Office for the Eastern District of New York, and the United States Attorney's Office for the Northern District of West Virginia (collectively, the 'Department') and HSBC Bank USA, N.A. ('HSBC Bank USA') and HSBC Holdings plc ('HSBC Holdings'); and as part of a separate Deferred Prosecution Agreement between the New York County District Attorney's Office ('DANY') and HSBC Holdings (2012).
30   John Christensen, 'HSBC and the world's oldest drug cartel', Tax Justice Network, 2015; Eric Toussaint, 'HSBC: The bank with a shameful past and scandalous present', Committee for the Abolition of Illegitimate Debt (CADTM), 2014.
31   Christensen, 'HSBC and the world's oldest drug cartel'.
32   amaBhungane and Scorpio, '#GuptaLeaks: Meet the money launderers', *fin24*, 2017. Available at: https://www.news24.com/Fin24/guptaleaks-meet-the-money-launderers-20180118, accessed 31 August 2022.
33   Gabriele Stenhauser and Margot Patrick, 'From the WSJ: The Guptas used HSBC accounts for transactions linked to suspected SA kickbacks', *Business Day*, 2017. Available at: https://www.businesslive.co.za/bd/national/2017-11-10-from-the-wsj-hsbc-accounts-used-for-transactions-linked-to-suspected-sa-kickbacks/, accessed 31 August 2022.
34   Cronje and Smith, 'Transnet Disbands Scandal-Plagued Acquisition and Disposal Committee', *Fin24*, 20 July 2018. Available at: https://www.news24.com/Fin24/transnet-disbands-scandal-plagued-acquisition-and-disposal-committee-20180720, accessed 30 August 2022.
35   Khadija Sharife, 'Guptas, big banks linked to South African-Chinese locomotive deal', OCCRP, 2017.
36   Sharife, 'Guptas, big banks linked to South African-Chinese locomotive deal'.
37   Sharife, 'Guptas, big banks linked to South African-Chinese locomotive deal'.

38 The Guardian, 'HSBC shut down accounts linked to Gupta scandal', *The Guardian*, 1 November 2017.

39 Sharife, 'Guptas, big banks linked to South African-Chinese locomotive deal'.

40 HSBC, *Violation Tracker*.

41 Philip Mattera, 'HSBC: Corporate Rap Sheet', Corporate Research Project, 2018.

42 HSBC, *Violation Tracker*.

43 Patrick Radden Keefe, 'Why Corrupt Bankers Avoid Jail', *New Yorker*, 24 July 2017.

44 Kalyeena Makortoff, Franz Wild and Ben Stockton, 'HSBC faces questions over alleged disclosure of money laundering to monitors', *The Guardian*, 28 July 2021. Available at: https://www.theguardian.com/business/2021/jul/28/hsbc-faces-questions-over-disclosure-of-alleged-money-laundering-to-monitors, accessed 31 August 2022.

45 Tabelo Timse and Stefaans Brümmer, 'Guptas' farm cash cows in Free State', *Mail & Guardian*, 2013. Available at: https://mg.co.za/article/2013-05-31-00-guptas-farm-cash-cows-in-free-state/, accessed 31 August 2022.

46 Shadow World Investigations, Submission to the Commission of Inquiry into Allegations of State Capture regarding the Estina/Vrede Integrated Dairy Project, November 2019.

47 Daily Maverick, 'Explainer: The eight Gupta-linked suspects who appeared in court', *Daily Maverick*, 15 February 2018. Available at: https://www.dailymaverick.co.za/article/2018-02-15-explainer-the-eight-gupta-linked-suspects-who-appeared-in-court/, accessed 31 August 2022.

48 Zaakir Mohamed and Krevania Pillay, 'The Obligation to Report Suspicious Transactions in terms of S29 of the Financial Intelligence Centre Act', *CDH Dispute Resolution Alert*, 27 February 2019.

49 Timse and Brümmer, 'Guptas' farm cash cows in Free State'.

50 Commission of Inquiry into State Capture, 12 March 2019, Transcript: Standard Bank/Ian Sinton Testimony. Available at: https://www.statecapture.org.za/site/files/documents/74/U10._Ian_Sinton_-_Statement_&_Annexure.pdf, accessed 31 August 2022.

51 Commission of Inquiry into State Capture, 12 March 2019, Transcript: Standard Bank/Ian Sinton Testimony, p. 74.

52 Commission of Inquiry into State Capture, 12 March 2019, Transcript: Standard Bank/Ian Sinton Testimony, p. 74.

53 Zaakir Mohamed and Krevania Pillay, 'The Obligation to Report Suspicious Transactions in terms of S29 of the Financial Intelligence Centre Act'.
54 Email from Standard Bank (through Ross Linstrom) to SWI and Open Secrets, 9 October 2019.
55 Commission of Inquiry into State Capture, 12 March 2019, Transcript: Standard Bank/Ian Sinton Testimony.
56 Commission of Inquiry into State Capture, 18 September 2018, Transcript: Johan Burger Testimony, p. 19. Available at: https://www.statecapture.org.za/site/files/transcript/21/18_September_2018_SESSION_1_%E2%80%93_2.pdf, accessed 31 August 2022.
57 Free State Legislature: Question Paper: Wednesday, 4 March 2015 [No. 1 – 2015] Second Session, Fifth Legislature, Ms S.M. Mlamleli, Acting MEC Agriculture and Rural Development, 28 April 2015.
58 Michael Marchant, Mamello Mosiana, Paul Holden and Hennie van Vuuren, 'The Enablers: The Bankers, Accountants and Lawyers that Cashed in on State Capture', Report submitted to the Zondo Commission of Inquiry into State Capture, Open Secrets & Shadow World Investigations, 2020, p. 104.
59 Joseph Hanlon, 'Mozambique: Credit Suisse is liable for the $2bn secret debt', *Committee for the Abolition of Illegitimate Debt (CADTM)*, 17 March 2020.
60 World Bank, 'World Development Indicators: Mozambique', Data Bank.
61 'Mozambique to seek extradition of ex-Credit Suisse bankers involved in $2 billion debt scandal', Reuters, 21 October 2020. Available at: https://www.reuters.com/article/us-mozambique-credit-suisse-banking-idUSKBN2762KS, accessed 31 August 2022.
62 Karin Strohecker, 'Factbox: Mozambique debt crisis - What does the country owe, and to whom?', Reuters, 9 September 2019. Available at: https://www.reuters.com/article/us-mozambique-debt-creditors-factbox-idUSKCN1VU1WE, accessed 31 August 2022.
63 Joseph Hanlon, 'Mozambique: Credit Suisse is liable for the $2bn secret debt', Committee for the Abolition of Illegitimate Debt (CADTM), 17 March 2020.
64 Mary Serumaga, 'The Mozambican debt crisis: How a sovereign state was sold', Committee for the Abolition of Illegitimate Debt (CADTM), 9 February 2017.
65 Serumaga, 'The Mozambican debt crisis: How a sovereign state was sold'.

66 Hanlon, 'Mozambique: Credit Suisse is liable for the $2bn secret debt'.
67 Serumaga, 'The Mozambican debt crisis: How a sovereign state was sold'.
68 Kroll Associates, Executive Summary: Independent audit related to loans contracted by ProIndicus S.A., EMATUM S.A. and Mozambique Asset Management S.A., Report prepared for The Office of the Public Prosecutor of the Republic of Mozambique, 23 June 2017, pp. 40–44.
69 Cate Reid, 'Mozambique: The anatomy of corruption', *The Africa Report*, 26 June 2018.
70 Hanlon, 'Mozambique: Credit Suisse is liable for the $2bn secret debt'.
71 Reid, 'Mozambique: the anatomy of corruption'.
72 Hanlon, 'Mozambique: Credit Suisse is liable for the $2bn secret debt'.
73 Reid, 'Mozambique: The anatomy of corruption'.
74 Margot Patrick and Patrick Wirz, 'For love and money in Mozambique: How a Credit Suisse banker helped fuel an alleged $2 billion debt fraud', *Wall Street Journal*, 2 December 2019.
75 Patrick and Wirz, 'For love and money in Mozambique'.
76 Joseph Hanlon, 'Kroll suggests Credit Suisse acted improperly – turning a blind eye and loan pushing', *Mozambique: News Reports and Clippings*, 7 September 2017.
77 Hanlon, 'Kroll suggests Credit Suisse acted improperly – turning a blind eye and loan pushing'.
78 'Mozambique files case against Credit Suisse', *BBC*, 28 February 2019.
79 Reid, 'Mozambique: The anatomy of corruption'.
80 Will Fitzgibbon, 'Unchecked by Global Banks, Dirty Cash Destroys Dreams and Lives', *OCCRP*, 20 September 2020. Available at: https://www.icij.org/investigations/fincen-files/unchecked-by-global-banks-dirty-cash-destroys-dreams-and-lives/, accessed 31 August 2022.
81 Christina Maza, 'Bank that allegedly planned to finance Trump Tower Moscow purchased leading Russian TV station from oligarch Roman Abramovich', *Newsweek*, 3 July 2019. Available at: https://www.newsweek.com/bank-allegedly-planned-finance-trump-tower-moscow-purchased-leading-russian-1355045, accessed 31 August 2022.
82 US Department of the Treasury, 'Announcement of additional Treasury sanctions on Russian financial institutions and on a defense technology entity', 29 July 2014.
83 Reuters, 'Russia's VTB, bank subsidiary hit with $5 million penalty for false trades: CFTC', 19 September 2016.
84 Euromoney, 'Interview by Alexei Yakovitsky, Global CEO at VTB Capital,

for Euromoney', *VTB* Capital, 3 November 2016.

85 Kroll Associates, Executive Summary: Independent audit related to loans contracted by ProIndicus S.A., EMATUM S.A. and Mozambique Asset Management S.A., Report prepared for The Office of the Public Prosecutor of the Republic of Mozambique, 23 June 2017, p. 35, para. 3.5.1.

86 *The Republic of Mozambique vs. Credit Suisse International, Credit Suisse AG, Mr. Surjan Singh, Mr. Andrew Pearse, Ms. Detelina Subeva, Privinvest Shipbuilding Investments LLC, Logistics International SAL (offshore), Logistics International Investments LLC, Credit Suisse Securities (Europe) Limited and Mr. Iskandar Safa*, in. the Court of Appeal (Civil Division) on Appeal from the High Court of Justice Business and Property Courts of England and Wales Commercial Court (QBD) (Case no. A4/2020/1467), para 16.

87 United States District Court Eastern District of New York, 'United States of America against Jean Boustani and others', Case 1:18-cr-00681-WFK, 19 December 2018, p. 12; 27, para 38; p. 76.

88 Kroll Associates, Executive Summary: Independent audit related to loans contracted by ProIndicus S.A., EMATUM S.A. and Mozambique Asset Management S.A., Report prepared for The Office of the Public Prosecutor of the Republic of Mozambique, 23 June 2017.

89 Jake Ruditsky, Henry Meyer and Patricia Hurtado, 'Russia's VTB Bribe Claim May Set Back Kremlin Bank's Africa Ambitions', *Bloomberg*, 8 November 2019. Available at: https://www.themoscowtimes.com/2019/11/08/russias-vtb-bribe-claim-kremlin-bank-africa-ambitions-a68100, accessed 31 August 2022.

90 Kroll Associates, Executive Summary: Independent audit related to loans contracted by ProIndicus S.A., EMATUM S.A. and Mozambique Asset Management S.A., Report prepared for The Office of the Public Prosecutor of the Republic of Mozambique, 23 June 2017.

91 *VTB Capital PLC vs. The Republic of Mozambique and Mozambique Asset Management SA*, in the High Courts of Justice Business and Property Courts of England and Wales Commercial Court (QBD).

92 France24, 'Mozambique court annuls loans of $1.4 bn', 13 May 2020. Available at: https://www.france24.com/en/20200513-mozambique-court-annuls-loans-of-1-4-bn, accessed 31 August 2022.

93 Jubilee Debt Campaign, 'Reaction to Russian bank suing Mozambique in London', 7 January 2020.

94 UNDP, 'Briefing note for countries on the 2020 Human Development

Report: Mozambique', *Human Development Report – The Next Frontier: Human Development and the Anthropocene*, 7 January 2020.

Section 6: Failing Auditors

1   Michael Marchant and Mamello Mosiana, *The Corporations and Economic Crime Report: The Auditors*, Vol. 2, Open Secrets, Cape Town, 2020.
2   Ben Chapman, 'PwC, KPMG, Deloitte and EY all fail to meet audit quality targets after string of high-profile failures', *Independent*, 10 July 2019.
3   Odd-Helge Fjeldstad, Sigrid Jacobsen, Peter Ringstad and Honest Ngowi (eds), *Lifting the Veil of Secrecy: Perspectives on International Taxation and Capital Flight from Africa*, Michelsen Institute, 2017, pp. 70–71.
4   Barclay Ballard, 'Top 5 biggest financial scandals of all time', *World Finance*, 2018.
5   Deloitte website, 'Our heritage'. Available at: https://www2.deloitte.com/global/en/pages/about-deloitte/articles/deloitte175.html, accessed 30 August 2022.
6   Jan Cronje, 'Top 5 things to know about the PwC report into Steinhoff and questions that still remain', *Fin24*, 18 March 2019. Available at: https://www.news24.com/Fin24/the-top-5-things-to-know-about-the-pwc-report-into-steinhoff-and-the-questions-that-still-remain-20190318, accessed 31 August 2022.
7   PwC forensic investigation into Steinhoff, quoted in Tim Cohen, 'PwC's Steinhoff report suggests profit was boosted R106bn in seven years', *Daily Maverick*, 17 March 2019.
8   Summary: Key Findings of the PwC Investigation, Tongaat Hulett Limited, 29 November 2019.
9   Rob Rose, 'Deloitte's R11,8 billion pickle', *Financial Mail*, 12 December 2019. Available at: https://www.businesslive.co.za/fm/opinion/editors-note/2019-12-12-rob-rose-deloittes-r118bn-pickle/, accessed 31 August 2022.
10 Rob Rose, *Steinheist*, Tafelberg,, 2018, p. 3.
11 Rob Rose, 'Hawks "don't have the budget" for Steinhoff probe', *Financial Mail*, 4 March 2021. Available at: https://www.businesslive.co.za/fm/fm-fox/2021-03-04-hawks-dont-have-the-budget-for-steinhoff-probe/, accessed 31 August 2022.
12 Cohen, 'PwC's Steinhoff report suggests profit was boosted R106bn in seven years'.

13   Steinhoff 1999 Annual Report.
14   Tehillah Nieselow, 'We did the right thing with Steinhoff – Deloitte', *Fin24*, 19 January 2018. Available at: https://www.news24.com/Fin24/exclusive-we-did-the-right-thing-with-steinhoff-deloitte-20180119, accessed 31 August 2022.
15   ISA 200, Overall Objectives of the Independent Auditor and the Conduct of an Audit in Accordance with International Standards on Auditing.
16   Financial Mail, 'EDITORIAL: Media victory in the battle for Steinhoff's forensic report', 11 May 2022. Available at: https://www.businesslive.co.za/fm/opinion/editorial/2022-05-11-editorial-media-victory-in-the-battle-for-steinhoffs-forensic-report/, accessed 31 August 2022.
17   JG Jenkins and JD Stanley, 'A current evaluation of independence as a foundational element of the auditing profession in the United States', *American Accounting Association Journals* (2018), pp. 1–2.
18   Susan Comrie, 'The dirt on Deloitte's consulting dealings at Eskom, Part 2', *amaBhungane* for *News24*, 16 January 2020. Available at: https://amabhungane.org/stories/the-dirt-on-deloittes-consulting-deals-at-eskom-part-2/, accessed 31 August 2022.
19   Tebogo Tshwane, 'Eskom accuses Deloitte of corruption and (maybe) plagiarism', *Moneyweb*, 23 October 2019. Available at: https://www.moneyweb.co.za/news/south-africa/eskom-accuses-deloitte-of-corruption-and-maybe-plagiarism/, accessed 31 August 2022.
20   Carol Paton, 'Eskom goes after Deloitte for Corruption', *Business Day*, 21 October 2019. Available at: https://www.businesslive.co.za/bd/national/2019-10-21-eskom-goes-after-deloitte-for-corruption/, accessed 31 August 2022.
21   Tebogo Tshwane, 'Eskom accuses Deloitte of corruption and (maybe) plagiarism'.
22   Paton, 'Eskom goes after Deloitte for Corruption'.
23   Comrie, 'The Dirt on Deloitte's Consulting Dealings at Eskom Part 1'.
24   Sikonathi Mantshantsha, 'Eskom: We paid Deloitte R60-million for three weeks of work in two corrupt contracts', *Business Maverick*, 23 October 2019.
25   Comrie, 'The Dirt on Deloitte's Consulting Dealings at Eskom Part 1'.
26   Comrie, 'The Dirt on Deloitte's Consulting Dealings at Eskom Part 2'.
27   *Joint Statement between Eskom and Deloitte Consulting*, 20 March 2020, Deloitte & Eskom.
28   Comrie, 'The Dirt on Deloitte's Consulting Dealings at Eskom Part 2'.
29   Susan Comrie, 'In the wake of Eskom scandal, two Deloitte directors

resign', amaBhungane, 9 April 2020.

30   Deloitte, '2019 Transparency Report', 31 March 2020. Available at: https://www2.deloitte.com/za/en/pages/about-deloitte/articles/2019-transparency-report.html, accessed 30 August 2022.

31   Rosalind Z. Wiggins, Rosalind L. Bennett and Andrew Metric, 'The Lehman Brothers Bankruptcy D: The Role of Ernst & Young,' *Journal of Financial Crises*, Vol 1, Issue 1, (2019), p. 108–113.

32   Olaf Storbeck, 'Wirecard: The frantic final months of a fraudulent operation', *Financial Times*, 25 August 2020. Available at: https://www.ft.com/content/6a660a5f-4e8c-41d5-b129-ad5bf9782256, accessed 31 August 2022.

33   Olaf Storbeck, 'EY audit failings on Wirecard laid bare in 'dynamite' report', *The Financial Times*, 21 May 2021. Available at: https://www.ft.com/content/68c699dc-7427-4c24-a57e-0980fb1371ec, accessed 31 August 2022.

34   Olaf Storbeck, 'EY and Wirecard: anatomy of a flawed audit', *Financial Times*, 26 October 2021. Available at: https://www.ft.com/content/bcadbdcb-5cd7-487e-afdd-1e926831e9b7, accessed 31 August 2022.

35   Karin Strohecker, 'Fact box: Mozambique debt crisis - What does the country owe, and to whom?', Reuters, 9 September 2019.

36   Peter Fabricius, 'Former Mozambican finance minister a step closer to a US courtroom after appeal rejected', 27 July 2022, *Daily Maverick*. Available at: https://www.dailymaverick.co.za/article/2022-07-27-former-mozambican-finance-minister-chang-a-step-closer-to-a-us-courtroom-after-appeal-rejected/, accessed 31 August 2022.

37   Mary Serumaga, 'The Mozambican debt crisis: How a sovereign state was sold', Committee for the Abolition of Illegitimate Debt (CADTM), 9 February 2017.

38   Cate Reid, 'Mozambique: the anatomy of corruption', 26 June 2018, *The Africa Report*. Available at: https://www.theafricareport.com/607/mozambique-the-anatomy-of-corruption/, accessed 31 August 2022.

39   Kroll Associates, Independent audit related to loans contracted by ProIndicus S.A., EMATUM S.A. and Mozambique Asset Management S.A., Report prepared for The Office of the Public Prosecutor of the Republic of Mozambique. 23 June 2017, p130. Section 5.7.1. Available at: https://www.opensecrets.org.za/wp-content/uploads/Kroll-Independent-Audit-Executive-Summary-English-REDACTED-FOR-PUBLISHING.pdf, accessed 31 August 2022.

40   Kroll Associates, 'Independent audit related to loans contracted by

ProIndicus', p. 130.
41 Kroll Associates, 'Independent audit related to loans contracted by ProIndicus', p. 131, section 5.7.2.
42 IFAC' international auditing standard 240 sets out an auditor's responsibility to consider fraud during an audit.
43 Kroll Associates, 'Independent audit related to loans contracted by ProIndicus', p. 32, section 3.4.5. para 1.
44 Kroll Associates, Independent audit related to loans contracted by ProIndicus, p. 32, section 3.4.5 para 2.
45 Kroll Associates, 'Independent audit related to loans contracted by ProIndicus', p. 116, para 1 – EMATUM did not give Kroll information on the identity of the recipient.
46 Kroll Associates, 'Independent audit related to loans contracted by ProIndicus', p. 115, section 5.4 para 2.
47 Kroll Associates, 'Independent audit related to loans contracted by ProIndicus', p. 32.
48 Kroll Associates, 'Independent audit related to loans contracted by ProIndicus', p. 132.
49 Kroll Associates, 'Independent audit related to loans contracted by ProIndicus', p. 134, section 5.7.5.
50 Kroll Associates, 'Independent audit related to loans contracted by ProIndicus', p. 134.
51 Kroll Associates, 'Independent audit related to loans contracted by ProIndicus', p. 132, section 5.
52 Kroll Associates, 'Independent audit related to loans contracted by ProIndicus', p. 134, para 3.
53 Kroll Associates, 'Independent audit related to loans contracted by ProIndicus', p. 131.
54 Kroll Associates, 'Independent audit related to loans contracted by ProIndicus', p. 49, section 3.6.5.2.
55 Kroll Associates, 'Independent audit related to loans contracted by ProIndicus', p. 52, para 2.
56 Kroll Associates, 'Independent audit related to loans contracted by ProIndicus', p. 193, 9.2.1 paras 1–3.
57 Kroll Associates, 'Independent audit related to loans contracted by ProIndicus', p. 195, section 9.24.
58 Kroll Associates, 'Independent audit related to loans contracted by ProIndicus', p. 196, para 3.
59 Kroll Associates, 'Independent audit related to loans contracted by

ProIndicus', p. 16, 3.2.2.
60 Kroll Associates, 'Independent audit related to loans contracted by ProIndicus', p. 30, table 5.
61 Kroll Associates, 'Independent audit related to loans contracted by ProIndicus', p. 30, para 1.
62 Spotlight on Corruption, 'Cleaning up the audit sector: Why the government should consider banning Ernst & Young from public contracts', 2020.
63 Marianne Merten, 'State capture wipes out a third SA's R4,9 trillion GDP – never mind lost trust, confidence, opportunity', *Daily Maverick*, 1 March 2019. Available at: https://www.dailymaverick.co.za/article/2019-03-01-state-capture-wipes-out-third-of-sas-r4-9-trillion-gdp-never-mind-lost-trust-confidence-opportunity/, accessed 31 August 2022.
64 Michael Marchant, Mamello Mosiana, Paul Holden and Hennie van Vuuren, 'The Enablers: The Bankers, Accountants and Lawyers that Cashed in on State Capture', Report submitted to the Zondo Commission of Inquiry into State Capture, Open Secrets & Shadow World Investigations, 2020.
65 Kyle Cowan, 'SARS and the 'rogue' unit: the ultimate guide', *Fin24*, 5 July 2019. Available at: https://www.news24.com/fin24/Economy/sars-and-the-rogue-unit-the-ultimate-guide-20190705, accessed 31 August 2022.
66 Pieter du Toit, 'Secret intelligence report into SARS unit a 'travesty' and 'false', says former taxman', *News24*, 2 October 2019. Available at: https://www.news24.com/news24/SouthAfrica/News/secret-intelligence-report-into-sars-unit-a-travesty-and-false-says-former-taxman-20191002, accessed 31 August 2022.
67 Jeanette Chabalala, 'Ntsebeza inquiry: Claims that KPMG "rogue unit" report was cut-and-paste job', *News24*, 27 June 2018. Available at: https://www.news24.com/Fin24/sars-inquiry-claims-that-kpmg-rogue-unit-report-was-cut-and-paste-job-20180627, accessed 31 August 2022.
68 Chabalala, 'Ntsebeza inquiry: Claims that KPMG "rogue unit" report was cut-and-paste job'.
69 Chabalala, 'Ntsebeza inquiry: Claims that KPMG "rogue unit" report was cut-and-paste job'.
70 Chabalala, 'Ntsebeza inquiry: Claims that KPMG "rogue unit" report was cut-and-paste job'.

71 Pauli van Wyk, 'KPMG: "Weak" apology suggests company saw no evil, heard no evil therefore did no evil', *Daily Maverick*, 15 September 2019. Available at: https://www.dailymaverick.co.za/article/2017-09-15-kpmg-weak-apology-suggests-company-saw-no-evil-heard-no-evil-therefore-did-no-evil/, accessed 31 August 2022.

72 Van Wyk, 'KPMG: "Weak" apology suggests company saw no evil, heard no evil therefore did no evil'.

73 Hajra Omarjee, '"I would do this for anyone": Zuma's lawyer Muzi Sikhakhane', *Power987*, 16 July 2019.

74 Sibongile Khumalo, 'Gupta wedding under scrutiny as IRBA wraps up disciplinary of ex-KPMG auditor', *Fin24*, 6 August 2018. Available at: https://www.news24.com/Fin24/gupta-wedding-under-scrutiny-as-irba-wraps-up-disciplinary-of-ex-kpmg-auditor-20180806, accessed 31 August 2022.

75 Pieter-Louis Myburgh, 'Gupta associate "advised" Magashule on Vrede dairy project', *News24*, 12 July 2018.

76 Tabelo Timse and Stefaans Brümmer, 'Guptas' farm cash cows in Free State', *Mail & Guardian*, 2013.

77 Pieter-Louis Myburgh, 'Gupta associate 'advised' Magashule on Vrede dairy project', *News24*, 12 July 2018.

78 Shadow World Investigations, Submission to the Commission of Inquiry into Allegations of State Capture regarding the Estina/Vrede Integrated Dairy Project, November 2019.

79 SKhumalo, 'Gupta wedding under scrutiny as IRBA wraps up disciplinary of ex-KPMG auditor'.

80 AmaBhungane and Scorpio, 'The Dubai Laundromat – How KPMG saw no evil at the Sun City Wedding, *News24*, 30 June 2017. Available at: https://www.news24.com/News24/guptaleaks-the-dubai-laundromat-how-kpmg-saw-no-evil-at-the-sun-city-wedding-20170629, accessed 31 August 2022.

81 AmaBhungane and Scorpio, 'The Dubai Laundromat – How KPMG saw no evil at the Sun City Wedding'.

82 'Linkway Trading Auditor deregistered – ordered to contribute to costs', Independent Regulatory Board for Auditors (IRBA), 23 March 2019.

83 Terry Motau SC, *The Great Bank Heist: Investigator's Report to the Prudential Authority*, 30 September 2018. Available at: https://www.opensecrets.org.za/wp-content/uploads/VBS-Mutual-Bank-The-Great-Bank-Heist.pdf, accessed 31 August 2022.

84 Pauli van Wyk, 'Five VBS robbers-in-chief – R2.7 billion gone (R800

million more than previously thought) – still zero criminal prosecutions', *Daily Maverick*, 7 November 2019. Available at: https://www.dailymaverick.co.za/article/2019-11-07-five-vbs-robbers-in-chief-r2-7-bn-gone-r800-million-more-than-previously-thought-still-zero-criminal-prosecutions/, accessed 31 August 2022.

85 Sipho Masondo and Dewald Van Rensburg, 'How VBS Mutual Bank was plundered', *Fin24*, 24 June 2018.

86 Terry Motau SC, *The Great Bank Heist: Investigator's Report to the Prudential Authority*, 30 September 2018, p. 10.

87 Hannah Ziady, 'Regulator reveals KPMG waved no red flags over Guptas and VBS', *Business Day*, 13 April 2018. Available at: https://www.businesslive.co.za/bd/companies/2018-04-13-regulator-reveals-kpmg-waved-no-red-flags-over-guptas-and-vbs/, accessed 31 August 2022.

88 Terry Motau SC, *The Great Bank Heist: Investigator's Report to the Prudential Authority*, 30 September 2018, p. 18.

89 Kabelo Khumalo, 'KPMG auditor paid R34 million to cover up #VBSBankHeist', *Business Report*, 11 October 2018. Available: https://www.iol.co.za/business-report/companies/kpmg-auditor-paid-r34m-to-cover-up-vbsbankheist-17439815, accessed 31 August 2022.

90 Kabelo Khumalo, 'KPMG auditor paid R34 million to cover up #VBSBankHeist'.

91 Terry Motau SC, *The Great Bank Heist: Investigator's Report to the Prudential Authority*, 30 September 2018, p. 76.

92 Terry Motau SC, *The Great Bank Heist: Investigator's Report to the Prudential Authority*, 30 September 2018, pp. 84–85.

93 Terry Motau SC, *The Great Bank Heist: Investigator's Report to the Prudential Authority*, 30 September 2018, p. 83.

94 Terry Motau SC, *The Great Bank Heist: Investigator's Report to the Prudential Authority*, 30 September 2018, p. 83.

95 'KPMG to donate R40m it earned in fees from Gupta-related entities to NGOs', *Mail & Guardian*, 15 September 2015. Available: https://mg.co.za/article/2017-09-15-kpmg-to-donate-r40m-it-earned-in-fees-from-gupta-related-entities-to-ngos/, accessed 31 August 2022.

96 'Appropriation Bill & Special Appropriation Bill: National Treasury Briefings', 4 May 2021, Standing Committee on Appropriations, South African Parliament.

97 Sarah Smit, 'Austerity budget unpacked', *Mail & Guardian*, 4 March 2021. Available at: https://mg.co.za/business/2021-03-04-austerity-budget-unpacked/, accessed 31 August 2022.

98 Sunday Times, 'About 2,700 SAA workers to lose jobs as retrenchment package deal reached', *TimesLive*, 7 July 2020. Available at: https://www.timeslive.co.za/news/south-africa/2020-07-07-about-2700-saa-workers-to-lose-jobs-as-retrenchment-package-deal-reached/, accessed 31 August 2022.

99 James Mahlokwane, 'Unions take SAA to court over salaries', *Pretoria News*, 2 February 2021.

100 Joe Bavier, 'SAA can operate for 12–36 months with R3bn investment – consortium', *MoneyWeb*, 11 June 2021. Available at: https://www.moneyweb.co.za/news/south-africa/saa-can-operate-for-12-36-months-with-r3bn-investment-consortium/, accessed 31 August 2022.

101 *Organisation Undoing Tax Abuse and Another v Myeni and Others* (15996/2017) [2020] ZAGPPHC 169 at para 265.

102 *Organisation Undoing Tax Abuse and Another v Myeni and Others* (15996/2017) [2020] ZAGPPHC 169 at para 272.

103 'SIU Investigation into SAA and Denel', Standing Committee on Public Accounts, South African Parliament, 3 March 2021.

104 Jan Gerber, 'State capture reports: Here's what the SIU has in its sights after Zondo's investigations', *News24*, 11 May 2022.

105 Rob Rose, 'PwC chokes on a cracker', *Financial Mail*, 15 April 2021. Available at: https://www.businesslive.co.za/fm/opinion/editors-note/2021-04-15-rob-rose-pwc-chokes-on-a-cracker/, accessed 31 August 2022.

106 Makhosandile Zulu, 'Not all auditing steps were inalized at SAA, PwC auditor tells Zondo', *The Citizen*, 16 July 2020. Available at: https://citizen.co.za/news/south-africa/state-capture/2322745/not-all-auditing-steps-were-finalised-at-saa-pwc-auditor-tells-zondo/, accessed 31 August 2022.

107 Auditor-General of South Africa, 'Report of the Auditor-General', as contained the South African Airways Annual Financial Statements for year ended 31 March 2017, 8 December 2017.

108 Auditor-General of South Africa, 'Report of the Auditor-General'.

109 Auditor-General of South Africa, 'Report of the Auditor-General'.

110 Nomahlubi Jordaan, 'State capture inquiry: PwC admits mistake in not saying SAA had not complied with Public Finance Management Act', *TimesLive*, 16 July 2020. Available at: https://www.timeslive.co.za/politics/2020-07-16-state-capture-inquiry-pwc-admits-mistake-in-not-saying-saa-had-not-complied-with-public-finance-act/, accessed 31 August 2022.

111 Jordaan, 'State capture inquiry: PwC admits mistake in not saying SAA had not complied with Public Finance Management Act'.
112 IRBA, 'There have been cracks: but lessons learnt and new strategic moves will pave a better future', Independent Regulatory Board for Auditors Newsletter, January–March Issue 53, 2021, p. 10.
113 IRBA, 'There have been cracks'.
114 Deloitte's Independent Auditor's Report, As contained in the South African Airways Annual Financial Statements for year ended 31 March 2011, 2012.
115 Antoinette Slabbert, 'The biscuit maker, the big shot auditor, and the SAA cover-up', *The Citizen*, 28 May 2018. Available at: https://citizen.co.za/news/south-africa/1939019/the-biscuit-maker-the-big-shot-auditor-and-the-saa-cover-up/, accessed 31 August 2022.
116 Siyakhula Vilakazi, 'SAA Chief Audit Executive affidavit to Institute of Internal Auditors South Africa', 16 March 2017.
117 Rose, 'PwC chokes on a cracker', *Financial Mail*.
118 Justice RMM Zondo, 'Judicial Commission of Inquiry into State Capture Report: Part I', p. 347, para 850.
119 IRBA, 'There have been cracks'.
120 Ann Crotty, 'SAA, PwC – and Irba: A case of regulatory capture?', *Moneyweb*, 21 April 2021. Available at: https://www.moneyweb.co.za/news/companies-and-deals/saa-pwc-and-irba-a-case-of-regulatory-capture/, accessed 31 August 2022.
121 Michael Marchant, Mamello Mosiana, Paul Holden and Hennie van Vuuren, 'The Enablers: The Bankers, Accountants and Lawyers that Cashed in on State Capture', Report submitted to the Zondo Commission of Inquiry into State Capture, Open Secrets & Shadow World Investigations.
122 IRBA Website: https://www.irba.co.za/, accessed 31 August 2022.
123 Londiwe Buthelezi, 'Deloitte should not have missed African Bank red flags, says auditing board', *Business Day*, 3 December 2018. Available at: https://www.businesslive.co.za/bd/companies/financial-services/2018-12-03-deloitte-should-not-have-missed-african-bank-red-flags-says-auditing-board/, accessed 31 August 2022.
124 Justin Brown, 'Audit watchdog accuses Deloitte of 'auditing disaster' at African Bank, Part One', *Daily Maverick*, 15 June 2020. Available at: https://www.dailymaverick.co.za/article/2020-06-15-part-one-audit-watchdog-accuses-deloitte-of-auditing-disaster-at-african-bank/, accessed 31 August 2022.

125 Londiwe Buthelezi, 'Six years later, Deloitte auditor walks away with the slightest sentence for African Bank', *Fin24*, 11 December 2020. Available at: https://www.news24.com/fin24/companies/financial-services/six-years-later-deloitte-auditor-walks-away-with-the-slightest-sentence-for-african-bank-20201210, accessed 31 August 2022.

126 Buthelezi, 'Six years later, Deloitte auditor walks away with the slightest sentence for African Bank'.

127 Independent Regulatory Board for Auditors (2019), Annual Report, p. 61.

128 Ann Crotty, 'EXCLUSIVE: Another major auditing firm drawn into SAA scandal', *Financial Mail*, 25 October 2017. Available at: https://www.businesslive.co.za/fm/fm-fox/2017-10-25-exclusive-another-major-auditing-firm-drawn-into-saa-scandal/, accessed 31 August 2022.

129 Bernard Agulhas, 'IRBA responds regarding actions against auditors of VBS', Independent Regulatory Board for Auditors (IRBA), 7 November 2018. Available at: https://www.irba.co.za/news-headlines/press-releases/irba-responds-regarding-actions-against-auditors-of-vbs, accessed 31 August 2022.

130 Auditing Profession Amendment Bill, Republic of South Africa, 2020.

131 Open Secrets, *Submission to Standing Committee on Finance concerning the Auditing Profession Act Amendment Bill*, 12 October 2020. Available at: https://www.opensecrets.org.za/wp-content/uploads/Open-Secrets-Submission_Auditing-Profession-Amendement-Bill-1.pdf, accessed 31 August 2022.

132 Rob Rose, 'EXCLUSIVE: Tension as Jenitha John takes charge at Irba', *Financial Mail*, 4 June 2020. Available at: https://www.businesslive.co.za/fm/fm-fox/2020-06-04-tension-as-jenitha-john-takes-charge-at-irba/, accessed 31 August 2022.

133 Rob Rose, 'Fear and loathing at audit watchdog Irba', *Financial Mail*, 5 November 2020. Available at: https://www.businesslive.co.za/fm/features/cover-story/2020-11-05-fear-and-loathing-at-audit-watchdog-irba/, accessed 31 August 2022.

134 Rob Rose, 'Tongaat: what happened behind closed doors', *Financial Mail*, 5 November 2020. Available at: https://www.businesslive.co.za/fm/features/cover-story/2020-11-05-tongaat-what-happened-behind-closed-doors/, accessed 31 August 2022.

Section 7: Conspiring Consultants

1. Duff McDonald, *The Firm: The Story of McKinsey and Its Secret Influence on American Business*, Simon & Schuster, 2013, p. 8.
2. McDonald, *The Firm*, pp. 12–13.
3. 'McKinsey: Overview', *Craft*; CNBC, *How McKinsey Became One of the Most Powerful Companies in the World*, CNBC YouTube, 6 June 2019. Available at: https://www.youtube.com/watch?v=jEJJz-8uG64&t=15s, accessed 31 August 2022.
4. 'McKinsey: Overview', *Craft*.
5. CNBC, *How McKinsey Became One of the Most Powerful Companies in the World*.
6. Statement by McKinsey on *New York Times* article, 16 December 2018.
7. Open Secrets and Shadow World Investigations, 'Why Zondo must summon banks, lawyers and consultants to answer for enabling state capture', *Financial Mail*, 6 February 2020. Available at: https://www.businesslive.co.za/fm/features/cover-story/2020-02-06-the-enablers-of-state-capture-banks-lawyers-and-consultants/, accessed 31 August 2022.
8. McKinsey website, 'Our Work: Public Sector in South Africa', *McKinsey*.
9. Sally Evans, 'How McKinsey and Trillian Ripped R1.6bn from Eskom – and Planned to Take R7.8bn More', *#GuptaLeaks*, 2017. Available at: http://www.gupta-leaks.com/salim-essa/how-mckinsey-and-trillian-ripped-r1-6bn-from-eskom-and-planned-to-take-r7-8bn-more/, accessed 31 August 2022.
10. Fundudzi Forensic Services, 'Final Report: Forensic Investigation into Various Allegations at Transnet and Eskom, Chapter II: McKinsey, Trillian and Regiments', *National Treasury*, 2018, p. 22, para 5.7.74.
11. Fundudzi Forensic Services, 'Final Report: Forensic Investigation into Various Allegations at Transnet and Eskom, Chapter II: McKinsey, Trillian and Regiments', *National Treasury*, 2018, pp. 22–23, para 5.7.79.
12. Justice RMM Zondo, 'Judicial Commission of Inquiry into State Capture Report: Part II, Volume 1: Transnet', 2022, p. 175, para 393.
13. Fundudzi Forensic Services, 'Final Report: Forensic Investigation into Various Allegations at Transnet and Eskom', *National Treasury*, 2018, 5.9.9.10.
14. Fundudzi Forensic Services, 'Final Report: Forensic Investigation into Various Allegations at Transnet and Eskom', *National Treasury*, 2018, 5.9.12.35.

15   Justice RMM Zondo, 'Judicial Commission of Inquiry into State Capture Report: Part II, Volume 1: Transnet', 2022, p. 175, para. 39.
16   Fundudzi Forensic Services, 'Final Report: Forensic Investigation into Various Allegations at Transnet and Eskom, *National Treasury*, 2018.
17   Fin24, 'McKinsey to pay back R870 million in Transnet fees', *Fin24*, 25 May 2021. Available at: https://www.news24.com/fin24/companies/mckinsey-to-pay-back-r870-million-in-transnet-fees-20210525, accessed 31 August 2022.
18   Sikhonathi Mantshantsha, 'McKinsey pays back interest coming from Eskom contract', *Business Day*, 6 September 2018. Available at: https://www.businesslive.co.za/bd/companies/2018-09-06-mckinsey-pays-back-interest-arising-from-eskom-contract/, accessed 31 August 2022.
19   Walt Bogdanich and Michael Forsythe, 'How McKinsey lost its way in South Africa', *New York Times*, 26 June 2018. Available at: https://www.nytimes.com/2018/06/26/world/africa/mckinsey-south-africa-eskom.html, accessed 31 August 2022.
20   Bogdanich and Forsythe, 'How McKinsey lost its way in South Africa'.
21   Jackie Cameron, '#JoiningTheDots: Meet McKinsey Gupta mole Vikas Sagar', *BizNews*, 14 July 2017. Available at: https://www.biznews.com/sa-investing/2017/07/14/vikas-sagar-mckinsey, accessed 31 August 2022.
22   Stephan Hofstatter. 'McKinsey Stands Firm on SOE Pricing Model', *Business Day*, 10 July 2018. Available at: https://www.businesslive.co.za/bd/companies/financial-services/2018-07-10-mckinsey-stands-firm-on-soe-pricing-model/, accessed 31 August 2022.
23   Stephan Hofstatter, 'McKinsey Stands Firm on SOE Pricing Model'.
24   Stephan Hofstatter, 'McKinsey Stands Firm on SOE Pricing Model'.
25   Sally Evans, 'How McKinsey and Trillian Ripped R1.6bn from Eskom – and Planned to Take R7.8bn More', 20 September 2017, *#GuptaLeaks*. Available at: http://www.gupta-leaks.com/salim-essa/how-mckinsey-and-trillian-ripped-r1-6bn-from-eskom-and-planned-to-take-r7-8bn-more/, accessed 31 August 2022.
26   Portfolio Committee on Public Enterprises, Report of The Portfolio Committee on Public Enterprises on the Inquiry into Governance, Procurement and the Financial Sustainability of Eskom, *Parliament of South Africa*, 2018, p. 54. Available at: https://www.parliament.gov.za/storage/app/media/Links/2018/November%202018/28-11-2018/Final%20Report%20-%20Eskom%20Inquiry%2028%20NOV.pdf, accessed 31 August 2022.

27. Jackie Cameron, '#JoiningTheDots: Meet McKinsey Gupta mole Vikas Sagar'.
28. Geoff Budlender, 'Report for T.M. Sexwale (Chairperson, Trillian Capital Partners pt.), on Allegations with Regard to the Trillian Group of Companies and Related Matters', 2017, *Trillian Capital Partners*, p. 39, para. 99. Available at: https://www.opensecrets.org.za/wp-content/uploads/6.-Budlender-Trillian-Final-Report-with-Annexures.pdf, accessed 31 August 2022.
29. Portfolio Committee on Public Enterprises, Report of The Portfolio Committee on Public Enterprises on the Inquiry into Governance, Procurement and the Financial Sustainability of Eskom, *Parliament of South Africa*, 2018, p. 54.
30. Budlender, 'Report for T.M. Sexwale (Chairperson, Trillian Capital Partners Pty.), para 97.
31. Budlender, 'Report for T.M. Sexwale (Chairperson, Trillian Capital Partners Pty), pp. 39–41.
32. Bogdanich and Forsythe, 'How McKinsey lost its way in South Africa'.
33. Bogdanich and Forsythe, 'How McKinsey lost its way in South Africa'.
34. McKinsey & Company, *McKinsey's statement on its settlement with Transnet SOC Ltd*, 26 May 2021. Available at: https://www.mckinsey.com/za/our-work/mckinsey-statement-on-its-settlement-with-transnet, accessed 31 August 2022.
35. McKinsey & Company, *McKinsey's statement on its settlement with Transnet SOC Ltd*.
36. Walt Bogdanich and Michael Forsythe, 'How McKinsey Has Helped Raise the Stature of Authoritarian Governments', *New York Times*. Available at: https://www.nytimes.com/2018/12/15/world/asia/mckinsey-china-russia.html, accessed 31 August 2022.
37. 'McKinsey Takes Heat for Its Saudi Work', *New York Times*, 22 October 2022. Available at: https://www.nytimes.com/2018/12/15/world/asia/mckinsey-china-russia.html, accessed 31 August 2022.
38. McKinsey & Company, 21 October 2018, Twitter Post.
39. Bogdanich and Forsythe, 'How McKinsey Has Helped Raise the Stature of Authoritarian Governments'.
40. Forbes Profile, 'Bain & Company', and Bain & Company Website, 'About Bain'. Available at: https://www.forbes.com/companies/bain-and-company/?sh=110f46765f5a, accessed 31 August 2022.
41. Forbes Profile, 'Bain & Company'.
42. Bain & Company Website, 'Bain Office: Johannesburg'. Available at:

43 Bain & Company Website, 'Bain Office: Johannesburg'. https://www.bain.com/about/offices/, accessed 31 August 2022.
44 Nancy Perry, 'A consulting firm too hot to handle?', *Fortune* magazine, 27 April 1987. Available at: https://archive.fortune.com/magazines/fortune/fortune_archive/1987/04/27/68952/index.htm, accessed 31 August 2022.
45 Perry, 'A consulting firm too hot to handle?'.
46 Vernon Wessels, 'Bain sets aside fees earned from SARS', *Bloomberg*, 10 September 2018. Available at: https://www.bnnbloomberg.ca/bain-sets-aside-fees-earned-from-south-african-tax-agency-1.1135194, accessed 31 August 2022.
47 Vittorio Massone, Affidavit before the Commission of Inquiry into tax administration and governance by the South African Revenue Service, (Pretoria), 2018, p. 3, para 8–9.
48 Ambrobrite (Pty) Ltd and Bain & Company (2013), Business Development and Stakeholder Management Contract.
49 Ambrobrite (Pty) Ltd and Bain & Company (2013), Business Development and Stakeholder Management Contract.
50 Ambrobrite (Pty) Ltd and Bain & Company (2013), Business Development and Stakeholder Management Contract.
51 Vittorio Massone, Affidavit before the Commission of Inquiry into tax administration and governance by the South African Revenue Service, (Pretoria), 2018, p. 12, para 43.1
52 Judge R Nugent, 'Final Report of the Commission of Inquiry into Tax Administration and Governance at SARS', p. 34, para 25, 11 December 2018.
53 Christopher Spillane, 'Bain wins Telkom contract 'without open bidding', *Business Day*, 29 July 2014. Available at: https://www.bloomberg.com/news/articles/2014-07-28/telkom-hired-bain-to-advise-on-strategy-without-bidding-process#xj4y7vzkg, accessed 31 August 2022.
54 Pauli van Wyk, 'The Bain Files, Part 1: Massone knew in advance Moyane would become SARS head and Bain would get restructuring contract', *Daily Maverick*, 5 October 2018. Available at: https://www.dailymaverick.co.za/article/2018-10-05-the-bain-files-part-1-massone-knew-in-advance-moyane-would-become-sars-head-and-bain-would-get-restructuring-contract/, accessed 31 August 2022.
55 eNCA, 'Moyane appointed as SARS Commissioner', *eNCA*, 23 September 2014. Available at: https://www.enca.com/moyane-appointed-sars-commissioner, accessed 31 August 2022.

56 News24, 'Bosasa bribes scandal: Agrizzi implicates Tom Moyane', *News24*, 21 January 2019. Available at: https://www.news24.com/News24/bosasa-bribes-scandal-agrizzi-implicates-tom-moyane-20190121, accessed 31 August 2022.
57 Judge R Nugent, 'Final Report of the Commission of Inquiry into Tax Administration and Governance at SARS', p. 37, para 36–37, 11 December 2018.
58 eNCA, 'Moyane appointed as SARS Commissioner'.
59 Email from John Beaumont to Stephane Timpano and Vittorio Massone, 28 August 2014, 'Subject: RE'.
60 Judge R Nugent, 'Final Report of the Commission of Inquiry into Tax Administration and Governance at SARS', p. 50, para 6, 11 December 2018.
61 Judge R Nugent, 'Final Report of the Commission of Inquiry into Tax Administration and Governance at SARS', p. 50, para 6, 11 December 2018.
62 Pauli van Wyk, 'Jonas Makwakwa's swift rise to power, and his abuse of it', *Daily Maverick*, 29 June 2018. Available at: https://www.dailymaverick.co.za/article/2018-06-29-jonas-makwakwas-swift-rise-to-power-and-his-abuse-of-it/, accessed 31 August 2022.
63 amaBhungane, 'Jonas Makwakwa, then SARS No 2 executive, secured a job for his girlfriend', *Daily Maverick*, 2 October 2016. Available at: https://www.dailymaverick.co.za/article/2016-10-02-amabhungane-jonas-makwakwa-then-sars-no-2-executive-secured-a-job-for-his-girlfriend/, accessed 31 August 2022.
64 Pauli van Wyk, 'The Makwakwa Dossier, Part 2 – SARS No. 2 was paid a bonus worth nearly R1 million ... while on suspension', *Daily Maverick: Scorpio*, 23 November 2017. Available at: https://www.dailymaverick.co.za/article/2017-11-23-scorpio-the-makwakwa-dossier-part-2-sars-no-2-was-paid-a-bonus-worth-nearly-r1-million-while-on-suspension/, accessed 31 August 2022.
65 Judge R Nugent, Final Report of the Commission of Inquiry into Tax Administration and Governance at SARS", p. 27, para 1, 11 December 2018.
66 Judge R Nugent, 'Final Report of the Commission of Inquiry into Tax Administration and Governance at SARS', p. 21, para 3, 11 December 2018.
67 L. Smith, 'The power of politics: The performance of the South African Revenue Service and some of its implications', GSDRC: Applied

knowledge Services, 2003.
68 Judge R Nugent, 'Final Report of the Commission of Inquiry into Tax Administration and Governance at SARS', p. 120, para 8, 11 December 2018.
69 Fin24, '5 key takeaways from Bain's statement on SARS', *Fin24*, 18 December 2018. Available at: https://www.news24.com/Fin24/5-key-takeaways-from-bains-statement-on-sars-20181218, accessed 31 August 2022.
70 Barry Bateman, '"Ill" Vittorio Massone a no-show as Nugent Inquiry Resumes', *Eyewitness News*, 25 September 2018. Available at: https://ewn.co.za/2018/09/25/ill-vittorio-massone-a-no-show-as-nugent-inquiry-resumes, accessed 31 August 2022.
71 Roxanne Henderson and Prinesha Naidoo, 'Ex-partner hired to fix Bain South Africa turns against firm', *Bloomberg*, 19 December 2019. Available at: https://www.bloomberg.com/news/articles/2019-12-19/ex-partner-hired-to-fix-bain-south-africa-turns-against-firm#xj4y7vzkg, accessed 31 August 2022.
72 Londiwe Buthelezi, 'Bain "fixer" Williams: "I've been through hell the last 2 months"', *Fin24*, 20 December 2019. Available at: https://www.news24.com/fin24/Companies/Financial-Services/bain-fixer-williams-ive-been-through-hell-the-last-2-months-20191220, accessed 31 August 2022.
73 Bain & Company, Statement on SARS, 20 December 2019. Available at: https://www.bain.com/offices/johannesburg/sars-statement-dec20/, accessed 31 August 2022.
74 Boston Consulting Group Website, 2022. Available at: https://www.bcg.com/about/overview, accessed 31 August 2022.
75 Boston Consulting Group Website, 2022.
76 Sydney P. Friedberg, Scilla Alecci, Will Fitzgibbon, Douglas Dalby and Delphine Reuter, 'How Africa's richest woman exploited family ties, shell companies and inside deals to build an empire', *International Consortium of Investigative Journalists*, 19 January 2020. Available at: https://www.icij.org/investigations/luanda-leaks/how-africas-richest-woman-exploited-family-ties-shell-companies-and-inside-deals-to-build-an-empire/, accessed 31 August 2022.
77 Forbes, 'How Africa's richest woman Isabel Dos Santos went broke', *Forbes*, 10 February 2021. Available at: https://www.forbes.com/profile/isabel-dos-santos/, accessed 31 August 2022.
78 Freedberg, Alecci, Fitzgibbon, Dalby and Reuter, 'How Africa's richest

woman exploited family ties'.

79 Freedberg, Alecci, Fitzgibbon, Dalby and Reuter, 'How Africa's richest woman exploited family ties'.

80 David Pegg, 'How Angola's state oil firm was left with just $309 in its account', *The Guardian*, 19 January 2020. Available at: https://www.theguardian.com/world/2020/jan/19/angola-state-oil-company-sonangol-isabel-dos-santos-investigation, accessed 31 August 2022.

81 Will Fitzgibbon, 'Banking documents reveal consulting giants' cash windfall under Angolan billionaire Isabel dos Santos', *International Consortium of Investigative Journalists*, 15 February 2021. Available at: https://www.icij.org/investigations/luanda-leaks/banking-documents-reveal-consulting-giants-cash-windfall-under-angolan-billionaire-isabel-dos-santos/, accessed 31 August 2022.

82 Will Fitzgibbon and Morgan Torres, 'Read the Luanda Leaks documents', *International Consortium of Investigative Journalists*, 19 January 2020.

83 Freedberg, Alecci, Fitzgibbon, Dalby and Reuter, 'How Africa's richest woman exploited family ties'.

84 Will Fitzgibbon, 'Banking documents reveal consulting giants' cash windfall'.

85 Joseph Cotterill, 'Global firms under scrutiny in Isabel dos Santos alleged corruption leak', *Financial Times*, 20 January 2020.

86 Fitzgibbon, 'Banking documents reveal consulting giants' cash windfall'.

87 Freedberg, Alecci, Fitzgibbon, Dalby and Reuter, 'How Africa's richest woman exploited family ties'.

88 Pegg, 'How Angola's state oil firm was left with just $309 in its account'.

89 Fitzgibbon, 'Banking documents reveal consulting giants' cash windfall'.

90 Freedberg, Alecci, Fitzgibbon, Dalby and Reuter, 'How Africa's richest woman exploited family ties'.

91 Ben Hallman, Kyra Gurney, Scilla Alecci and Max de Haldevang, 'Western advisers helped an autocrat's daughter amass and shield a fortune', *International Consortium of Investigative Journalists*, 19 January 2020. Available at: https://www.icij.org/investigations/luanda-leaks/western-advisers-helped-an-autocrats-daughter-amass-and-shield-a-fortune/, accessed 31 August 2022.

92 Hallman, Gurney, Alecci and De Haldevang, 'Western advisers helped an autocrat's daughter amass and shield a fortune'.

93 Hallman, Gurney, Alecci and De Haldevang, 'Western advisers helped an autocrat's daughter amass and shield a fortune'.

94 Hallman, Gurney, Alecci and De Haldevang, 'Western advisers helped an

autocrat's daughter amass and shield a fortune'.
95 Will Fitzgibbon, 'Banking documents reveal consulting giants' cash windfall'.
96 World Bank, 'Macro Poverty Outlook for Angola: April 2022'. Available at: https://documents1.worldbank.org/curated/en/099922304182222324/pdf/IDU087b6285c05e64047bf0b7530c21ca3a47d94.pdf, accessed 31 August 2022.
97 Will Fitzgibbon, 'US sanctions Angolan billionaire Isabel dos Santos for corruption', *International Consortium of Investigative Journalists*, 9 December 2021. Available at: https://www.icij.org/investigations/luanda-leaks/us-sanctions-angolan-billionaire-isabel-dos-santos-for-corruption/, accessed 30 August 2022.
98 Fitzgibbon, 'US Sanctions Angolan billionaire Isabel dos Santos for corruption'.
99 Michael Forsythe, Mark Mazzetti, Ben Hubbard and Walt Bogdanich, 'Consulting firms keep lucrative Saudi alliance shaping crown prince's vision', *New York Times*, 4 November 2018. Available at: https://www.nytimes.com/2018/11/04/world/middleeast/mckinsey-bcg-booz-allen-saudi-khashoggi.html, accessed 31 August 2022.
100 Human Rights Watch, 'World Report 2021: Saudi Arabia', 2021. Available at: https://www.hrw.org/world-report/2021/country-chapters/saudi-arabia, accessed 31 August 2022.
101 Arwa Youssef, 'US should sanction Saudi crown prince', *Human Rights Watch*, 3 March 2019. Available at: https://www.hrw.org/news/2021/03/03/us-should-sanction-saudi-crown-prince, accessed 31 August 2022.
102 Forsythe, Mazzetti, Hubbard and Bogdanich, 'Consulting firms keep lucrative Saudi alliance shaping crown prince's vision'.
103 Forsythe, Mazzetti, Hubbard and Bogdanich, 'Consulting firms keep lucrative Saudi alliance shaping crown prince's vision'.
104 Forsythe, Mazzetti, Hubbard and Bogdanich, 'Consulting firms keep lucrative Saudi alliance shaping crown prince's vision'.
105 Misk Website: https://misk.org.sa/en/about-misk/, accessed 31 August 2022.
106 Rachel Wolcott, 'Reputation launderers,' disinformation campaigns hinder sanctions and financial crime compliance efforts', *Thomson Reuters*, 9 June 2022. Available at: https://www.thomsonreuters.com/en-us/posts/news-and-media/reputation-launderers-evade-sanctions/, accessed 31 August 2022.

107 Ruth Michaelson, '"It's being built on our blood": The true cost of Saudi Arabia's $500bn megacity', *The Guardian*, 4 May 2020. Available at: https://www.theguardian.com/global-development/2020/may/04/its-being-built-on-our-blood-the-true-cost-of-saudi-arabia-5bn-megacity-neom, accessed 31 August 2022.

108 James Reini, 'Western firms complicit in human cost of Saudi Arabia's dystopian Neom megacity', *The New Arab*, 5 June 2020. Available: https://english.alaraby.co.uk/analysis/human-cost-saudi-arabias-dystopian-neom-megacity, accessed 31 August 2022.

109 Reini, 'Western firms complicit in human cost of Saudi Arabia's dystopian Neom megacity'.

110 Reini, 'Western firms complicit in human cost of Saudi Arabia's dystopian Neom megacity'.

Section 8: Bad Lawyers

1 Shamila Batohi, 'NPA Annual Report', 2020. Available at: https://www.npa.gov.za/media/npa-annual-report-20192020, accessed 31 August 2022.

2 Lukas Muntingh, 'Key issues in the NPA: Knowledge, skills, and human resources', [Issue Paper 2], Africa Criminal Justice Reform and Dullah Omar Institute, 2020.

3 Civil Society Working Group on State Capture, *Agenda for Action*, Submission to the Zondo Commission, 2020. Available at: https://www.opensecrets.org.za/wp-content/uploads/An-Agenda-for-Action_A-Joint-Submission-_Civil-Society-Working-Group-on-State-Capture.pdf, accessed 31 August 2022.

4 T.F. Mathibedi, L. Vilakazi, K. Ramaimela, Z. Madlanga, Recordal Of The Versions Of Dr Jacobus Petrus Pretorius ('Dr Pretorius'), Advocates George Baloyi ('Baloyi'), Khehla Masenyani Andrew Chauke ('Chauke'), Gladstone Sello Maema ('Maema'), Khulekani Raymond Mathenjwa ('Mathenjwa'), Anthony Mosing ('Mosing'), Marshall Mokgatlhe ('Mokgatlhe'), and Michael Mashuga ('Mashuga') ('The Implicated Prosecutors'), in Response to Allegations Implicating Them in State Capture Made to the Commission by Witnesses Who Can No Longer Be Cross Examined Due to the Commission's Operational Constraints, Submission to the Zondo Commission, 2020.

5 Linda Ensor, 'Low-yield NPA unable to prosecute all cases from Zondo commission', *BusinessLive*, 8 December 2021. Available at: https://www.

Notes

businesslive.co.za/bd/national/2021-12-08-low-yield-npa-unable-to-prosecute-all-cases-from-zondo-commission/, accessed 31 August 2022.

6   Rodney de Kock memorandum to Shamila Batohi, 'Reconsideration of authorisations in terms of section 2(1) (e) and (f) of the prevention of organised act, 121 of 1998', 27 June 2019. Available at: https://www.opensecrets.org.za/wp-content/uploads/2022/06/27.06.2019-De-Kock-Report.pdf, accessed 31 August 2022.

7   SANews, 'NPA seized with 37 high profile State Capture cases', *SANews*, 16 February 2022. Available at: https://www.sanews.gov.za/south-africa/npa-seized-37-high-profile-state-capture-cases, accessed 31 August 2022.

8   Eyewitness News, 'NPA boss Batohi on Cronje's resignation: We are not in a crisis, there is no infighting', 6 December 2021. Available at: https://ewn.co.za/2021/12/06/batohi-npa-is-not-in-crisis-and-there-s-no-infighting, accessed 31 August 2022.

9   Eyewitness News, 'NPA boss Batohi on Cronje's resignation: We are not in a crisis, there is no infighting'.

10 FTI Consulting and Corruption Watch, 'Deferred Prosecution Agreements: A Solution to Prosecuting Backlog', Webinar, 2021.

11 Eyewitness News, 'NPA boss Batohi on Cronje's resignation: We are not in a crisis, there is no infighting'.

12 Shamila Batohi. 2020. NPA Annual Report.

13 Eyewitness News, 'NPA boss Batohi on Cronje's resignation: We are not in a crisis, there is no infighting'.

14 Eyewitness News, 'NPA boss Batohi on Cronje's resignation: We are not in a crisis, there is no infighting'.

15 Sipho Masondo, 'Prosecute, or else! NPA, Batohi threatened with legal action over sluggish investigations', *News24*, 2021.

16 Azarrah Karrim, Kyle Cowan and Sipho Masondo, 'Corruption boiling point: Eskom could consider private prosecutions if NPA don't show progress soon', *News24*, 29 November 2021. Available at: https://www.news24.com/news24/newsletters/gmsa/featured2/corruption-boiling-point-eskom-could-consider-private-prosecutions-if-npa-dont-show-progress-soon-20211129-2, accessed 31 August 2022.

17 Andrew Meldrum, 'Apartheid spy clears prosecutor' *The Guardian*, , 21 October 2003. Available at: https://www.theguardian.com/world/2003/oct/22/southafrica.andrewmeldrum, accessed 31 August 2022.

18 Frene Ginwala, 'Report of the Enquiry into the Fitness of Advocate VP Pikoli to Hold the Office of National Director of Public Prosecutions',

2008, p. 69.
19 The Presidency of RSA, 'Government and Adv. Vusi Pikoli reach out-of-court settlement', 2009.
20 Ginwala, 'Report of the Enquiry into the Fitness of Advocate VP Pikoli to Hold the Office of NDPP'.
21 *Zuma v Democratic Alliance and Others; Acting National Director of Public Prosecutions and Another v Democratic Alliance and Another* (771/2016, 1170/2016). [2017].
22 Karen van Rensburg, 'Affidavit Regarding the National Prosecuting Authority', Submission to the Judicial Commission of Inquiry into Allegations of State Capture, Corruption and Fraud in the Public Sector Including Organs of State, 2020.
23 Van Rensburg, 'Affidavit Regarding the National Prosecuting Authority', p. 8.
24 Johan Booysen, Affidavit and Annexures of Johan Wessel Booysen, 2019, Submission to the Zondo Commission. p. 29.
25 Rodney de Kock memorandum to Shamila Batohi, 'Reconsideration of authorisations in terms of section 2(1) (e) and (f) of the prevention of organised act, 121 of 1998', 27 June 2019.
26 Franny Rabkin, 'Booysen: I was prosecuted because I got in Edward Zuma's way', *Mail & Guardian*, 2019.
27 Rodney de Kock memorandum to Shamila Batohi, 'Reconsideration of authorisations in terms of section 2(1) (e) and (f) of the prevention of organised act, 121 of 1998', 27 June 2019.
28 Terrence Joubert, Affidavit and Annexures of Terrence Joubert, 2020, Submission to the Zondo Commission.
29 NPA Prosecution Policy. Available at: https://www.opensecrets.org.za/wp-content/uploads/2022/06/Zondo-Commission_NPA-Prosecution-Policy.pdf, accessed 31 August 2022.
30 NPA Prosecution Policy.
31 Rodney de Kock memorandum to Shamila Batohi, 'Reconsideration of authorisations in terms of section 2(1) (e) and (f) of the prevention of organised act, 121 of 1998', 27 June 2019.
32 Afriforum, 'NPA still refuses to issue nolle prosequi-certificate for the private prosecution of Jiba', 23 March 2022. Available at: https://afriforum.co.za/en/npa-still-refuses-to-issue-nolle-prosequi-certificate-for-the-private-prosecution-of-jiba/, accessed 31 August 2022.
33 Afriforum, 'NPA still refuses to issue nolle prosequi-certificate for the

private prosecution of Jiba'.
34 Jacques Pauw and Carien du Plessis, 'Mdluli's 'pledge' to Zuma', *City Press*, 5 May 2012. Available at: https://www.news24.com/citypress/Politics/News/Mdlulis-pledge-to-Zuma-20120505, accessed 31 August 2022.
35 Karen van Rensburg, 'Affidavit Regarding the National Prosecuting Authority', Submission to the Judicial Commission of Inquiry into Allegations of State Capture, Corruption and Fraud in the Public Sector Including Organs of State, 2020.
36 Karen van Rensburg, 'Affidavit Regarding the National Prosecuting Authority', Submission to the Judicial Commission of Inquiry into Allegations of State Capture, Corruption and Fraud in the Public Sector Including Organs of State, 2020.
37 Karen van Rensburg, 'Affidavit Regarding the National Prosecuting Authority', Submission to the Judicial Commission of Inquiry into Allegations of State Capture, Corruption and Fraud in the Public Sector Including Organs of State, 2020.
38 Karen van Rensburg, 'Affidavit Regarding the National Prosecuting Authority', Submission to the Judicial Commission of Inquiry into Allegations of State Capture, Corruption and Fraud in the Public Sector Including Organs of State, 2020.
39 Shamila Batohi, NPA Annual Report, 2020.
40 Brian McKechnie, 'Modernist icon shimmers above Joburg once more'. *Heritage Portal*, 28 October 2015. Available at: https://www.theheritageportal.co.za/article/modernist-icon-shimmers-above-joburg-once-more, accessed 31 August 2022.
41 The National Prosecuting Authority Act, 1998 Act 32 of 1998.
42 Andrew Chauke, 'Application to Cross-Examine Booysen and Mlotshwa at the State Capture Inquiry', 15 February 2021. Available at: https://www.opensecrets.org.za/wp-content/uploads/2022/06/Zondo-Commission_Andrew-Chauke_AffidavitAnnexures.pdf, accessed 31 August 2022.
43 Phindi Mjonondwane email correspondence to Open Secrets, 28 June 2022.
44 *Booysen v Acting National Director of Public Prosecutions and Others* (4665/2010) [2014].
45 NPA, 'NDPP to Withdraw Racketeering Charges in the Matter of State vs Booysen and Others Following a Review Process', 2019.
46 Andrew Chauke, 'Application to Cross-Examine Booysen and Mlotshwa

at the State Capture Inquiry', 15 February 2021, p. 31.
47 Rodney de Kock memorandum to Shamila Batohi, 'Reconsideration of authorisations in terms of section 2(1) (e) and (f) of the prevention of organised act, 121 of 1998', 27 June 2019.
48 Andrew Chauke, 'Application to Cross-Examine Booysen and Mlotshwa at the State Capture Inquiry', 15 February 2021, p. 31.
49 Andrew Chauke, 'Application to Cross-Examine Booysen and Mlotshwa at the State Capture Inquiry', 15 February 2021, p. 31.
50 Justice Yvonne Mokgoro, 'Enquiry In Terms Of Section 12(6) Of The National Prosecuting Authority Act 32 of 1998', 1 April 2019. Available at: https://www.opensecrets.org.za/wp-content/uploads/2022/06/Section-126-Mokgoro-Enquiry-report-unabridged-version.pdf, accessed 31 August 2022.
51 NPA Prosecution Policy.
52 Indictment: Mabula and Others, (2020).
53 Indictment: Mabula and Others, (2020).
54 For reasons of protecting the source, we would not be able to provide a specific citation for this.
55 Jeff Wicks, 'Kidnappings, beatings and torture: Prosecution of ex-Hawks general stalls', *News24*, 7 October 2020. Available at: https://www.news24.com/news24/southafrica/news/kidnappings-beatings-and-torture-prosecution-of-ex-hawks-general-stalls-20201006-2, accessed 31 August 2022.
56 Jeff Wicks, 'Gauteng DPP Andrew Chauke called to heel by NPA prosecutions boss over 'torture cops' bungle', *News24*, 18 November 2020. Available at: https://www.news24.com/news24/southafrica/investigations/gauteng-dpp-andrew-chauke-called-to-heel-by-npa-prosecutions-boss-over-torture-cops-bungle-20201118, accessed 31 August 2022.
57 Wicks, 'Gauteng DPP Andrew Chauke called to heel by NPA prosecutions boss over 'torture cops' bungle'.
58 Julia Evans, 'Former SAPS 'rogue' cops accused of extortion, assault and kidnapping listen to gruesome torture testimony', *Daily Maverick*, 10 May 2022. Available at: https://www.dailymaverick.co.za/article/2022-05-10-former-saps-rogue-cops-accused-of-extortion-assault-and-kidnapping-listen-to-gruesome-torture-testimony/, accessed 31 August 2022.
59 Citizen Reporter, 'NPA boss reportedly on warpath against Joburg head over his prosecution decisions', *The Citizen*, 6 June 2021. Available at:

https://www.citizen.co.za/news/2514344/npa-boss-reportedly-on-warpath-against-joburg-head-over-his-prosecution-decisions/, accessed 31 August 2022.
60   Special Investigating Unit, 'Investigation into certain affairs of the Gauteng Department of Health', 14 May 2010. Available at: https://www.opensecrets.org.za/wp-content/uploads/2022/06/SIU-Report-on-Gauteng-Department-of-Health.pdf, accessed 31 August 2022.
61   Special Investigating Unit, 'Investigation into certain affairs of the Gauteng Department of Health'.
62   Bheki Simelane, 'Former Gauteng health MEC Brian Hlongwa and co-accused granted bail in decade-old R221m tender graft case', 7 December 2021, *Daily Maverick*. Available at: https://www.dailymaverick.co.za/article/2021-12-07-former-gauteng-health-mec-brian-hlongwa-and-co-accused-granted-bail-in-decade-old-r221m-tender-graft-case/, accessed 31 August 2022.
63   WhatsApp message from Sello Maema to Open Secrets, 26 July 2022.
64   Rodney de Kock memorandum to Shamila Batohi, 'Reconsideration of authorisations in terms of section 2(1) (e) and (f) of the prevention of organised act, 121 of 1998', 27 June 2019.
65   Franny Rabkin (2019), 'Booysen: I was prosecuted because I got in Edward Zuma's way', *Mail & Guardian*.
66   Rodney de Kock memorandum to Shamila Batohi, 'Reconsideration of authorisations in terms of section 2(1) (e) and (f) of the prevention of organised act, 121 of 1998', 27 June 2019.
67   Rodney de Kock memorandum to Shamila Batohi, 'Reconsideration of authorisations in terms of section 2(1) (e) and (f) of the prevention of organised act, 121 of 1998', 27 June 2019.
68   Rodney de Kock memorandum to Shamila Batohi, 'Reconsideration of authorisations in terms of section 2(1) (e) and (f) of the prevention of organised act, 121 of 1998', 27 June 2019.
69   Rodney de Kock memorandum to Shamila Batohi, 'Reconsideration of authorisations in terms of section 2(1) (e) and (f) of the prevention of organised act, 121 of 1998', 27 June 2019, p. 31.
70   Rodney de Kock memorandum to Shamila Batohi, 'Reconsideration of authorisations in terms of section 2(1) (e) and (f) of the prevention of organised act, 121 of 1998', 27 June 2019, p. 39.
71   Rodney de Kock memorandum to Shamila Batohi, 'Reconsideration of authorisations in terms of section 2(1) (e) and (f) of the prevention of organised act, 121 of 1998', 27 June 2019., p. 39.

72 Aristeidis Danikas, 'Daily Maverick apolgises to Aristeidis Dankias, affords him right of reply', *Daily Maverick,* 27 May 2021. Available at: https://www.dailymaverick.co.za/article/2021-05-27-daily-maverick-apologises-to-aristeidis-danikas-affords-him-right-of-reply/, accessed 30 August 2022.

73 Johan Booysen, Sworn statement against Maema, 2016, submitted to the Hawks.

74 Sello Maema, 'Application for Condonation and Leave to Cross-Examine', Submission to the Zondo Commission, 2021.

75 T.F. Mathibedi, L. Vilakazi, K. Ramaimela, Z. Madlanga, (2021), Recordal Of The Versions Of Dr Jacobus Petrus Pretorius ('Dr Pretorius'), Advocates George Baloyi ('Baloyi'), Khehla Masenyani Andrew Chauke ('Chauke'), Gladstone Sello Maema ('Maema'), Khulekani Raymond Mathenjwa ('Mathenjwa'), Anthony Mosing ('Mosing'), Marshall Mokgatlhe ('Mokgatlhe'), and Michael Mashuga ('Mashuga') ('The Implicated Prosecutors'), in Response to Allegations Implicating Them in State Capture Made to the Commission by Witnesses Who Can No Longer Be Cross Examined Due to the Commission's Operational Constraints. Submission to the Zondo Commission. p. 32.

76 Sello Maema, 'Application for Condonation and Leave to Cross-Examine, Submission to the Zondo Commission', 2021.

77 Sello Maema, 'Application for Condonation and Leave to Cross-Examine, Submission to the Zondo Commission', 2021, p. 7.

78 Sello Maema, 'Application for Condonation and Leave to Cross-Examine, Submission to the Zondo Commission', 2021, p. 12.

79 Robert McBride, 'Affidavit and Annexure of Robert McBride', Submission to the Zondo Commission, 2019, p. 29.

80 Kingdom Mabuza, 'NPA drops fraud charges against Robert McBride', *TimesLive,* 1 November 2016. Available at: https://www.timeslive.co.za/politics/2016-11-01-npa-drops-fraud-charges-against-robert-mcbride/, accessed 31 August 2022.

81 Sello Maema, 'Application for Condonation and Leave to Cross-Examine, Submission to the Zondo Commission', 2021, p. 12.

82 Sello Maema, 'Application for Condonation and Leave to Cross-Examine, Submission to the Zondo Commission', 2021, p. 12.

83 Judge R Nugent, Commission Of Inquiry into Tax Administration and Governance: First interim report, 2018.

84 Matthew Savides, 'Criminal charges to be dropped in SARS' "rogue unit" case', *TimesLive,* 7 February 2020. Available at: https://www.

timeslive.co.za/news/south-africa/2020-02-07-criminal-charges-to-be-dropped-in-sars-rogue-unit-case/, accessed 31 August 2022.
85   Matthew Savides, 'Criminal charges to be dropped in Sars 'rogue unit' case'.

We have not forgotten

1   Sarah Smit,'What the FICA? South Africa's possible greylisting in black and white', 5 August 2022, *Mail & Guardian*. Available at: https://mg.co.za/business/2022-08-05-what-the-fica-south-africas-possible-greylisting-in-black-and-white/, accessed 31 August 2022.

Index

1064 locomotives deal 115–117, 119, 120–121, 201–202, 207, 218, 284

A

A-M Consulting Engineers 136
Abrahams, Shaun 310, 313, 317, 321–323, 326, 333, 335–337, 341
Accurate Investments (Gupta company) 118, 258
Aerohaven (Gupta company) 216
Africa Criminal Justice Reform (ACJR) 309–310
Africa Wealth Report 13
African Bank 236, 243, 256, 272–273
African National Congress (ANC) 36, 142
Afro 4000 locomotives 133, 135
Al-Yamamah deal 70
Alexander Forbes 173, 178
AM Investments 136
amaBhungane 120, 186, 216, 240–242
Anti-Apartheid Movement 49
anti-corruption 251
Anti-Corruption Task Team (ACTT) 330–331
Anti-Money Laundering (AML) banking standards 206, 208, 210–211
apartheid 52–54, 57, 71, 78, 108, 114, 345
(*See also* post-apartheid.)
apartheid profiteers 14, 15, 19–22
apartheid-style abuses 328

Archive for Contemporary Affairs 24
Arms Acquisition Council 72
Arms Deal Commission 65, 99
Armscor 40–45, 78, 158
Asset Forfeiture Unit (AFU) 309
Auditing Profession Amendment Bill 235
Auditor-General's Draft Final Management Report (2015) 125
auditors 13, 15, 16, 233, 235–236, 238–240, 245, 247–248, 256–260, 263, 265, 267–269, 271–276, 323
(*See also* Independent Regulatory Board for Auditors (IRBA))

B

'bad lawyers' 15, 307
BAE Systems (formerly British Aerospace) 69–76, 77–89, 91–99
Bain & Company 118, 161, 219, 255, 281, 291–299, 305, 340
Banco Nacional de Investimento (BCI, Lisbon) 248
Bank of Baroda 119, 197–199, 203, 215
Batohi, Shamila (NDPP) 122, 309, 313–315, 323, 327, 334, 336, 337, 340
BDK Attorneys 329
Bekker, Koos 32
Bell Pottinger 54, 87, 305
Bellingcat 106–107
Bid Evaluation Committee (BEC) 129

417

'Big Four' (accounting and audit firms) 15, 199, 219–220, 235–236, 239–240, 253, 256–257, 271–272, 275, 277, 281
'Big Three' (accounting and audit firms) 15, 281–283, 291, 299, 305
Board of Control (BOC) 127, 128
Booysen, Johan (former KZN Hawks boss) 313, 317, 320–322, 326–328, 331, 333–341
Boston Consulting Group (BCG Consulting) 119, 281, 299–305
Botha, Pik 31
Botha, PW 24–26, 29–31, 44–45, 51–52
Braun, Markus (KPMG auditor) 246
Bredenkamp, John 73, 77–81, 92
broad-based black economic empowerment (B-BBEE) 117, 133
Broadcasting Complaints Committee of South Africa (BCCSA) 158
Brown, Lynne (ex-Minister of Public Enterprise) 158–159
Brown, Mike (Chief executive, Nedbank) 197, 201
Bureau of State Security (BOSS) 32
Business and Individual Tax (BAIT) 294–295
Buthelezi, Sfiso 126, 128, 149–156

C

Cadiz Holdings 150, 152
Century General Trading (CGT) 117, 119–120, 207
Chang, Manuel 225, 229, 247
Chauke, Andrew (DPP) 325–332, 334
China North Rail (CNR) 116–118, 120
China Railway Rolling-Stock Corporation (CRRC) 115, 116–117, 120–122, 207
China South Rail (CSR) 116–117, 120, 207, 208
Chinese Railway Rolling Stock Corporation (CRRC) 115–117, 207
Civil Society Working Group on State Capture 310

China South Rail (CSR) 116–117, 120, 207–208
(*See also* Chinese Railway Rolling Stock Corporation.)
China North Rail (CNR) 116–118, 120
(*See also* Chinese Railway Rolling Stock Corporation)
Chinese Railway Rolling Stock Corporation (CRRC [Zhuzhou Locomotive Co. Ltd]) 116–117, 120–122, 207
CRRC E-Loco Supply 122
Civil Society Working Group on State Capture 310
Committee for the Abolition of Illegitimate Debt (CADTM) 227
Companies and Intellectual Property Commission (CIPC) 144, 148
Complaints and Compliance Committee 158
Compliance and Enforcement Division (Financial Surveillance Department, Reserve Bank) 137
consequences of non-prosecution of crimes against the state 61
Constitution 323
Constitutional Court 168, 184–185, 188, 189
constitutional
democracy 109
duties 296
responsibility 122
right(s) 34, 66–67, 167
values 108
consultants 15, 236, 240, 245, 247–248, 250–251, 255–257, 279, 281–283, 286, 290, 294, 299–304, 340, 345
Corporations and Economic Crimes Report (CECR) 235, 267, 275
corruption 13–17, 34, 38, 46, 52, 57, 61–66, 76, 79, 87, 99, 113–114, 121, 123–132, 138–139, 141–142, 145–148, 150–152, 160–163, 195–196, 201, 205, 208–209, 226–227, 235, 242–243, 248, 252, 253, 263, 265,

Index

269, 281, 284, 290, 297, 299–300, 302–303, 305, 309, 310, 313–317, 319, 323, 325–326, 329–330, 332, 334, 339, 340, 343–345
(*see also* BAE, grand corruption, PRASA)
apartheid 52
arms deal 76, 79, 84
global arms trade 57–58
high-profile cases 315
Corruption Watch 65
Coutinho, Caro & Co (CCC) 49–51, 53
Covid-19 pandemic 101, 114, 167, 183, 188, 223, 231, 253, 263, 291
Social Relief of Distress (SRD) grant 167, 183, 263
Credit Suisse 36, 223–231, 246–249, 252
Criminal Procedure Act 331
Cross-Functional Sourcing Committee (CFSC) 129, 132

D
Danikas, Ari 335–337
Dawoood, Adam 335
De Klerk, FW 21–22, 24–25, 27, 31
Nobel Peace Prize 21
De Kock, Rodney 326–329, 334, 336
De Kock report 320, 327–328, 335, 336
Defence Advisory Board 25, 51
Defence Export Service Organisation (DESO) 71
Dekker, Leendert 44–45
Deloitte 118, 235, 237–243, 256, 265, 267, 272–273, 276
Democratic Alliance 137
Denel Munitions (RDM) 59, 83, 103, 157–161, 163
Rheinmetall Denel Munition (subsidiary) 103, 106–107
Department of Defence 71
Dingiswayo, Fani 129, 143–146
Directorate for Priority Crimes Investigation (DPCI/Hawks) 46, 64, 79, 93, 99, 126, 130, 136, 138, 139, 148, 154, 155, 313, 317, 318, 319,

321, 326, 330, 337–339, 340
Dlamini, Bathabile 188
Dlamini-Zuma, Nkosazana 58
Dlodlo, Ayanda 88
Downer, Billy, Advocate 67
Dramat, Anwa (national head of DPCI/Hawks) 321–322, 338–339
Du Plessis, Barend (former Finance Minister) 37–38

E
economic crime(s) 13–17, 57, 99, 157, 175, 196, 235, 271, 299, 343–344, 347
People's Tribunal on Economic Crime 57
Ematum 224–225, 228, 231, 247–252
(*See also* Credit Suisse, SISE)
Ernst & Young *see* EY
Erwin, Alec 75
Eskom 118, 119, 200, 208, 218, 219, 241–243, 256, 284–288, 299, 315, 319
Essa, Salim 120, 198, 207–210, 286
Estina 118, 119, 198, 213–222, 255, 257, 269
Vrede Dairy Project *see* Vrede Dairy Project]
EY (Ernst & Young) 119, 235, 236, 245–252, 257

F
Ferreira, Mario 126, 147
FIFA World Cup (2010) 124, 150
Financial Intelligence Centre (FIC) 198, 217
Financial Intelligence Centre Act (FICA) 198–200, 217
Financial Sector Conduct Authority (FSCA) 170, 173–175, 178, 180–181
Financial Services Board (FSB) 170–171, 173, 175, 178, 180, 181
forensic investigation 119, 125, 128, 129, 136, 143, 150–152, 238, 254, 265
Free State Department of Agriculture 118, 214–216, 220-221
Freedom Under Law 321
Fundudzi Report 152, 284–285

G

Gama, Siyabonga 114–115
'Germany's Enron' 246
Ginwala, Frene 316
Godongwana, Enoch (Finance Minister) 159
Gordhan, Pravin 128, 255, 321–322
Government Employees Pension Fund (GEPF) 238, 256
grand corruption 15, 63, 205, 281, 309, 310, 314–315, 323, 345
Gripen craft 71–72, 75, 77, 80, 85, 92–95
GroundUp News 126, 188–189
Gupta, Atul 258
Gupta, Tony 88, 128
Gupta family/enterprise 31, 34, 61, 77, 87–88, 99, 113, 115, 117, 118–119, 120, 152, 158–163, 195–199, 201, 205–210, 213–216, 219, 286, 345
  #GuptaLeaks investigation 34, 120, 207, 214–216, 255
  attempted capture of Denel 158–159
  Bell Pottinger 54, 87, 305
  capture of SARS 161–162
  Eskom *see* the main entry for Eskom
  link with Jacob Zuma 122
  linked firms (network/front companies/related businesses)) 115, 117, 119–122, 205, 207–210, 213–215, 220–221, 241, 255, 257–258, 261, 269, 283–284, 345
  looting of South African public funds 54
  racketeering enterprise 195
  state capture network 25, 255
  Sun City wedding (2013) 255–259
  Transnet *see* the main entry for Transnet
  (*See also* Salim Essa, Anoj Singh)

H

Hail Way Trading 147–148
Harber, Anton 33
Hawk craft 71-72, 75, 77, 80, 92–95
Hawks *see* Directorate for Priority Crimes Investigation
Hlongwa, Brian 325–326, 329–331
Hlongwane, Fana ('Styles') 54, 73, 81, 83–89, 91–99, 316
Hlongwane Consulting 84–86, 95, 97–98
Hodeidah massacre 106–107
Hodge, Margaret, Dame (nee Watson) 47–49, 53–54
Holele, Tiro 143–147
Horwath Forensics (now Crowe Forensics) 136–137, 153–155
HSBC Holdings plc 45, 119, 196, 205–211, 285
Hugo, Chantal 171
human rights 13, 107, 283
  abuses 108, 206, 281, 289, 303–305
    in Saudi Arabia 69, 303–305
    watchdog 305
  abuses/violations of by Saudi Arabia, in Yemen 69
  aiding and abetting violations, during apartheid 36
  groups 304
  impact of infringement of 46
  infringement of 14
  obligations 69
  of pension fund members 173
  poor records 283
  undermining of 13
  violations, 36, 52, 53, 59, 103, 108, 109, 304

I

Independent Communications Authority of South Africa (ICASA) 158
Independent Regulatory Board for Auditors (IRBA) 235, 239, 240, 243, 258–259, 267–269, 271–277
inequality 13, 113–114, 169, 345
Innes Chamber (NPA HQ) 323
insurance industry regulator 173
International Monetary fund (IMF) 223, 225 Authority of South Africa (ICASA) 158–227, 231

Intrinsic Investments 53
Investigating Directorate (NPA ID) 115, 203, 314, 318, 325, 337
Islandsite Investments (Gupta company) 258

J
Jacob Zuma Foundation 138
Jagati, Ratan (Gupta associate) 117, 129, 207
Janse van Rensburg 333, 339
Jiba, Nomgcobo 310, 313, 317, 320–323, 326–328, 333
JJ Trading (JJT) 119–120, 207
Johannesburg Stock Exchange (JSE) 51, 119, 150, 236, 256
John, Jenitha 275–276
Jonas, Mcebisi 88, 128
Jooste, Markus 25, 175, 181, 237–238
(*See also* Steinhoff)
Judicial Conduct Committee 66
Judicial Services Commission 65, 163

K
K2B 171, 172
Kayswell Services 79–80
KBL (subsidiary of Kredietbank) 40–46
Kgoedi, Paul, torture in detention 328–329
Kgosana, Moses (ex-KPMG CEO) 255, 258
Khana, Major-General (Hawks) 154–156
Know Your Customer (KYC) banking standards 206, 208
KPMG (Gupta auditing company) 118, 170, 172, 179, 214, 235, 246, 253–261, 274
  #GuptaLeaks investigation 255
  Zondo Commission, appearance before 253–254
  (*See also* Accurate Investments, Linkway Trading, Jacques Wessels)
Kredietbank (now KBC Bank) 39–45
KwaZulu-Natal high court 66

L
Langa, Bheki 142
Lawyers for Human Rights 109
Lebeya, Godfrey, General (head of Hawks) 46
Liberty Corporate (insurance company) 169–174
Linkway Trading (Gupta company) 118, 214, 255, 257, 258, 260, 393
Logistics International 249
Lotz, Rudiger 140, 370
Lurie, Richard 51–53

M
Mabula, Jan (Major-General, former senior Hawks official) 326, 328–329
Mabunda, Makhensa 126, 137–138, 141
Madonsela, Thuli 124–125, 142, 151–152
  allegations of corruption and maladministration at Prasa (2015) 124
  Public Protector's report 129, 178
Maema, Sello 321–322, 333–341
  Hawks case opened against 337
Mafori Finance Vryheid 133
Mainline Passenger Services (MPS) 131
Major, John (former UK Prime Minister) 71
Makana Investment Corporation 150, 152–155
Makana Trust 150
Makwakwa, Jonas 294–295
Malaba, Sipho (Gupta associate) 257, 260–261
Malema, Julius (leader of EF) 254
Mamorokolo Makoele (MM) Trust 136
Mandela, Nelson 21–22, 47, 71, 108
  Nobel Peace Prize 22
Mandela/Mbeki administrations 21
Manuel, Trevor 75
Marsalek, Jan (KPMG CFO) 246
Martins, Ben 127–128
Mashaba, Auswell 132–139
Mashiane Moodley and Monama (MMM) 254–255

Massone, Vittorio 292–294, 297
Maswanganyi, Joe 127, 146
Mbeki, Thabo (former President) 57, 71, 75, 93, 95, 316
McBride, Robert 313, 322, 333, 338–342
McCarthy, Leonard (head of Scorpions) 64, 317
Mkhwebane, Busisiwe (Public Protector) 152, 178
McKinsey and Company 119, 219, 241, 281–282, 283–290, 299, 301, 303, 304–305
Mdluli, Richard 322, 339
'Medical Protector Compensation Loan' 96–97
Metrorail 124–125
Mhlongo, Welcome, Colonel 320
Minister of Transport (Dipuo Peters) 126, 127, 146
Minister of Transport (Jeff Radebe) 150
Mitchley, Michelle (whistleblower) 171
Mjonondwane, Phindi 326, 328, 329, 331
Mlotshwa, Simphiwe 327–328
Modise, Joe (ex-Minister of Defence) 72, 74–75, 84–85
Moemi, Alec 131–132
Molefe, Brian 117, 285
Molefe, Popo 125–127, 139, 145–147, 153, 155
Mokgoro Inquiry (2019) 327–328
Mokgoro, Yvonne, Justice 321
Mokoena, Refiloe 157–163
Montana, Lucky 125, 126, 128, 129, 132, 133, 137, 142–144, 151–153, 155
Moodley, Roy 126, 141–148
Motau, Moamela, General 158
Motau, Terry (advocate) 259–260
Moyane, Tom 161–162, 254–255, 293–296, 340
Mozambique 15, 99, 196, 223–231, 246–250
Mozambique Asset Management (MAM) 224–225, 228–230, 246–247
Mozambique Budget Monitoring Forum 231

Mozambique Constitutional Court 231
Mozambique Ministry of Finance 249–250
Mpofu, Dali, SC 67
Mpshe, Mokotedi (Acting NDPP) 65–66, 316–317
Mrwebi, Lawrence 327
Mthimkhulu, Daniel 132–133, 137
Myeni, Duduzile 263–266

N
Nasionale Pers (Naspers) 22, 29–34, 275
National Conventional Arms Control Committee (NCACC) 101, 105, 107–109
National Credit Regulator 187
National Director of Public Prosecutions (NDPP) 46, 64, 122, 309, 313, 325
Deputy 317, 321, 333
(*See also* Chauke)
National Household Travel Survey (NHTS – 2000) 123
National Intelligence Agency *see* State Security Agency
National Party 21–25, 27, 29–30, 32–33, 44
National Prosecuting Authority Act 32 of 1998 148, 243, 323, 334
National Prosecuting Authority (NPA) 15, 17, 46, 64, 66–67, 79, 115, 122, 130, 148, 203, 238, 243, 255, 261, 264 309–311, 313–341, 344
National Treasury
Investigation into 216 contracts awarded by Prasa from 2012-2015 123–124
investigation into Estina Vrede Dairy Project 216
Nduli, Zondi 260
Ndamazela, Portia 75
Ngcuka, Bulelani 64, 315–317
Ngoye, Martha 129, 145, 146
Ngwane Aerospace 95–98
Nkandla (Jacob Zuma's private residence) upgrades 322, 339

Index

Nkonki (partner to PwC) 256, 263, 265–268, 273–274
Nkosazana Dlamini-Zuma 58
Nkosi Sabelo 138
Non-Proliferation of Weapons of Mass Destruction Act 322
  Investigating Directorate (ID) 115, 203, 314, 318, 325, 337
  Prosecution Policy 328
Ntsebeza, Dumisa, Advocate 254–255
Nuclear Energy Act 322
Nugent Commission (Commission of Inquiry into SARS, led by Judge Nugent) 118, 161–162 294–297, 340
Nxasana, Mxolisi 317, 319, 320
Nyanda, Siphiwe, General 86, 91–92, 94–99

O

Oakbay Investments (Gupta company) 118, 161–162, 214, 216
Optimum Coal Mine 119, 198, 218
Organisation Undoing Tax Abuse (OUTA) 88, 139, 264, 275–276
Organised Crime and Corruption Reporting Project (OCCRP) 198, 208

P

#Prasaleaks 126
Parliamentary Standing Committee on Transport 126
Passenger Rail Agency of South Africa *see* Prasa
Pearse, Andrew (Credit Suisse banker) 224, 226, 229, 249, 251
Pelissier, Julian 80
pension fund(s) 15, 168, 169–173, 175, 177–179, 181, 238, 256, 346
People's Tribunal on Economic Crime 57
Peters, Dipuo (Minister of Transport) 126, 127, 146
Phahlane, Khomotso (National Police Commissioner) 339, 340
Pikoli, Vusi 316
Pillay, Ivan 254, 255, 321, 333, 339
Pilllay, Niven (Director of Regiments Health) 330
Pillay, Thiru 242
Political Party Funding Act 6 of 2018 27
Portfolio Committee on Justice and Correctional Services 265
post-apartheid
  'amnesia' 26
  arms deal scandal 78
  contracts 72
  government acquisition 71
  military procurement contract 98
  period 54
Prasa (Passenger Rail Agency of South Africa) 16, 113, 114, 123–156, 319, 325
  Lucky Montana (CEO) 125, 129
  Corporate Security 143
  capture of 127, 128
  complaints made by SATAWU
  corrupt contracts 123
  damage to rail infrastructure and rail fleets 130
  decline in services 123
  destruction of passenger rail in South Africa 123
  effect of corruption and maladministration 129
  erosion of passenger train services 123
  FIFA World Cup (2010) 124
  formation of 124
  increased funding 124
  irregularity in service appointments 143
  irregularity in extensions of security contracts 143
  proposed modernisation and upgrading of locomotive fleet 124
  report on allegations of corruption and maladministration (Thuli Madonsela – 2015) 124
  serious maladministration 125
  Supply Chain Management (SCM) team 144
  systemic corruption 124

423

Prevention of Organised Crime Act 331
Priority Crimes Litigation Unit (PCLU) 322
Privinvest 225–226, 228–229, 247, 249
Prodigy Business Services 144–148
ProIndicus 224–228, 246–247
profiteers 13–15, 22, 55, 57, 59, 109, 111, 165, 168, 183, 191
Protea Holdings 49–53
Protea International 49–51
Protection of Constitutional Democracy Against Terrorist and Related Activities Act 322
psychiatric camps 52–53
Public Finance Management Act (PFMA) 128, 143, 149–151, 156, 242, 265–268
Public Protector *see* Thuli Madonsela
Public Service Commission 316
PwC 235, 238, 240, 256, 263–269, 273, 301–302
    forensic report re: Steinhoff collapse 273
    IRBA's findings against, and against Nkonki 273

R
Radebe, Jeff (Minister of Transport) 150
Railway Safety Regulator (RSR) 135
Red Diamond Trading 74, 79
Regiments Capital 119, 202, 284, 285, 287, 330
Rheinmetall Denel Munition (RDM) *see* Denel Munitions
Right2Know Campaign 65
'rogue' unit' report 254–255
Royal Security 142–144, 148

S
S-Investments (Pty) Ltd 137–138
SAAB (also BAE-SAAB) 71, 85–87, 92, 94–95
Sagar, Vikas 286–289
SANIP 85–86, 95, 98
Scorpions 64, 73, 79, 84, 92, 317
SARS (South African Revenue Service) 118, 120, 121–123, 158, 161–163, 219, 253–255, 257, 261, 291–299, 321–322, 333, 338–341
    (*See also* 1064, Bain and Company, CRRC, CRRC E-Loco, Nugent Commission, Prasa, Swifambo Rail Leasing, Transnet)
SARS 'rogue unit' 254, 257, 322, 333, 338–340
Saudi Arabia, human rights abuses in 303–305
Sebenza Forwarding and Shipping 150, 153–155
Sector Education and Training Authority (SETA) 144
Selebi, Jackie 316
Serious Fraud Office (UK – SFO) 70, 73–76, 79–81, 84–85, 92
Seriti, Willie, Judge 65–66
Seriti Commission 80, 86–87, 99
Shaik, Schabir 61–64, 66–67, 80, 99
Shosholoza Meyl 124, 131
Sibiya, Shadrack (former head of Hawks) 321–322, 329, 338, 339
Sigcau, Stella 75
Sikhakhane, Musi 254–255
Simelane, Menzi 316
Similex 138
Singh, Anoj (Eskom) 241, 284–285
Singh, Power 109
Singh, Surjan 224, 226
Sinton, Ian 217, 220
Serviço de Informação e Segurança do Estado (SISE – Mozambique's intelligence services) 224, 246–248
Shadow World Investigations (SWI) 11, 65, 91, 113, 121, 195, 199, 214, 217, 221
Sithole, Abel 178–180
Siyangena Technologies 126, 129, 139, 145, 147–148, 155
Siyaya Rail Infrastructure Solutions Technology (Pty) 137
Sonangol 256, 300–302
Soni, Vas 141

Index

South African Air Force (SAAF) 71–72, 77, 83,
South African Airways (SAA) 38, 236, 256, 263–269, 271, 273–274, 277, 289
South African Airways Pilots Association (SAAPA) 264
South African History Archive (SAHA) 173
South African National Defence Force (SANDF) 86, 91–92, 94–98
South African Rail Commuter Corporation (SARCC) 150
South African Reserve Bank (SARB) 41, 121–122, 259
South African Social Security Agency (SASSA) 167–168, 183–185, 187–190
South African Transport and Allied Workers Union (SATAWU) 125
South African Trust Fund (SAFIT) 37
Southern African Litigation Centre 109
Southern Centre for Inequality Studies and World Inequality Database 13
spatial apartheid 123
Special Investigating Unit (SIU) 121–122, 265, 315, 319, 330
Specialised Commercial Crime Unit 330
Spotlight on Corruption (Phd – UK) 251
spy tapes scandal 64–65, 317
Stalingrad strategy 64–67
Standing Committees (Appropriations, Finance, Transport) 126, 149, 156, 235, 275
StanLib (Liberty Corporate subsidiary) 172
state capture 11, 14–16, 25, 27, 31, 45–46, 54, 57, 61, 98, 102, 113–115, 118, 121–123, 129, 139–140, 155, 157–158, 161, 163, 195–199, 203, 205, 207–211, 213–214, 222–223, 237, 241–243, 253–255, 269, 273, 281–285, 289, 291, 293, 295, 297–299, 309–311, 314–315, 317, 319–320, 322–323, 325, 330, 332–333, 338, 344–346
condemnation of 322
prosecutions 323
(*See also* Zondo Commission)
State Capture Commission (of Inquiry) 88, 113, 129, 265, 284–285, 289, 320
state-owned enterprises (SOEs) 16, 113, 114, 117, 123–125, 127, 129, 141, 146–147, 149, 156–159, 199, 201, 241, 283, 286
State Security Agency (previously National Intelligence Agency) 254
Steinhoff 25, 175, 236–240, 242–243, 256, 271, 273, 277
Stemcor 49-51
Stow, Peter (Senior Engineer, Transnet Freight Rail) 133
Strategic Defence Procurement Package (SDPP) 57, 70–71
Supreme Court of Appeal (SCA) 64, 66, 133–134, 316–317
Surty, Envre (Justice Minister) 316
Survé, Iqbal 34, 181
suspicious transaction reports (STRs) 217
Swifambo Holdings 135
Swifambo Rail Leasing (previously Mafori Finance Vryheid) 126, 129, 132–139, 141, 145, 147, 153–155
Swiss People's Party (SVP) 38

T
Telkom 141–143, 158, 292–293
Tequesta Group Limited 119, 120–121, 207–210
Thales 61–63, 66–67, 80, 99, 317
Thatcher, Margaret 53–54, 70
Tongaat Hulett 236–238, 243, 256, 275–277
Transnet 16, 114–123, 133, 152, 201–203, 205, 207–208, 218, 241, 284–285, 287, 289, 299
Transnet Freight Rail 133, 135
Trillian Capital Management 114, 119, 219, 241, 284–289

Truth and Reconciliation Commission (TRC) 27, 34, 46, 310
Tshidi, Dube 171, 175, 178–181
Tutu, Desmond, Archbishop 30, 34

U

uMkhonto weSizwe 83, 94
Union Bank of Switzerland (UBS) 37
#UniteBehind 126, 139–140, 152
United Nations Convention Against Corruption (UNCAC) 122
Unpaid Benefits Campaign 173

V

Van Loggerenberg, Johann 255, 333, 339
Van Rensburg, Karen 317, 322
Vasram, Kamal 215–216
VBS Mutual Bank 257, 259–260, 274
Vosloo, Ton 31–34
Vossloh España 131–139, 141, 153, 155
Vossloh Kiepe 137, 155
Vrede Dairy Project 198, 213–214, 216–217, 221, 255
 [*See also* Estina.]
VTB Capital 223–224, 228–231, 246–247

W

Waligora, Roy 254
war profiteers 14, 55, 57, 59, 109
Waterkloof Air Force Base 213, 255, 318
welfare profiteers 14, 165, 183–192
Werksmans 126, 141, 143, 147, 156
Wessels, Jacques (KPMG partner – auditor) 258
White Paper on National Defence 58
Wirecard 245–246
WKH Landgrebe 136
World Trade Organization (WTO) 73
Wood, Eric 115, 287, 288

Y

Yemen, human rights abuses 69
Yengeni, Tony 99

Z

Zhuzhou Locomotive Co. Ltd *see* Chinese Railway Rolling Stock Corporation (CRRC)
Zondo Commission (of Inquiry into State Capture) 11, 27, 113, 115, 121, 122, 125–127, 139, 141–155, 159–161, 195, 197–203, 210, 217, 220, 222, 253, 266–268, 293, 298, 310, 317, 318, 322–323, 327, 337–340
Zuma, Jacob 16, 31, 45, 61–67, 80, 88, 91, 99, 107, 122, 127, 128, 138, 150, 155, 156, 161, 254, 293, 295, 310, 317, 321, 339, 340
 MEC for Economic Development (KZN) 128, 150
 post-Zuma-era 315
 state capture 61
Zuma, Duduzane 88, 128
Zuma, Edward 138, 317, 326, 334
Zuma-Thales trial 67
Zwane, Mosebenzi 201, 216